D1573086

MASTERING
INTERNET VIDEO

A GUIDE TO STREAMING
AND ON-DEMAND VIDEO

MASTERING INTERNET VIDEO

A GUIDE TO STREAMING AND ON-DEMAND VIDEO

DAMIEN STOLARZ

✦ Addison-Wesley

Boston • San Francisco • New York • Toronto • Montreal
London • Munich • Paris • Madrid
Capetown • Sydney • Tokyo • Singapore • Mexico City

Copyright © 2005 by Pearson Education, Inc.

All rights reserved. No part of this publication may be reproduced, stored in a retrieval system, or transmitted, in any form, or by any means, electronic, mechanical, photocopying, recording, or otherwise, without the prior consent of the publisher. Printed in the United States of America. Published simultaneously in Canada.

For information on obtaining permission for use of material from this work, please submit a written request to:

Pearson Education, Inc.
Rights and Contracts Department
75 Arlington Street, Suite 300
Boston, MA 02116
Fax: (617) 848-7047
ISBN 0-321-12246-1
LOC 2004105901

Text printed on recycled paper

1 2 3 4 5 6 7 8 9 10—MA--0605040302

First printing, August 2004

Many of the designations used by manufacturers and sellers to distinguish their products are claimed as trademarks. Where those designations appear in this book, and Addison-Wesley was aware of a trademark claim, the designations have been printed with initial capital letters or in all capitals.

The authors and publisher have taken care in the preparation of this book, but make no expressed or implied warranty of any kind and assume no responsibility for errors or omissions. No liability is assumed for incidental or consequential damages in connection with or arising out of the use of the information or programs contained herein.

The publisher offers discounts on this book when ordered in quantity for bulk purchases and special sales. For more information, please contact:

U.S. Corporate and Government Sales
(800) 382-3419
corpsales@pearsontechgroup.com

For sales outside of the U.S., please contact:

International Sales
(317) 581-3793
international@pearsontechgroup.com

Visit Addison-Wesley on the Web: www.awprofessional.com

Library of Congress Cataloging-in-Publication Data

A CIP catalog record for this book can be obtained from the Library of Congress

Acquisitions Editor: *Mary Franz*
Editorial Assistant: *Noreen Regina*
Marketing Manager: *Robin O'Brien*
Marketing Specialist: *Kathleen Addis*
Publicity: *Heather Fox*
Managing Editor: *Gina Kanouse*
Production: *Ginny Bess Munroe, Angela Calvert Johnson*
Cover Design: *Alan Clements*
Manufacturing Buyer: *Dan Uhrig*

To Jacob Riskin,
Daniel Gordon-Levitt,
and
Reverend Dr. Brian Wingfield Morrison III, Esquire

CONTENTS AT A GLANCE

CONTENTS

ABOUT THE AUTHOR

Damien is an entrepreneur with 15 years of experience making computers talk to each other. He cofounded static.com (also known as Blue Falcon Networks, which is now akimbo.com) in 1995, where in his long tenure as Chief Technology Officer, he led the development of numerous technologies including an online service, networked multiplayer games, and peer-to-peer cost-reduction

 *software for video streaming. In 2002, he started Robot Army Corporation (www. robotarmy.com), a software consultancy and R&D house, which continues to develop large-scale media delivery software among other secret projects. In 2004, Robot Army spun off Carbot, Inc. (www.carbotpc.com), which designs and manufactures in-car entertainment of computers. Damien holds a bachelor or science degree in computer science/engineering from UCLA.*

FOREWORD

As a global network, the Internet has brought many new possibilities for professionals who want to offer new services. As a side effect, the Internet has also dramatically lowered the access threshold to common users. Today, anybody can "set up shop" with his own personal website.

This is true if the website contains standard web pages with characters, graphics, natural pictures, and so on. This is not always the case if the website contains time-dependent media: audio and video. In this case, it is a rare occurrence to see a single person with the breadth of technical knowledge required to deal with the number of problems that must be solved to get video in the right analog format, convert it to a digital format, compress it, store it, and stream it on an intranet. However, the number of people who have the need to set up services that require handling time-dependent media on the Internet is growing, and with it grows the need for a less cumbersome and time-consuming way to access the necessary information.

Mastering Internet Video is an important step toward making Internet video a mainstream technology that is accessible to many. This is not an easy task for a number of reasons. The first reason is the sheer number of disciplines required for all but the most straightforward instances of Internet video. A short list includes video production, television broadcasting, telecommunications, computer programming, data compression, encryption, computer networking, and other Internet technologies.

A second reason it is a difficult task to make Internet video technologies accessible is the isolated nature of Internet video disciplines. Video production and television broadcasting have been coupled in business for a long period of time, but telecommunication is just "another field" with regard to tradition and the mind set. Computers and telecommunication occasionally merge, but their traditions and mind sets are vastly different.

In addition, the deliberate attempt of some vendors to obscure interdisciplinary issues in an effort to promote their own solutions creates obstacles in making Internet video accessible to all.

Internet video is not just a complex set of technical fields, but also one that is undergoing a fast-moving evolution. Decisions that people have to make should not only take into account what is available today, but also what the next step in technology or implementation can make possible tomorrow.

This book is a service to the industry at large in that it provides technical descriptions of the different fields, taking the time to define the many terms from different industries that are required by those who want to read even the most basic instructions. It also separates marketing buzzwords from substance, and it puts issues into a time perspective.

I am grateful for a detailed account of the most critical technologies: audio and video compression. MPEG-1, MPEG-2, and MPEG-4 are described in a way that shows how compression technology is the enabler of digital media on the Internet today and will continue to be the driving force toward a realization of the dream in which the global digital network supports the global and unrestricted flow of digital audio and video.

—Leonardo Chiariglione, MPEG Founder

INTRODUCTION

GOALS OF THIS BOOK

This book has the primary (and ambitious) goal of making Internet video understandable to anyone, through a carefully planned, complete, and entertaining sequence of definitions and illustrations.

Perhaps Internet video will eventually be easier to understand, well explained in a tidy package that protects the new student from all the gory details. Right now, the beginner who tries to dissect the marketing claims made by a variety of vendors finds himself quickly put to sleep by technical explanations in almost any direction he looks. In this book, we attempt to arm the reader with sufficient weaponry—by providing both a strong conceptual understanding and a high-level technical understanding—to confront these gory details head-on.

In addition, we intend for this book to be the basic text on the core technology of Internet video. That's a daunting task for any work with "Internet" in the title, but through our disciplined avoidance of many brand names, fleeting product lines, and easily dated technologies—and a focus on the unchanging fundamentals of these fields—*Mastering Internet Video* should stand as an accurate description of the basics of Internet video for years to come.

This is not a tutorial book. We won't walk you through the dialog boxes or tell you which buttons to push. Rather, our goal is to educate you well enough so that you know what all the options in the dialogs mean and what steps to take when you're unhappy with your initial results.

Although there are many fine books on compression, networking, and video editing, this is, we believe, the first book that pulls together all these disciplines into a single coherent picture of Internet video from beginning to end.

WHO THIS BOOK IS FOR

Our aim with *Mastering Internet Video* is to create a book that works for all the disparate specialists involved in the whole process.

For the website designer or web developer, it aims to be compelling page-turner—a picture book that can be read cover to cover in a few sittings, which comfortably conveys a thorough mechanical understanding of getting video online.

For the technical manager, it aims to convey a deep conceptual understanding of every knowledge domain relevant to Internet video, so that business decisions can be readily made without having to constantly defer to experts.

For the venture capitalist, it aims to provide an instant mastery of a broad array of technical fields, enabling them to make more insightful decisions on where their markets of interest are headed.

For the technology hobbyist, it aims to be an entertaining look inside Internet video, showing how it really works and providing a deep well of insight for intelligent cocktail party banter.

For programmers and software engineers, this book aims to convey a complete, accessible grounding in all the relevant technologies of video delivery over TCP/IP networks. The hard-won collection of data in this book usually takes years to accumulate, and most of the books in the market do not attempt to give a complete picture of the art and science of Internet video.

Last, but not least, this book is for the people deep in the trenches: the system administrators and people tasked with keeping large-scale Internet video services up and running while constantly improving performance, broadening their scale, and adding large amounts of new content on an almost daily basis.

ORGANIZATION OF THIS BOOK

Following is an outline of the book's content. As you can see, the first seven chapters of this book walk sequentially through the steps involved in making video available on the Internet. The final chapter discusses Internet video standards.

Chapter 1, "Video Preparation and Capture," describes the process and technology of *preparing* and *capturing* the video (getting high-quality video into the computer in a digital form).

Chapter 2, "Video Compression," explains video *compression*, the methods of making video files (which are very large) small enough to work with and deliver over the Internet.

Chapter 3, "Video Storage File Formats," describes the many different *file formats* in which video is stored on a computer and their different uses.

Chapter 4, "Streaming Media Server Software," describes *streaming servers*, software, and hardware that is better suited for delivering real-time video data over the Internet than web servers.

Chapter 5, "Video Transport Protocols," describes *video transport protocols*, the languages spoken between computers when transporting video data over a network, such as the Internet. This chapter also gives an excellent tutorial on how the Internet works (and doesn't work) for real-time data delivery.

 Chapter 6, "Enterprise Multicast," describes *enterprise multicasting*, the highly efficient video transport protocol that most closely approximates traditional television broadcasting and that is used more in the corporate environment than within the Internet at large.

 Chapter 7, "Video Security and Digital Rights Management (DRM)," describes the technology behind *Digital Rights Management*, the technologies used by content owners to control how Internet video is used by its audience.

 Chapter 8, "Internet Video Standards," describes Internet video standards in general.

 Appendix A, "A Quick List of Problems and Concise Solutions," offers a toolbox of solutions to the routine problems encountered in the process of setting up Internet video. The chapter also outlines many specific scenarios in which people want to use Internet video and offers several potential approaches to their implementation.

 Appendix B, "The MPEG-4 Standard," discusses in more detail the MPEG-4 standard.

WORD PROBLEMS

In the process of writing this book, the heaviest emphasis was on defining everything in an easily readable way. Each technical term is defined when it is first used.

Internet video, as a subject, presents a particularly steep learning curve for many people. Some of the reasons for this are:

- It contains technical terms from many different fields.
- It is explained with poorly named, easily misunderstood, or the incorrect terms.
- It is clouded by marketing buzzwords that have little real meaning.

TECHNICAL TERMS FROM TOO MANY DIFFERENT FIELDS

As a discipline, Internet video borrows words and concepts from many different fields. Most "mature" subjects like math or physics have only one set of technical terms that you have to learn. In trying to understand Internet video, however, you instantly encounter sophisticated terminology from the fields of electronics, physics, video production, television broadcasting, telecommunications, encryption, data compression, computer networking and Internet, and computer programming.

To address this problem, we've attempted to define every word in these fields with a straightforward, conceptual definition and a comprehensible explanation.

COUNTERINTUITIVE NAMING

In addition to the problem of too many technical terms, there is simply bad naming of terms. Professionals in the originating fields admit that the words have always been confusing, or that they should be renamed, but "that's what we've always called it." Sometimes the terms were invented by technicians who were already confused, and their misuse is continued as a matter of tradition.

To address this problem, we've attempted not only to define these terms, but also to point out when they are poorly named, and to reiterate the explanations several different ways to explain them clearly and thoroughly. We've done our best, however, not to introduce new terms, as there has been enough confusion already.

BUZZWORD OVERLOAD

Another major challenge to understanding Internet video is misleading marketing-speak. Examples abound in subjects like digital rights management and content control (where no truly foolproof system exists). The urge to stand out from competitors results in different cool-sounding buzzwords for the exact same technologies. Potential consumers of the technology thus have very little information on which to base their decisions. They can read low-level technical discussions, which makes all the technologies sound like the same gibberish, or they can study marketing buzz-speak designed to make nearly identical approaches sound unique and better than the rest. In truth, many technology vendors use similar systems and make minor compromises and enhancements to make their systems unique.

HOW THIS BOOK IS WRITTEN

This book was written with the following strategies in mind:

- Define each term used.
- Illustrate as much as possible.
- Eliminate unnecessary detail.
- Use analogies to illustrate concepts.
- Explain everything.
- Start light, and then go technically deep.
- Don't be overawed by technology.
- Stay interesting!

We hope you learn a lot!

1

VIDEO PREPARATION AND CAPTURE

HOW TO GET HIGH-QUALITY VIDEO INTO THE COMPUTER

IN THIS CHAPTER

- Video Basics
- Capturing Video
- Creating New Internet Video Content

This chapter shows you how to put your video into the computer. It assumes you have either prerecorded content and want to convert it to Internet video or that you intend to film and then import it into the computer for online delivery.

The first part of this chapter walks you through the basics of video storage and playback for both cinematic film and broadcast television media.

The second part of this chapter goes into more specific detail about cinema standards, television broadcast, and tape standards. Because digital television, digital cinema, and Internet video share the same underlying technologies, an understanding of each of these areas enhances the overall understanding of the subject.

The third part of this chapter briefly discusses ways to create professional-looking video on the Internet. Although it isn't intended as a mini-course on cinematography or scriptwriting, the last section provides a few pointers as to the formats and approaches that get you the best results.

1

VIDEO BASICS

The word movie is an abbreviation of moving picture. Video, like film, creates the illusion of movement by showing a series of slightly different still images in rapid sequence, as in the flipbook shown in Figure 1-1. At a certain speed, we interpret these pictures, typically called frames, as movement, as in the filmstrip shown in Figure 1-2.

Figure 1-1   *A flipbook creates the illusion of moving video.*

Figure 1-2   *Moving video is composed of many still frames.*

FRAME RATE

The speed at which the frames are displayed is called the *frame rate*. Frame rates of less than 10 frames per second (fps) basically look like a slide show. At 10 fps, the video conveys motion. Silent movies were filmed at 16 fps. When sound was added to movies, the frame rate was increased to 24 fps, which is still used today. See Figure 1-3.

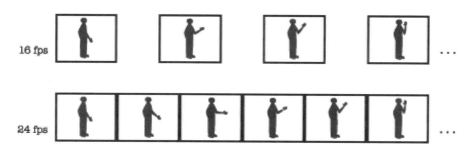

Figure 1-3 *In 16 fps film, there are four frames every quarter of a second. In 24 fps film, there are six frames every quarter of a second.*

FLICKER

Flicker is the perception that the pictures are flashing on and off, like a strobe light. To reduce flicker, the frame rate needs to be almost twice the rate of film. Twenty-four frames per second is the lowest tolerable frame rate for convincingly synchronizing lips with voice; however, higher frame rates are needed to reduce flicker. Movie screens usually flash each unique picture two or three times on the movie screen, effectively doubling or tripling the number of frames shown to the viewer to 48 fps or even 72 fps, as shown in Figure 1-4. However, there are still only 24 unique frames.

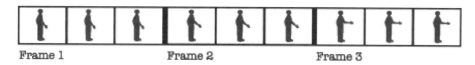

Frame 1   Frame 2   Frame 3

Figure 1-4 *The same frame can be flashed two or three times to reduce flicker.*

TELEVISION VIDEO VERSUS FILM

The first television sets used a picture tube (as do modern TVs that are not flat-screen or rear-projection). The way these televisions work is that a beam of electricity (technically called a cathode ray) sweeps or scans across the inside of the tube from top left to bottom right, creating the image by lighting up chemicals on the inside of the picture tube, as shown in Figure 1-5. The chemicals stay lit for a fraction of a second, and then fade back to black. To display moving pictures on the screen, the screen is constantly redrawn. The scanning electrical beam draws about 500 (in U.S. systems) to 600 (in European systems) lines from top to bottom.

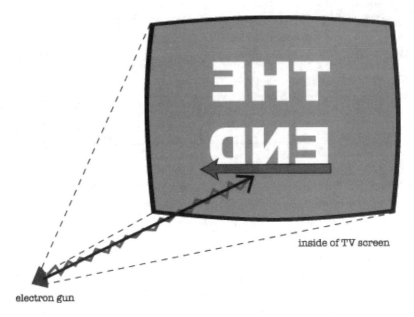

inside of TV screen

electron gun

Figure 1-5 *A beam of electricity scans across the inside of the TV screen, creating the picture.*

Initially, the inventors of television considered showing pictures at 24 fps, like in film. However, at this frame rate, the flicker was unbearable because the chemicals on the picture tube were too slow in responding to the electrical beam. To get around this, a scheme of interlacing the image was developed. Instead of redrawing the whole image 24 times each second, they chose to redraw half a frame 25 to 30 times per second (depending on the country), scanning every other line. This is depicted in Figure 1-6.

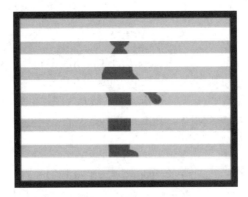

Figure 1-6 *The TV draws only half the screen at once (also called interlacing).*

A half frame is called a *field,* and it consists of every other line of the video, as shown in Figure 1-7. The odd fields contain lines 1, 3, 5, 7, and so on. The even fields consist of lines 2, 4, 6, 8, and so on.

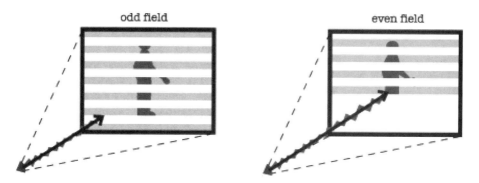

Figure 1-7   *The alternating lines of video on a TV screen are called fields.*

Interlacing accomplished several things:

- It effectively transmitted 50 to 60 different images per second, but with a video signal no bigger than progressive (noninterlaced) 25 to 30 fps video.

- The lingering brightness effect of the screen chemical coating, combined with the high screen-refresh rate, reduced the flicker of the image.

- When video was filmed with television cameras, it captured 50 to 60 unique moments in time (50 to 60 different fields), so fast motion worked very well on the screen.

Why Is Broadcast TV Video Interlaced?

TV signals were sent over the air (to antennas) via radio waves. To make the best use of the available radio waves by fitting the largest number of channels into those waves, it was necessary to make the video data as small as possible.

Another factor that went into interlacing was flicker reduction. Although TV designers could have standardized on the 24 fps used by film, the chemicals on the inside of the TV screen had a longer lingering brightness than movie screens. So, a higher refresh rate was needed to reduce the flicker to a tolerable level.

A final factor was the different electrical systems in different countries. Film would transfer a lot easier to television if TV had standardized on 48 fps.

This would have been sufficient to eliminate flicker, and converting movies to TV would have simply required turning each frame into two fields. However, it was much cheaper and easier to engineer a receiver that ran at 50 fps in Europe and 60 fps in North and South America because this matched the oscillating frequency of the electrical power in these countries.

INTERLACED AND PROGRESSIVE VIDEO TRADEOFFS

As we've seen, the two major types of video are progressive (frame-based) and interlaced (alternating even and odd fields). You might see the letters p and i used in conjunction with the number of frames. Thus, modern film would be 24p, and television would be 60i (U.S. and Japan) or 50i (Europe). Figure 1-8 shows the difference between film and television.

film (24 frames per second)

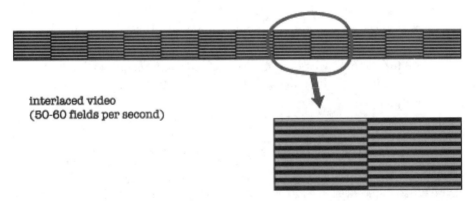

interlaced video
(50-60 fields per second)

Figure 1-8   *Moving images on film are composed of frames. Moving television images are composed of interlaced fields.*

Film, with its full, progressively displayed frames, is much more pleasant to look at in still shots, as shown in Figure 1-9, whereas television is much better for showing the fast motion of a football game. Capturing more slices of time captures motion more effectively.

progressive video (film)   interlaced video (television)

Figure 1-9   *A still frame of film looks good, whereas a "still" of interlaced video is jagged.*

Here is what you need to know about progressive and interlaced images:

- Film projectors and computer monitors display progressive images. Televisions display interlaced images.
- Progressive images have to be converted to display on televisions. Interlaced video has to be converted to play back on computer monitors.

For an experiential view of the difference between film and television, check out the flipbook movies in the margins of this book.

FILM-TO-VIDEO CONVERSION

When 24 fps film needs to be converted for broadcast on 60 fps television, there are not enough frames to fill a second. For every four frames of film, 10 fields of video are needed.

Thus, a conversion technique was developed to spread 24 frames over 60 fields. It is called 3:2 pulldown because it pulls down film frames into alternating fields of three and two, as shown in Figure 1-10.

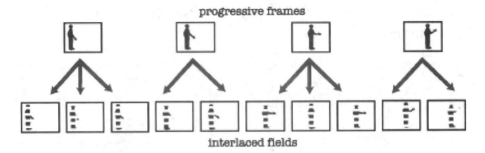

Figure 1-10   *With 3:2 pulldown, film frames are converted into alternating fields of three and two.*

You might wonder what this does to the image quality. Mainly, the motion results in *judder,* the less-than-smooth motion of objects as they are displayed at slightly changing speeds. However, the increased frame rate, combined with the smoothing effect of most tube televisions, evens this out. People have watched films for years on television and are basically satisfied with the results.

Telecine and Pulldown

This process is also called *Telecine,* a word that refers to the original machine that was used to do film-to-TV conversion.

In Europe or other regions that use 50 fps interlaced video, the content goes through a simpler process called *2:2 pulldown.* In this process, each frame film (which is 24 fps) is split into two fields, doubling to 48 frames. So what becomes of the other two fields? European systems simply play the films faster. A 50-minute film ends in 48 minutes.

FILM-TO-VIDEO-TO-FILM CONVERSION

Usually, the content projected in movie theatres is created only at 24p. Because DVD and videocassette are the primary distribution mechanisms for almost all consumer and studio-grade video, however, most films eventually end up in the form of TV-ready video. This presents a problem when the films need to be played on computers. In other words, interlaced video needs to be converted back to its original progressive form.

Luckily, the 3:2 conversion is usually reversible, through a process called *inverse 3:2 pulldown* or inverse Telecine. Media preparation software often features an option called *3:2 pulldown detection.* In Figure 1-11, you can see that by recombining the right fields, you can go back to the original 24 frames.

This works fine unless the video has been edited. Because there are ten video fields for each of the four film frames, missing fields might cause incomplete frames. If the video has been edited throughout, it might be a bit of a hunt to find the new beginning of the 3:2 pattern and reconstruct the correct frames. The process needs to detect when this editing has occurred. Good software does indeed figure out the starting field and starts the conversion correctly, but it's far better to work from a version that hasn't been edited. Of course, working with a progressive video instead of an interlaced file is best of all.

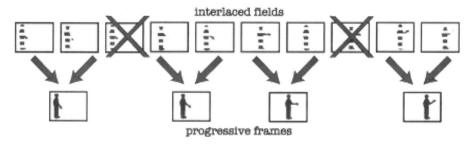

Figure 1-11   *Inverse 3:2 pulldown.*

FRAME SHAPE (ASPECT RATIO)

The relationship between the width and height of a frame is called the *aspect ratio,* and it is expressed in the form *horizontal:vertical.* The shape of the television screen was designed to match film when it was first developed, where the width was a third greater than the height, as shown in Figure 1-12. This ratio can be written as 1.33:1, or more simply as 4:3. Computer screens traditionally had aspect ratios of 1.33:1 as well.

1.33:1 (4:3)

Figure 1-12   *Traditional aspect ratio for computer screens and televisions.*

When you go to the movies now or watch "letterbox" DVDs, you see ratios such as 1.85:1 (wide) or even 2.35:1 (very wide). Newer, flat-panel computer screens are wider than 4:3 to play wide-format movies. Also, the new standard for high-definition television (HDTV) has a ratio of 1.78:1, more commonly written as 16:9. These ratios are shown in Figure 1-13. For a comparison of all four aspect ratios, see Figure 1-14.

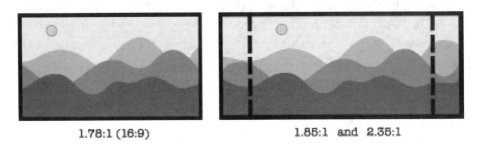

1.78:1 (16:9)   1.85:1 and 2.35:1

Figure 1-13   *HDTV and widescreen aspect ratios.*

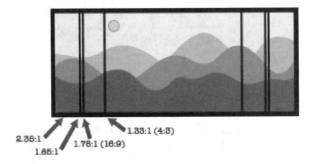

Figure 1-14   *Composite showing all four common aspect ratios.*

ANALOG VERSUS DIGITAL

We talked about how many pictures or fields are displayed in a second, and whether they are widescreen or not. But the biggest difference between traditional moving images (film and TV) and computer and DVD video is whether the media is analog or digital.

What is analog? When phonographs play back audio, the vibrations of the speaker correspond to the indentations on a vinyl record. You can say that the sound is analogous to the small pits and bumps on the record. When video is stored in an analog form, the frames are stored on a physical medium, such as film or tape.

When a still or movie camera captures an image, the patterns of light and shadow expose the silver in the film to represent the image, as shown in Figure 1-15.

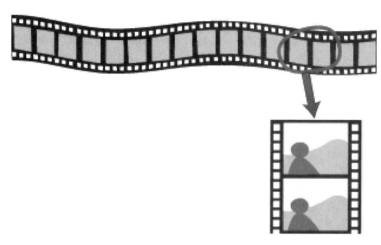

Figure 1-15   *Most motion pictures are stored on the same sort of 35mm film you use in a camera.*

When sound is stored on audiotape, the sound waves and volume create patterns in the metal that coats the tape, using an electrically controlled magnet. Video is stored on videotape in a similar process. The colors and brightness of the lines of video, which are to be beamed onto the TV screen, are stored as patterns on the metal-coated tape, as shown in Figure 1-16.

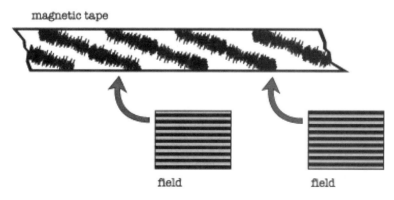

Figure 1-16   *Each stripe on the tape contains a field.*

Digital content is represented not by altering physical media (the vinyl in records or the silver in film), but by a series of numbers. Digital is not inherently better than analog; in fact, it's far from it. Despite huge advances in digital technology, high-quality analog media is still superior to digital in many cases. Although it might seem that digital is just a buzz phrase used to sell new and not always better products, the real reason everything is going digital is that digital information can be processed, stored, and manipulated by computers.

Also, after it is in digital form, content can be stored much more compactly, as shown in Figure 1-17. It takes many large reels of film to make up a two-hour movie, whereas a single DVD or hard disk (or even a flash memory stick) can contain the whole movie with plenty of room to spare. (Yes, a videocassette can also store a movie, but at less than one-tenth the quality of film, this is not quite a fair comparison.)

reels of film   VHS tapes   hard drive   flash disk

Figure 1-17   *Comparative sizes of storage devices.*

Another plus for digital storage is that digital is far less prone to degradation over time. Film becomes discolored, faded, and brittle with age. Old VHS (video home system) tapes get more and more distorted with each passing year. Also, an analog copy of a film or tape is slightly worse than the original, and over several generations the content becomes unusable.

The benefit of digital is that digital files can be copied over and over with no loss of quality, and many identical copies can be made so that there is virtually no risk of losing the original. With analog film and audiotape, the original (the negatives of the film or the original audio tape) is extremely valuable because they cannot be copied without some degradation.

ANALOG-TO-DIGITAL (A/D) CONVERSION

So how do you convert something analog into digital form? The basic approach of analog-to-digital conversion consists of the following steps:

1. Establish the feature you want to convert, such as color, brightness, loudness, and so on.

2. Sample it—that is, use a device and measure it. For photographic material, a grid of brightness and color sensors is used. For audio, a system that senses sound loudness and frequency is used.

3. Using an appropriate scale, assign a number to represent the measured quantities.

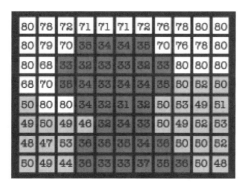

4. Repeat this procedure for many samples until the entire piece of media has been turned into numbers.

Currently the highest quality method of film scanning is called *flying spot scanning,* depicted in Figure 1-18. A bright light (that can be aimed and scanned around) is swept across the picture vertically, and this light is split into red, green, and blue. The intensity of each color for that spot that the light shines through is measured with a light sensor. The flying spot can be moved finely or coarsely, taking more or fewer samples per inch as desired.

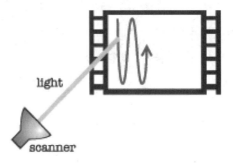

Figure 1-18   *Flying spot scanning converts film-to-digital form at a very high resolution.*

Each spot is then represented by three numbers, representing the intensity of red, green, and blue for that spot, as shown in Figure 1-19. Several thousand spots are recorded horizontally and vertically. After this process is complete, the millions of samples or pixels are stored on some sort of computer storage medium, such as hard disk.

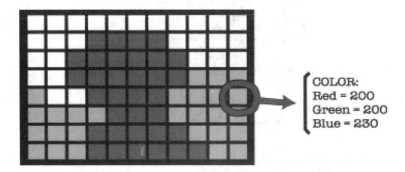

Figure 1-19   *Each pixel is shown as three numbers, representing the intensity of red, green, and blue.*

Capturing video from VCRs, camcorders, or broadcast television requires a different approach because the video is already in an electrical form, albeit analog. As a simplified explanation, the analog data would normally trigger a scanning stream of electricity to paint the picture on a TV tube. Instead, the data that would have triggered the electrical stream is measured, line by line, and sampled at specific intervals, generating pixels. Video that has been broadcast or recorded on tape is already far, far lower quality than film—usually analog-to-digital capture of video captures about 640 horizontal samples by 480 vertical samples.

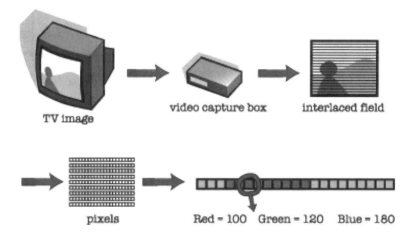

Figure 1-20   *Capturing video from TV. Each line of the field is cut into pixels, and then each pixel is assigned values for red, green, and blue.*

Of course, all these numbers make no sense to our human eyes and ears until they are converted into sound waves or light and color. To play back digital media, it must undergo digital-to-analog (D/A) conversion.

The basic approach of digital-to-analog conversion involves the following steps:

1. Retrieve all the numbers from the original sample.

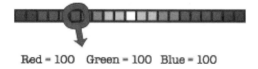

Red = 100   Green = 100   Blue = 100

2. Transform each number into the corresponding real-world perceivable quality it represents. For instance, if the numbers represent sounds, send them to a chip that translates the sounds into voltages that power a speaker. If the samples are levels of brightness and color, use a chip on a video card to translate the numbers into voltages that create appropriate colors on a monitor or video projector.

RESOLUTION

In the analog world, *resolution* means how much information there is in a picture or how much detail is recorded in the picture. Most commercial films are recorded on 70mm film, which offers four times the resolution (double the width and the height) of 35mm film, as shown in Figure 1-21.

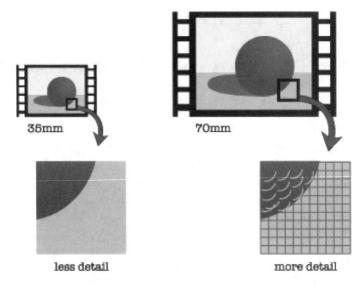

35mm — less detail

70mm — more detail

Figure 1-21 *70mm film has much higher resolution than 35mm film.*

In the digital world, resolution means much the same thing, but it specifically means how many horizontal dots or pixels of color make up the picture. Digital resolution is typically measured in dots (pixels) per inch (dpi). As shown in

Figure 1-22, when you scan a photo on a flatbed scanner at 600 dpi, each resulting pixel is $1/600$ of an inch wide. When you scan at screen resolution (72 ppi), each pixel is just $1/72$ of an inch.

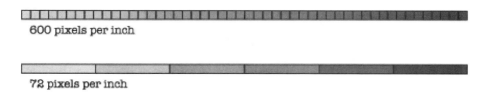

600 pixels per inch

72 pixels per inch

Figure 1-22 *Comparison of number of pixels in $1/12$ of an inch (not to scale).*

It's important to note that scanning resolution numbers refer to the horizontal aspect, whereas digital cameras refer to resolution in both aspects. That is, a 600 dpi scanner actually captures 360,000 pixels. A 4-megapixel (4 million pixels) camera captures 2,000 pixels along both the horizontal and vertical axes. Analog film is actually very high resolution when compared to current digital film standards. It would require something on the order of 10,000 horizontal and 10,000 vertical pixels of resolution (measured spots) to capture every detail in 35mm film, so that absolutely no detail from the analog film is lost. This would create a 100-megapixel image, excessively large compared to what works in practice. Normal film scanning resolutions for cinema work are 2,048 pixels wide and 1,556 pixels tall (called 2K in film jargon, which is not to be confused with 2 megapixels), which winds up being about 3.2 megapixels per frame, and for a higher resolution, 4,096 pixels wide and 3,112 pixels tall (4K), at around 12 megapixels. When digital graphics or backgrounds are made for film, to be combined with analog camera work they are usually created 5,000 pixels wide. The differences in resolution are depicted in Figure 1-23. These resolutions are generally considered good enough so that the digital effects and touchups look right when the image is blown up and projected on a movie screen.

In general, when editing video on a computer, you want to work with the highest resolution available, but within reasonable limits based on the power of your computer and the available hard disk space. You can never increase the quality of an image from the original resolution you captured at or worked in, so start high.

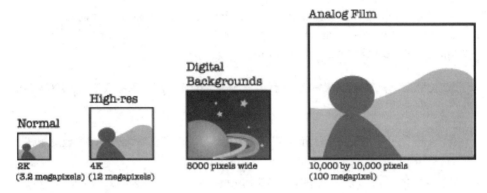

Figure 1-23   *Even super high-resolution digital images don't come near the resolution of plain 35mm analog film.*

SCAN LINES (VERTICAL RESOLUTION)

The resolution of analog TV is far lower than film. However, unlike film, it does have a set number of scan lines going from left to right, stacked one on top of another. The number of these scan lines is equivalent to the vertical resolution of the TV. Each scan line is not transmitted as distinct dots, but rather as rows of light intensities and colors. It is accurate to say that television displays around 480 (U.S. and Japan) to 576 (Europe) horizontal scan lines, as shown in Figure 1-24.

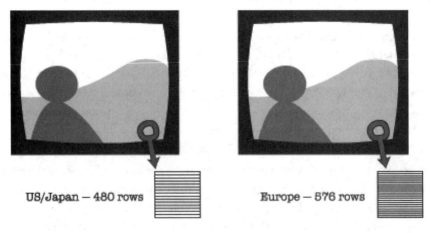

Figure 1-24   *Comparison of scan lines.*

LINES OF HORIZONTAL RESOLUTION

There is no fixed horizontal resolution for TV, nor are there distinct dots or pixels in a scan line. Essentially, the horizontal resolution varies depending on the equipment, but always stretches to fit the screen. If you look closely at a television tube, you can distinguish scan lines (left to right), but you will not find any distinct vertical lines. However, different monitors have different amounts of fine detail that can be displayed.

Technically, TV engineers defined horizontal resolution relative to the height of the TV, so that the measurement is independent of the shape of the TV tube. As shown in Figure 1-25, when you see a 4:3 television that can display 600 lines of horizontal resolution, the actual number of effective pixels is 800 across. If the TV has only a horizontal resolution of 400, it would be about 533 pixels. If a 16:9 widescreen TV had the same 600 lines of horizontal resolution, it would actually be more than 1,000 pixels across.

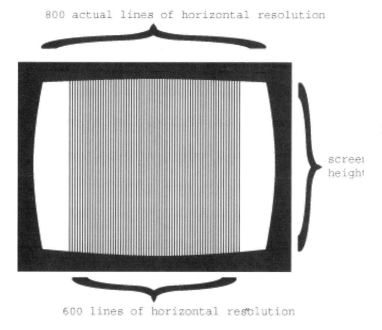

Figure 1-25 *Horizontal resolution is relative to the height of the screen.*

This terminology is confusing, and mistakes are often made because of it. When vendors of TVs and camcorders say their device records or displays a number of

lines of resolution or horizontal lines of resolution, they actually mean the number of vertical lines in the square shown in Figure 1-25.

For another example, a camera might record a 720×480 picture, but advertise "540 lines of horizontal resolution." A consumer might think, "How do I get 720 pixels if the camera can record only 540 lines?" In fact, according to this formula, the camera captures 540 * $^4/_3$ = 720 pixels. The formula is depicted in Figure 1-26.

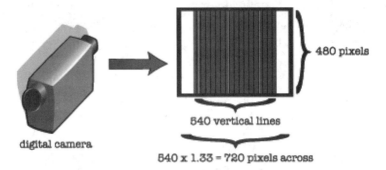

digital camera

480 pixels

540 vertical lines

540 x 1.33 = 720 pixels across

Figure 1-26 *Lines of resolution multiplied by screen resolution yields the number of pixels.*

To measure the horizontal lines of resolution of a particular TV or camera, many parallel black and white lines are put on the screen or camera in increasing density. At a certain number, they blur together and you won't be able to see alternating black and white lines. When you can no longer resolve, or see these lines distinctly, you have exceeded the horizontal resolution of that TV, as shown in Figure 1-27.

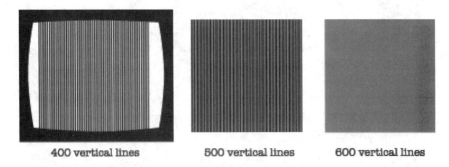

400 vertical lines   500 vertical lines   600 vertical lines

Figure 1-27 *This television has between 500 and 600 lines of horizontal resolution; any more than that and the lines start to blur together.*

The amount of effective horizontal resolution displayed depends on:

- The quality of the television
- The quality of the video signal

Because of the scanning lines in a television, it is misleading to state that an analog television has a resolution, such as 640×480 or 720×480; modern digital TVs actually do have a fixed number of dots that they can display vertically. However, TV video is usually captured into a computer at a resolution of either 720×480 or 640×480 pixels. This translates to about 0.3 megapixels—remarkably small compared to film—and yet a television still provides a very high quality image.

Figure 1-28 offers a summary of our resolution discussion, including vertical resolution, horizontal resolution, and horizontal lines of resolution.

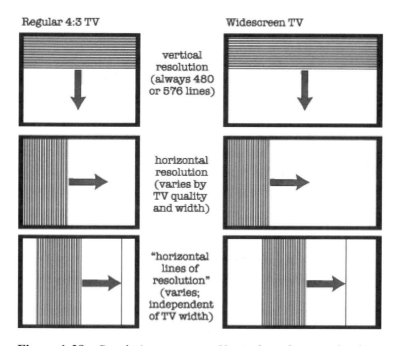

Figure 1-28 *Resolution summary: Vertical resolution is fixed; effective horizontal resolution displayed depends on the signal source and TV quality.*

HIGHER AND LOWER RESOLUTION SOURCES

TV always displays 480 (U.S. and Japan) or 576 (Europe) horizontal lines and, as discussed in the previous section, has characteristic horizontal lines of resolution. High-end TVs and analog studio monitors can display horizontal resolutions of 500, 600, 800, or even 1,000. Low-end televisions can have a horizontal resolution in the 200s, meaning they blur together the horizontal details, but they are still viewable.

The resolution of the information sent to the television can be lower or higher than the resolutions of the sets, as shown in Figure 1-29. The source of the television signal could be video camera, DVD, laser disc, broadcast video, or digital cable, all of which store a different number of horizontal lines. For instance, a low-quality VCR might record only 200 lines of resolution. This low resolution just shows up as fuzziness and indistinct image features, especially when the video is paused.

TV broadcast (330 dots/row)   VHS (200 dots/row)

Figure 1-29   *VCR playback can be blurry.*

A laser disc or high-definition digital cable signal has lines of resolution in the 500s. Even on a low-end TV with less than 500 lines, a DVD looks better than VHS because the better the input, the better the output. As a comparison, analog broadcast video transmits about 440 effective dots on each scan line and thus is rated 330 horizontal lines of resolution. See Figure 1-30.

With all this talk of specific line numbers, you may have gotten the impression that all that matters to image quality is the horizontal and vertical resolution. In fact, a lot more goes into it. For one thing, the quality of the electronics of a recording device and the quality of the analog-to-digital converters greatly affect the quality of the signal before it is recorded or broadcasted.

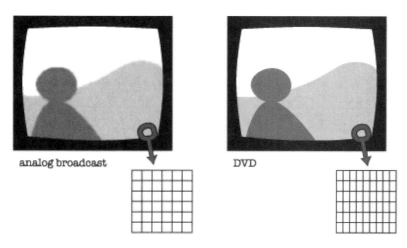

Figure 1-30 *Analog broadcast has fewer dots per row than DVD.*

When an image is scanned or created at a higher resolution than the destination playback device, that extra resolution is never wasted. The best output comes from much higher resolution input, especially if the data goes through some sort of digital translation or analog transport. For example, a very high-resolution digital signal might be squeezed down to a lower resolution (but still digital) signal in the process of being broadcast (for instance, a broadcaster needs to fit more channels into the same wire, so he cuts the size in half).

The better this signal is to begin with, the less degradation it experiences in the many stages it goes through in the process of getting in front of the viewer's eyes. And this applies especially in Internet video, where the signal has to be severely compressed to get to the viewer. If possible, work with high-resolution digital images from start to finish.

COLOR RESOLUTION

Many complaints about broadcast video revolve around its color quality. If you go into a TV store, you'll notice that the colors vary widely from set to set. This shows some of the color drawbacks of broadcast and videotaped video. Attempts have been made throughout the years to improve the situation, but the fundamental standards of broadcast video (and its subsequent storage formats on videotape) are weighed down by its analog heritage.

Part of the reason that color can go bad is the way it is transmitted. In U.S. broadcast, color was actually an afterthought, and had to be hacked onto the existing black and white standard. The resolution of the color is actually lower than the resolution of the brightness, as shown in Figure 1-31. So where the horizontal resolution is around 330 lines for broadcast video, the actual color resolution might be only one-fourth of that. This lack of color information doesn't affect viewer enjoyment too much; if you look closely, you will sometimes see color bleeding around shapes and edges, but most of the time it looks fairly acceptable.

brightness data

color data

Figure 1-31 *The resolution of the color data is only one-fourth the resolution of the brightness data.*

This reduction of color resolution is not limited to analog. Digital video formats apply the same technique to reducing the amount of data they store. You will find that the differentiation between various digital video formats relates to whether the color resolution is the same as, half as much as, or even one-fourth the resolution of the image itself. (As we explain in Chapter 2, "Video Compression," brightness information has more to do with picture quality than color data does.)

Another problem that leads to color inconsistency besides low color resolution is the fact that all the video signals (brightness, different colors) are squeezed onto one pair of wires. This leads to our next discussion: video connectors.

CONNECTORS AND IMAGE QUALITY

If you examine the video cable connector to your computer, shown in Figure 1-32, you'll see 15 different wires, six of which carry color and brightness information between the computer and the monitor. Consumer video devices often cram color and brightness signals onto one pair of wires, whereas computers separate the colors red, green, and blue and transmit them on different wires.

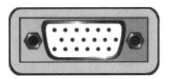

Figure 1-32   *Video cable connector on computer.*

Television sets and VCRs connect via two different types of wires. One is the wire that connects the antenna or cable feed and VCR to the television, shown in Figure 1-33. It squeezes together all the different channels, audio, and video on one coaxial cable.

United States   Europe

Figure 1-33   *Coaxial cables.*

The other method of connecting TV video devices isn't much better. It uses RCA connectors, shown in Figure 1-34. These connectors separate the two channels of audio, but the video signal is still composite, meaning that brightness and the three different colors are still squished together.

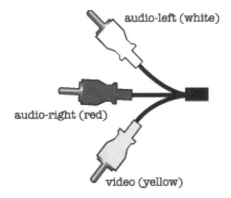

audio-left (white)

audio-right (red)

video (yellow)

Figure 1-34   *RCA composite connectors.*

A slight improvement was made to separate the color from the brightness signal, which you see on the higher-end consumer gear. Shown in Figure 1-35,

S-video is round with four pins and a little rectangular shape. S-video is sharper and brighter than the composite video that travels over the ubiquitous yellow RCA cable.

Figure 1-35   *S-video.*

When importing video stored on VHS tapes (such as into a computer with consumer equipment), S-video is the only cable to use. If your VCR or video import device does not have S-video, then you need to purchase one that does.

Component video connectors are the best choice for analog video because they break the signal into different color components. When the color is sent this way, it has the least degradation due to transmission, and thus can retain broadcast quality even when going through editing, re-recordings, and so on. We highly suggest that you have access to component video equipment for importing into the computer.

The appropriate cables for component transmission are called BNC (Bayonet Neill Concelman), shown in Figure 1-36. There are three to five component wires going between devices—three for color and sometimes two more for horizontal and vertical synchronization, especially when the video signal can have different refresh rates and pixel resolutions, such as computer monitors.

For television signals, the color components are split into three, but they aren't RGB because broadcast signals are not broken into those components. On higher-end DVD players, shown in Figure 1-37, you see three connectors labeled either Y Pb Pr or Y Cr Cb. The brightness of the whole picture and green color information go on one cable (Y), and the blue (Pb) and red (Pr) color signals alone (without brightness) go on the other two cables. These usually connect with either BNC cables or special higher quality RCA cables that are color-coded to match. (For more information on different types of component color, see Chapter 2).

You won't find consumer analog-to-digital capture systems that accept component video; these systems primarily consist of a method of getting better signal from a DVD player or digital set-top box out to the television with cleaner, more consistent color and signal quality.

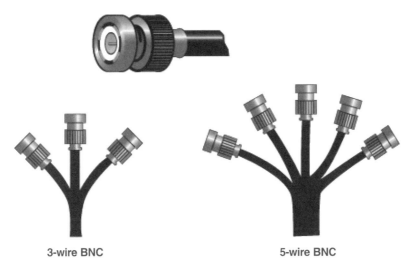

3-wire BNC   5-wire BNC

Figure 1-36 *BNC cables.*

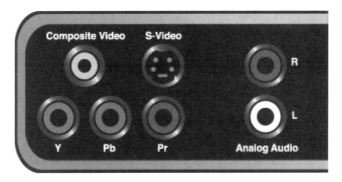

Figure 1-37 *Higher-end DVD players and TVs have component video connectors (Y Pb Pr).*

Recent developments lean toward all-digital transmission between devices. Flat-screen TVs and computer displays, unlike analog tube monitors and TVs, are digital internally. Thus, these devices degrade quality to reduce the DVD or digital cable signal (digital) to component video (analog) and then send it to a flat screen (digital).

DVI (Digital Visual Interface), shown in Figure 1-38, provides a completely digital path from computer or video playback device to display. However, these interfaces cannot be used for importing video into a computer; they are strictly one-way interfaces by design. These interfaces have built-in copy protection where the playback device authorizes the TV to play back the video only if it

trusts the make and brand of the TV. So, although DVI may enhance the way a DVD plays back on your big-screen TV, it isn't capable of transferring video content into a computer.

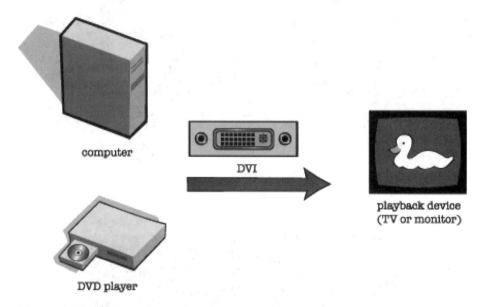

computer

DVI

playback device
(TV or monitor)

DVD player

Figure 1-38   *DVI provides a completely digital path from computer or DVD player to a monitor or TV.*

A digital interface that is designed to go into a computer is the IEEE 1394 connector, also called FireWire, or i.Link, shown in Figure 1-39. The Institute of Electrical and Electronics Engineers (IEEE) specified the standard; Apple was the first computer company to promote it heavily for video editing under the trademark FireWire. Sony promotes the connection on all their video cameras and computers as i.Link.

The IEEE1394 connector is found mainly on digital video cameras, but is also seen on digital cable and set-top boxes as well as stand-alone DVD recorders. It is also used for connecting computers to each other, and connecting small portable hard drives (and Apple's iPods) to computers.

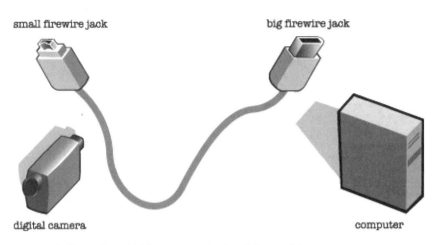

small firewire jack   big firewire jack

digital camera   computer

Figure 1-39   *The 1394/FireWire i.Link cables and jacks.*

RECTANGULAR PIXELS AND NON-SQUARE PROJECTION

Almost all computer monitors work with square pixels. The pixels have the same width and height, relative to the dots per inch (dpi) of the monitor. Thus, a circle would have the same number of pixels across as it would down, as shown in Figure 1-40.

square pixels   rectangular pixels

Figure 1-40   *Computers use square pixels, where-as video sometimes has rectangular pixels.*

Film and television do not always use square pixels. The horizontal resolution can vary from source to source, and if it is scanned at a different width, the pixels will not have a 1:1 ratio (square). Theoretically, an image could have vertical resolution much higher or much lower than the horizontal resolution, but still look right when displayed only on a 4:3 ratio screen.

TELEVISION

When DVD video was standardized, instead of going with a 4:3 ratio of pixels, a slightly higher 720×480 (U.S. and Japan) and 720×576 (Europe) pixel resolution was used. Note that the corresponding aspect ratios for these are 1.5:1 and

1.25:1, respectively. Nonetheless, these are displayed at a 4:3 ratio on TV screens, resulting in a pixel aspect ratio of .9:1, as shown in Figure 1-41. These pictures are only 90 percent as wide as they are tall.

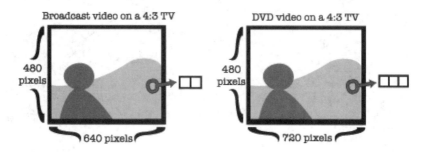

Figure 1-41 *Broadcast video has 640 square pixels across, whereas DVD video fits 720 tall pixels across.*

Because computers can display only square pixels, DV video can appear slightly narrowly on the computer screen. These non-square pixels are sometimes be called DV or D1 pixels.

Sometimes 4:3 video is stored in resolutions such as 480×480. This does not mean that the image is supposed to be square—even though it looks square on a monitor, as shown in Figure 1-42.

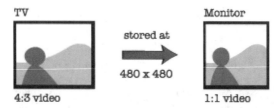

Figure 1-42 *Square storage of wide pixel video.*

Figure 1-43 shows how the image is supposed to look.

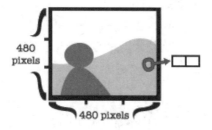

Figure 1-43 *Wide, non-square pixels.*

Video software will properly deal with resolutions as long as you tell the program the correct pixel aspect ratio (often it can guess correctly). Also, when you combine computer-generated, square-pixel art with non-square imported video, one of the two images will be resampled, meaning that its pixels will be scaled up or down to fit the other image. So you will need to be aware of the subtle changes made in resizing the pixels to ensure that the combination of images is acceptable.

FILM

A similar phenomenon occurs in the film world, where 35mm film has been used for almost a century. Originally, movies were shot and projected in a 4:3 aspect ratio (1.33:1), as shown in Figure 1-44.

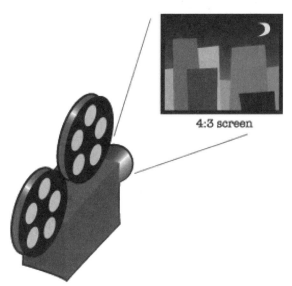

4:3 screen

Figure 1-44 *Traditional movies are shot and projected in a 4:3 aspect ratio.*

When filmmakers started making wider screen shoots, such as 1.85:1 (a very popular modern format), the solution was simply to shrink the height of the image on the film and put masks around the projector output so that it would block the extra film area—the so-called letterbox shown in Figure 1-45.

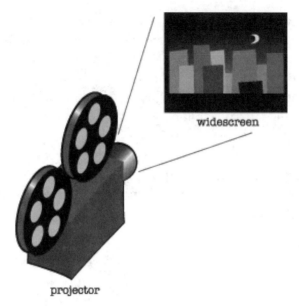

Figure 1-45   *widescreen movies are shrunk and letterboxed.*

Letterbox wastes a bit of film (the portions above and below the image aren't being shown), and it uses less film for a bigger image, effectively lowering the resolution. When it came time to project very wide formats, such as 2.35–2.40:1, a technique for using all the film area was developed. The image is squeezed in half horizontally onto the film, and then the horizontal is doubled again when projected, using an anamorphic lens, as shown in Figure 1-46.

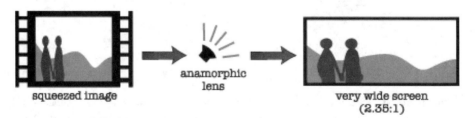

Figure 1-46   *Anamorphic film.*

Because the film measures about 1.33:1 in physical dimensions but the image will be projected at about 2.35:1, you should be able to see that the horizontal direction gets less resolution than the vertical direction.

When anamorphic film is projected, the full resolution of the film itself shows up on the screen. When it is distributed on digital cable or DVD, however, it has to be digitized, captured, and converted to pixels. Each of the resulting pixels has a rectangular aspect of about 1.76:1 (U.S.and Europe). The math is not the interesting point; the point is that the pixels are not square.

When the DVD plays it back on a 4:3 television, it looks squished, just like the left-side image in Figure 1-46. If the DVD player or the television is smart enough, it will create letterboxing and center the image on the screen. If the TV set is a 16:9 widescreen, then it will do some letterboxing but will expand the image to the width of the screen. The benefit of these "anamorphic DVDs" and digital broadcasts is that they provide the full resolution of the image to the DVD player and TV, and then allow those devices to make appropriate decisions about how to display that information. Ordinary letterboxed DVDs have the black bars preinstalled so to speak, and thus provide only half the picture resolution of anamorphic DVDs.

So, an anamorphic widescreen movie stored on DVD will be stored at 720×480, but the 720 pixels will be resampled and stretched (by creating new pixels) to fill 1280 pixels horizontally, as shown in Figure 1-47.

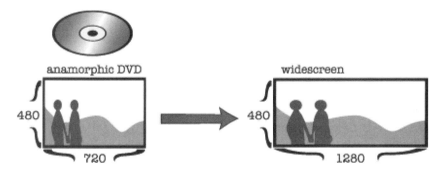

Figure 1-47   *Anamorphic DVD.*

As stated earlier in this section, non-square pixels aren't really a problem so much as they are confusing. They can be easily converted into square pixels— or not—when the video is digitized into the computer.

BROADCAST STANDARDS

We mentioned several different frame rates and resolutions in the previous discussions, and drew a distinction between U.S., Japan, and Europe. Figure 1-48 shows the different broadcast standards used around the world.

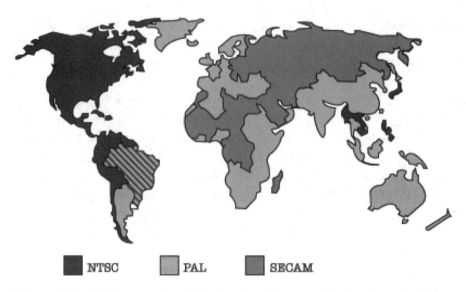

Figure 1-48   *There are essentially three broadcast standards across the globe.*

The international standards for analog broadcast are:

- National Television System Committee (NTSC, 1953). The TV standard used in the U.S., Japan, Canada, parts of South America, and elsewhere. It has 480 visible horizontal scan lines and 60 interlaced fields per second (60i). It has the highest frame rate of the interlaced formats, and thus the smoothest motion for content recorded on video camera.

> **Note**   It's important to note that 60 fields per second is actually usually 59.94 fields per second, and thus the 30 pairs of fields per second actually play back 29.97 times per second. Source material that has been converted from another format, such as film or PAL or computer, may be in 30 fields per second and may need to be slightly changed in speed for audio to sync exactly. You will often see 30 and 60 used when they really mean 29.97 and 59.94. NTSC is sometimes incorrectly called 30 interlaced frames per second, but this can be misleading because each field cap-tures a unique moment in time.

- Phase Alternation by Line (PAL, 1967). The TV standard used by much of Western Europe, United Kingdom, and many other parts of the world. It has better color than NTSC, being a newer design, and has 576 visible horizontal scan lines. However, it is slower, at 50 interlaced fields per second (50i). The name comes from the technical description of the way color is transmitted. Brazil uses a slightly different version of PAL that runs at 59.94/60i.

- Systeme Electronique Couleur Avec Memoir (SECAM, 1967). This electronic color system with memory (describing the technical manner in which color is transmitted) is used in France, Russia, much of Eastern Europe, and everywhere else PAL and NTSC are not used. It has 576 visible horizontal scan lines and 50 interlaced fields per second (50i), like PAL. It differs mainly in the way color is transmitted. Content is usually produced in NTSC or PAL, and is converted to this format at the end.

Broadcast-quality videotape in the U.S. is in NTSC, and broadcast-quality videotape in Europe is in PAL or SECAM. The cameras used in these countries produce video in the corresponding format.

The resolutions corresponding to traditional analog are called Standard Definition (SD), and the new higher resolution digital formats are High-Definition Television, or HDTV. Table 1-1 shows the standard definition formats.

Table 1-1   Standard Definition Formats

480/60i	640×480 pixels, 60 interlaced fps (NTSC Broadcast).
480/60i	640×480 pixels, 60 interlaced fps (NTSC DVD).
576/50i	720×576 pixels, 50 interlaced fps (PAL/SECAM Broadcast).

The worldwide conversion to digital and HDTV is still in progress, and will be for years. Because of the need for backwards compatibility with film, European, and U.S. broadcast video, the standard has grown to include several dozen potential combinations of resolutions, frame rates, and interlace options. A couple primary examples are shown in Table 1-2.

Table 1-2   Example Digital High Definition (HD) Formats

480/60p	720×480 pixels, 60 progressive fps (Progressive NTSC DVD).
576/50p	720×480 pixels, 50 progressive fps (PAL/SECAM).

continues

Table 1-2 Example Digital High Definition (HD) Formats *continued*

720/60i	1280×720 pixels, 60 interlaced fps. This is a high-resolution NTSC format.
720/30p	1280×720 pixels, 30 progressive fps. This is a high-resolution NTSC format.
720/24p	1280×720 pixels, 24 progressive fps. This is a good format for broadcasting film, as it provides high resolution and native 24 fps with no interlacing.
1080/24p	1920×1080 pixels, 24 progressive fps. This is the highest quality film recording and playback format in the Digital TV standards, and is comparable to 2K digital film scanning.
1080/60i	1920×1080 pixels, 60 interlaced fps. This is a very high-resolution image at NTSC refresh.
1080/60p	1920×1080 pixels, 60 progressive fps. This is a very high-resolution 60 fps image.

Although you might not be able to deliver at these rates over high-speed Internet connections, the source video you deal with will most likely be in one of these formats.

> **Note** As a terminology note, you will often see the refresh omitted when televisions are being marketed, as it always the same in a particular country. Thus, you will see HDTV sets labeled as supporting 480p, 720p, or 1080i. These correspond (in the U.S.) to 480/30i, 720/30p, 1080/60i, and so on.

VIDEO BASICS SUMMARY

In this section we tried to give you the basics of the most common video formats so that you better appreciate the process of getting this content into the computer. The key data are:

- It takes a frame rate of 10 fps to convincingly simulate motion.
- It takes a frame rate greater than 24 fps (film) for speech to match the lips well.

- It takes a frame rate of 48 or higher to mask perceptible flicker.
- Films have frames; TVs have alternating interlaced fields.
- 24p means 24 progressive frames per second.
- 50i means 50 interlaced fields per second.
- Analog video must be converted to digital to get into the computer.
- Low-resolution digital is worse than high-resolution analog.
- Work with video in as high a resolution as possible because you can go down, but you cannot go up.
- Use digital interconnects for digital video transfer, and use the best analog interconnects available when transferring analog. Don't use composite video for copying or importing video.
- Pixels aren't always square, a fact you need to account for when importing TV content to computers and combining it with computer graphics.

CAPTURING VIDEO

To get video online, you need to capture it. We discuss four general sources: digital tape, analog film, analog tape, and computer graphics. Each of these sources is captured into the computer in a different way, as shown in Figure 1-49:

- If the video is on a digital tape format, it needs to be captured but not converted.
- If the video is on film, it needs to be converted from analog to digital, transferred to a tape format, and then captured, unless cinema quality scanning at 2K or 4K is available, which is a much more expensive process.
- If the video is on an analog tape format, it needs to be analog-to-digital converted in the capture process.
- If the video is created on a computer (for example, synthetic computer graphics, such as 2D or 3D animation), it does not have to be captured; however, it needs to be exported into a high-resolution source format for editing.

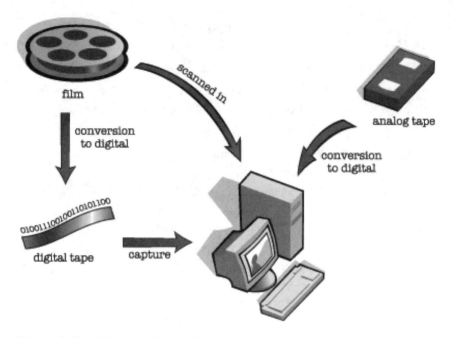

Figure 1-49 *Major methods of capturing video.*

Compression, the science of reducing the amount of data it takes to represent video (or audio, still images, text, and so on), is the subject of Chapter 2. To get video to fit through modems and even high-speed connections, it needs to be squished down, and even lowered in resolution, as shown in Figure 1-50. In our discussion on resolution, we described a variety of sizes from 4096×3072 (high-resolution film scan) down to 640×480 (captured broadcast television). Internet resolutions are even lower than this, often 320×240.

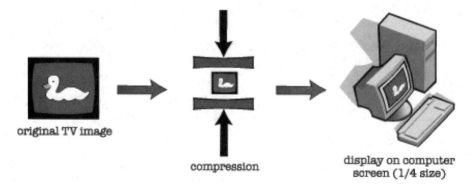

Figure 1-50 *Even low-resolution video must be further compressed for Internet broadcast.*

The fact that the eventual resolution will be low does not mean that you can simply scan the video in at that resolution. Source video should always be scanned in at as high a resolution as possible, because editing and compression work best on high-quality, high-resolution source material. When producing smaller resolution versions of video, it is better to have more than twice the destination resolution in the source. Creating 320×240 video from 640×480 video works well, but creating it from 400×300 video is problematic.

At the beginning of this chapter, we discussed the differences between progressive and interlaced video. Most inexpensive recording devices, such as video cameras and VCRs, are for television, and thus are interlaced; however, only television sets display interlaced video well. Computers can really display progressive frames. Thus, interlaced video must be converted to progressive video when or after it is captured. Even DVD movies have to be converted to progressive as they are played back on a computer. Because deinterlacing involves merging fields or creating new frames, there are many different ways to do it. This is part of why capturing and compressing video effectively is something of an art.

DIGITAL TAPE FORMATS

There are hundreds of different film and tape video formats. The range of equipment you will have to deal with is much smaller. Here we present the more common options.

We start with the most popular format for getting video into a computer: consumer digital videotape (DV). There are many kinds of professional digital videotape because there are many competing companies, and there are both consumer and professional studio needs and requirements. But the term DV has been marketed to mean the standard data format for consumer digital video.

DV was designed with computers and consumer-level video editing in mind. People use DV cameras to shoot feature-length cinematic films, so the quality of the format is certainly quite sufficient for Internet video work. Consumer DV stores interlaced video at 720×480 or 720×576 pixels (480/60i or 576/50i, respectively). The video is stored digitally onto the tape at 25 megabits per second (about 4 megabytes per second) and thus is sometimes technically called DV25. Color information is sampled at one-fourth the resolution of the image (in contrast to professional formats that sample it at half the image resolution.)

DV data is stored in several different tape sizes, shown in Figure 1-51. MiniDV is pretty much the standard DV tape format, and it fits into everything from small handheld video recorders to large digital filmmaker cameras. In addition to MiniDV tapes, you will encounter the larger DV tapes. Both MiniDV and DV tapes sometimes say DVC (for digital video cassette) on the package.

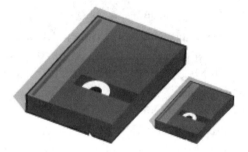

Figure 1-51 *MiniDV and DV tapes.*

Two variants of DV tapes are DVCam and DVCPRO. These tape formats store less time on a single tape but are more durable, can survive more playbacks, and degrade less over time. They look the same as DV and MiniDV tapes, but are labeled DVCam and DVCPRO. Tape decks for these special formats can play back normal DV tapes as well, but not the other way around.

Digital 8mm is a format used by Sony in some of its DV cameras, shown in Figure 1-52. The tapes are the same size and shape as Hi8 and 8mm analog tapes. Digital 8mm cameras can also play analog 8mm tapes.

Figure 1-52 *Hi8 8mm Digital 8 tape.*

Note All of these DV tapes store the same information: a digital picture with about 540 lines of horizontal resolution (720 pixels at a 4:3 ratio). They all have the same information recorded on them at 25Mbps.

Almost all consumer and pro-consumer DV cameras have an IEEE1394 connection. This connector was designed in conjunction with the DV standard, and it is the dominant way to get video into and out of the camera digitally.

There is also a recent consumer D-VHS standard that records digital and even HD video on normal VHS videocassettes. IEEE 1394 connections are finding their way into home entertainment equipment, and you will find several VCRs on the market with IEEE 1394 connections. Some of these store HD and regular broadcast television on tape over a DV connection (in a more compressed, non-DV format), but they can also be used to play existing analog VHS tapes out to standard DV data streams.

The other dominant digital standard in the professional world is DigiBeta, which is higher quality than DV. DigiBeta, shown in Figure 1-53, is used extensively for portable filming of news events. It uses larger tapes than DV, and tends to hold less video because the tape runs faster to store the extra signal quality. It is the standard broadcast quality television studio format. For this standard, color information is sampled at half the image resolution, twice that of DV. Another DV format, DV50, has the same color resolution as DigiBeta.

The increased color resolution in these formats helps when actors are filmed in front of a blue or green screen (a process called chroma keying) because the edge between the actor and the background (which has to be replaced with a digital backdrop) is sharper.

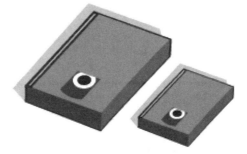

Figure 1-53   *DigiBeta tape.*

There are many, many other digital tape and camera-to-computer connection standards and a corresponding alphabet soup of acronyms and marketing names. If you have to deal with media in these formats, you will probably need to use a service bureau because the professional equipment is often 10 to 100 times more expensive than consumer gear. You will also see the word Pro appended to all sorts of tape formats, and you will see different sizes of tape. You may run into formats such as D-1, D-2, D-5, D-9, and so on. Each of these is a different digital format developed to handle a high-end studio digital need. Some of these formats do full-resolution color sampling; although this is necessary for high-end image editing, it is overkill for Internet video because it greatly increases the bandwidth requirements.

Sometimes you will see the letters HD next to a digital standard, designating standards for recording HDTV at resolutions such as 1280×720 and 1920×1080. These resolutions are far higher than even today's DV, so they've started to come up with new formats, such as DV100, as well as other non-DV based formats. The point to keep in mind is that digital tape is designed for broadcast quality and higher, and thus a digital tape is certainly suitable for lower-resolution Internet video.

DIGITAL VIDEO CAMERAS

Now that we've seen the different digital videotape format, let's take a look at digital camera technology. Just because you record on digital videotape at DV resolution does not mean that one camera will produce as good a picture as any other. As in most things, you get what you pay for, and you can spend anywhere from $300 to $30,000 for a DV-based camera. However, before you go out and spend $30,000, it's important to understand the differences in technology and where the additional cost comes from.

NUMBER OF CCDs

The device inside a video camera that actually takes the picture is a two-dimensional grid of light sensors called a CCD, or charge-coupled device. In a CCD, each of the light-sensing elements in the grid is connected to coupled (or linked) elements, which pass along a charge or voltage that represents the amount of light they received. Most low-cost digital video cameras have a single CCD that records the brightness and color of the image. Higher-end and professional video cameras separate red, green, and blue, sending each color light to a different CCD to be measured, as shown in Figure 1-54. This is your first purchase consideration: Is it a one-CCC or three-CCD camera?

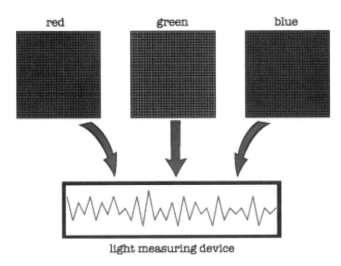

Figure 1-54 *CCDs (charge-coupled devices) measure light intensity.*

INTERNAL RESOLUTION

All these cameras have an internal resolution that depends on the size of the CCD. The internal resolution can be higher or lower than the standard resolution of DV cameras (720×480). The higher-end cameras can produce the full 540 lines (720 pixels) on DV, and the brighter, cleaner, clearer, better colored image stored on the exact same DV tape will look better at the same resolution than a single-CCD camera.

Lower resolution, single-CCD cameras will still store 720 pixels, but they will interpolate the missing pixels by averaging two adjacent pixels and inserting a new pixel between them. This is also called upsampling. As you can imagine, creating new pixels practically out of thin air does not really increase the quality; it increases the size and usually decreases the quality.

LENS QUALITY

The camera lens also affects the quality of the image. The small lens in a hand-held portable MiniDV camera does not compare to the large, studio-issued lens used for portable field journalism and news gathering.

We aren't necessarily trying to tell you what digital camera you should buy, as ultimately your needs and budget will determine that. We do want to point out some of the factors to consider when using a digital camera for Internet video.

Much of the information you find about digital cameras relates to their suitability as a replacement for budget filmmaking. A large number of resources can be found online, which show you how to get a film look while shooting video. As discussed earlier, the big differences between digital video and film are interlacing and the higher frame rate. Fortunately, all the information about how to get a film look from your digital camera is exactly the information that points the way to the best online delivery of your digital video. The usual first steps in preparing video for Internet delivery are:

- Making sure the frames are progressive
- Reducing the frame rate

Some special DV cameras actually have a progressive mode where the film they shoot is stored on DV tape, but it contains 24 progressive frames. They target digital filmmakers who intend to transfer their project to film and project it in a theater, but they are just as useful for an Internet broadcaster seeking clean, low-frame rate, progressive content. If you have access to one of these cameras, by all means, use it for shooting your Internet video.

FILM FORMATS

Often times the content you might want to put online is available only in analog format. Here we take a brief look at popular film formats.

8mm film and Super 8 were the old home movie formats. A lot of this consumer footage has been converted to video. However, in the video conversion, it was probably copied onto VHS tape, which is interlaced and fairly low quality.

Regular 8   Super 8

Figure 1-55   *Regular 8mm and Super8 film.*

16mm film, shown in Figure 1-56, is used for student and educational films, and in the past, 35mm films were converted to 16mm for TV broadcast. A lot of archival material exists on 16mm.

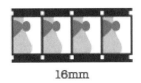

Figure 1-56   *16mm film.*

35mm film, shown in Figure 1-57, is the staple film used in cinema today, and is used in a variety of different formats and aspect ratios.

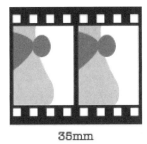

Figure 1-57   *35mm film.*

There are many ways to capture film into the computer, many of which yield unsatisfactory results. The goal is to get film into the computer at a high resolution (720×480 or higher), non-interlaced, and in a direct-to-digital format, never going through analog television videotape.

Here are some methods of importing film to the computer, from very bad to excellent:

- Project the film on the wall and videotape it, then import the tape. This technique is extremely low-quality, but it works.
- Use an at-home film transfer kit and a video camera. This is definitely low-quality.
- Convert it professionally to analog videotape and then capture the tape with an analog capture card. This approach is low-quality, interlaced, and analog. VHS tape mangles color and has a low resolution when captured into the computer.
- Have a service bureau convert it to DVD. This yields variable quality because the service bureau might use an analog capture process instead of going straight to digital. DVD video is designed for watching and is hard to edit or convert.

- Have a service bureau convert it to interlaced DV, which is designed to be edited on a computer and can be transferred into the computer digitally without degrading the signal. The presence of interlacing will require some work on the computer side, as the 30 separate fields (60i) have to be spliced back into 24p progressive frames (deinterlaced); however, this can be done without a major loss of quality.

- Have a service bureau convert it to progressive DV. Many of the new systems have a way of storing 24p directly on DV tape, so that it can be imported onto the computer with little conversion needed and no de-interlacing.

- Have the service bureau scan the film at high resolution (2KB, 4KB) and deliver it on computer disk as progressive uncompressed or losslessly compressed video.

We recommend only the last three options. The reason is that analog film, as discussed, has the potential to store at least 4000×3000 pixels of resolution. Converting it through another analog format, such as VHS tape, can decimate the effective pixel resolution down to around 330×480 pixels and reduce the color resolution. Downsampling works best when you have more than twice the resolution you need. VHS resolution is already low, and the generally lousy color of VHS tape—which blurs out the details a bit more—just compounds the problem. Then there's the need to reverse the 3:2 pulldown of the video. Although video can still be constructed from this, it's an awful thing to do to your film. As Figure 1-58 indicates, avoid the use of VHS in your conversion process.

Having the service bureau convert to a DVD is a possibility, but only if you know they will do it correctly. Studio-made DVDs are high-enough quality to be used for Internet video without question, but a cheap conversion service might put the film through analog video before it is saved on DVD. You want to ensure that the film goes straight into a CCD and digitally onto a tape or hard disk.

Also, if you import video from a DVD, do not play the DVD recorder into an analog capture card! Put the DVD into the DVD drive of the computer and pull the files off directly. Figure 1-59 makes the point.

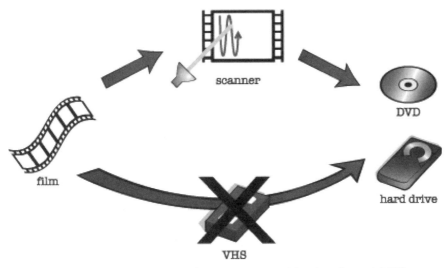

Figure 1-58   *In analog to digital conversion, avoid going through VHS.*

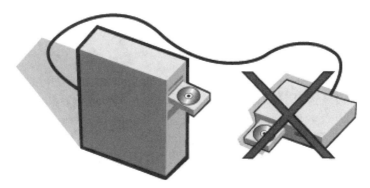

Figure 1-59   *Import using your computer's DVD drive, not analog cables.*

In summary, film is already analog. Every step in converting the film should be digital. Use high-resolution scans, and don't let your film conversion come anywhere near analog video!

ANALOG TAPE FORMATS AND CAMERAS

There are many analog videotape standards. You are likely to encounter only a few of these, however, and all others can be transferred at a service bureau.

VHS tape, shown in Figure 1-60, is the dominant consumer standard and is the tape you put in your VCR. Although there have been several attempts to market higher-resolution versions of VHS, most consumer video is recorded on VHS. Some video cameras use a compact version of VHS, called C-VHS, which can play in a normal VCR using an adapter.

VHS tape records only 220–250 lines of horizontal resolution; it stores video on $1/2$ inch tape and if the tape is run slower, it records at a lower quality but stores up to eight hours on a videotape. VHS stores the color essentially as a composite signal on the tape. Copies of VHS tapes are almost always of unacceptable quality; VHS tapes of studio movies are made from a higher quality master source, not other VHS tapes.

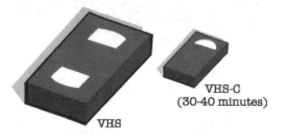

Figure 1-60   *VHS and C-VHS tapes.*

Video8 and Hi8, shown in Figure 1-61, are 8mm tape minicassette formats for digital cameras. Like VHS, Video8 can be run at a slower speed for longer video at lower quality. 8mm was about the same as VHS quality at about 250 lines of horizontal resolution; Hi8 improved this significantly to 415, and separated color and brightness in storage. These tapes are upward compatible with the Digital 8mm standard of modern digital cameras in that the tapes play back through the IEEE 1394 port for easier DV importing.

Figure 1-61   *Video8 and Hi8 tapes.*

Betacam SP or BetaSP, or just Beta, shown in Figure 1-62, is the dominant professional analog standard. Introduced in the mid-1980s, it became the standard for broadcast quality studio recording and in-the-field news reporting. Betacam SP stores about an hour on a tape, and about 340 lines of horizontal resolution. However, unlike consumer formats, it stores component video, meaning that the brightness and individual colors are split into separate signals. This factor alone results in a format that can be copied over several generations without a significant drop in quality.

Betacam

Figure 1-62 *Beta tape format.*

ANALOG CAPTURE

With so much video recorded on VHS and 8mm/Hi8 video cameras throughout the last few decades, you certainly will find that you need to capture it into the computer. There are a number of ways to do this, again in increasing order of preference:

- Aim your webcam at a television set that plays your video.
- Capture the video using an inexpensive USB 1.1 video capture device connected to the composite video out jack of a 15-year-old VCR.
- Capture the video using an analog capture card, shown in Figure 1-63, that plugs into the computer, using S-video jacks to connect to a newer VCR or tape deck.

Figure 1-63 *PCI capture card.*

- Use an analog-to-DV converter box, shown in Figure 1-64, that is hooked to the S-video cable of a newer VCR or video camera.

Figure 1-64   *The back of a DV converter box.*

- Use a VCR (VHS) or digital camcorder (Video8 or Hi8) with DV out.
- Get the content converted by a service bureau that has professional decks designed to recover the most color and quality from lower resolution videotape.

Importing Betacam SP usually involves a service bureau with the appropriate equipment, but because the video is broadcast quality to begin with, it transfers nicely to digital when the component connections are used (don't just dump it to S-video or composite connectors).

Betacam SP or Hi8, with a high-quality camera, are the only recommended formats if you must use analog recording equipment or cameras.

Sometimes, if you do your own analog capture and conversion, it can help to use the exact same unit for playback that you recorded on. VCRs and cameras that are out of calibration may produce recordings that play back correctly only in that device. (This is the only exception to the "don't use an old VCR" rule).

For live video broadcasting on the Internet, using an analog capture card makes sense, especially if a composite or S-video feed is the only thing available from the video crew.

If you use an analog capture card (as in the third option), the most compatible choice is Viewcast Corporation's Osprey cards. Just about everyone uses them; more importantly, they are the cards best supported by the major vendors of live encoding software (including Microsoft and Real).

As mentioned previously, DV has become the best-supported way to get video cleanly into the computer, so you should use DV as the import mechanism, even for analog video.

Finally, service bureaus with experience in importing low-quality footage might have equipment or know-how to convert VHS tapes into something that can be successfully imported into a computer.

COMPUTER GRAPHICS

Synthetic computer graphics don't have to be imported, as they are already in the computer; however, they often must be converted to formats suitable for Internet delivery. In most graphics creation programs, such as 3D rendering programs or animation programs, there is an option to export a high-quality or uncompressed image, or to save out the individual frames. You want to save your graphics in an uncompressed full-frame movie format (one file, not individual frames), as shown in Figure 1-65. For more information, see Chapters 2 and 3, "Video Storage File Formats."

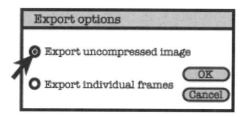

Figure 1-65 *Exporting computer graphics.*

CREATING NEW INTERNET VIDEO CONTENT

It should be clear to you that only digital equipment should be used to create new content for Internet delivery. The cleaner the input signal is, the more effectively you can squeeze it down for Internet delivery. The only exception is if studio-grade, analog component video equipment (Beta SP) is available to you.

Up until now we have assumed that your content destined for the Internet has already been produced and edited. If you are completely new to shooting video, do some research online or get a book on digital filmmaking. As stated before, most of the advice on how to get a film look on digital equipment translates well to producing a high-quality Internet video product.

If you feel relatively confident as a videographer, the following sections provide additional considerations to improve the quality of your video when it is translated for Internet delivery.

AUDIENCE INTERNET CONNECTION

The primary obstacle to delivering high-quality Internet video is the speed of the viewer's Internet connection. If modem users are part of the target audience, only low-motion video (talking heads, newscasts, and slow still scenes) can be squeezed down to fit in their connection. If the target audience has broadband, then full-motion video will be feasible. Also, if the users are willing to wait to download the whole video before watching and don't need to see video the instant they click, then even full-screen movies will be a viable delivery option. Chapters 2 and 5, "Video Transport Protocols," go over this in detail.

SHOOTING

Although this is not a book on cinematography, some basic rules of shooting video apply:

- Have a script or a plan of what you're going to shoot.
- Make sure there is plenty of light on the people or objects in the scene and that the light is not facing the camera.
- Shoot more film than you need and edit it later.
- Try to match the lighting conditions if you shoot in more than one place (so they blend well).
- Use external microphones connected to the camera and near the people who are talking; don't rely on the built-in camera microphone.

The following is a list of Internet-specific advice on how to shoot video. These points apply mainly to environments in which the video must be highly compressed to fit into Internet connections:

- Use a tripod for everything. Don't hold the camera.
- If the target audience uses modems, don't even move the camera. Choose a single shot, and film that position for the entire video.
- Don't zoom. Zooming is hard for the computer to compress, and won't come across well at Internet resolutions.
- If you have to pan (move camera sideways), do it slowly and evenly, and preferably not at all.
- Reduce clutter in scenes, including unnecessary objects, patterns, colors, pictures, and backgrounds.

- Minimize the use of scene changes. Keep most of the video in the same scene.

- Minimize the use of complex scene transitions, such as fading from one scene to another or having the old scene move out while the new scene moves in. These effects don't compress well and tend to look choppy.

- Make the subject (people or action you're filming) of the scene larger by zooming in (but then leave Zoom button alone). When the video is reduced in size and blurred, a small subject is hard to make out.

- Minimize the motion of the subject itself.

You might interpret all this advice to mean that you should shoot a perfectly still person on an empty white background. Although this is a bit extreme, it is true that motion and detail are the problematic factors for Internet-delivered video. It is just a fact of life that sitcoms look consistently better than kung-fu movies when compressed for Internet delivery. High-quality, cinematic video is possible on the Internet, but it takes longer to download, is accessible to less of the audience, and tends to cost more to deliver. These tradeoffs are discussed in more detail in Chapters 2, 4, and 5. Your goal should be to use the available resources to convey the most important aspects of the subject of your video, and not waste resources on non-essential features.

EDITING

Almost all currently shipping personal computers come with video editing software. There are many consumer and professional editing applications to choose from. Operating systems now come bundled with video editing applications, and the major computer vendors include their own custom software as well. The consumer editing applications often come with built-in features for saving directly to Internet video, whereas others are more oriented for exporting to DVD.

Almost any editing application is sufficient for creating Internet video. As discussed in this chapter, a minimum of transitions and other visual fluff are desired. The best use of editing is to make Internet video as short as possible, preserving only those video segments that contribute to the message you want to convey in your video.

SUMMARY

After reading a few pages of this chapter, you might have asked, "If I want to work with Internet video, why must I read about cinema and television broadcasts?" We went into detail because much of the content that is put online comes from film or TV. Also, you can hardly use computer software for creating, editing, or preparing Internet video without encountering terminology from these industries.

The most important points are:

- Don't ever use composite video for importing if you can avoid it.
- Use digital capture, connectors, and conversion for everything.
- Capture at a high resolution.
- If you want to shoot video for the Internet, focus on the subject and minimize both scene and camera motion.

CHAPTER

2

VIDEO COMPRESSION

HOW TO MAKE VIDEO SMALL ENOUGH SO YOU CAN WORK WITH IT

IN THIS CHAPTER

- Compression: How Much Is Bad?
- What Codec Should I Use?
- The Decision-Making Process
- Basic Settings
- Advanced Settings
- A Brief History of Internet Codecs
- Video Compression: Under the Hood
- Recommending a Codec for Your Content

In this chapter, we clear up any new or confusing compression termi-nology you may have run into, and define the specialized terms you hear or see most often while trying to use compression programs. Then we explain the main ways that audio and video are compressed for use on the Internet. Finally, we give you some guidelines on how to choose the best way to compress data, and how to make decisions about what kind of compression you should use for your specific project.

COMPRESSION: HOW MUCH IS BAD?

Compression, the process of making a file smaller, is a critical part of the digital video process. Uncompressed video represents simply massive file sizes. Consider standard television. Normal North American television video is approximately 720×525 pixels. There are 30 frames per second. The frames are interlaced, so in each frame only half the lines are updated (720×262). The color of a pixel can be encoded in 2 or 3 bytes. So if an analog television signal were simply converted to digital, it would require approximately 200 megabits/second. HDTV, an even higher quality, represents about a gigabit of uncompressed data per second. To put these bandwidth requirements into perspective, standard 100-Megabit Ethernet could not carry this. The point is, video is big and gets very big, very fast.

We can safely assume that your audience will consist of broadband users (modem users might click on a video link once, but surely they won't do it twice!). That can mean anything from a 128 kilobits per second (Kbps) ISDN connection to a 1544Kbps T-1 and of course speeds are variable based on network traffic and other factors (see Figure 2-1). Add to this the fact that the speed of decompression and playback is dependent on the client machine's processing speed, and you're dealing with some very tight constraints.

Figure 2-1 *Relative size of bandwidth pipes.*

When looking at compression for the Internet, the practical question boils down to, "How bad do you want your video to be?" Compared to watching DVD, a VHS tape, or even a CD-ROM, Internet video is terrible. It's slow, it's choppy, it's blurry, frames drop out, audio drops out, and so on. That's the nature of the

Internet. When you compress your video for Internet delivery, you need to make some substantial compromises in quality. There are a number of factors that can help guide you in making that decision, such as the nature of the content (talking heads or fast motion, see Figure 2-2), the quality requirements of your audience (news programming or feature film), and the fundamental bandwidth limitations of your audience.

Action clips
(high-motion)

News and talk shows
(low-motion)

Figure 2-2   *High-motion video (left) requires more data to match the image quality of low-motion video (right).*

This chapter helps you to understand where the dividing line between aggressive compression and unacceptable quality degradation lies, and more importantly, what you can do to maintain the highest quality given the bandwidth available to your specific audience. Although you can certainly just jump into your encoding application of choice and step through a wizard, this book provides a solid technical understanding of what the various terms mean so you can make the most informed decisions. Thus, before we get into the practical questions of compressing and encoding in Real, Windows Media, QuickTime, and MPEG formats, we look at the technical theory of how video compression works and how it affects what you do.

WHAT CODEC SHOULD I USE?

Compression is the process of making a video file smaller. The software that performs this shrinking function is called a *compressor.* Uncompressed video is simply huge. So a compressor decreases the size of the video using a variety of techniques and produces a file small enough to be delivered to the intended viewer.

Now that the viewer has received the file, their machine must decompress the file to display the video. The process of decompressing is essentially the opposite of compressing—whatever steps were taken to compress the video are now reversed. Like making juice from concentrate, this is the "just add water" step to get back something resembling what was started with.

Because the compression and decompression steps are closely related, the software that performs these tasks is usually bundled together in a package called *codec*. The word itself is a combination of compressor and decompressor, and can describe either the technique being used to compress the video or the software on the computer that actually performs the compression and decompression.

Sometimes a viewer's machine may have only the decompressor. For instance, most computers can play DVDs but not necessarily create them. Nonetheless, the word "codec" is still used to describe the decompressor software and method.

Figure 2-3 shows the basic process of delivering video via the Internet.

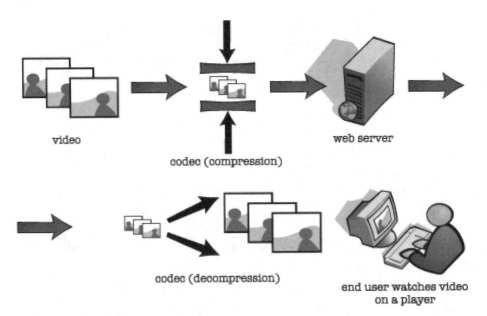

video

codec (compression)

web server

codec (decompression)

end user watches video
on a player

Figure 2-3   *Video is compressed with a codec for online delivery. The same codec decompresses the video for playback.*

This compressed video file is stored on a web or media server and downloaded by end users. Although the software on the user's machine is typically referred to as the *player*, and in fact there are two separate pieces of software on the user's machine:

- The player, which simply knows how to play video
- The codec, which knows how to decode the compressed stream

Because the two are discrete units of software, it is certainly possible to install different codecs for use by the player; you are not locked into the codec that ships with the player. Thus, your compression options are more expansive than simply using the default codec for the system you've chosen.

So which codec do you pick? One approach is to "pick your religion" (Real, Windows Media, QuickTime/MPEG-4, Macromedia Flash), and then learn how to tweak within that platform's codec. The hype from the major media player providers is designed to convince you that no one will ever see your content unless you choose the player that comes bundled with the world's most popular operating system, or is the most installed across platforms, or has been deploying streaming media solutions longer than anyone else, or is installed in more web browsers than all the rest. We'd like to suggest, however, that your religion isn't actually important. If you have compelling content, users will download the software they need to play it if they have the ability to install software on the machine they are using.

That doesn't mean you can choose some totally obscure player and assume all your users will download it. You are quite safe if you choose from one of the Big Three video players—Real, Windows Media, and QuickTime—or if you use Macromedia Flash MX Player, with its addition of the Sorenson Spark codec, which is now a viable way to deliver video with interactivity.

The point is, if Real gives you the best quality for your particular content, you should use Real. If Windows Media gives you better quality, use that. If you need interactivity, use Flash MX and its video features. Within the confines of the big three media players—Microsoft, Real, and Apple—home users will download the appropriate player in order to see your content—that is, if your content is compelling. If you want to target broadband users, you can assume that:

- Your audience may already have all the Big Three media players and some version of the Flash Player.
- Downloading these players on a high-speed connection is fairly trivial.
- Installation of the players, via wizards and automated web installation, is trivial and non-threatening. (This is not always true for people at work, however, who may not be able to install things on their machines).

It's easy to suggest that you use the codec that works best, but what are the metrics for measuring "best?" We can offer one absolute recommendation: The most recent codec is the superior codec. Remember, Microsoft, Real, Apple, and all the MPEG-4 and codec vendors are locked into a battle for market share superiority. They are constantly trying to outdo each other, and are constantly tweaking their codecs to deliver a little better quality at a little better compression than the competition. If your only concern is to use the most efficient codec in existence, and if Microsoft's codec is two months more recent than Real's, you will probably want to go with Microsoft; however, it is very unlikely that the latest and greatest is your only concern.

We do not address issues of video capture and editing in this chapter; these topics were discussed in some depth in Chapter 1, "Video Preparation and Capture." We assume that all the creative work is finished; what we are interested in here is how to compress your creations into the smallest possible file size while maintaining the best quality. That said, there is a connection between creative and compression (see Figure 2-4). If you cannot achieve acceptable quality in any of the competing systems, the culprit is likely the content itself. Because video compression generally has a hard time with both fast motion and rapid scene changes, you may choose to re-edit to match the speed of the action with the compressor's ability to encode at an acceptable quality level.

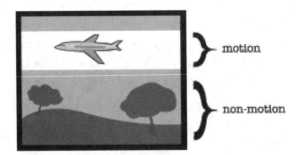

Figure 2-4   *Limiting the motion to a smaller area of your frame makes compression easier.*

THE DECISION-MAKING PROCESS

As stated in the previous section, the actual codec you use is just one small part of the compression decision-making process. In fact, there are a number of facts to gather in order to make your decision.

The decision-making process consists of the following steps:

1. Choose how you'll deliver the video (whether it's going to be on a website, streaming server, email, and so on).
2. Determine the bandwidth of your audience and the bit rate to use for encoding.

3. Establish whether the user can wait for higher-quality video or needs to see the content playing immediately.

4. Choose which player you want the audience to use.

5. Decide on the format (codec) for encoding the content.

6. Find an encoding system (software, hardware) that can process all your content in a timely manner (real-time versus nonreal-time).

DELIVERY METHOD

Is the content going to be delivered on a web site, streaming server, or via email?

If it's email, the main consideration is file size. Many email servers and ISPs have limits for file attachments—typically a few megabytes. Therefore, video has to be limited in order to fit into an email. If you're sending video to more than a few people, a better idea is to simply upload the video to a website and include the link in your email (see Figure 2-5).

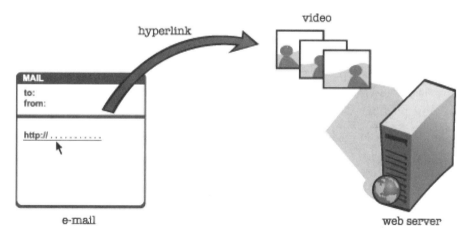

Figure 2-5 *Video delivery via email is possible simply by including links into an HTML email message.*

If you choose to serve your media from a web server, it isn't difficult to choose which format. Pick one of the standard formats, encode, and then upload it to the web server.

If you're using a media server (sometimes called a *streaming server),* it's important to establish the limits of your hosting provider (unless you're choosing a provider based on the streaming systems they provide or support). For instance, many providers offer Windows Media or Real servers, but not QuickTime servers. QuickTime streaming servers can be run on Windows, Linux, and Mac-intosh hosts, but only if the hosting company is willing to set it up.

If your provider's limits don't work with the decisions you've made, you might need to find a different provider. Don't let their limitations drive your whole process.

BANDWIDTH TARGET

It's important to determine the bandwidth of your audience. Of course, your audience might consist of a variety of bandwidths, but even then you must determine the relative size and importance of the bandwidth categories. For instance, if you're deploying a streaming audio service, you might assume that at least half the audience will be using modems, and you might do a lot of work trying to get the most amount of quality into that little pipe. If you then find that two-thirds of your audience is using broadband pipes (cable modems, DSL, or corporate LANs with decent bandwidth), you'll have wasted a lot of computer power serving the wrong audience.

Don't forget that bandwidth is often the most expensive part of a streaming system. Smaller is always better from a cost perspective. Even if the target audience can all view, say, a 300Kbps stream (broadband is usually a minimum of 384Kbps downstream and around 128Kbps upstream), a 300Kbps stream costs three times as much as a 100Kbps stream because hosting companies charge for bandwidth by the megabyte transferred. The bean counters in your outfit will want you to use the lowest resolution possible, while the artists will want the best resolution. Your job is to balance cost and quality.

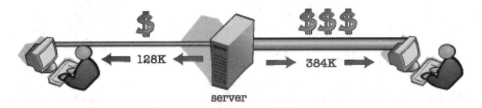

Figure 2-6 *It takes three times as much money to deliver a 300Kbps stream than a 100Kbps.*

If you want to stream in real-time, as opposed to a download, 100Kbps is probably your best lowest common-denominator target. The slowest broadband connections are 128Kbps or less, so 100Kbps is viewable by all broadband users.
Also, 100Kbps streams maximize the number of users who can be served by single Internet connection. For instance, Figure 2-7 shows that a server with a T-1
connection can serve almost 15 people with 100Kbps streams, whereas the same
T-1 can serve only five people with 300Kbps streams.

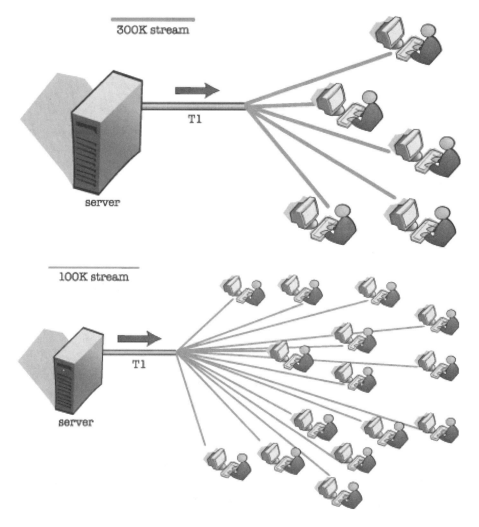

Figure 2-7   *Reducing the bit rate can increase audience capacity substantially.*

If you choose to encode with multiple bit rates (which is a built-in feature in Real's codecs, as well as Microsoft's), make sure you realize that the number of times you will have to encode is multiplied by the number of different formats you encode in. For instance, if you try to deliver 56Kbps, 128Kbps, and 300Kbps in three media formats, you'll wind up with nine separate encodes and seven files to keep track of (Real keeps the different bit rates in the same file). So don't try to please everyone if you don't have to.

The bottom line on bandwidth is this: Pick the smallest bit rate you can get away with. Bandwidth is the largest expense you will run into in creating a streaming application.

PLAYER CHOICE

Unlike television encoding, which is pretty much standard across a country or continent, there are essentially three or more types of "television" on the Internet.

- Microsoft Windows Media
- Real Media
- Apple's QuickTime/MPEG-4
- Macromedia Flash

Your choice of format between Microsoft, Real, and QuickTime shouldn't be determined by fear that the player doesn't have a big enough installed base. All Big Three players are massively installed, and anyone on a broadband connection will download one of these players to view content they want. If your content isn't compelling, it won't matter which format it's encoded in.

A variety of systems exist that can help write and compress content, sometimes in real time, into one of the three "standard" formats. Although these might be applicable to large web sites (news sites, for instance) that need to work with whatever a user already has installed, it can be tremendously simpler to standardize, for a given site, on one of the three players.

Each player has its own benefits and drawbacks, most of which relate to cost and complexity rather than meaningful technological differences. Whatever your choice is, you'll create content in the format understood by a given player.

CODEC/FORMAT

There are two general approaches to compression from the perspective of complexity: symmetric and asymmetric. MPEG video standards are asymmetric. You can spend many, many hours to produce the best encoding for a DVD, so you can watch the video in just an hour. Teleconferencing codecs, such as H.261, can be more symmetric—the complexity (and speed) of compressing and decompressing have to be similar because they are likely to be used in real time.

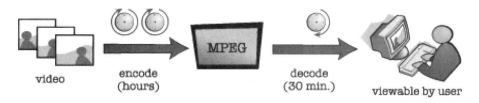

video   encode   MPEG   decode   viewable by user
             (hours)   (30 min.)

Figure 2-8   *An asymmetric codec takes much longer to encode than to decode.*

This book tends to focus on asymmetric codecs, with the assumption that a great deal of Internet video involves broadcasting live or on-demand content to end users.

MPEG-2 is an excellent asymmetric codec for broadcast-quality video, but its high bit rate (which, in layman's terms, means long hours of downloading) makes it inapplicable to our medium—broadband Internet viewing. Various MPEG-2 codecs can be installed in Microsoft, Real, and QuickTime players, although the players do not, in their basic form, decode MPEG-2. MPEG-4 and its competitors have been designed for lower bit rates and are the codecs of choice for Internet video applications.

MPEG-4 promises to be the first compression format that actually works across all the players and is installed along with each player. Traditionally, each player uses its own unique file type and unique set of codecs. Until MPEG-4, codecs were almost always incompatible between the players. A variety of MPEG-4 encoders and decoders have been produced that work in the QuickTime, Real, and Microsoft streaming systems. The earliest codec of this sort was Microsoft's MS MPEG-4 codec, an early MPEG-4 implementation for movie content stored in a proprietary Microsoft package. (Although this codec was based on MPEG-4, it did not fully comply with the MPEG-4 standard, and content stored in this format did not play in true MPEG-4 players.) Note that MPEG-4 is an arena of competition; various vendors will be able to compete on the quality of their implementations and on which subsets of the MPEG-4 suite they choose to focus.

You are not bound by the codecs that Microsoft or Real happen to include, although there are certainly advantages to using them:

- Those codecs have been tweaked to work best with the vendors' system.
- Those codecs are included in the player distributions, so your audience with Windows Media Player, for instance, can just click a button and start viewing your broadcast.

Although that's a huge argument in favor of sticking with the built-in codecs, it's not a complete lock-in. There are several excellent third-party codecs that offer a relatively easy install process. Just as people will download a player they don't have in order to view desirable content, they'll also download a new codec—if they want the content bad enough (and if you can convince them that downloading the new codec will make the experience that much better).

In any event, it is necessary to decide on in what codec(s) the content will be encoded (based on the desired compression), and the codecs that will be available to the audience.

ENCODING SYSTEMS

The decision on what to use to encode depends on how much content is compressed, how frequent a task it is, and how many formats are supported. For a one-time compression of a reasonable set of files, it is probably best to work with the native encoders for each format. Versions of these tools can be downloaded for free or for nominal fees (with encouragement to upgrade from Real and Apple) from the vendor's web site.

For live applications, multi-bit rate applications, and multi-format applications, however, it might be a good idea to look into hardware systems and/or third-party software systems that can target multiple bit rates and formats for the same source file, and can batch process large groups of files.

BASIC SETTINGS

In any Internet video compression system, you have the ability to adjust a variety of settings in order to achieve the desired audio/visual experience.

These include:

- Audio Bit Rate
- Audio Codec
- Video Bit Rate
- Video Codec
- Frame Size
- Frame Rate
- Quality (Compression)

Here is an example of the output settings generated by Windows Media Encoder:

```
Profile name:      WM Video for DSL/Cable Delivery (250Kbps,
320x240, 30fps)
Description:     Use for streaming delivery of video and audio
content. Target audience has a cable modem, xDSL (any type of
Digital Subscriber Line), or equivalent connection.

Audio bandwidth:      40 Kbps
Audio codec:      Windows Media Audio
Audio format:      40 Kbps, 32 kHz, stereo

Video bit rate:   202 Kbps
Video codec:      Windows Media Video
Video size:      320 x 240
Video stream 202 Kbps:     30 fps, 10 seconds per key frame,
Quality: 75
```

When choosing encoding parameters, you are bound the most by the target bandwidth of the audience; that is, you have to balance size, frame rate, and compression, both for audio and for video. These tradeoffs depend on the following:

- Whether the video or the audio is the key part of the experience, and whether the video is high motion (requiring more bandwidth)
- Whether the audio is speech, music, or something else
- How small a bandwidth you want to fit everything into

BALANCING AUDIO AND VIDEO BIT RATES

To begin with, consider the audio and video bit rates. This profile assumes the audience will have bandwidth of 250 kilobits per second (Kbps), and it divides

that available bandwidth into 202Kbps for the video and 40Kbps for the audio, for a total of 242Kbps. 8Kbps are left for "headroom," a small amount of unused bandwidth that compensates for variables like a sudden drop in available band-width or the possibility that other applications might need to receive or send data. If you want to produce a music video, the first thing you might want to do is beef up your audio to 64Kbps and cut your video back to 178Kbps.

Figure 2-9   *Bandwidth usage.*

CODECS

For any playback system, there is a variety of codecs to choose from, both old and new. When choosing a codec, the general rule is this: the older the codec, the larger the audience to readily view the content. The trade-off is that the newer the codec, the more efficient is the compression, and thus the higher qual-ity for a given target audience and bit rate. Also, some codecs are better suited for particular kinds of content. For instance, MP3 is a great codec for music, but is fairly inefficient at compressing voice. If spoken word is being compressed, other codecs exist that can get far higher quality for a given bit rate.

FRAME RATE

Frame rate is a very important factor in the perceived smoothness of video. Films are shown at 24 frames per second (fps). European television plays at 50 fields per second, and North American television plays at roughly 60 fields per second. If you use anything less than 10fps, your video ceases to look animated and begins to resemble a slide show.

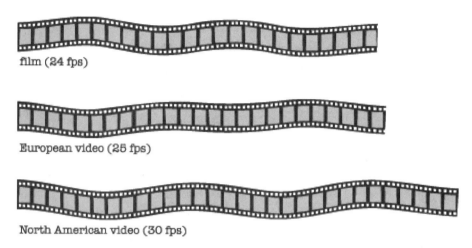

film (24 fps)

European video (25 fps)

North American video (30 fps)

Figure 2-10   *How many frames in a second of video? It varies.*

A standard way of saving bandwidth is to cut the video frame rate—and thus the amount of data to send—in half, down to 15, 12.5, or 12fps, respectively. If you choose to cut frames in some other proportion, make sure to use a divisor of the original frame rate so dropped frames are evenly distributed. Dropping frames can make the video look jerky, but truthfully it's better than encoding at a higher frame rate and having the encoder or decoder drop frames randomly because it can't keep up.

When broadcasting over modems, a slide show is all that can be reasonably expected; thus, content in which the audio is more important than the video (concerts, news broadcasts) are better suited for modem connections, because they can endure a very low frame rate. For high-motion video, a low frame rate might be unacceptable. You may have to focus on size and compression.

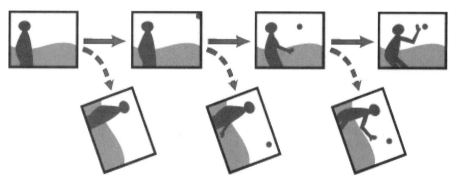

Figure 2-11   *For applications where jerky video display is acceptable, dropping the frame rate by half can reduce file size substantially.*

VIDEO SIZE

Video size, or resolution, is the horizontal and vertical number of pixels that is actually in your video, as well as the rectangular shape in which video will be shown. There are a couple of things to know here regarding resolution.

There are various pre-established sizes of video that the systems are more comfortable playing back.

The number of pixels in the video needs to be an even number, and that usually means it needs to be a multiple of 4 because, for most compression systems, the video is split into 4×4 or 8×8 squares.

Here you also have the issue of aspect ratio. Aspect ratio refers to how wide the picture is compared to how tall. Aspect ratios are written in the form *horizontal: vertical*. A screen with an aspect ratio of 16:9 might be 8 inches horizontally by 4 1/2 vertically, or 16 feet wide (horizontal) and 9 feet high (vertical). This ratio can also be boiled down to a denominator of 1. The ratio 1.78:1 has the same value as the ratio 16:9.

Computer screens traditionally have had aspect ratios of 4:3 or 1.33:1, such as 640×480, or 1,024×768 pixels. 4:3 aspect ratios, such as 320×240, are common for online video, partially because these match the native resolution of most computer screens and the TV screens with which we're familiar.

4:3 or 1.33:1

Figure 2-12 *Traditional 4:3 computer screen aspect ratio.*

When low-resolution video is played back on computers with high-resolution screens (say, 320×240 video played back on a 1,280×1024 screen), the user will tend to show the video at "double size" or "full screen" in order to make it display bigger. This is typically done by simply doubling or quadrupling the size of the pixels (for instance, showing each pixel as a square of 4 pixels of that color). This also requires the computer to do more work; higher resolutions are always harder to do and thus are usually slower than lower resolutions. This translates into delays, jitters, and slow redrawing that reduces the frame rate. So, even if the computer is receiving 30fps, it might only be able to smoothly draw 15fps at that resolution.

Some players are smart enough to actually lower the computer resolution when playing in full-screen mode: They reduce the screen resolution to 640×480, so that 320×240 is only doubled in size (4 pixels per 1 pixel). This also makes the pixels much bigger on the screen and less grainy. And at 640×480, computers have no trouble smoothly displaying more than 30fps . Video players that do this can provide a smooth full-screen video experience for viewers.

The first video conferencing and video phone systems (using what are called the H.261 and H.263 compression standards) established several standard resolutions, as well: Common Interchange Format (CIF) at 360×248 and Quarter CIF (QCIF) at 180×144, both with an aspect ratio of 1.25:1. You sometimes see these resolutions in encoding programs because a lot of media playback software and hardware has been designed to play back video of this resolution.

1.25:1

Figure 2-13   *Common Interchange Format (CIF) 1.25:1 screen aspect ratio.*

When you watch widescreen DVDs or go to the movies, you're dealing with ratios such as 1.85:1 or even 2.35:1, meaning the width can be more than twice the height. widescreen HDTVs and widescreen computer monitors are both designed to natively display wider aspect ratios than the traditional 4:3 ratio.

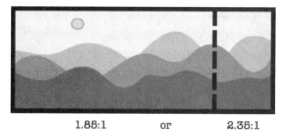

1.85:1   or   2.35:1

Figure 2-14   *widescreen aspect ratios.*

Generally, when choosing a video size, pick one of the standards that is suggested by the encoding software because they are designed to handle those sizes best. Choose a size that shows the level of visual detail necessary for the type of video shown, but no larger; too large a video reduces how much bandwidth can be allocated to frame rate. And make sure your size and shape play back correctly on all the machines you expect it to play back on, especially if some of the viewers will be using handheld mobile devices.

QUALITY

Most still and motion video codecs have an ambiguous "quality" parameter. In general, higher quality requires more time to compress and more bandwidth. The compressor can take more time to deliver higher quality video at a given bit rate, up to a limit. If you tell the compressor that the quality must be a certain level, then the bit rate will have to increase, possibly beyond what is available.

Quality is also changed by the complexity of the codec. A higher quality codec can often achieve better-looking video at the same bit rate, but requires a more powerful computer at the receiving end to actually decode the video. This is the case for many complex codecs, where a cell phone or PDA might not have the computational power to decode the higher quality, though a personal computer or set-top box would.

ADVANCED SETTINGS

After you've chosen a codec, there are a number of decisions you need to make about the encoding process. Regardless of the system you've chosen, you'll run into most of the following options in your compression software:

- Quality-based versus bit-rate–based compression
- Constant/variable bit rate
- 1-pass/2-pass encoding
- Key frame frequency
- Frame dropping
- Temporal compression versus spatial compression
- Bandwidth scalability

To understand what these options mean and how and when to use them, it is necessary to delve into compression technology.

QUALITY-BASED VERSUS BIT RATE-BASED COMPRESSION

Should the encoder put more emphasis on maintaining quality or maintaining delivery of a certain number of bits per second?

In the process of making trade-offs between the different video parameters, the target bit rate of the video is usually fixed, and thus the only ways to increase visual picture quality (meaning, the quality of a single frame of video) are to decrease either the frame rate or the resolution. But decreasing the resolution also decreases the quality, and decreasing the frame rate degrades the motion quality.

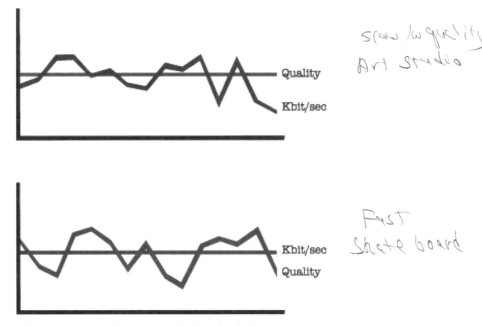

slow lw quality
Art Studio

Fast
Skate board

Figure 2-15 *With a fixed quality target, bit rate is allowed to vary. With a fixed bit-rate target, quality is allowed to vary.*

Thus, the settings really depend on what is displayed. A walk through an art gallery, with long still shots, might benefit from a higher resolution, a higher quality, and a lower frame rate. A skateboard video might need higher frame rates and look acceptable at a lower resolution.

CONSTANT BIT RATE (CBR)

The video's bit rate is always constant regardless of the complexity of the content at that moment. Complex scenes are encoded at lower quality, maintaining the bit rate; simpler scenes are encoded at higher quality, maintaining the bit rate.

VARIABLE BIT RATE (VBR)

The bit rate can change depending on how much data is contained in a given frame. Simpler scenes are encoded at a lower bit rate, and complex scenes are encoded at a higher bit rate. This keeps the visual quality fairly constant; the spare bandwidth available during low-complexity scenes is used to send the data for upcoming high-complexity scenes.

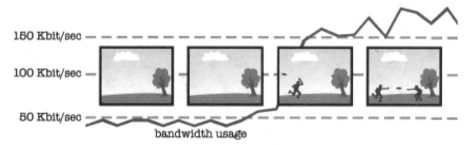

Figure 2-16   *VBR: Bit rate changes according to the needs of each frame.*

1-PASS AND 2-PASS ENCODING

In the encoding process, the encoder analyzes what is happening in your video. Elements such as scene changes, motion direction, and color changes all affect the trade-offs made by the codec in achieving the target bit rate. In the first pass, the encoder analyzes the content on a fairly localized basis. With a second pass, the codec has a complete picture of the complexity of the entire video, can balance its bandwidth use across all the complex or high-motion portions, and thus achieve a consistent and higher quality level at the target bit rate. Just as natur-ally, making that second pass takes additional time.

KEY FRAMES

Video compression involves not sending all the data for each frame, but in predicting what will happen in the next several frames. Key frames contain a full picture; the intermediate frames contain only changes from earlier frames. This can work quite well within a scene, but when the video changes to a new frame, you want to be sure to start with a new key frame (a frame for which you have complete data). Ideally, each new scene and camera angle needs to start on a key frame.

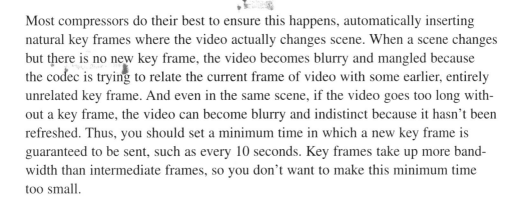

keyframe   intermediate frames   keyframe

Figure 2-17 *Intermediate frames can be extrapolated from key frames.*

Most compressors do their best to ensure this happens, automatically inserting natural key frames where the video actually changes scene. When a scene changes but there is no new key frame, the video becomes blurry and mangled because the codec is trying to relate the current frame of video with some earlier, entirely unrelated key frame. And even in the same scene, if the video goes too long without a key frame, the video can become blurry and indistinct because it hasn't been refreshed. Thus, you should set a minimum time in which a new key frame is guaranteed to be sent, such as every 10 seconds. Key frames take up more bandwidth than intermediate frames, so you don't want to make this minimum time too small.

FRAME DROPPING

Some Internet video applications have an option for dropping some frames out of the stream if things get too backlogged. This is not really a compression option; it's an option to help with streaming performance. Without it, when the stream gets backlogged, it will simply slog along until things get better. This option helps plan for circumstances when you know you have a bad connection. (We'll discuss frame dropping in more detail in Chapter 4, "Streaming Server Software.")

BANDWIDTH SCALABILITY

The ability to send an appropriately encoded stream for users with different bandwidths is a feature of most of the major streaming servers. Some of them use feedback about the stream quality to determine whether to raise or lower the bit rate; some of them simply match the Choose your bandwidth setting the user selected when the player was installed. Some codecs have a separate copy of each bit rate and select the appropriate one when the user first connects. Some codecs encode all the various bit rates into the same file, and save space in this way.

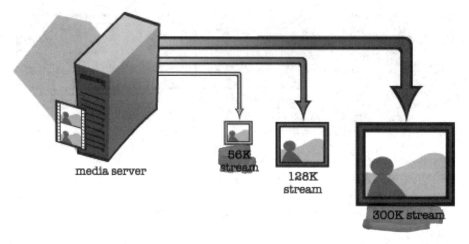

Figure 2-18   *Bandwidth scaling applications can send out the appropriate stream for each user.*

A BRIEF HISTORY OF INTERNET CODECS

To help you get your "codec legs," this section offers a history of video compression standards and products. This should help you understand the basic features of each major technology and how each built on the preceding technologies.

Audio at a Glance

A little explanation of digital audio helps here. Conceptually, sampling audio involves taking "snapshots" of the sound thousands of times per second and then using a number of bits to represent those snapshots. The number of snapshots or samples per second is the *sampling frequency*.

The lower the sampling frequency, the more high-frequency sound is lost, and the muddier and duller the sound is. In a different way, the number of bits used to encode these samples determines how glitchy or smooth the sound is. Just like a 24-bit palette has far more colors than an 8-bit palette, 16-bit sampling has a lot more sound fidelity than 8-bit samples.

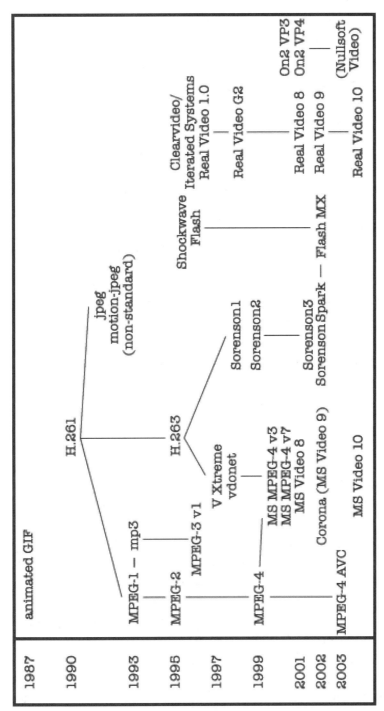

Figure 2-19   *Family tree of Internet video codecs.*

EARLY 1980S: DAT AND CD AUDIO

In the early days of digital audio recording, CD audio did not yet exist, and digital audio tape (DAT) was becoming a standard in professional audio. The DAT standard sampled data at a high rate—48kHz, 16 bit sampling—but did not compress it. CD audio was being standardized as well—44.1kHz sampling (about twice the 22050Hz humans can hear), 16-bit sampling.

1984: MACINTOSH AUDIO

In 1984, Macintosh computers were the first to arrive with built-in, 8-bit sound quality, sufficient to have actual recorded sounds instead of mere simple audio tones. Just playing the sounds was enough work, so the sound wasn't additionally compressed much. A computer would pull the sound file—probably sampled at 8 bits—off the disk, and people would fill their hard drives with these little samples, which always sounded muddy and washed out compared to the originals. This is because the 8-bit, low kHz sampling tended to cut off the high end, muffling the sound and making it sound like AM radio. An 8-mHz CPU would barely be able to play the sound, much less decompress it, so the first sound compression was basically achieved through low sampling rates.

MID-1980S: GIF

On the graphics front, similar things were happening. People were going online in the 1980s and downloading graphics and text files from bulletin board systems. They used rudimentary hand scanners to get bitmapped, grayscale graphics into their computers. People generated pictures on their computers, and once again the low resolution and color sampling rate was the only compression that took place.

Graphics Interchange Format, (GIF) came about in 1987 through work done by CompuServe, who wanted an image format that contained its own compression and that could be displayed on different platforms of different qualities. One of the keys to its success was the ability to reduce the size of the palette.

Every computer today can display 24-bit or 32-bit color (so-called "true color" resolution), but at the time, most computers could display only 8 bits (256 colors) at best. Today's machine's routinely boast hundreds to thousands of megabytes of RAM; at the time, high-end machines had one megabyte of RAM. Thus, GIF's capability to choose the most important 256 colors in an image represented a break-through in image quality.

Here's how the palette feature of GIF can be used:

1. The software analyzes an image, identifies the colors present, and creates a palette or index of 256 colors.
2. Each pixel in the original image is then mapped to the closest available color in the index.
3. Each color is assigned a spot in the palette, so color data is replaced with index data.

More importantly for our purposes is GIF's built-in compression scheme: run-length encoding. With this method, GIF compressed data by representing runs of identical data with a shorthand notation. For instance, assume that the color black is assigned to the last spot in the index (255). Without run-length encoding, a run of 32 white pixels would be represented as

255255255255255255255255255255255255255255255255255255255255255255255255255255255255255255255255

With run-length encoding, it looks something like 32-255. The longer the run, the more benefit there is to encoding the run.

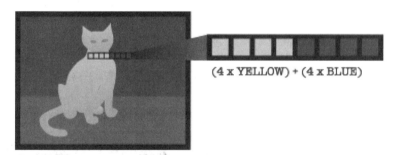

(4 x YELLOW) + (4 x BLUE)

Figure 2-20 *Run-length encoding offers a compressed way to reference runs of identical data.*

At this time, each major platform (Apple, Amiga, Atari, IBM-PC) had a native graphics format as well, but these were closely tied to the way graphics were stored on these systems. Amiga's had 16-bit color and Macintoshes had only 8 bits, and sometimes 4 bits (16 colors!) without a special card. VGA had only 16 colors. In the late '80s and early '90s, the video resolution of most computers was 640×480 or less. At this time, very few computers had consistent graphical capabilities. Each had differing levels of sound output and graphical output.

The existence of a standard format (GIF) for encoding images caused a vast proliferation of programs to create and view this format. It was a lingua franca between computers, which at that time was unusual. I could make an image on my computer and save it as a GIF—and it would be viewable on your computer!

MID-1980S: AMIGA MOD AND MIDI

Another codec of sorts was Amiga MOD (short for module) files and general MIDI or .MID files. Musical Instrument Digital Interface (MIDI) is generally known as that cheesy prerecorded music you sometimes hear when you visit a poorly produced personal web page. But that's not an accurate reflection. MIDI is in fact a text format consisting of instructions on what pitches to use, what voices to use, what sounds to loop, and so on. The reason MIDI on the Web sounds so horrid is that MIDI support on personal computers consists of low-quality digital synthesizers with bad voices; dedicated MIDI instruments, on the other hand, produce rich, realistic sounds.

MOD files had a combination of voice triggers, such as MIDI, and the ability to embed sound clips. These files became the most popular music format of their time. People would pass MOD files around—like they do with MP3s today—and hit songs would be re-authored in MOD (instrumentally, of course, or with simple, short looping voice samples) and uploaded to bulletin boards. The point is that authoring is a form of compression. If you're just creating instructions and allowing the end user's machine to render them, you can work with much smaller files than when sampling existing audio or video.

LATE 1980S: VIDEOCONFERENCING AND H.261

In the late 1980s, work began on standards for videoconferencing over telephone lines, specifically ISDN (which runs at 64Kbps) and 128Kbps with two channels. From 1988–1990, telephone companies developed the H.261 standard, which was intended for videoconferencing and video telephone applications. It was designed to run over any bandwidth multiple of 64Kbps, with a baseline of 64Kbps, and it is thus sometimes referred to as a p×64 codec. H.261 had all the basic ingredients now found in MPEG for motion video compression: interframe prediction (just sending the difference between frames), transform coding (crazy math), and motion compensation (moving the same blocks in the image between frames). We cover these in the "Video Compression: Under the Hood" section.

H.261 works with two video resolutions:

- CIF, at 352×288 pixel resolution
- QCIF, at 176×144 pixel resolution

This standard worked on special videoconferencing hardware at this time; computers did not yet have enough computational power to do the compression in real time.

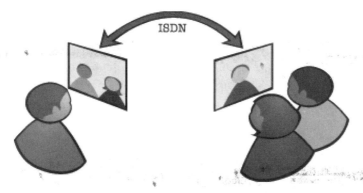

Figure 2-21 *Videoconferencing over H.261.*

As we entered the '90s, computers were getting fast enough that people were starting to play with video. Amiga computers were sold with special software and hardware and packaged as a "Video Toaster." They used hardware to overlay computer graphics on real broadcast-quality images. These titling systems did all their work using custom analog video chips on an expansion card, which was kind of cheating; the broadcast video was never digitized or saved on the hard disk.

EARLY 1990S: JPEG

JPEG was another still file format that came out in the early 1990s. Created by the Joint Photographic Experts Group, this standard focused on making "photo quality" images for display on screens. GIF was very good for text and precise palates ("spot color"), but more sophisticated image compression was becoming possible due to the fact that machines were now as fast as 20–33MHz. MPEG uses something similar to JPEG techniques to encode "key frames" (technically, interframes) in the video.

EARLY 1990S: QUICKTIME

In the early 1990s, Apple introduced QuickTime. For really the first time, you could play video on an off-the-shelf personal computer. Of course, the video was initially the size of a postage stamp, was jumpy in the extreme, and dropped audio. Computers were still too slow to decompress and display video at the same time effectively, so uncompressed video clips played back the best, but they filled up the hard disk quickly.

EARLY 1990S: CINEPAK

Cinepak is a codec still used today and was perhaps the first cross-platform multimedia codec for PCs. It is simple to decode, which is its main strength. As computers became a little faster and Intel 80386 (PC) and Motorola 68040 (Mac) machines sped up, at 20–40MHz these computers could decode almost-full-screen Cinepak video off a double-speed (2x) CD-ROM. Most of the "interactive" CD-ROM titles of that time had Cinepak encoding—even on PCs, which used it in video games. Cinepak did not achieve extremely high compression, and is unsuitable for Internet use for the most part, but it was a great achievement for its time.

1991: MPEG-1

MPEG-1 is the compression technique used in video CDs, on some game CDs in the mid-1990s (such as PlayStation), CD-Interactive, and commonly seen in .mpg files. Created by the Motion Picture Experts Group, this standard basically defines how you store an hour of video onto a standard 680MB CD, and how you play it back with about a 150Kbps/sec (1200Kbps, about the speed of a T-1 Internet connection or a 1-speed CD-ROM) bit rate. MPEG-1 was useful mostly for computer playback of video. It couldn't handle interlacing, which TV signals use. Computers were nowhere near decoding MPEG-1 in real time in the early '90s without add-on decoding boards. (MP3 audio is actually part of the MPEG-1 standard; its full name is MPEG-1 Layer III Audio.)

1995: H.263 AND MPEG-2

H.263 continued to improve upon H.261 with MPEG-like interframe coding (predictive frames) as well as much higher resolutions than CIF (352×288 pixel resolution). H.263 was developed around the same time as MPEG-1, and they use many of the same techniques.

MPEG-2 is a probably the most widely deployed digital video standard. It grew out of MPEG-1 but is a substantial improvement. MPEG-2 is the standard used by digital satellite systems (DSS), DVD players, and digital cable systems. It uses higher bit rates, supports interlacing, and allows several hours of video to fit onto 4.7-gigabyte (GB) DVD disks.

What happened to MPEG-3? Not to be confused with MP3 (part of MPEG-1), MPEG-3 was originally intended to be the compression system for HDTV, but it turned out that MPEG-2 could handle it. Thus, development of an MPEG-3 standard was discontinued in the early 90s.

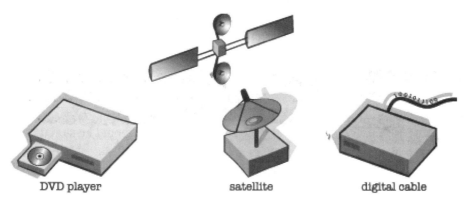

DVD player   satellite   digital cable

Figure 2-22   *Uses of MPEG-2.*

1996: SORENSON

QuickTime found itself playing catch-up with Real and other compression systems, so it licensed a codec from a company called Sorenson. This Sorenson codec, and its several revisions, used similar compression techniques to the MPEG codecs, but targeted the bit rates, computational power, and video systems on personal computers. Sorenson's kept Apple competitive with Real and Microsoft for years, and now supplies the video codec used by Flash MX.

1996: MP3

MP3, or MPEG-1 Layer III audio, was for years an obscure audio codec. It was technically part of the MPEG-1 standard, but it took a lot of processor power to implement. MPEG-1 Video and MPEG-1 Layer II audio (MP2), which did much lighter compression, were used in video CDs and CD-Interactive, and almost no

commercial implementations of MPEG-1, including special chips that implemented it and supported the MP3 part of the standard. MP3 was and still is a very good compression format, providing 12:1 compression for audio.

When people first started using the MP3 codec in the mid 1990s, the Intel 80486 PC computers of the time weren't even fast enough to play back MP3s in real-time. MP3 was used as a sort of "Zip file" for CDs and records they imported. People would take a CD full of audio and wait many hours for it to compress (like video compression today). MP3 was then used to swap music on dial-up bulletin board systems long before the Internet had reached mainstream popularity, despite the many hours it took to compress, upload, download, and then decompress the music. Usually at this time, the MP3 would be burned onto a CD because just an album or two (which was uncompressed) would fill the not-yet-gigabyte hard disks of the time.

Although MP3 slowly gained momentum, the real turning point for MP3 was when average consumer processor speeds got up to about 90–100Mhz. An Intel Pentium at 90Mhz or higher could play back MP3s without having to expand them into large files first, and thus 10 CDs worth of music could be stored on an average hard disk. After computers reached 200MHz, MP3s could be ripped (pulled off of CDs) and encoded in real time (meaning a 70-minute CD took 70 minutes or less to grab).

By 1999 or so, computers were fast enough and broadband was widespread enough that "MP3 audio" became a household term through the popularity of applications such as Napster. A near-CD quality song could be downloaded in 10 minutes or so even with a modem. MP3 became the audio codec of choice for tens of millions of consumers and changed an industry. The history of the MP3 audio codec (invented before 1991!) illustrates how it can take many years before other variables such as computer power, plentiful storage, and bandwidth line to reveal the true power of some of these standards.

1997 TO THE PRESENT: COMMERCIAL EFFORTS

If you recall, the Internet became extremely popular in 1996 and 1997. The sudden commercial interest in the Internet spawned streaming approaches to delivering video over the Net. Many companies began working on ways to deliver Internet video.

In 1997, the focus on making many asymmetric codecs, which could pump some usable bit of video down a thin, thin 28.8Kbps modem pipe, became very important. Several companies jumped in (Vdonet, Vxtreme, and Iterated Systems) and began working on alternative technologies.

Although the history of the proprietary codecs is less well documented than the standardized MPEG series; the math behind these approaches is fairly well known. Some of the general techniques in this area were different transforms than MPEG's DCT, such as wavelets and fractal-based compressors that zoom in on areas of pictures to find repeating data (making it easier to compress). An example of this was RealVideo 1.0, based on Iterated's codec, which was one of the first to have audio, video, and streaming (instant-on) capabilities on the Internet.

The general outcome here was that these companies were absorbed into Microsoft and Real, and these companies used them for their own approaches. Real and Microsoft continue to battle for the hearts, minds, and pocketbooks of video developers.

1997 TO THE PRESENT: MACROMEDIA FLASH

Macromedia Flash appeared on the scene around this time as well. Coming from a different perspective entirely, Flash is based on animating vector graphics as opposed to bitmap graphics. Instead of taking video from some other source in the analog world and trying to decompose, send, and reconstitute it, Flash gives you the capability to create the various pieces of the content in question (lines and shapes) and animate them using motion sequences.

Recent versions of Flash (MX 2004) include the capability to import movies as part of Flash presentations, using the Sorenson Spark codec, and a scripting language that enables dynamic loading and playback of video. Flash combines the bitmap world of video with vector-based (lines and curves) technology for interface design and titling and low bit rate animations.

1998: QUAKE

Quake is worth noting as a compression scheme. At this time, many aborted attempts to create online virtual reality were being explored. Yet with Quake, ID Software had actually created it. In Quake, a thin (modem-capable) real-time data stream could not only download textures to the Quake video game, but it could animate the characters fighting in real time, at high enough frame rates for people to compete in vast numbers. Recordings were made of master players competing or passing the levels in record times. These were then downloaded and watched from many different camera angles. Granted, in order to view these, you needed a custom player (the game), and you need to have already downloaded the textures and 3D models. But Quake represented an innovative delivery mechanism for what would become the overused buzzwords "3D interactive content."

2000: SCALABLE CODECS

Real's G2 player is notable in that it was designed to be scalable within the codec. From the early days of streaming media, Real had focused on low bandwidth users and had done a lot of work on codecs that could handle dropped frames and packets (by having redundancy between packets and extra data). Real also concentrated on scaling down size, quality, and frame rate independently with the same file.

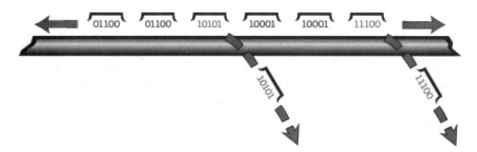

Figure 2-23 *Redundancy allows for dropped packets of data.*

Real was also unique in bundling together various bit rates for a piece of content in one file, which MPEG-type codecs were not designed to do. Real could bundle, say, a 28KB, 56KB, and 128KB file into a file smaller than all three individual files. Some of this was achieved because Real controlled the encoder-publishing system and could correctly adjust the stream for a given client, but this also required good customized work on the codec itself.

In 1998, Microsoft decided, predictably, to compete with Real and make its own "advanced" streaming formats for the Internet. It had already acquired or invested in several codec companies (including licensing Real's codecs for $30 million) and began working on its own internal codecs.

Figure 2-24 *Bundling allows multiple bit rates of a file to be sent together.*

PRESENT: MPEG-4

MPEG-4 was standardized in 1999, but extensions to the standard are still being worked on. MPEG-4 is the first of the standards to focus on the Internet and networked delivery of video. It encompasses much more than the latest ways to squish video. When Microsoft and several other companies implemented the first versions of "MPEG-4 video," they improved greatly on MPEG-2 and MPEG-1 for video at those low Internet bit rates. It is somewhat misleading to call these "MPEG-4," however, because they implemented only the basic layer of the simplest compression for video. These early implementations used few of MPEG-4's new approaches to compression; they arguably could be considered essentially "MPEG-2+ for low bit rates."

As far as compression goes, MPEG-4 is a vast and encompassing standard, and it will take years to implement and exploit every last benefit. For more detail on MPEG-4, see Appendix B.

VIDEO COMPRESSION: UNDER THE HOOD

Although we talk a lot about Real, Microsoft, and QuickTime video for Internet distribution, these programs do not operate in a vacuum. Research into compression and digital video technology has been ongoing for several decades. The MPEG standard is one of the culminations of this work, and the work of most of the commercial digital video companies spills over into the MPEG standard.

Just as almost all cars use internal combustion engines and compete on issues like manufacturing quality and ride comfort, most of the video companies use the same basic compression technology. Understanding how compression works in MPEG and JPEG, the standard for still image compression, provides a lot of insight into how the commercial vendors' compression systems work as well.

All video compression boils down to two basic techniques: spatial compression and temporal compression. Spatial compression involves compressing the data within a single frame, much like a JPEG file is a compressed version of a photograph.

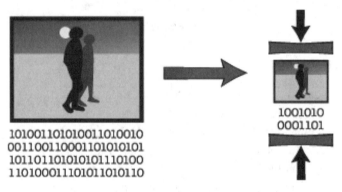

Figure 2-25 *Spatial compression simply reduces the amount of data it takes to represent a single frame.*

Temporal compression essentially applies compression over time. In Figure 2-26, the people move to the right, and the moon moves to the left. Rather than send each compressed frame, temporal compression predicts where the people and the moon are in each incremental frame.

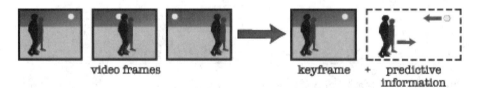

Figure 2-26 *Temporal compression reduces the amount of information required to show action over time.*

Using only spatial compression, a video would contain essentially a bunch of compressed frames (Motion JPEG is an implementation of this idea). With both spatial and temporal compression, the video includes some compressed frames and enough data to predict the content of the other frames.

SPATIAL COMPRESSION: JPEG

Intraframes, also known as key frames, are the building blocks of MPEG and most other codecs, but they are not just uncompressed pictures. Intraframes are compressed much like JPEGs. For this discussion, we look at the technology of JPEG itself.

Let's start with the official description of what happens when you convert an image to JPEG. Then we describe each step in some detail. Our aim is to provide just enough information to give you a conceptual understanding of the process that is at the heart of video compression.

There are five basic steps in JPEG compression:

1. **Color Space Transform.** Transform the color space from RGB.
2. **Downsampling.** Average together color values for groups of pixels.
3. **Transform.** Group pixels into 8×8 blocks and transform them from visual data to frequency data.
4. **Quantization.** Basically, the coefficients created by the frequency transform step are rounded off. This is where the compression really occurs.
5. **Entropy Encode and Output.**

STEP 1: COLOR SPACE TRANSFORM

Just as there are often several ways to accomplish the same result in a computer program, there are different ways to represent the same data—for instance RGB (Red-Green-Blue) color versus CMYK (Cyan-Magenta-Yellow-Black) color. Shifting between different ways of representing the same information is called a *transform.* Of course, RGB and CMYK are not completely interchangeable; the colors in the two modes are similar but not identical. Shifting modes sometimes causes changes; that's an unavoidable fact about transforms.

Another reason for transforms is that different color spaces are better suited to different tasks. If you're working on a print piece, you need to transform to CMYK because presses print in cyan, magenta, yellow, and black; RGB simply doesn't apply to putting ink on paper. If you're going for compression, it makes sense to work in a color space that maximizes the quality of data that the human eye easily perceives and minimizes the storage space used by data that is less easily perceived. Thus, JPEG uses luminance/chrominance color spaces because the human eye easily distinguishes changes in luminance (brightness), but is more forgiving about changes in chrominance (color).

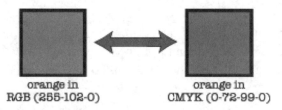

orange in
RGB (255-102-0)

orange in
CMYK (0-72-99-0)

Figure 2-27   *Color transforms: The value of a single pixel can be given in different forms—for instance, RGB or CMYK.*

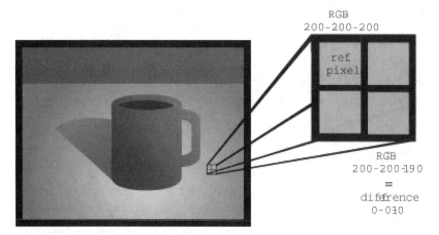

Figure 2-28   *In a block of pixels, if the value of one reference pixel is known, then the values for all the other pixels can be stated in terms of their difference from that reference pixel.*

To understand the idea of luminance and chrominance, think about a black and white photograph. Photography simply records how much light (brightness) coming in through the lens makes it to the film. In a black and white photo, we have essentially all the information we need to recognize the image as a realistic representation of reality. Figure 2-29 shows the luminance of a color photograph.

Figure 2-29 *Luma channel of a color image.*

As you can see, this image contains a huge amount of information about the scene: highlights, shadows, midtones, background and foreground, depth, detail, and so on. All that's missing is a little color.

Digital compression systems use a color space called Y'C$_r$C$_b$. In this color space, the Y' channel contains a combination of red, green, and blue brightness, or *luminance*, called *luma*, and the other two channels carry color information about red (C$_r$ = chrominance-red) and blue (C$_b$ = chrominance-blue) color, without luminance.

The benefit of using such a seemingly weird color space is that it separates most of the brightness into a separate channel, so that color information can be treated separately and in proportion to their visual importance.

Although Y would simply be the luminosity of the image, the Y' ("Y prime") channel is a combination of different luminosities for each color, reflecting how the human visual system works. It contains roughly 60 percent green brightness, 30 percent red brightness, and 10 percent blue brightness.

Figures 2-30 and 2-31 show the color information for this picture. As you can see in the grayscale, this information offers little help in making out the image and merely provides color information.

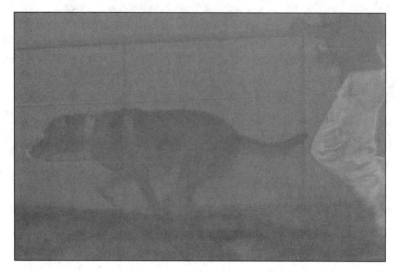

Figure 2-30 *The C$_r$ channel of the image in Y'C$_r$C$_b$ color space.*

Figure 2-31 *The C$_b$ channel of the image in Y'C$_r$C$_b$ color space.*

You might also run into the YUV and YIQ color spaces. YUV is used in European television broadcasting; YIQ is the North American broadcast equivalent. Both of these are similar to Y'C$_r$C$_b$. Often YUV is used interchangeably with Y'C$_r$C$_b$. The only real difference is that they contain slightly different ratios of red, green, and blue. The important thing to know about these color spaces is that they allow us to separate color from brightness and deal with it separately.

STEP 2: DOWNSAMPLING

Sometimes you will see three numbers with colons between them, such as 4:2:2. In simple terms, these three numbers correspond to $Y':C_r:C_b$ and describe how much resolution (dots) to give each component. Because the color components are less important than the luminance component, they are downsampled; that is to say, they sample the colors with less resolution ("down"). While Y' is sampled once for every pixel, C_r, and C_b might be sampled only every other pixel or even every fourth pixel. This downsampled information is then compressed in the subsequent steps.

Just like you can look at just the red, green, or blue part of an image, JPEG compression handles each color component separately as a grayscale image. It's as if you took only the red in the picture, so you have just a red image; and then you compressed it alone, then the blue, and then the green. However, in JPEG, it is Y', C_r, and C_b that are all compressed separately, and then recombined in the end.

If you see 4:4:4, this means no downsampling has occurred; the color channels are at the same resolution as the luminance channels.

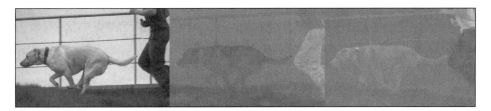

Figure 2-32 *Y', C_r, and C_b channels of a 4:4:4 picture.*

4:2:2 is the downsampling commonly used in professional video equipment. This means that for every four pixels of intensity information, there are only two pixels for each channel of color information. C_r, and C_b are sampled every other pixel.

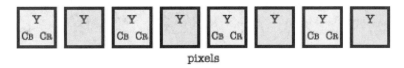

Figure 2-33 *4:2:2 downsampling.*

Figure 2-34   *Y', C$_r$, and C$_b$ channels of a 4:2:2 picture.*

4:1:1 is more common in consumer video equipment; it fits a lot more video because while the video intensity is sampled for every pixel, the C$_r$, and C$_b$ are sampled together every fourth pixel, with four pixels of intensity for every one pixel of color information.

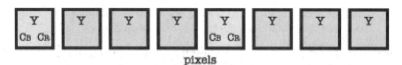

Figure 2-35   *4:1:1 downsampling.*

Figure 2-36   *Y', C$_r$, and C$_b$ channels of a 4:1:1 or 4:2:0 picture.*

You also see 4:2:0 used in the MPEG and JPEG compression process. This doesn't mean that C$_b$ is downsampled to 0; it means that the numbering scheme was poorly designed. There are actually multiple different 4:2:0s, complicating matters. It's similar in quality to 4:1:1, but sampled differently: C_r is sampled every other pixel on the first line, then C_b is sampled every other pixel on the second line, and son on.

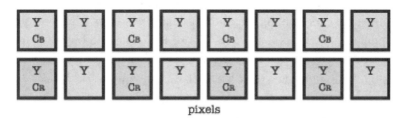

pixels

Figure 2-37   *4:2:0 downsampling.*

If you see 4:4:4:4, this means there is another channel of some sort, which also isn't downsampled. If you see other numbers between columns (such as 6:4:4), it means that some other subsampling approach was used, and that other channels of visual data might be involved. You shouldn't be intimidated by these numbers, just know they simply indicate how much the color information was reduced and by what ratios.

STEP 3: FREQUENCY TRANSFORM

If you have ever tried using JPEG's low quality setting in a graphic editor, you have probably seen blocking in the image, as shown in Figure 2-38.

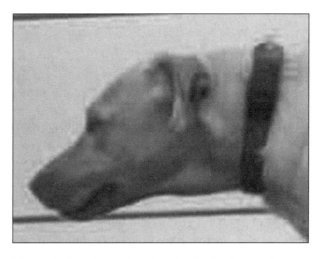

Figure 2-38   *Note the blocking in the image due to the 8×8 sample blocks.*

JPEG takes each channel—Y', $C_r C_b$—splits them into 8×8 blocks, and applies a mathematical process that essentially transforms the individual pixel values in those blocks into a representation of the spatial frequencies of change in the block.

The purpose of this transform is to represent the general pattern or shape of the block without having to transmit the value, luma, and color of every single pixel. That is, instead of representing that block as an 8×8 bitmap, it's represented as a sort of swatch or pattern. Is it a "busy" block? Is it a smooth block? Is it jagged or grainy? This transform can represent the general shape character of the block by analyzing the frequencies, or repeating patterns, within the block.

A block with lots of dramatic changes in brightness or color would be high frequency. Typically, high-frequency blocks show edges, such as where a window meets a wall, or the hairs in a man's beard. In our sample image, the edge of the building against the sky is high frequency, and the lines between the tiles are high frequency; the rest of the image (the sky and the tiles themselves) are extremely low frequency as we shall see. Low frequency, thus, means blocks where there are no or few changes in brightness.

Named after the French mathematician Jean Baptiste Joseph Fourier, fourier transforms can represent any oddly shaped curve on a graph as the sum of a bunch of sine and cosine waves added and subtracted together.

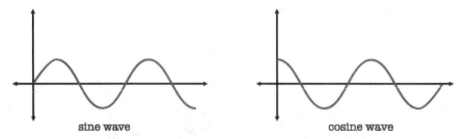

Figure 2-39 *Sine and cosine waves.*

In other words, any complicated curving line can be represented by a series of numbers representing the size and position of these waves. Because this is not a mathematics textbook, let us stick to the essential point: you are transforming a set of values from one system of representation to another in such a way that you can reduce the amount of data required to represent the line, edge, or shape.

Certain shapes take a lot of sine waves to build up (it's hard to build squares out of curves), but with enough curves, it looks good enough. This gives another unique property to Fourier transforms: you can make them more or less precise, depending on how many curves (data) you use. You can approximate a curve with only a few waves. The waves are represented with a few numbers (called coefficients—add 2 of this wave and subtract 3 of this wave, and so on). So what you are doing is representing a general pattern or shape with a few (or many) numbers. And you can see that even with just one number (the first wave is labeled $n=1$ as shown in Figure 2-40), you roughly have the basic shape of the square. In the same way, this technique is used to represent the basic shape in a two-dimensional patch of color.

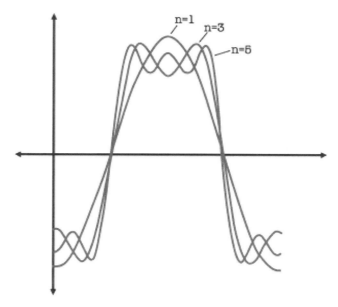

Figure 2-40   *Waves with different coefficient values.*

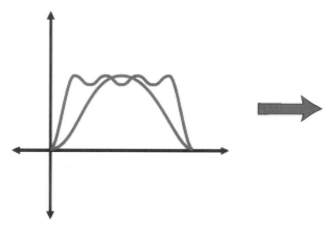

Figure 2-41   *Approximating a shape by adding cosine waves.*

Fourier's system worked on continuous, smooth lines. Similar techniques can be used on discrete points, namely pixels. Discrete cosine transform (DCT) is the name of the type of Fourier transform that uses discrete points (as opposed to continuous lines). It uses cosines (sine waves, just shifted to the left half of a wave) to do this. DCT is really a lossless part of compressing data; it just restates the same data in a different way by transforming it.

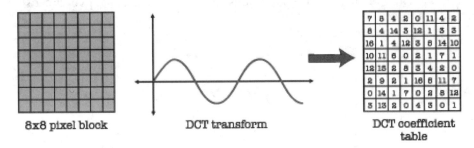

8x8 pixel block   DCT transform   DCT coefficient
                                                table

Figure 2-42 *The DCT transform converts color pixel information to a DCT coefficient table, a measurement of frequency variation.*

On any given 8×8 block (or 16×16 block in MPEG), a DCT is applied in both the horizontal and vertical directions (for example, from left to right, then top to bottom). The result is an 8×8 table of values that describe the frequency values of the block. Notice that these coefficients don't describe each pixel but rather describe the frequencies (slow or rapid changes of color or brightness) present in the block.

The $Y':C_rC_b$-to-DCT transform then is a move from color space to frequency space.

Take a look at these 8×8 blocks, 64 pixels, from the Y' channel of a graphic image. It's important to note that we're not looking at a JPEG: no DCT transforms have taken place. So far we've just been getting pixels in shape for DCT to do its thing.

The block on the left is not complicated. We see clear bands of horizontal rows that are relatively smooth gradients. The rows basically go from light on the top to dark on the bottom.

The block on the right is complicated. There are no smooth gradients; certain pixels stand out differently. These interruptions are areas of higher frequency.

It should be clear that it will not take much more data to depict the pattern on the right than the pattern on the left.

Figure 2-43   *8×8 blocks of pixels exhibit low frequency (left) and high frequency (right).*

To summarize the whole DCT frequency transform, we have changed a square of pixel colors into a square of coefficients that represent the changes in frequency and thus the pattern in the square.

STEP 4: QUANTIZATION

Step 4 is the truly lossy step of JPEG. Quantization is essentially rounding (for instance, changing the values 19 and 21 to 20). This achieves a lot of compression because the fewer values there are, the more compression. In this step, we basically round off the high frequency numbers in the DCT table for each block. Conceptually, we make the 8×8 blocks "fuzzier" or less distinct by rounding off the values we use to represent them. Based on the quality level requested by the user, different tables are used of 8×8 values that quantize the original 8×8 values from Step 3.

Remember, the new 8×8 blocks don't correspond to pixels; they correspond to frequencies of change. Had we tried to round off the squares without completing the DCT step, we would have destroyed not only the color but the shape as well. Because of DCT, we make only the shape a little less precise by rounding off.

The tables are designed to aggressively throw away small variations while preserving higher frequencies, and to reduce unneeded detail on larger changes in frequency. There are different tables for brightness and color, based once again on the sensitivity of the human visual system.

JPEG is based on the assumption that the pictures will depict natural scenery with smooth gradations—in other words, low frequency is the norm, and adjacent pixels will be close in value. As long as this is the case, we can discard higher frequency information quite aggressively. When this is not the case (basically at the edges), you see errors in the form of artifacts, visual features that were not part of the original picture but were added by the process of compression and decompression.

Figure 2-44 shows how quantization creates errors in high-frequency areas of an image. As you can see, MPEG and JPEG compression doesn't deal as well with high-contrast images like the stark black-and-white difference in printed text. This ringing or mosquito noise occurs around high contrast edges in a single frame or due to changing edges between frames.

Figure 2-44 *Notice all the artifacting ("ringing") around the high-frequency borders between text and background.*

Mosquito noise can be observed on digital cable or DVD when the scene changes rapidly, or on poorly made DVD movies. It appears as sort of a halo of rectangles or squares of incorrect color around the edges of objects, people, or text in the credits of a movie.

Step 5: Output

Although quantization has been completed, conventional lossless compression (similar to .ZIP files) is performed on the values. This is called *entropy coding,* and it shrinks the size of the image without getting rid of any information.

Because all the reductions were achieved in ways that the human visual system isn't as sensitive to, JPEG pictures come out looking like the original with a lot less data. For example, a 1-megabyte photo might compress to a 150-kilobyte file as a high-quality JPEG, 28-kilobytes as a medium-quality image, and only 8 kilobytes as a low-quality image.

Temporal Compression: MPEG

We now look at a harder problem: compressing not just the spatial information in a single image, but compressing a whole bunch of images over time. Using only intraframes, a medium-quality, 4-minute music video at 15fps could run as large as 100 megabytes. Obviously just performing JPEG compression on each frame doesn't provide enough file savings. That procedure is inefficient, because most of the data is the same between one frame and the next. If you've ever held a roll of motion picture film up to the light, you've noticed how little difference there is between any two adjacent frames.

This insight—that most of the content is unchanged—led to creation of cel animation back in the early days of motion pictures. Animators devised a system of breaking an image into different layers and just working on the parts of the image that changed in each frame. This meant that they didn't have to redraw the scenery for each frame, which saved a huge amount of work. Similarly, they would draw the background scenery on sheets much larger than the final frame and simply move the scenery in front of the camera.

Where the classic animators wanted to save labor, we want to save bits. Temporal compression is an attempt to work as efficiently as animators. In animation, it's fairly easy—even for a computer—to see what's changed and what hasn't. In full-motion, live-action video, it's quite a different matter.

MPEG provides techniques for temporal compression and for reducing the amount of information needed to reproduce a series of frames rather than a single image. The major techniques are:

- **Motion vectors**: Deciding the direction an object moves.
- **Bidirectional prediction:** Using past and future frames to build an in-between frame.

In the world of MPEG, there are three kinds of frames:

- **Intraframe**: Essentially, a key frame; that is, a stand-alone frame that is encoded in its entirety (compressed, of course), and doesn't depend on information from any other frames. Think of this as a single JPEG image.
- **Predictive**: A frame whose contents are predicted based on a previous frame using predictive (what changed) information.
- **Bidirectional**: A frame whose contents are calculated based on both previous and future intraframes or predictive frames. Essentially, this is like a tween frame in Flash animation: Given a starting frame and an ending frame, the software can calculate the position of the objects in each "in-between" frame.

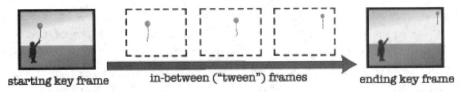

Figure 2-45 *Bidirectional (in-between) frames are calculated from two key frames.*

MPEG-1, MPEG-2, H.263, MPEG-4, and most of the proprietary codecs from Real, Microsoft, and Sorenson all use these same approaches. The basic goal is to send as few intraframes (complete, stand-alone frames) as possible, while sending the most compact predictive information, and using that to draw all the other frames from the few available key frames. The technique in each case involves splitting the pictures into blocks and trying to identify changed blocks.

The MPEG-4 standard throws in almost every good idea about compression available during its design, and represents the merging of vector- and image-based compression schemes. MPEG-4 incorporates the entire MPEG-1 and MPEG-2 legacy and improves upon it for image compression, focusing on Internet low bit rates, taking advantage of the many years of computer speed increases. It augments this with the concept of objects, and creates a new way to both compress pre-made video and author new video.

Where as MPEG-2 might try to find similar blocks between two frames that represented a moving ball, MPEG-4 can actually have a ball object, which has been transmitted once with its own texture, move across the screen.

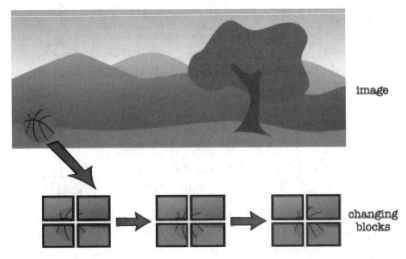

Figure 2-46 *MPEG-2: Similar blocks are compared and moved.*

Figure 2-47 *MPEG-4: The ball object is separated from the rest of the image.*

MPEG-4 adds a whole set of compositing tools for overlays of text and the composition of video and authored scenes. This means that subtitles (which compress poorly when treated like video) can be sent as a separate text track, and that high-quality vector-based objects (squares and boxes), which are already extremely compact, do not have to be turned into large bitmaps before they are sent. Part of MPEG-4 focuses as well on the needs of so-called "interactive content" and standardizes approaches for areas traditionally addressed by video game and Flash developers.

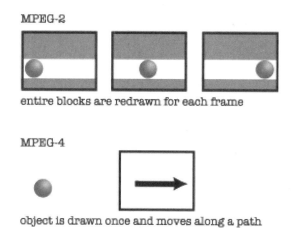

Figure 2-48 *MPEG-4 vastly simplifies the problem of determining motion by separating objects from background data, much as in cel animation.*

In short, MPEG-4 could be considered to have combined the best of completely different kinds of codecs:

- Animation data for pre-rendered object scenes, as in virtual reality.
- Object-based compositing for combinations of captured and authored content.
- Vector and image tools.
- The ability to author content in the same compact form it can be delivered in.

Many of the features in MPEG-4 were anticipated here or there in earlier products; the strength with MPEG-4 is that, like the earlier MPEGs, a compliant decoder (player) can decompress any standard encoded (compressed) stream. Because of this, companies can innovate incredibly and make faster, more sophisticated, and higher quality images and squeeze them into a compliant MPEG-4 stream.

> **Note** It is worth noting that not all implementations of MPEG-4 incorporate these new object detection approaches. The amount of computation (and thus time and cost) needed to detect objects in the video makes it far easier to use MPEG-4 as an improved MPEG-2 for low bit rates. In fact, the more recent additions to the MPEG-4 standard make it twice as efficient as MPEG-2—for example, half the bit rate at the same quality, and this *without* using object features. In fact, MPEG-4 is much like a toolbox, and vendors can select pieces of it they see fit. The full list of tools available in MPEG-4 is covered in Chapter 8.

RECOMMENDING A CODEC FOR YOUR CONTENT

The procedures described in the previous sections help to figure out some of the settings you'll need to use, but they don't necessarily answer the question outright: Which codec should you use? As we said earlier, the type of content you're dealing with says a lot about the codec you'll use and the settings you'll choose. For instance, if you're creating a music video, you'll place a premium on audio quality, whereas video quality is of lesser importance. For adult content, video quality is of prime importance, whereas audio is not very important.

Table 2-1 lists a number of classes of video. We describe them in terms of video settings and codec capabilities, and then we recommend your best codec bets—at least as of this writing. Because we're dealing with fast-moving technology here, you'll have more success with whatever codecs are most recent.

Table 2-1 Types of Video Content and Codec Recommendations

Content Description	Compression Description	Compression Technology	Recommendation	Realistic bit rates
Cartoon	Large areas of contiguous color, easily predictable motion.	Flash/Flash MX, Real G2 codec, QT Animation and graphics codec, Motion-compensating codecs—Real, Microsoft QuickTime, MPEG, and Flash MX.	If at all possible, author/compose the cartoon on the computer for better compression—digitized captured cartoons compress less.	40Kbps or lower if authored in Flash or other vector techniques.
Motion graphics	Lots of type and geometric shapes, motion blurs, graphic animation, and more.	Flash/Flash MX PowerPoint QuickTime animation and graphics codec.	Flash has the most mature toolset. QuickTime can work as well, and PowerPoint even has its own web publishing tools with Windows Media.	20Kbps achievable with judicious use of Flash or PowerPoint.
Rock concert	Music quality is very important, video less so. Moderate movement.	Motion-compensating codecs—Real, Microsoft, QuickTime, MPEG, Flash MX (for high frame rates > 12fps). Motion JPEG (lower frame rates < 12).	Choose minimum acceptable audio quality, then use left-over bandwidth for video. Slide shows (< 12fps) are still somewhat acceptable depending on the audience. Audio helps maintain illusion. If you have a low frame rate, each frame might as well be a keyframe (too much change between frames).	40Kbps for slide show; 100Kbps for something viewable. 32Kbps minimum for the audio portion; good stereo music; whatever is left for video.

continues

Table 2-1 Types of Video Content and Codec Recommendations (continued)

Content Description	Compression Description	Compression Technology	Recommendation	Realistic bit rates
Music video	Music quality very important, video less so. Many scene changes.	Motion-compensating codecs—Real, Microsoft, QuickTime, MPEG, and Sorenson Spark/Flash (for high frame rates > 12fps).	Choose minimum acceptable audio quality, then use left-over bandwidth for video.	100–300k minimum 32k minimum for the audio portion good stereo music; whatever is left for video.
High-action (fight scenes, car chases and so on)	Doesn't tolerate lower quality settings; high likelihood of excessive blurring and artifacting.	Variable-bit rate motion-compensating codecs—Real, Microsoft, QuickTime, MPEG, and Flash MX.	Ideally, earlier low-motion scene can be bit-starved (lower bit rate) so that this scene can spike over target bit rate.	250KB minimum
Sitcom	Bright color, few lighting effects, no soundtrack, very little action, intermittent sound, minimal camera motion, and scene changes.	Fixed bit rate motion-compensating codecs—Real and H.263 can be used as well. Microsoft, QuickTime, and MPEG. Flash MX.	Similar to news broadcast—talking heads, static background.	100Kbps minimum
Adult content	Video quality very important, audio unimportant, maintaining realistic skin tones important.	Motion JPEG (low frame rate). Motion JPEG (high frame rate). Motion-compensating codecs—Microsoft, Real, QuickTime,	Opposite of music video—video quality overrides audio. Also, individual frames must be crisp (using JPEG), so motion compensating	100Kbps for low-frame rate motion JPEGs; for 300Kbps, minimum motion-compensating codecs.

		and MPEG (very high bit rates—more than 500KB). Voice-oriented audio codecs (Real codec; Qualcomm Pure voice; MPEG-4 voice codecs, and so forth)	codecs should not be used unless frame rate is high or the key frames are kept close together.	
News show	Chroma keying (blue screen), very little movement (but spliced-in video of varying quality), and voice clarity important.	Compositing video codecs such as Sorenson, MPEG-4 for blue screen, plus talking head. Voice-oriented audio codecs (Real audio codec; Qualcomm codec; and so on).	Codecs with the ability to send the background once and then simply animate the talking head are preferred.	40Kbps possible; 100Kbps to avoid smearing.
Documentary/reality-based programming	Video is (sometimes) intentionally choppy, jagged, footage perhaps shot on the run. Digital camera look acceptable. Audio degradation okay.	Motion-compensating codecs: MPEG-4, Real, QuickTime, Microsoft. Quality audio codec (voice codec or MP3, and so on).	Sound should always be crisp and audible; video should retain original motion.	100Kbps minimum; 16Kbps or more for audio; remainder for video.
3D Museum walkthroughs	Video quality, 3D rendering crucial, audio probably non-existent or voice, and light background music.	QT3D with JPEG compressors, MPEG-4 IPix plugin, VRML/Web3D plugins, and Flash.	QuickTime is best choice for authoring interactive content of this nature because it can use a variety of codecs, in addition to the 3D display. MPEG-4 includes features to solve this as well and will be the best option when its toolset matures.	100Kbps and higher. For decent quality, a modem will still not work.

continues

Table 2-1 Types of Video Content and Codec Recommendations (continued)

Content Description	Compression Description	Compression Technology	Recommendation	Realistic bit rates
Sports	Moments of high-action, combination of long shots, action frame shots, and close-ups.	Motion-compensating variable bit rate codec: MPEG, Real, Microsoft, and QuickTime.	MPEG-4 shows most promise for this kind of content; no strong codecs for live video right now. MPEG-2 is the reigning king, but only at broadcast bit rates (2Mbps and higher).	300Kbps and up; best as on-demand (down-loaded clips).
Slide presentations (PowerPoint)	Essentially slide shows, but sometimes with sound and animation effects.	PowerPoint and Flash.	Flash is better for graphically rich presentations with anima-tion; PowerPoint requires PowerPoint, player, or plug-in on client. Also, Real and Microsoft have features to efficiently broadcast Power-Point presentations with sound; custom Java can be used in the browser to send timed slides; third-party applications can con-vert PowerPoint to Flash format.	20–40k possible with Flash and light PowerPoint; as always, higher quality equals higher bandwidth.
Conferencing	Basically symmetrical, talking heads, voice quality important, and the white board should be readable.	Proprietary conferencing codecs, H.261, H.263, and custom conferencing codecs.	Compression must be very real-time (low latency) for interactive use. Some newer codecs actually send a 3D model of the head and animate it based on motion capture.	1 fps possible on modem; 64Kbps minimum for H.261; 128Kbps and up begins to be usable.

Interactive games/video games	Texture maps, rich scenery, transitions between scenes and angles, needs to be programmed.	Game itself: Flash/Shockwave; custom 3D engine (Quake, Unreal engine). Cut scenes: MPEG-1, MPEG-4, or latest high bit-rate motion compensating codec.	3D models and textures are downloaded before game starts; modem bandwidths usable for multi-player gaming (only animation commands are sent, not video).	1.5 megabytes for cut scenes; 30–40 Kbps for interactive game move data.
Video for re-editing	Footage that needs to be readily manipulated without slow decompression and degradation.	DV (digital video), Motion JPEG, and Apple Pixlet codec.	DV is light compression and files are large. Motion JPEG has no motion compensation; each frame is a key frame. Thus, cutting, editing, and rearranging is easier. Pixlet provides lossless video editing for broadcast up to film quality.	2 megabits/second and up for motion. JPEG DV: 25–50 megabits/second. Pixlet: Up to hundreds of megabits/second.
High-quality broadcast or editing	Stock footage or archival footage that needs to be in high-quality source format.	MPEG-2, MPEG-4, and MPEG-1.	MPEG-2 is DVD and digital satellite format; very high-quality MPEG is best non-proprietary choice for permanent footage if uncompressed is not an option.	4 megabits/second (4,000kilobits/second) and up.

SUMMARY

Although MPEG-1 and MPEG-2 provide great quality—good enough for DVDs and HDTV—they're not really appropriate for the Internet. A whole array of low-bit rate codecs have been designed for the Internet.

As Real, Windows Media, and QuickTime are the major streaming video players, it's likely you'll choose to use one of their codecs; however, there are other possibilities. Each media player has a system for third-party codec insertion, and it may be appropriate for your application to use a special codec. Codec quality is rarely the only factor in deciding which media system to use. The fierce competition between different codec vendors, even within MPEG-4 vendors, provides many choices for compression technology.

Any current vendor naturally aims to make or use state-of-the-art codecs; thus, the claims each vendor makes on how well its codecs work over the others should be verified by you for your application. Take some of your source video, choose your destination bit rate, and use the free tools these vendors provide. Using a machine similar to your expected audience machine (in speed, connectivity, and so on), try playing back each of the streams. You will then be able to choose, if you even need to, which codec to use over the others.

Digital video compression draws terminology from mathematics, computers, television, electronics, and the physics of light, to name a few. You now know and understand the major terms and symbols that you are likely to encounter.

A lot of complicated techniques go into compressing motion video, but similar techniques are used by all the systems. Understanding these basics can give some perspective from which to evaluate new technologies and claims from vendors.

CHAPTER

3

VIDEO STORAGE FILE FORMATS

HOW TO STORE VIDEO ON A COMPUTER

IN THIS CHAPTER

- An Ideal File Format for Video Storage
- Common Internet File Formats
- File Formats Versus Codecs: "How Do I Play Back an AVI?"
- A Brief History of File Formats
- Common Features

Faced with the decision of what delivery system to use for Internet video, nobody asks, "Which file format should I choose?" With the Web, you can choose between several standard formats (GIF, JPEG, and PNG) with clear strengths and weaknesses; however, video delivery systems come with their own set of proprietary file formats.

Even though file formats are generally not a user-defined option, many of the features provided by the different streaming media systems (security, bandwidth awareness, interoperability) depend on the file format developed by that vendor. Also, it is often desirable to export content stored in one file format into another, and understanding which codecs can be stored in which file formats helps determine if such translations are possible.

New video file formats (and the corresponding three-letter extensions) are invented all the time. Knowing how to identify and categorize file formats by their different functions helps you make sense of the bewildering quantity of file types you can encounter when working with Internet video.

111

Consider some of the questions addressed by file formats:

- *Should the content be stored in separate files or interleaved into a single file?*
- *How well do audio and video data synch up?*
- *Should the format hold any other kind of data besides the video and audio content?*
- *Can the user fast-forward and rewind through the file?*
- *Can the file contain different kinds of compressed audio and video (and different codecs)?*
- *How does the format deal with slow modem connections or lost packets?*
- *How do broadband users and dialup users both receive and view the video with the appropriate resolution?*

> **Note** Note that in this chapter we are concerned exclusively with matters of *storage* (what is the actual data stored in the file and how is it stored there?) as opposed to *transport* (how do we move the data to the user?).

AN IDEAL FILE FORMAT FOR VIDEO STORAGE

In this section, we delve into the formats for the major Internet video systems. For now, though, it makes sense to acquire a technical grounding into why and how file formats are used. Various file formats exist to store data not only because competing companies create their own formats and push their ideas into standards bodies, but also because of legitimate differing needs in the marketplace. We have yet to see a single be-all-and-end-all format that meets everyone's needs. The following sections analyze some characteristics common to all file formats by building up an example file format. Then we look at how each of the major formats addresses these various needs.

REQUIREMENTS OF INTERNET VIDEO FILE FORMATS

We can distill the job of a video file format into 12 requirements:

- Store the audio and video data (obviously).
- Provide for efficient (fast, real-time) playback on the target-viewing platform.

- Provide for efficient *scrubbing* (fast-forward and rewind while previewing).
- Provide for efficient seeking (jumping to any point in the video).
- Store data regarding what codecs were used for the audio and video.
- Store *metadata* (data about the content, such as copyright data, authorship, dates of creation, ownership, and so on).
- Store additional tracks and multimedia data, including thumbnails, subtitle tracks, alternate language audio tracks, alternate video tracks, and more.
- Allow for multiple resolutions of video depending on the viewing platform.
- Lock the file so that it can't be tampered with, possibly preventing even viewing the file without authorization.
- Allow for video editing (cutting and pasting portions of footage).
- Provide for checking the integrity of a file, either against tampering or because of losses incurred during transport, and recovering from errors.
- Segment the audio and video portions into packets so that they can be efficiently transmitted via the Internet.

Each of these requirements is discussed in the following sections.

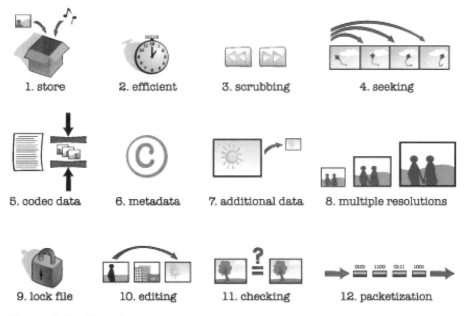

Figure 3-1 *Video format requirements.*

STORE COMPRESSED AUDIO/VIDEO

The straightforward way to store compressed video and audio is to sequentially store the video data into one file and the compressed audio into another file

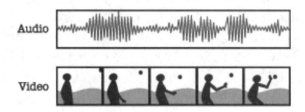

Figure 3-2 *Audio and video stored in two separate files.*

A better way to store compressed video is to put both video and audio into the same file, with some information specifying when the audio ends and the video starts.

Figure 3-3 *Audio and video stored in a single file.*

When dealing with file formats, there are two concepts you should know:

- Logical is the abstract view of what the format is supposed to hold.
- Physical is how it is formatted on the disk.

The logical format of audio and video synchronized in time, depicted in Figure 3-4, gives the impression that there is an audio track and a video rack in parallel from start to finish.

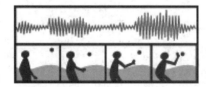

Figure 3-4 *A logical file format where audio and video are parallel tracks.*

While logical file formats are useful for thinking about or visualizing file organization, they don't reflect how the file is physically laid out onto disk. The arrangement of data on the hard disk tremendously affects how efficiently the computer can access the file. The diagrams in the following sections realistically show how a file is written to a disk.

EFFICIENT PLAYBACK

Playing back multimedia that is stored in the manner shown in Figure 3-5 would require the hard drive to frantically seek back and forth: first to get a little bit of video, then to get a bit of audio, and then more video, then audio, on and on until the playback is complete. It would be better to work with two tracks and interleave them—for example, to store them in alternating segments.

Because of the extreme nature of streaming media (it pushes the limits of bandwidth, storage, and computing power), it's necessary to not only put the audio and video in a single file, but also to break them into small segments that are spliced together. AVI and other interleaving formats use a scheme that looks like Figure 3-5.

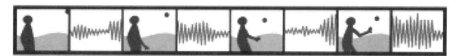

Figure 3-5 *Audio and video are broken into small segments and spliced together in an interleaved file.*

With this simple format, we can efficiently play back the video with a minimum of disk resources. With luck, the audio and video contain some information to allow the decompressor in the player to match them up, so the audio and video are synchronized.

EFFICIENT SCRUBBING

Scrubbing is rapid playback of the video, either forward or backward, so that the user can see the content fly by. This is easy enough, because digital video consists of keyframes and interpolated frames. Interpolated frames are calculated from the data in keyframes. Keyframes contain all their data themselves; they don't rely on any other frame. (For technical details of this aspect of video compression, see Chapter 2, "Video Compression.") We can use keyframes to "scrub" through a video—like fast-forwarding or rewinding on a VCR—by displaying only keyframes (or only some keyframes) while the user drags the FF or REW buttons on the player.

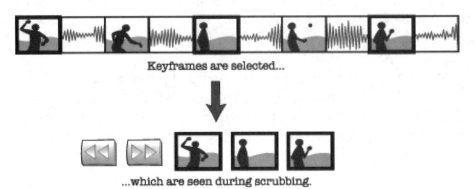

Figure 3-6 *Scrubbing through a file can be accomplished by displaying keyframe and skipping interpolated frames.*

EFFICIENT SEEKING

MPEG and similar compression systems rely on past (and possibly future) keyframes to decide on the current frame. Thus, digital video is not a linear affair, where the data for 30:00 can be assumed to directly follow the data for 29:59. The data for 30:00 may derive from a keyframe at 29:32 and another keyframe at 31:01. Additionally, because video frames vary in size, if you asked to seek to exactly 30:00:00 minutes into the video, our file format requires the decoder to go into each segment of video to see if it might have frame 30:00.00. This would take awhile. So we need a map of which segments of interleaved audio and video represent which segments of time. We'll put this index segment at the beginning of the file so it can be quickly read when the file is opened.

Figure 3-7 *An index at the start of the file quickly looks up the physical location of any given timecode.*

DEFINING CODECS

How does the player software know which codec to use to decompress the audio and video data? For instance, a file might contain MP3 audio and MPEG-1 video. We need to store that information somewhere, so we add a header (a chunk of information) at the head of the file:

> Video codec: Windows Media Video
> Video bit rate: 202 Kbps
> Video size: 320 x 240
> Video stream: 202 Kbps, 30 fps, 10 sec. per keyframe
> Quality: 75
> Audio codec: Windows Media Audio
> 40 Kbps, 32 kHz, stereo

Figure 3-8 *The header contains information about codecs and other file details.*

OTHER HEADER INFORMATION: METADATA

What else should we put in the header? What about copyright data, such as ©*Disney Corp. All Rights Reserved?* What about authorship, dates of creation, ownership, and more? We can also store keywords that describe the content itself, a practice that offers deeper searching capabilities than just title, creator, and so on. We can put all our *metadata* (information about the file) into this header, perhaps in different subsegments but all easy to access at the beginning of the file.

Figure 3-9 *A header with metadata (extra descriptive data about the video file).*

NON-VIDEO CONTENT

You may have other content that you need to encode along with the video. Perhaps you have an animated GIF for applications to use as a preview, several sizes of thumbnail views, or images of different scenes (such as in a DVD). All of this would be added as sections of the header as well.

MULTIPLE BIT RATES

The Internet is bandwidth-heterogeneous—that is, different users have different connection speeds, and we want to offer streams with more or less data for different users. Unless the codec has some sort of capability to produce different bit rates, we'll want to simply cram the different target bit rates into the same file. This means, for instance, putting the 56k, 100k, and 300k versions all in a row. Note that physically, you would still want to interleave the audio portion for these different bit rates with the corresponding video. Thus, we have what appears in Figure 3-10.

Figure 3-10 *An interleaved file with three different bandwidth settings stored sequentially.*

PROTECTING FILES AGAINST UNAUTHORIZED USE

Exercising strong control over Internet media is a highly technical feat of almost mystical wizardry. The whole area of technology is often termed Digital Rights Management, or DRM. Anything that offers content providers a measure of control regarding when and how their content is consumed comes under this heading. This includes password-protected media files, required payment systems, files that expire after a certain time, copy protection, and more. DRM tends to be implemented by storing all the audio and video data in some sort of DRM wrapper, which surrounds and protects the video and audio from unauthorized access.

This is usually achieved by encrypting (scrambling and locking) the data and then separately delivering the keys (needed to unlock the media) to the user after the user has been properly authorized to view it. For simplicity, we simply put all the video data in a DRM wrapper and then put a DRM block at the beginning of the file. This DRM block would contain information such as the web site of where to go to become authorized to view the file, the website where the keys can be retrieved, the expiration date of the file, and so on. (DRM is discussed in substantial detail in Chapter 7, "Digital Rights Management [DRM].")

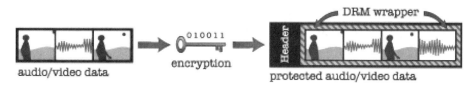

Figure 3-11   *A video stream protected by a Digital Rights Management (DRM) wrapper.*

VIDEO EDITING

Naturally, editing video, rearranging the order of video segments, deleting portions, and adding scene transitions is going to require more CPU power and disk access than simply watching video. Editing can be achieved simply by changing the index portion of the header. By changing the index, you can re-arrange or delete scenes without actually moving or removing them.

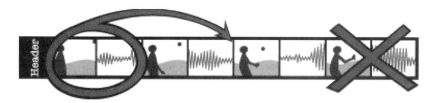

Figure 3-12   *In an edited file, some scenes are transposed and others are deleted. Changes can be reflected in the index without resequencing the data.*

After a file has been extensively edited, however, it needs to go through some sort of re-sequencing. For instance, imagine the editor cuts the first half of the file, pastes it after the second half, then copies a small portion of the middle of the file and puts it at the beginning, and then deletes a large portion of the second half. This can be easily re-indexed in the index block without moving the data in the audio-video portions.

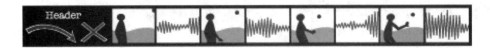

Figure 3-13 *A re-indexed file.*

But now playing back the file requires more processing by the computer. The decoder has to go on a scavenger hunt—rewind, fast-forward—to play the video in sequence. The file needs to resaved and resequenced so that the index is once again a relatively straightforward task.

Figure 3-14 *In a resequenced file, the video is physically reordered so that index mapping is relatively simple.*

CHECKING FILE INTEGRITY

Checking for file integrity ensures that the file has not been damaged or altered in transit. There are two approaches for checking a file's integrity:

- Checksums involve a technique to find out if something's been altered in transit. The receiver can sum all the data received and check if the total adds up to the right number. In our file format, we include checksums with each audio or video segment.

Figure 3-15 *Checksums verify file integrity.*

- Digital signatures ensure not only the integrity of the stream but can positively verify who sent it. So we include a digital signature in our file format as well. It works like this: The publisher of the file calculates a checksum, then scrambles the checksum, and locks it with a secret key or passcode that only that publisher knows, but which can be unlocked with a key that is publicly available. The player software uses the public key to unlock the checksum, and compares it with the calculated checksum. If they match, the file was not altered in transit, because only the author who knew the checksum to begin with could have produced it. (For more on public key encryption, see Chapter 7, "Video Security and Digital Rights Management [DRM].")

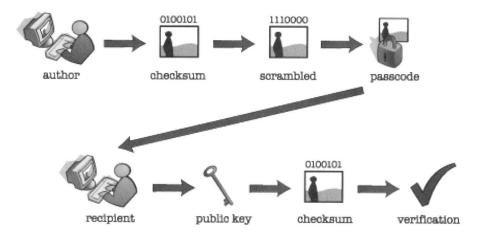

Figure 3-16 *Digital signatures can positively verify the sender of the stream.*

PACKETIZATION

Ultimately, the video file needs to be streamed over the Internet. Streaming involves breaking the file down into kilobyte-sized chunks called packets. Getting the data from the streaming server to the media player requires that the audio and video synch up, that the video is sent fast enough but not too fast, and that packets that are lost on the network can be quickly detected and resent. The process of breaking up the video into these chunks is called *packetization.* In order to reduce the work of the media servers, the work of organizing the file into these chunks is sometimes done beforehand in a process called *hinting*. Hinting involves adding additional data to the video file (a hint track) to tell the media server how to packetize it when it is served. Hint tracks contain data about not only what chunks of audio and video exist, but how large a chunk to send over the Internet and at what time intervals.

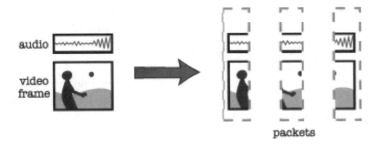

Figure 3-17 *Packetization of a video frame.*

We just constructed a hypothetical video storage file format. Real-world file formats of this type have most or all of these features. There aren't too many substantial differences between the major file formats; each of them achieves the goals in one way or another. The things to compare have more to do with how flexible the format is, how many operating systems it works on, and how supported it is by different software companies.

COMMON INTERNET FILE FORMATS

File formats relating to Internet video actually fall into three major categories:

- **Category 1:** Video container file formats, hierarchical in structure, hold many different kinds of media (audio, video, and text) synchronized in time. These files contain the audio and video data; they can be as small as several kilobytes (for a short audio clip) to megabytes or even gigabytes for hours of video. The ideal format described in this chapter is of this type.

- **Category 2:** Simple raw storage or stream formats hold the compressed video data without extra headers or metadata. These are essentially a live audio-video stream saved to disk.

- **Category 3:** Playlist, index, and scripting formats do not contain the actual media files, only pointers and commands that indicate where the files are located and how to present the media in the player. These formats are usually small text files, containing a list of URLs to play in a row, or a list of audio and video to put together as a slide show. These files give instructions to a media player to retrieve the actual video files from somewhere else, and perhaps to arrange the timing in which this retrieval is performed.

INTERNET VIDEO CONTAINER FILE FORMATS

ASF, MOV, AVI, RM, and MP4 are all container formats. They store various types of media. They differ only in what they hold and how they hold it.

- AVI (Audio Video Interleaved) can hold just about anything. It works on every platform, and it's wide open—the video content itself is accessible to anyone who wants to go in and get it. Unfortunately, it doesn't do the best job of synching audio and video, and seeking is slower than it needs to be. This is because the file index used to be located at the end of the file instead of the beginning. Newer versions of AVI attempt to solve this problem; however, the format has been extended so much that that many AVI files contain content that can't be played on mainstream AVI players. In addition, AVI is not at all suited for streaming because it has no standard way of storing packetization data.

- MOV, the format of Apple's QuickTime, is just as open as AVI, but it does a much better job of synching audio and video. And it goes much further than AVI in providing a rich context for holding and linking multimedia content, such as Flash, animation "sprites," text, scene transitions, and more. As with AVI, several third-party tools are available, as well as Apple's rich QuickTime API for Windows and Linux. MOV is the most flexible and extensive media format in this group.

- ASF (Advanced Streaming Format), Microsoft's proprietary format, is dominant as an Internet delivery format. Currently branded *Windows Media* (it often shows up as .WMV or .WMA), it is potentially as versatile a storage format as AVI, with better streaming capabilities. It is primarily designed to hold synchronized audio and video.

- RM (RealMedia), the format for Real's streaming media files, can be extended to hold all types of multimedia. It was designed from the ground up for streaming efficiency, and it works hand in hand with Real's streaming server product. On the openness front, it is *only* accessed through Real's software interfaces; however, Real has always provided them on every conceivable media platform including Linux, so the commercial availability of support is good. Known file formats supported by RM include MPEG-2, MPEG-4, Real, and H263.

- MP4 (MPEG-4) is a container format that is almost identical to MOV; however, for simple reasons of compatibility, MPEG-4-compliant playback devices can handle only MPEG-4 related audio, video, and multimedia. (Unless the player also knows explicitly how to handle MOV files; for instance, Apple's QuickTime 6 player also handles MPEG-4 content.)

- SWF, SWV (Shockwave Flash), the format for Flash movies, typically contains vector-drawn animations with scripting controls. It can simply play an animation, or it can allow for extensive user interaction. A player (usually installed as a browser plug-in) is required. Besides vector animation, SWF supports certain video codecs (SWV files), JPEG still images, remote loading of other SWF files, XML data, and raw text. The file format has been published, but development of the format is very much in the hands of Macromedia.

- NSV (NullSoft Video) is a format recently developed by NullSoft (a division of AOL) used to contain the video streamed by ShoutCast/IceCast video servers. Like most of the other formats, it can hold audio and video, and can be streamed or downloaded.

Some of these formats, such as MOV or MP4, are designed to hold other multimedia elements in addition to audio and video, such as 3D objects, textures, still images, and more. Some of them have evolved mainly as holder formats for disk-based or streaming audio or video, such as ASF/WMF, .RA, .RM, and so on. But they all have very similar approaches to the problem. (See Chapter 8, "Internet Video Standards," for more detailed technical information.)

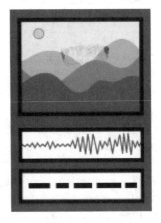

Figure 3-18 *The container format holds video, audio, text, and more in one file.*

SIMPLE RAW OR STREAM VIDEO FORMATS

Besides the major streaming video formats, you should know about some of the simple raw formats used with video and audio in other contexts:

- MPEG-1 and MPEG-2 each have their own file formats, but those formats are transient. The files are almost never played on a personal computer, but are delivered via satellite, cable, or DVD. MPEG-2 is usually encrypted into a .VOB file on a DVD. MPEG-1 is also found in a .DAT file on a video CD. They basically contain the encoded data written raw onto disk.

  MPEG streams are composed of interleaved audio and video data arranged into sections called *groups of pictures*. Just like TV, you can "tune in" to the stream at any point, but unlike hierarchical formats, there is no table of contents, index, copyright information, and so on. In the MPEG-1 and MPEG-2 standards, this data is usually delivered outside of the .MPG file:

- MP3 started as little more than the raw bytes of MP3-encoded audio; there was no real file format of which to speak—just the raw bytes of a single track (or stereo track) of audio data. This is primarily because the MP3 format, part of the MPEG-1 standard, evolved outside of any standards committee work. Eventually, metadata was added to the media data; the file format held the artist, title, album, track number, even album art as a JPEG, which could be embedded into this chunk. These "tags" were prepended to the file and went through several design iterations—ID1, ID2, and finally ID3 tags, the current standard. Now most CD-ripping programs grab the album data from a central database and properly fill out the ID3 portion of the MP3 file when connected to the database that stores this information.

- DV (digital video) is produced by modern digital cameras, usually named .DV files. They are used by video editing software.

Other raw file formats pop up now and then, too:

- .263 is a file format that contains video compressed with the H.263 codec.

- .RTP files contain the raw network stream for an RTP (Real Time Protocol) saved to disk. Raw formats are usually created when software developers want to quickly save video to disk instead of using some pre-existing file format.

INTERNET PLAYLIST, INDEX, AND SCRIPTING FORMATS

Index formats are simple pointer files. Each of the video storage formats has a corresponding index format.

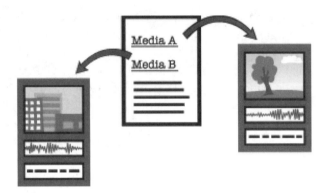

Figure 3-19 *An index file (center) uses the http protocol to point to container files.*

- MOV has several formats that don't contain actual audio or video at all, but merely point to other files. The simplest of these are reference movies. Reference movies are just a few kilobytes in size and point to several other movies. They are used to select different actual movies depending on the language or bandwidth of the viewer. They still have a *.mov* suffix.

- RAM (RealAudio Metafile) is Real's index file format, which simply points to the URL of the actual media file (RealMedia .RM or Real-Audio .RA). It was developed as a way to make sure that the RealPlayer would launch if it was installed. The browsers see a file of type RAM and launch RealPlayer; RealPlayer then reads the actual URL from the RAM file, grabs that, and connects to the Internet. RAM files can also play a list of URLs in sequence.

- ASX (Active Streaming index) files are index files that work in the Windows Media system and point to the content held in an ASF media file. These can consist of just one URL or a long list (as in playlists). They can also be nested—for example, an ASX can point to a list of ASX files, which in turn point to actual playable Windows Media files, just like a web page can forward you to another web page, which forwards you to the actual web page.

- SMIL (Synchronized Multimedia Integration Language) provides instructions to a media player on how to present a multimedia interface and what content to display in various media containers. You can think of it as a sort of HTML for media players. It allows you to place text, still graphics, and media clips in different positions within the media player view, as well as compose the order in which clips are played. A SMIL file basically draws the geometry of the interface (with commands to a compliant player) to display particular video, text, and audio content to display in the different areas. (Real, QuickTime, and Microsoft's Internet Explorer all understand SMIL.)

FILE FORMATS VERSUS CODECS: HOW DO I PLAY BACK AN AVI?

What video goes into what file format?

The question of what file format to use is less frequent than the question of what codec to use. Invariably, the file format really depends on the codec, which in turn depends on what platform it is viewed. Until the Internet became popular, each of the various file formats (MOV, AVI) were capable in practice of holding any of the available codecs—the handful of audio codecs, Cinepak video, Motion JPEG, and so on. The rise of the Internet required companies to stake their claims, and the various competitive (though very similar) file formats began specializing and restricting what they would contain, even though in theory they can hold anything. As a result of this general-purpose nature, file formats often became confused with the data they hold. "How do I play an AVI?" is actually the wrong question; the correct question might be, "How do I play an AVI with Microsoft MPEG-4 version 3 video and MP3 audio?"

To compound this problem, vendors continually improve the quality of their proprietary codecs, so that an ASF file created with codecs available in 2005 is not playable in the Windows Media Player available in 2002. Also, slight incompatibilities and many "levels" of compatibility hinder even "standard" codecs, so not all MPEG-4 streams play back in all MPEG-4 players.

Although the media player can automatically download popular codecs from the vendor's web site in this situation, some codecs were only installed along with

media-editing boards, video cards, and so on. For instance, some real-
o editing cards install a special Motion-JPEG codec and store their
media in an *AVI* file. However, when this file is taken to any other machine, it
does not play back because the codec requires the actual hardware on that board
to function correctly! In this case, the fact that it is an AVI file is of no help,
and most likely only the audio will play back on other computers.

To avoid these sorts of compatibility problems, it is key to:

- Ensure that video is published on the Web and that it last for years in
  a mainstream video player format.
- Ensure that video is archived, is encoded at as high a quality as possible,
  and kept in a relatively open file container format (or a closed one for
  which tools are guaranteed to exist in the future).

There are many different ways that video will be manipulated or produced
on a computer, and each one suggests both a different codec and a different
file format—editing, streaming, archival storage, Internet video-on-demand,
satellite/cable delivery, and so on. For instance, to edit digital video on a computer, it is best to store it in a raw DV format (simply the audio and video right
off a digital consumer video camera.) Another popular editing format is Motion-
JPEG stored in AVI files. In both of these formats, the audio and video are
arranged logically and physically (not interleaved), so that actions like rearranging tracks and cutting tracks are fast and efficient. However, for something such
as broadcasting video from a satellite to consumer set-top boxes, the best format
is MPEG-2 or MPEG-4. These formats are not good for editing at all, but are
excellent for high-quality playback.

Table 3-1 summarizes the file formats we've discussed in this section along
with some other formats you might encounter.

Table 3-1 Video File Formats	
File Extension	**Description**
.AVI	Audio-Video Interleaved container file.
.ASF, .WMA, .WMV, .WM	Windows Media formats. The extensions stand for (in order) Advanced Streaming Format, Windows Media Audio, and Windows Media Video. .WM is a container file for Windows Media content.

File Extension	Description
.MPG, .MPEG, .VOB	MPEG-1 or MPEG-2 audio/video stream.
.DAT	VideoCD and CD-Interactive MPEG-1 video stream file.
.MOV	QuickTime movie container file.
.MP4	MPEG-4 media container file.
.ASX	Advanced Streaming Index, a list of one or more URLs to media that a Windows media player can play in sequence.
.RA, .RM., .RAM	Real formats. .RA is for RealAudio, .RM is for Real-Media, and .RAM is a pointer file for Real content.
.DIVX, .AVI	De facto standard consisting of an AVI file containing (usually) MPEG-4 video and MP3 audio, commonly used for movie distribution over the Internet.
.M3U	Playlist of MP3 URLs, playable by media players.
.DV	Digital video stream from a digital camcorder, and saved to a raw file on disk.
.RTP	Real Time Protocol, a format containing audio or video streams and RTP network transport information.
.SWF, .FLA, .FLV	Shockwave Flash format, used to deliver Flash movies over the Internet.
.SML, .SMIL	Simple Multimedia Integration Language, used by RealPlayer, QuickTime player, and Internet Explorer to combine different multimedia elements into a time-based presentation.
.NSV	NullSsoft Video, used by Shoutcast and played back by Winamp audio/video players.
.OGG	A container format developed by ziph.org to house its open source and patent-free audio and video content.

A BRIEF HISTORY OF FILE FORMATS

When computers first began storing digital video in the early 1990s with very little compression (the CPU wasn't fast enough yet), it was quite a feat just getting the data off the disk. For instance, the *CD-ROM standard (MPEG-1* video at 150Kbps/sec) was a breakthrough; early personal computers required special hardware to get smooth full-screen playback of MPEG-1 in software.

CD-ROMs stored the data very carefully; video was located in well-placed rows on the physical disk. Most importantly, the audio and video were interleaved. This strategy reduced the odds (no guarantees) that the disk wouldn't be ready with the next chunk of media when needed, because less *seek time* was required.

Table 3-2 shows the history of major file formats.

Table 3-2 Video File Format Timeline

Year	Format
1985	IFF file format created by Electronic Arts for audio/video storage on Amiga computers.
1991	QuickTime .MOV format created by Apple.
1992	MPEG-1 stream format standardized.
1992	AVI (Audio-Video Interleaved) file format created by Microsoft.
1993	Video CD standardized with MPEG-1.DAT files on CD-ROM.
1994	MPEG-2 Stream format standardized.
1996	ASF (Advanced Streaming Format) created by Microsoft to replace AVI.
1997	MP3 (MPEG-1, Level 3) audio file format created with ID3 (such as artist identification) tags.
1997	Flash movie (Shockwave Flash, .SWF) format created.
1998	DivX file format (AVI + MS MPEG-4 video + MP3 audio) created.
2000	MPEG-4 file format based on MOV standardized; MPEG-4 stream format standardized.
2002	Sorenson Spark codec added to Flash .FLV files.
2003	NullSoft adds video support to its ShoutCast/WinAmp streaming system, creating .NSF files.

APPLE'S QUICKTIME: MOV FILES (.MOV)

The first standard for interleaved audio and video playback was Apple's *QuickTime* MOV format. Apple's MOV is a well-conceived storage format for holding many pieces of multimedia content. A QuickTime movie file is a container with links to tracks (media types), media (content), and atoms (content segments). MOV had been designed (heavily influenced by the more general *RIFF* format) with a concept of four-character *atoms* that described the various pieces of the file. (Atoms are conceptually identical to AVI's four-character segments.)

The first clips in QuickTime's *MOV* format were tiny—at 160×120, they were justifiably derided as jerky, "postage-stamp video"—and often managing only a few frames per second. Machines were limited at first by a variety of factors:

- Motherboard speeds established in the early 1980s were too slow to even get full-rate video to the video card.
- Video cards could not refresh full screen at 30fps.
- Computer screens turned out to be too sharp for satisfactory video display—everything looked grainy.

Neither Macintosh System 7 (MacOS) nor Windows 3.1 had true preemptive multitasking, so anything could interrupt the video (which it still does on modern operating systems, but less so now). By 1992, Apple had QuickTime 2.0 playing MOV files on Windows and Macintosh. Many interactive multimedia CD-ROM titles of the early '90s used QuickTime for movie playback. The next several years would see several other video playback systems for CD, but QuickTime was adopted broadly, and many early video clips were stored in the MOV format.

Apple's MOV files were structured to hold far more than just audio and video content; however, MOV was designed from the start to hold any multimedia content, and it has been extended to include support for images, animation data, Flash movies, text tracks, 3D walkthroughs, and more. MOV is also well supported on both Macintosh and Windows. Because of its flexible design, it was easily updated with "hint tracks" when Apple was ready to compete in the streaming wars.

After the Internet surged in popularity, QuickTime began improving rapidly in the online video arms race. In 1997, Apple received an exclusive license with

Sorenson for its H.263/MPEG family codec and added streaming capabilities. However, the file format had been so well designed that it kept up with the new needs of the Internet—multiple different codecs, conditional delivery of media elements, metadata, incorporation of MP3, and with version 4, the capability to stream. All these extensions were achieved through normal extensions within the QuickTime MOV file format and did not require the format to be redesigned.

QuickTime's hyper-extensibility has often made MOV a format of choice for complicated multimedia projects, including those distributed on CD-ROM, and it is well supported in video editing and creation tools on both PC and Macintosh platforms.

Container MOV files contain not only media content such as audio, video, graphics, QuickTime VR, QuickTime 3D, but also metadata, including user data, media data, media index, types of tracks, and compression/decompression information. In addition to container MOV files, however, there are also reference MOV files, which simply contain pointers to the container files that hold content, much like Real's .RAM format.

AUDIO-VIDEO INTERLEAVED: AVI FILES (.AVI)

AVI was the second major container format to come about. It was developed by Microsoft in 1992 and became the dominant format on the PC platform. AVI was a breakthrough in that Microsoft delivered for the first time real-time playback of video on a PC. Because codecs all contain different intellectual property, patent, and rights issues, and because bundles of codecs tend to become platform-differentiating features, the codec sets in QuickTime and Video for Windows immediately diverged. Even third-party codecs, and "standard" codecs, such as *H.261* and *H.263,* existed in forms just different enough that it was impractical to expect to author once and play back in any system. In some cases, the QuickTime system could open AVIs, and Microsoft's Video for Windows system could play back MOVs. This didn't last long, though, as new proprietary codecs soon came out, and as the Internet became more important.

AVI is based on the IFF file format (the basis of the WAV and TIFF formats). AVI has no inherent restrictions nor does it have any patents that encumber its use. With its IFF heritage, many programs can easily open and manipulate AVI files. When hard disks grew large and file sizes did as well, AVI 2.0 was standardized to allow file sizes greater than 2 gigabyte (GB) and to add an improved indexing system that is stored at the beginning of the file instead of at the end, a change that substantially improved seeking abilities.

AVI has been used to hold MP3 audio combined with MPEG-4 video (a new combination when it first appeared, not planned by the MPEG standards group) and playback tools have allowed this organically developed standard to play back on any platform imaginable. AVI is also frequently used as a utility format for PC video editing boards to store Motion JPEG. An all-purpose audio-video storage format, AVI is well established and straightforward.

MPEG-1 AND MPEG-2 (.MPG, .MPEG, .DAT, AND .VOB)

After MPEG-1 was standardized in 1992, it became popular in two offline formats delivered on CD-ROM. One was Video CD (VCD), a predecessor to DVD that was popular in Asia. A user could store up to 74 minutes of VHS-quality video on a single CD-ROM disk. Another format was CD-I (CD Interactive), which contained not only MPEG-1 video clips but interactive games, graphical table of contents, and other interactive features. Both of these formats ran on special players (with custom MPEG-1 decoding circuitry) that connected to television sets.

Over time, general-purpose computers gained the speed necessary to play back MPEG-1 video. Initially, it required custom expansion cards. Early Pentium chips were fast enough to decode MPEG-1 and display it full-screen. People began exchanging short MPEG-1 clips over the Internet. By 1998, the Linux and open source communities had developed tools for creating, converting, and playing back video in the open MPEG-1 format. The existence of a large body of MPEG-1 Video-CDs made it a natural choice for exchanging movies as high-speed Internet connectivity started to spread.

The contents of an MPEG file are simply the interleaved audio and video of the MPEG codec, called an *MPEG stream*. There is no header full of metadata, copyright information, or table of contents.

When DVDs (using the high-quality MPEG-2 codec) became mainstream, computers began to play those back as well. Initially, as with MPEG-1, DVD playback on computers required special decoding hardware. Once processor speeds exceeded 400MHz, however, the MPEG files on DVDs could be decoded and played back in real time, using only software.

In an effort to stop piracy, however, the video on DVDs was encrypted with a technique called Content Scramble System (CSS). For hardware or software companies to include DVD playback capabilities on their products, they had to license special software libraries to access and decode DVD video object *(VOB)* files, and agree to keep the encryption keys secret. A developer of a software DVD player failed to properly secure the DVD keys; soon enough the software had been reverse-engineered, and the keys obtained and made public. A CSS-decrypting program, DeCSS, was soon distributed over the Internet. This meant not only that software could be produced to let anyone play legitimately purchased DVDs (even with unlicensed software), but also that MPEG-2 video could now be extracted from DVDs just like MP3s were being ripped from CDs. Because there's no way to update millions of deployed DVD players and make new secret keys, all current and future standard DVDs can still be decoded this way. Unlike MP3s, MPEG-2 files are far too large to exchange quickly over the Internet, so they are typically re-encoded with a different codec, such as MPEG-1 or MPEG-4, which reduced the quality but still produced a very watchable version of the movie.

PROGRESSIVE NETWORKS: REAL AUDIO AND REALVIDEO (.RA, .RM, AND .RAM)

In 1995, RealNetworks (called Progressive Networks at the time) rocked the Web with the first audio streaming system—RealAudio 1.0. The RealAudio file format (.RA) was optimized for serving from the company's media servers. To integrate RealAudio with the Web, they also created a small pointer format, .RAM, a text file containing the URL of the .RA file to play. The Web browser would then hand the .RAM file to the Real player, which would extract the URL and play the media directly.

Real later created RealVideo, added support for both audio and video in the file, and changed the suffix from .RA to .RM (for RealMedia). An important addition was the ability to store different bit rate encodings of audio and video within the same file, so that the RealMedia server could send the appropriate content (audio only, audio and video, high bit rate audio, and video) depending on the detected connection speed of the client.

RealMedia (.RM) files are codec-agnostic, meaning they are structured to hold not only Real codecs but any industry standard codecs. Their file format is just as extensible as MOV, AVI, and ASF. Real has implemented MPEG-1, MP3, MPEG-2, MPEG-4, H.263, and many proprietary codecs for the RealMedia system. The benefits of the RealMedia storage format are that it is optimized with Real's media servers, it can contain multiple bit rate resolutions, and it allows for features like SureStream (providing a graceful increase/decrease of bit rate depending on viewer connectivity).

ADVANCED STREAMING FORMAT AND WINDOWS MEDIA FORMAT (.WMV, .WMA, .WMX, AND .ASF)

Microsoft's customers were telling the software giant that they wanted the capability to control rights, prevent tampering, and generally enforce licenses on media files. It was becoming obvious to everyone that digital media would soon be easy to copy, manipulate, and distribute over the Internet. AVI was certainly not designed for these robust rights controls.

ASF arguably represents a simple technical evolution from AVI; it updates the four-character codes to Microsoft's 16-byte GUIDs (Globally Unique IDs). It improves on some of AVI's synchronization and indexing issues and is better adapted for storing media in the exact format in which it will be streamed. There is no argument, however, about the most important features of ASF:

- Patenting the file format
- Publishing the ASF format with a license

In some ways, ASF is more of a legal development than a technological one. In 1998, Microsoft actually filed a patent for its new file format—*ASF (Advanced Streaming Format)*—which was eventually awarded in 2001. Although companies had been known to patent codecs, this was the first time a file format had been patented. This meant that programmers couldn't "crack open" the format to extract the goodies (the video and audio content). Microsoft could now legally prevent anyone from making tools that would extract video from ASF. Only Microsoft and its licensing partners could legally read and write to the ASF format.

In 2002, Microsoft published the ASF format and began operating somewhat more openly about the format, but even using that specification requires accepting a license agreement, the terms of which prevent the sort of *ripping* of content that the system was intended to prevent. But the license specifically prevents open source implementations of tools that handle ASF. By carefully binding anyone who implements ASF-compatible software to a license, however, Microsoft creates a legal trail of accountability when a file is compromised. If a switch in an ASF file says, "Don't copy this," programs produced under the licensing agreement must obey. Licensees of the documented file format must agree not to write software to weaken the format's security. Because the format itself is patented, programs that manipulate ASF must follow the licensing program.

The ASF format is not unique from a technical perspective. As a modern format, it has some features (timecode, and the capability to easily deal with MPEG-style codecs with several kinds of frames) that improve upon AVI. However, in the interest of intellectual property control, Microsoft has made it all but impossible to play content encoded in its advanced "MPEG-4-ish" (not interoperable with the standard) codecs unless it is stored in ASF. So, when large bodies of content are encoded in ASF with Microsoft MPEG-4 codecs, they are inseparable, and thus can only be delivered by a Microsoft-compatible streaming server or downloaded. Also notable is that these ASF files do not permit the audio to be encoded in MP3, only in the corresponding Microsoft audio codecs packaged with Microsoft's MPEG-4 codecs.

It is extremely difficult (if not impossible) to absolutely guarantee a file format will not be compromised, no matter what security system is used. ASF is clearly a response to content owners clamoring for more secure digital storage and distribution systems on PCs. Such security is delivered in ASF not only through technical means but by designing the format to give Microsoft strong legal protections.

DivX: A De Facto Standard

Around 1998, movies were being converted from DVDs to MPEG-1 files. Just when Microsoft's new MPEG-4 codecs were looked like a more efficient alternative, Microsoft crippled the codec so that it would play back only content stored in ASF (which Macintosh and Linux machines could not use). Then a crafty French programmer re-altered the Microsoft MPEG-4 codec so that it could once again play content stored in AVI. Now, with an even better codec than MPEG-1, a system emerged for ripping movies from DVD, consisting of Microsoft MPEG-4 version 3 for the video, MP3 for the audio, and AVI as the file container. This new rogue "standard" was dubbed DivX.This combination, although completely unplanned by any major commercial vendor, became the de facto standard of ripping movies online. The system was open, as many open source tools emerged for encoding and decoding MP3 audio and for reading and writing AVI files. Coders wrote players for Mac and Linux for these systems, using hacks of Microsoft's MPEG decoder on those platforms. It was quite a coup, the sort of technical activity expected with open source development and the corresponding attitudes about content openness. Shortly thereafter, the developer of DivX helped form a DivX company, which developed what is now a leading MPEG-4 codec and made it commercially available. Current DivX movies use this newer non-Microsoft codec, which is optimized for large file DVD-quality encoding.

SHOCKWAVE/FLASH (.SWF, .FLA, .FLV)

During all this time, a few other formats were being created, such as Flash's SWF. SWF is a file format closely tied to an authoring system. You don't really think of Flash as being a codec, but it is. SWF (Shockwave Flash) files basically contain graphics and commands for animating those graphics. The graphics are compressed with traditional methods similar to JPEG or GIF, and drawing is described with mathematical methods instead of large, raw bitmaps, making file sizes much smaller than traditional bitmap animations.

Instead of drawing a picture, then decomposing it, then recompressing it, then sending it, just the instructions to draw it are sent. In any event, the SWF file has a custom player that eventually was bundled with all the browsers, so that most people can go to a Flash-enabled website and play these files. Because of the small file sizes and the capability to display parts of the file even as others are still being downloaded, Flash has become an almost standard element in website design. With the addition of QuickTime support as well as Macromedia's integration of the Sorenson Spark codec, SWF can be used as a container for video, vector graphics, motion effects, and more.

Flash SWF files were designed to deliver compact animation files over the Internet. In its original incarnation, support was limited to vector-based graphics. In its latest version, support for JPEG files and QuickTime video is included. SWF is a tagged format, and the file structure is simply a header followed by a series of tagged data blocks.

The header contains information on file version, length of file, frame size, total number of frames, and so on. There are two main types of tags: definition tags define content, and control tags manipulate the content. For instance, a definition tag might define a triangle. Once defined, this object is placed in a dictionary. A control tag might move the triangle across the screen. When the necessary content and instructions have been received, a third tag, the ShowFrame tag, tells the player to render the frame.

SWF imposes a few rules on the order of tags:

- A tag can rely only on a previous tag, not a subsequent one.
- A definition tag must be sent before the control tag that accesses it.

So, unlike MPEG, SWF is a progressive format, meaning blocks are sent in their order of use. This restriction allows a Flash movie to be essentially streamed; the viewer can start watching it as soon as certain pieces arrive, and by the time they are finished watching, the entire movie has been received. The file format is structured so that this can occur without special server software; a Web server, the Flash content, and a Flash player are the only requirements.

SIMPLE MULTIMEDIA INTEGRATION LANGUAGE: SMIL (.SML, .SMIL)

SMIL occupies an interesting position in the universe of video file formats for the Internet. SMIL is not a container format—it does not itself contain any media. It is an XML-based, human-readable text file similar to HTML; however, it is far more than simple index format like .RAM or a list of URLs.

SMIL 1.0 was standardized in June 1998, and focused on the capability to synch-ronize media, combining multiple audio, video, and still images into a presentation. SMIL is in essence a simple multimedia-authoring format, sort of an "HTML for multimedia," with the ability to place graphics in exact positions, and splice together audio and video clips in real time. RealPlayer was the first media player to support SMIL files, and QuickTime followed suit. SMIL 2.0 was completed in 2001, and the standard is under continual improvement. Many of the customized multimedia navigation features produced in RealPlayer are implemented with SMIL.

SMIL takes a layers-based approach to laying out elements in a multimedia presentation. Elements can be set to start and stop, and layers can be made visible or invisible at various points in time. Still and moving video can be placed in different regions within the playback window. Different pieces of media can be synchronized either in a sequence (as in playlists) or in parallel (as in slide shows with audio narration).

MPEG-4 (.MPG, .MP4)

The MP4 file format is virtually indistinguishable from MOV (except of course that it holds only MPEG standard media elements). MOV is very extensible, and is specifically geared to handle many different kinds of media, a key design requirement for MPEG-4. Like MOV, MP4 consists of atoms, containing elements such as index points, durations, and pointers to the media data itself.

The top-level atom is called the movie atom. The content data itself is held separately, either contained within the MP4 file or simply linked through URLs. MP4 introduces several new atoms beyond the ones specified by MOV.

> **Note**   It should be noted, however, that the actual streaming does not depend on the file storage format, and MP4 is just a container. And it is only one such container—ASF and RM files both can hold MPEG-4 content as well. (It is not necessary to support the .MP4 file format to support MPEG-4, as in the case of mobile phone video.) Although standardized in 2000, it was not until MPEG-4 licensing terms were established in 2002 that many vendors began broadly releasing MPEG-4-compliant software and hardware. Microsoft had an MPEG-4 codec for several years in its ASF file format before Apple released its MPEG-4 codec and introduced .MP4 files in QuickTime 6.

COMMON FEATURES

The terminology and tools of offline video, such as tracks, influenced file formats. Professional multi-track audio recording studios have thick tapes that can synchronize many simultaneous different instruments into one performance. Similarly, these file formats allow a virtually unbounded number of parallel, time-synchronized tracks.

Most of these formats share several features:

- They are built around a concept of named file segments. AVI calls them *segments*. QuickTime calls them *atoms*. ASF calls them *objects*. Flash calls them *tags*.

- These segments usually start with an identifier and a segment size (in bytes). The identifier is unique and says what the segment stores—for instance, other segments, indexes, names, and so on.

- These segments are named uniquely. Many formats (QuickTime, AVI, and MPEG-4) use a four-character code system. ASF uses a 16-byte GUID, which is just a long number.

- They each have a set of known segments that are part of the original format. They have a concept of extensions to the original format as well, so those vendors can invent new segment types. Older tools simply ignore them. This is a feature of most extensible file formats, such as

RIFF and XML; however, it can create problems as well when too many incompatible extensions are made (as in AVI).

- Each format has a corresponding playlist/index file format, which facilitates Internet and media player integration. ASX files, RAM, and QuickTime reference MOVs all contain a list of one or more URLs to other media, and are handed to the appropriate media player by the browser.

The segment approach is common to all of these extensible formats. Hierarchically (segment within segment) stored chunks, with a name, size, and some contents make up the basic skeleton of these files. Then, as described in this section, specific-purpose segments hold metadata, indexes, audio clips, video frames, and more.

UNDER THE HOOD

You probably don't need to know how specific file formats are structured unless you are writing software to manipulate file formats. In fact, you will find that most of the file formats accomplish the same thing in very similar ways. But there's no harm in looking. For an example of how similar the competing file formats can be, take a look at these two files in Figure 3-20.

On the left is a movie trailer in MOV format. Another is the same trailer in DivX AVI format. Note the size of the chunks to the right of the atom/segment name. Also notice that MOV has a smaller header because the QuickTime header is compressed. Once decompressed, it contains similar data as AVI, containing information about the different audio video tracks in the file. The most important thing to note here is that things haven't changed much. MP4 files look like MOV files, which look like AVI files.

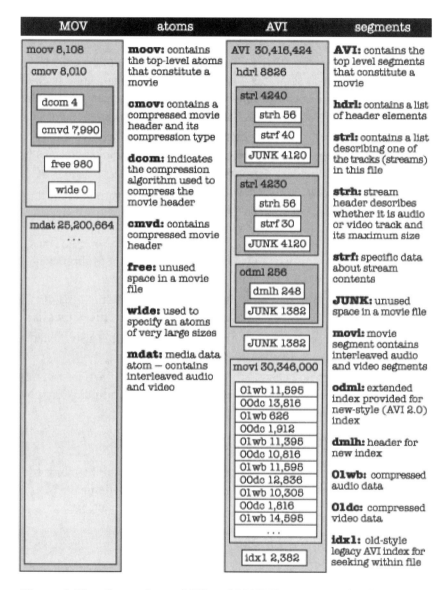

Figure 3-20 *Comparison of AVI and MOV file structures for the same movie trailer.*

SUMMARY

New file formats are developed all the time, and existing formats are subtly altered and renamed. Even as of this writing, a handful of new video formats (and related three-letter extensions) are being invented. New versions of Flash and MPEG-4 movies are being developed for handhelds, portable phones, and other small devices. New codecs are being developed constantly, and inevitably, the files that hold these will need to be renamed, not for technical reasons but to market them and differentiate them from earlier technologies.

The basics of these formats don't change, however. The most important things to understand about file formats are:

- File formats are independent of the type of compression used; thus, even if a player can read a given file format, it doesn't follow that it can read the compressed content inside.
- The structure of file formats is important to the system's capability to pull video and audio off disk and play it back in an efficient way.
- Other functionality (seeking, scrubbing, and son on) is also related to file format.
- There are two basic classes of rich media formats: container formats, which actually contain the media data, and pointer or index formats, which simply reference some container file.
- Legal and licensing constraints are currently more powerful than technical ones for DRM purposes.
- DRM technology is gradually being incorporated into the major file formats in order to more effectively enforce creator-defined rules on the use of content. DRM is discussed in depth in Chapter 6.

4

STREAMING MEDIA SERVER SOFTWARE

HOW TO SERVE VIDEO ON A NETWORK OR THE INTERNET

IN THIS CHAPTER

- Types of Internet Media Delivery: Streaming Versus Downloading
- Streaming Thoroughly Defined
- Internet Streaming Servers
- Conclusion: Choosing a Server

You've successfully imported your media into the computer using the capture system that came bundled with your system. You've also cleaned up the video and added some titles using the bundled editor program. Now you want to put the video online so your intended audience can see it. Can you simply put it on your web page? Or do you need a special web host that handles video? It depends on the experience you want to offer your viewers.

TYPES OF INTERNET MEDIA DELIVERY: STREAMING VERSUS DOWNLOADING

There are two basic ways to deliver audio, video, or other time-based multimedia on the Internet:

- Download the file to the user's hard disk.
- Stream the file.

In *downloading*, the entire file is downloaded to the user's machine before he or she can play a single frame, as depicted in Figure 4-1. In the download scenario, a standard web (HTTP) server can be used to serve the media file. The user must have the appropriate player.

Figure 4-1 *Downloading video.*

Downloading video is no different than downloading any multimedia file from the Web. Clicking on the link or entering the URL (Universal Resource Locator, a web address, such as http://www.masteringinternetvideo.com) sends an HTTP request to the server, which then initiates the transfer of the file to your hard disk. After download, the player software plays the file by reading it off the user's hard disk. Actually, most media players have the capability of playing a file while it is downloaded, as long as it downloads fast enough. But, if the video bit rate is too high for the user's bandwidth, he may have to wait until it fully downloads before it can be played back. When audio or video is too large to be listened to or viewed in real time, it must be downloaded to disk.

In this scenario, it doesn't really matter what the user's bandwidth is because the file will be read off the disk. As long as the user is willing to wait for the download (and as long as the connection doesn't fail), there is no limitation on bit rate or file size.

In *streaming*, a media server is used to send chunks of the file to the end user. As soon as a few frames are received, the media player can start playing. As new frames are received, they are stored in a *buffer* (a section of memory or disk space), displayed at the appropriate time, and then discarded. New video is pulled via the network to keep this buffer full. Streaming is depicted in Figure 4-2.

> **Note** Apple calls its server a "streaming server;" Windows calls it's server a "media server." We use the terms "media server," "streaming server," and "streaming media server" interchangably in this chapter.

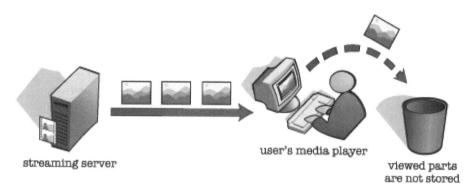

streaming server

user's media player

viewed parts are not stored

Figure 4-2 *Streaming video.*

Streams are *server-based* content, meaning all the video is kept on the media server, which only downloads a few frames of video at a time. The player does not (permanently) save the video to the hard disk. When the stream is finished, there is nothing left on the hard disk to watch.

Streaming from a media server to a media client allows relatively instantaneous viewing. Streaming can also allow viewers to skip around within the video with VCR-like controls, by sending these commands back to the streaming server. Because streaming is always intended to play back instantaneously, the bit rate of streamed video must be within the viewer's bandwidth to stream without constant pauses and rebuffering.

STREAMING THOROUGHLY DEFINED

The term streaming is presumably a metaphor used to describe the general technique of moving content to the user in small bits, as opposed to downloading a file. Of course, streaming applications are technically "downloading" content to the user's memory or hard disk (to create a buffer to improve the smoothness of playback. However, for many Internet viewers download merely means "any data coming down to my computer."

The term streaming becomes more confusing because of *HTTP streaming* and *progressive downloading*. Both these terms essentially refer to systems where the media can play as it downloads. Technically, the media is not streaming (it's downloading), but because the player can play the segments that have already downloaded, it sort of feels like streaming.

> **Note** Streaming isn't the only term that gets abused, misused, and confused in this topic. As mentioned in the Introduction, the marketing urge to differentiate essentially similar technologies has resulted in several names for all the major features of streaming servers. For that reason, this chapter has the unique feature of a "Buzzword Translator" in which we define the various terms used in streaming, in both their technically correct usage as well as their common industry usage, with example sentences of each.

Buzzword Translator: Streaming

Streaming:

Sending media (audio or video) at the same rate that it is played back, usually in such a way that the user is not able to directly access the media from his hard drive when playback is finished. *We opted for streaming instead of downloads because we didn't want people sharing our video.*

A generic term for any kind of Internet media delivery where the content can be played while it is downloaded. *We stream audio clips from our website.*

Download:

To obtain a computer file from another machine on a network. *Download the new program from his FTP site.*

Often used loosely to refer to any kind of data transfer. (Files are copied between disks on a local machine; they are downloaded from one computer to another over a network.) *I need to download my spreadsheet onto a floppy disk. I'm downloading the show to CD.*

HTTP streaming: Serving media file from a web server in such a way that viewers can view content as it is downloaded. *HTTP streaming lets our users save the movie trailers to disk, and enables them to watch videos the first time without a long delay.*

Progressive download: This is the same as HTTP streaming QuickTime.

INTERNET STREAMING SERVERS

What would the ideal server designed for streaming media look like? Well, there are numerous products out there in the real world, but for purposes of understanding the differences between Microsoft, Real, and Apple products, let's look at all the features we would like to see in a streaming media server. Figure 4-3 presents these features at a glance.

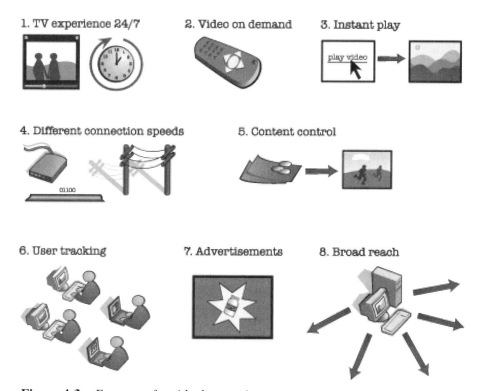

Figure 4-3 *Features of an ideal streaming server.*

Following is a description of the features:

- **Live streaming for a television-like experience.** The Internet makes everyone a potential publisher. In the same way, Internet streaming media should make everyone a potential TV broadcaster who is able to put up stations of 24/7 scheduled programming. Streaming servers should allow for easy setup of either live broadcast or pre-recorded set lists of content programming.

- **Video on Demand.** Many hotels and digital cable systems enable a video-on-demand feature where video is given to the viewer just like a VCR—they can start at will, pause, rewind, and so on. Streaming servers should provide that same experience to anyone on the Internet with enough bandwidth.

- **Instant gratification.** Most video systems not involving the Internet tend to be instant or have delays of less than a second. Cable, TV, satellite, DVD, VCRs, Video on Demand—most of these systems start showing video immediately when a button is pressed. An ideal streaming server translates this low-delay, instant-play experience to the Internet.

- **Support for different broadband speeds.** Whereas all TV sets can play basic video, digital video requires a special tuner, and new high-definition (HD) video requires new tuners and televisions to experience the full quality. During the long transition from traditional TV to HD, the old low-quality signal continues to be broadcast for backward compatibility. The Internet will always have audiences who connect using either a modem or high-capacity broadband. An ideal streaming server deals with this by providing the highest quality stream possible for any given viewer.

- **Content control and billing.** Broadcasters would like to have full control over who views what content, to ensure they've paid for it or watched the commercials that support it. Streaming servers should be able to ensure viewers watch things in the correct sequence and that they have paid for the content they watch.

- **Viewer tracking and statistics.** Because of the way the Internet directly connects viewers to the source of content, streaming servers can potentially have far better tracking than television ratings systems and even modern DVR (Digital Video Recorder, such as TiVo) rating systems.

- **Advertisements.** The range of advertisements possible on the Web is greater than on traditional TV. On the Internet, there are Flash animations, banner advertisements, entire websites that are an advertisement (as in those for movies), and interstitial (in-between) video ads, which most closely approximate television commercials. An ideal streaming server should facilitate the insertion and coordination of ads with the main video clips or programming being offered. Also, commercials can be regional, national, or sometimes global in scope, and an ideal server identifies viewers and determine its demographic to feed them the most appropriate ads.

- **Broad reach to large audiences.** Broadcast television reaches as far as antennas or satellite dishes can pick up the signal. Cable stations reach where local carriers in that country carry them. Internet streaming should side-step all that and be able reach anywhere in the world where viewers have broadband Internet. Also, the ideal server is just as scalable (if not more than) as today's traditional satellite or cable broadcasting systems. In practice, as an Internet broadcaster you can support hundreds of millions of simultaneous viewers!

TELEVISION EXPERIENCE: BROADCAST OR LIVE VIDEO

A primary feature of streaming media servers is to provide a television or radio-like live broadcast experience for consumers. Real Networks was one of the first to create a commercial platform for the broadcast of live events on the Internet, but a variety of rogue players (particularly Nullsoft) pioneered the radio station/MP3 technology that is predominant in audio streaming today.

There is far less 24/7 programmed TV-like content on the Internet than one would expect, due more to price concerns than a lack of technology. Internet advertising pays far, far less than television advertising (hundreds of times lower) yet television's current cost per viewer is far lower than that of Internet streaming. However, live streaming technology is used all the time to broadcast (or *webcast*) single events, mostly in the entertainment or technology space. Keynote speeches from CEOs at computer conferences, rock concerts, and board of director meetings for public companies are some of the most frequently live-broadcasted events.

"LIVE" VIDEO

In a broadcast event, all viewers are watching the same action at approximately the same time. Because streaming systems use buffering to keep smooth streams, viewers can witness the action anywhere from 15 seconds to several minutes behind real time. For all intents and purposes, though, viewers are watching in synch. Sometimes the media player allows pause control, and the viewer can "get behind" in watching the stream, but because it is essentially live, there are no fast-forward or rewind controls.

Streaming servers can be used to broadcast either live or pseudo-live events. Live includes both live and prerecorded events, which are beamed or reflected off the server from a media encoder/broadcaster, as shown in Figure 4-4.

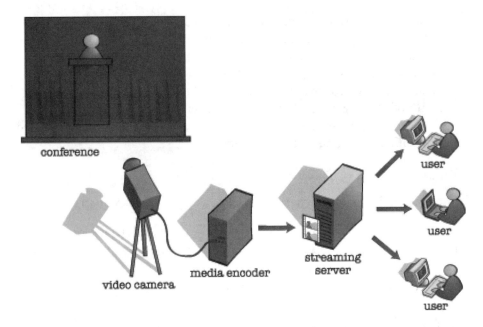

Figure 4-4 *The live broadcast happens now and is beamed simultaneously to all viewers.*

Pseudo-live broadcasting consists of video generated from a programmed play-list. It is television-like in that programs are scheduled for specific times and the video is *simulcast* (broadcast at the same time), as shown in Figure 4-5.

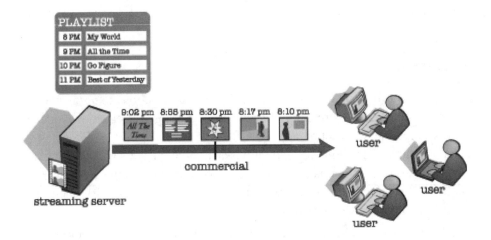

Figure 4-5 *A pseudo-live simulcast of programmed content playlist is beamed simultaneously to all viewers.*

Broadcasters can do anything with traditional television or cable that they can do in an online Internet format; however, content must be highly compressed to deliver it through the broadband connections of today's Internet audience. To repeat once more, in server terminology, *live* can mean "happening right now" and can also denote "viewed simultaneously" in contrast to *on demand.* *Unicasting*, depicted in Figure 4-6, describes the network function of sending a unique, single copy of a stream to each individual viewer; this contrasts with *multicasting*, which sends only one copy of a stream to multiple people.

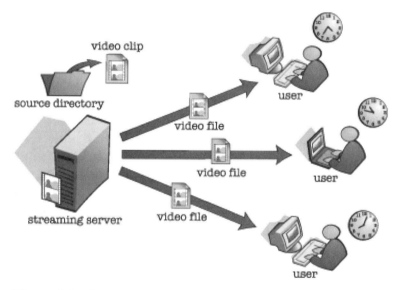

Figure 4-6 *Unicasting—each client has a direct connection to the server. Both live and on-demand streams can be delivered via unicast.*

Multicast, shown in Figure 4-7, is an important but limited network technology for efficiently broadcasting live media to large audiences. It is designed to use the Internet in an efficient way by sending only one copy of live video into any network, which is great except that it doesn't work on the public Internet—only private company or university networks! (See Chapter 6, "Enterprise Multicast.") Thus, almost all Internet streaming uses unicast.

One way to understand multicast is that it attempts to distribute video such as traditional cable, satellite, and TV broadcasts where one copy of the stream goes to millions of viewers.

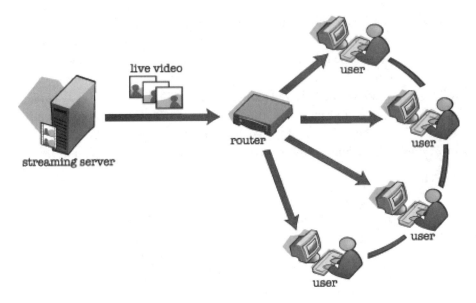

Figure 4-7 *Multicasting.*

Most of the streaming servers discussed here support multicasting, and have lots of documentation on the topic—so much that you'd think it was important or useful. Unfortunately, multicasting is only truly relevant for streaming in a controlled environment, such as a company's internal network. Because the main Internet media servers have to address the needs of corporate communications as well as entertainment, each has a well-developed multicasting compatibility for internal use. (For more explanation of the economics and technologies of streaming and multicasting, see Chapter 5, "Video Transport Protocols" and Chapter 6.)

Buzzword Translator: Live Video

Unicast: To deliver video to a single viewer via a server-to-client network connection. *On-demand streams are always unicast; live streams usually are.*

Live video:

1. Viewed while it is happening or seconds afterwards: *We watched a live event.*

2. Viewed simultaneously: *They put last year's awards show up on the server as a live broadcast.*

Simulcast: To deliver video simultaneously to all viewers: *The event was simulcast on Thursday at 8 p.m.*

Broadcast: To deliver video publicly and broadly, usually simultaneously to all viewers: *We broadcast the CEO's speech.*

Simulated live broadcast: Prerecorded video delivered at the same time to all viewers from a video file or playlist of files. Also called pseudo-live broadcast.

Multicast:

1. Technology for efficiently broadcasting to multiple viewers without redundant network traffic—only relevant on closed networks where multicast can be activated. *Our corporate network was set up for multicast.*

2. Generic term for multicast-like or multicast-alternative technologies; anything that delivers video to multiple viewers. *Their technology multicasts the video to everyone running their special client software.*

Reflected multicast: Receipt and redelivery of simultaneous video to many viewers via unicast. Not really multicast; just another term for broadcasting. *About 14,000 people viewed the reflected multicast of the rock concert over the course of the evening.*

Narrowcast: On the Internet, to deliver video to a niche market. *We narrowcasted the '06 Snail Olympics to the Gastropod Society members.*

VIDEO ON DEMAND (VOD)

One of the most common uses of streaming servers on the Internet is to provide video when the user asks for it, as opposed to broadcast television where viewers see content all at the same time. Streaming servers usually designate a folder or directory on their hard disk as the source directory. Without additional configuration, any media that is in this directory can be played back. VoD is depicted in Figure 4-8.

What's a *video clip*? This term usually means a short piece of video, but in this case it means any piece of video. (A two-hour movie, served on demand, would still be a *clip* in Real-speak, for instance.) Streaming media servers provide viewers with an enhanced ability to pause and move around within the video. Video from web servers can usually be paused and rewound, but if a five-hour video clip is accessed, only a streaming server would allow the viewer to fast-forward to the very end.

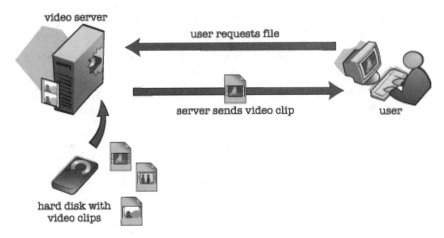

Figure 4-8 *Video on demand: Stored video comes off the hard disk and is served to the viewer.*

How does this work? The Real-Time Streaming Protocol (RTSP, discussed in Chapter 5) provides VCR-like control of video. Most streaming server vendors are now using this standard. With RTSP, the client sends a message to select, rewind, or fast-forward specific video clip. The server keeps track of where any particular viewer is in a file and what each viewer is watching. Naturally, with VoD, no one watches exactly the same thing at the same time, as shown in Figure 4-9.

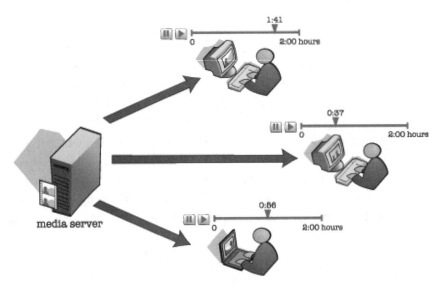

Figure 4-9 *Everyone watches video on his or her own schedule.*

Buzzword Translator: Video on Demand (VoD)

Video clip or clip:

1. A short piece of video. *I uploaded clips of my son skateboarding.*

2. A single piece of video of any length. *We assembled 12 two-hour clips into a day's broadcast.*

Buzzword Translator: Playlist

Playlists: Are simply lists of content that need to be played in a specific sequence. Although a variety of different names are available for the actual elements in a playlist, along with a variety of ways to make playlists, they boil down to simply a list of video URLs. Playlists are often implemented as SMIL files (for more information on SMIL files, see Chapter 3, "Video Storage File Formats"), and each streaming system has its own unique playlist format as well. The file extension can be .SMI, .RAM, .ASX, or .MOV, depending on the system.

Other terms for playlists are *programs* (used within older Windows Media), as in television *programming,* or *set list*, such as the list of songs in a performance.

The video in a playlist can be assembled by the client in *client-side playlists,* or assembled and fed to the client by the server in *server-side playlists.* A server-side playlist can be used to implement a broadcast, where everyone views the same thing at the same time; if someone shows up late, that person misses the beginning.

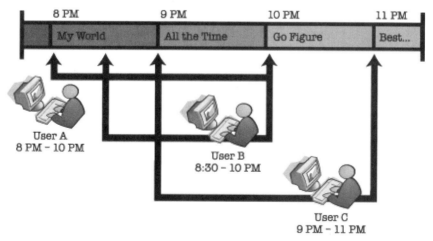

Figure 4-10 *Server-side playlists can generate a live video stream in which everyone views the same video at the same time.*

Server-side and client-side playlists can both be used to create a sequential viewing experience for the viewer. Depending on the rules in the playlist and the features of the player, the client might or might not be able to skip forward, skip commercials, and perform other tasks.

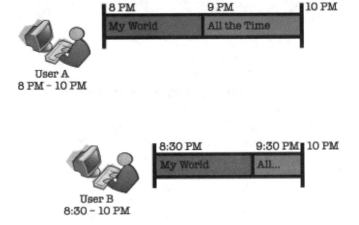

Figure 4-11 *Server-side playlists can also be configured to "start at the beginning," regardless of when the viewer starts watching, and can even allow the user to skip forward and backward in the playlist.*

If a simulated-live (prerecorded) simulcast is implemented using a playlist, it is important to note that all the video in the playlist must be encoded with identical compression settings and sizes. This applies to all the major streaming systems. Why? The codec and resolution (height and width in pixels) is communicated to the player the first time they connect, which can be anywhere during the stream.

If many different bit rates, sizes, or types of content are going to be integrated into a continuous stream, the playlist needs to be an on-demand type. A long client-side playlist can implement the same viewer experience as a live broadcast, except that the player is pulling all the content in an on-demand form. This is useful if synchronized viewing is unnecessary, or if playlists are customized on a viewer-by-viewer basis, but the intended experience is sequential, programmed video.

INSTANT GRATIFICATION: NETWORK CONDITION AND BANDWIDTH AWARENESS

Some of the television features we take for granted are very difficult to achieve on the Internet. Changing channels is an easy feat when all the channels are beamed to a TV set simultaneously and the receiver needs to only choose between them. TV sets are in essence passive—the video comes to them. And the channels are established and numbered; no complex URL such as http://www.cbs.comprimetime/show/insider/cbs_hp_redirec.php?chapter=16_03 is needed to simply watch CBS on TV

In contrast, all Internet video requires the player to somehow choose a channel and request the video, and then the server must send the video down to it. The simple action of flipping rapidly through 10 channels in a few seconds would generate so much back-and-forth network traffic that it would probably flood most broadband Internet connections. Unfortunately, the Internet is currently optimized for delivering web pages. (Chapter 5 explains the maze of networks that video must fight its way through to get to the viewer.)

Web servers just send the data as fast as it can go, and it's up to the client to choose the proper stream bit rate. Thus, one of the major reasons why you should choose a streaming server is due to network awareness—the fact that the streaming server helps obtain the correct signal to the viewer, whatever their connection may be. The first job of a streaming server is one of emulation: Creating an instant-gratification, TV-like environment out of the sluggish network called the Internet.

REAL-TIME VIEWING

The most basic feature of a media server would be that a viewer would receive media in *real time*. "Real time" is an abused term; technical purists would say that it has to do with systems that can consistently and without fail respond to requests in tiny fractions of a second. In Web marketing speak, it means roughly "really fast" or "what we'd like to brag as being really fast." It has come to mean that video or audio is playing at normal speed, and that it can play cleanly without skips or interruptions because it is downloaded at an acceptably fast rate. In other words, five minutes of video takes about five minutes to play.

Buzzword Translator: Networking

Real time:

1. Responding within a tiny, predictable time period: *They used a real-time computer to operate the nuclear reactor.*

2. Simultaneously, interactively, or immediately: *We chatted in real time. You can download our product literature in real time from our website.*

3. Fairly fast to really fast: *The video plays back in real time after it buffers for 20 seconds.*

We talk about the size of a stream as its *bit rate*, that is, the number of bits (measured in kilobits, thousands of bits) used to represent a second of audio or video. The bit rate is measured in *kilobits per second*, or *Kbps*, the same measurement used for Internet connection speeds. (For more explanation of bit rate, see Chapter 2, "Video Compression.") This is very handy because we need to compare a stream's bit rate to the user's bandwidth.

A media file can be delivered in realtime only if the bit rate of the stream is somewhat less than the speed of the viewer's Internet connection. For instance, a modem user with a 56K connection cannot watch streams up to 50K. A DSL subscriber with a 384K connection can watch only streams up to about 350K. The difference between the stream bit rate and the user's maximum bandwidth is called *headroom*, which represents the amount of bandwidth available for other applications while the stream plays.

Some viewers have a modem, whereas others have broadband. Even the definition of broadband is vague, meaning anything from 128Kbps up to many megabits per second. Also, if many people are sharing a single broadband connection, the effective bandwidth per user of this broadband connection can be as small as a modem connection.

People can already receive a real-time experience from web-served video content through HTTP streaming, shown in Figure 4-12. If the stream has a bit rate less than the bandwidth of the viewer's connection, the media will play smoothly and quickly. The entire file downloads to the hard disk, and because it is downloaded faster than it is played, there are no pauses or skips.

If, however, you are serving a high-quality high-bit rate stream (say, a 700Kbps DVD-quality MPEG-4 movie) to your audience and the viewer's bandwidth is less than that (for instance, 384Kbps), the player would not be able to play without interruption until the entire movie is downloaded to the hard disk. This task takes about twice as long as the length of the movie (a four-hour download for a two-hour movie). As depicted in Figure 4-13, this situation is typical when people download high-resolution movie trailers from a website. Of course, as we've already seen, many systems let users start playing movies before the entire file is downloaded, but this almost always results in a hard stop at some point during playback (because playback happens faster than data transfer).

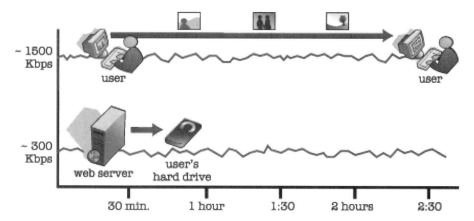

Figure 4-12 *HTTP streaming: The media download stream (300Kbps) is less than the user's connection (1,500Kbps).*

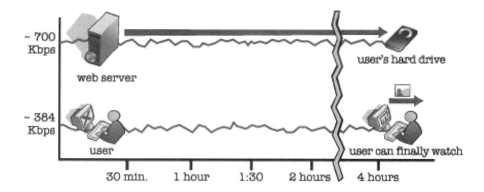

Figure 4-13 *If the media download stream is larger than the user's connection, the clip must be downloaded before viewing.*

So how should an ideal streaming server solve this problem of varying viewer bandwidth? The ideal streaming server delivers the stream in order to fill completely the viewer's bandwidth so he receives the absolute best picture possible, as shown in Figure 4-14.

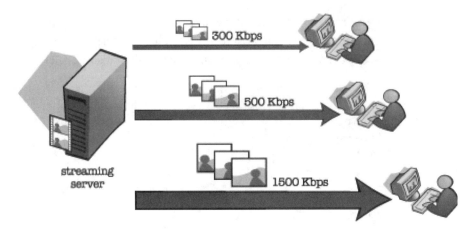

Figure 4-14 *Maximizing user bandwidth achieves optimal quality.*

TIME AWARENESS AND REAL-TIME DELIVERY

Web servers don't have a concept of how fast a movie should be sent to the viewer; they send as fast as they can and hope for the best. If the movie does not start playing quickly, the viewer often stops the playback and surfs for something else. The web server has no reporting mechanism to determine that the viewer was having a slow experience; the web server merely logged that a certain computer was requesting a specific file. That chunk of abandoned downloaded video, which may have been many megabytes in size, is wasted bandwidth—and over time it can add up.

Media servers waste less bandwidth than web servers by carefully controlling the speed at which media is served to viewers. First, by streaming, the video has been compressed down to a size likely to fit into common downstream Internet connections. Then, when the viewer tries to connect to the stream, the media server establishes direct two-way communication with the player. The player can send statistics, including how well the client receives the data, and the maximum *throughput* (the bit rate that can be consistently delivered) the client can receive.

The server sends audio and video down to the client, and the client sends acknowledgements back to the server, including acknowledgements of any data that was missing in what was sent. If a lot of data is missing, the client and server can agree that it is time to do something to solve the problem.

THROTTLING DOWN FOR NARROW PIPES OR CLOGGED CONNECTIONS

Streaming servers work with the media player to deal with different and changing connection speeds. On first connect, the server asks the client what speed of connection it has. Based on the answer, the media server chooses the appropriate bit rate in which to send the stream and starts sending. To support this feature, the stream must have been encoded at several different bit rates. In the QuickTime case, these different bit rates need to be individually encoded and stored. Another movie called a *reference movie* refers to these different bit rate movies, as shown in Figure 4-15.

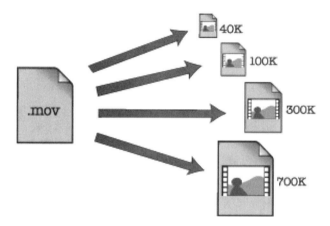

Figure 4-15 *QuickTime reference movies refer to the same clip at different bit rates.*

When the viewer first installed QuickTime, he was given the option to designate the speed of his Internet connection. Subsequently, when QuickTime encounters a reference movie, it automatically connects to the video with a bit rate lower than the viewer-established bandwidth. If the client overestimates his actual bandwidth, he is greeted with a choppy, hiccupping video experience. If he underestimates the bandwidth, he might receive a lower quality stream than he could enjoy.

Windows calls its techniques for handling bandwidth *intelligent streaming*, which is a more sophisticated approach than QuickTime. Windows combines all the different bit rate encodings into a single file, as shown in Figure 4-16.

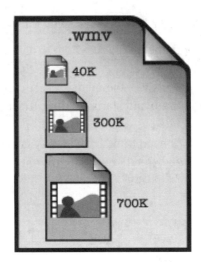

Figure 4-16 *Windows MBR (Multiple Bit-Rate) combines all the different bit rate encodings into a single video file.*

During playback, the server monitors the connection quality through statistics such as packet loss and delay (see Chapter 5, "Video Transport Protocols"), as well as client rebuffering and glitches. If the connection is suffering, the server forces a bit rate downgrade, say from 300KB to 150KB. If this does not solve the connectivity issue, it then employs *stream thinning* and lowers the frame rate—dropping it from 15fps to 7.5fps, for example. If this still does not handle the problem and the client is not getting a smooth stream, the system drops all video and sends only an audio stream. If the connectivity ever restores (for in-stance, if the source of bandwidth interference goes away), the server and client "throttle up" and restore the connection gradually up to the full frame rate and bit rate with which it started. Many codecs support stream thinning, but the server must also monitor connection quality to know when to thin the stream.

In Real's system, streams can be encoded using a technique called *SureStream*, where a single file contains not only the three or four target bit rates but a range of additional *distress streams* (for example, an 11Kbps and 18Kbps audio stream to support a 33Kbps audio stream in low bandwidth situations). With Sure-Stream, if the client reports to the server that it experiences packet loss (missing data due to Internet connection difficulties), the server "throttles down" the connection.

The Real server's multi-bit rate file, shown in Figure 4-17, has information to allow the stream to drop from, say, a 300KB file to a 150KB file, and do this without rebuffering or stopping; that is, the video gets more "blocky" but the stream keeps playing. Real's proprietary codecs have support for the SureStream features built in; Real was the first streaming media server with network awareness and has the most mature implementation of these features.

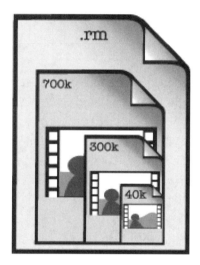

Figure 4-17 *RealMedia file with SureStream.*

Incidentally, Real can also use SMIL files the same way QuickTime uses reference movies. By providing alternative links for different bit rates within a .SMI file, it becomes the player's responsibility to choose the correct link; however, this approach makes more sense when switching between media served by web servers because media servers can already negotiate the bit rate-appropriate file.

Buzzword Translator: Choosing or Adjusting Stream Bit Rate Based on Client Capabilities

SureStream: Real technology for automatic adjustment of stream quality based on real-time network conditions.

Reference movies: A QuickTime system for linking to multiple bit rate files and having the client decide which one to play based on the viewer-selected bandwidth capabilities.

Intelligent streaming: A Microsoft system for scaling down the bit rate of a stream based on real-time network conditions.

Stream thinning: Any of a variety of techniques for lowering the frame rate of a stream to deal with impaired network conditions that rely on both the codec and the streaming server. Real's SureStream uses stream thinning as well as multiple bit rates, and Microsoft's literature also refers to stream thinning techniques.

FASTER STREAM STARTING

One of the late additions to Internet streaming client/server technology is a system for starting viewing right away. You might say to yourself, "What? I thought that's what streaming was all about."

Frustratingly, up until QuickTime version 6 and Windows Media Player version 9, when a viewer clicked a video link, he would invariably see a buffering status message, such as Buffering-29%, and would continue to see that for many seconds, up to a minute even, while the machine pulled down video without playing it.

The purpose of this buffer is to give the video a head start, so that if the Internet connection is clogged, the media player and server have time to recover without interrupting the viewer. If a 300K stream is delivered at 300Kbps, then naturally it takes 20 seconds to deliver 20 seconds of video. Because the network can choke a moment after the stream starts, the player usually has to wait until the desired safety buffer is full. Buffering is depicted in Figure 4-18.

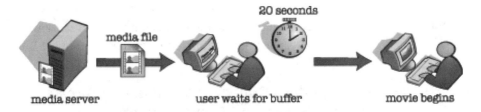

Figure 4-18 *Buffering gives the video a head start.*

Newer streaming servers can change the speed of initial content delivery, however. If the viewer's bandwidth is 1,500Kbps, the stream can be sent five times faster, as shown in Figure 4-19. And if the buffer is filled faster than it is emptied, the player can start playing almost immediately, as shown in Figure 4-20.

Figure 4-19 *High-speed Internet allows for a smaller buffer.*

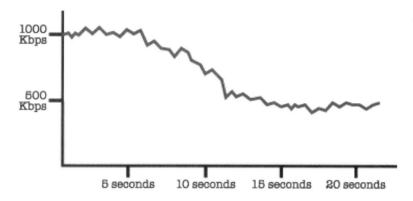

Figure 4-20 *Burst download at the beginning eliminates buffering time.*

Buzzword Translator: Rapid Playback Features

Instant On: Patent-pending QuickTime technology for rapid playback and seeking through files.

Fast Streaming: A group of Microsoft technologies relating to reducing buffering times when seeking through content including the following:

- **Fast Start:** Instant-on playback.
- **Fast Cache:** Download and cache the streaming content.
- **Fast Reconnect:** Automatically reconnect to a stream if interrupted.
- **Fast Recovery:** Use forward error correction.

TurboPlay: Real's rapid playback and seeking technology for broadband connections.

Forward error correction (FEC): A system to deal with packet loss from network error without having to resend lost packets.

These buffer-reduction technologies enable rapid movement within content as well. If the viewer fast-forwards or seeks to a later point in the video, the player can immediately start playing in the new location, as rapidly as when it started. And some of the systems even cache entire clips in a buffer, so that if the viewer rewinds, steps back, or performs another task, he can start watching instantly based on the local copy. Technically, these techniques blur the lines between downloading and streaming; however, the cached copy goes away when the player ends its connection with the server.

Forward Error Correction

The previously described technologies are the latest in the long line of products that deal with the variability of the Internet when delivering video to PCs. The new big market for video delivery is not the personal computer but handheld devices, such as mobile phones and handheld personal digital assistants (PDAs).

Mobile devices naturally have mobile network connections, and this creates an environment almost guaranteed to lose packets. Packet loss on mobile networks causes the glitches and dropouts with which all mobile phone users are familiar.

Forward-error correction (FEC), shown in Figure 4-21, is a system that controls errors in transmission when there is only one-way communication (for example, a satellite beaming the same video to millions of homes with a receiver dish). In these cases, there is no communication channel back to the source; there is no way for the receiver to individually say, "I'm sorry, I didn't get that last packet. Could you please resend it?"

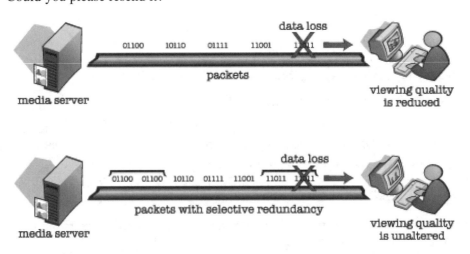

Figure 4-21 *Forward error correction.*

Error-correcting codes are extra information that goes along with the data that needs to be reliably received. The idea is that by adding extra information to all the packets in a transmission, the message can be reconstructed even if a few packets get lost.

A simplistic way to implement an error-correcting system is to simply send all packets twice, perhaps staggered by a few moments. This doubles the bandwidth of a video stream, and it also doubles the chance that the user receives a given packet.

In practice, error-correcting codes are more sophisticated than that. The amount of redundant information needed can be as low as 10–20 percent. The actual redundant information is spread out through a sequence of packets, such that a few of these packets can be reconstructed if they don't get across. RealNetworks and Microsoft both include FEC capabilities in their servers and players.

CONTENT TRACKING

One of the differences between streaming media and web-based browsing is that on the Web, it is difficult to track how long someone is actually visiting a website. Because a viewer can hit a web page, look at other pages for three days, and then click a link on the first one, it is difficult to establish exactly what the viewer looked at and how long he was there. Firewalls further confuse this issue, so that when many people in the same company visit a website, it is impossible to accurately count even how many people hit the site.

With video downloaded for a website, the same problem occurs. It is possible to track at least whether the viewer downloaded an entire file, but it is not possible with current web technology to see if he actually viewed the content.

USER EXPERIENCE TRACKING

With streaming servers, the viewer experience is different than the Web; media is viewed in sessions with a distinct beginning, middle, and end. Because the media player maintains a connection with the media server throughout the viewing session, it is possible to track exactly what was viewed and for how long. If the viewer rewatches something, or launches a second piece of content from a link in the first, the media server tracks that as well. Thus, once web browsing activity has launched a streaming media session, the ability to track viewer consumption (and thus ad consumption) is potentially far more accurate and complete.

Better Logging

Media servers track more than just successful viewership—they track the technical aspects of the viewing, such as how much bandwidth there was, what bit rate the viewer saw, and if there was any playback difficulties, such as packet loss or dropped frames. This sort of reporting can be used to see how a streaming provider or Internet service provider is performing and to isolate reasons why viewership might not be growing.

There are two sets of log files generated by most media servers, and they are similar to web servers. The *access log file* simply lists all the attempts to access media, and details when and if it was delivered, at what bit rate, to what IP address, and more. Most log files are stored in the standard format that is also used by most web servers. However, all the media servers are configured to add extra data to these logs (connection statistics, failure rates, packet loss, bit rates, and so on) that web servers cannot track.

Third-Party Verification and Reporting

Collected statistics can be audited by third parties for ad reporting. Also, media servers integrate well with banner and other ad insertion companies, and can provide ad-viewing statistics directly to separate verification companies.

Log Files

If you peruse much streaming server documentation, you'll see that the product's logs are "W3C-compliant." The World-wide Web Consortium (W3C), the standards body for the Web, created a set of standards for how to log visits to websites (as well as standards for every other Web technology). These same standards (with some enhancements) are used to store visitor and error information on streaming servers.

Many programs analyze simple W3C logs to tell you how many visitors came and from where, but the extended information in streaming log files includes extra information specific to streaming. There are usually two files: an access log, listing all the successful accesses of content by viewers, and an error log, listing server and connection errors.

In these log files, each line contains a specific event, such a viewer connecting, and specific values for that event separated by spaces.

An example Windows Media access log file follows:

```
#StartDate: 2006-10-06 03:34:45
#EndDate: YYYY-MM-DD HH:MM:SS
#TimeFormat: UTC
#EncodingFormat: UTF-8
#ServerName: www.masteringinternetvideo.com
#ServerIP: 216.250.117.146
#Software: Windows Media Services
#Version: 9.00.00.3372
#PublishingPoint: [Global]
#Fields: c-ip date time c-dns cs-uri-stem c-starttime x-duration c-rate c-
status c-playerid c-playerversion c-playerlanguage cs(Viewer-Agent)
cs(Referer) c-hostexe c-hostexever c-os c-osversion c-cpu filelength file-
size avgbandwidth protocol transport audiocodec videocodec channelURL sc-
bytes c-bytes s-pkts-sent c-pkts-received c-pkts-lost-client
c-pkts-lost-net c-pkts-lost-cont-net c-resendreqs c-pkts-recovered-ECC c-
pkts-recovered-resent c-buffercount c-totalbuffertime c-quality s-ip s-dns
s-totalclients s-cpu-util cs-viewer-name s-session-id s-content-path cs-
url cs-media-name c-max-bandwidth cs-media-role s-proxied
216.250.117.146 2006-10-06 03:37:31 www.masteringinternetvideo.com
/encoder_ad.wmv 0 2 3 200 {2749B6A4-A629-4309-AC3C-05BE27BCC949}
9.0.0.2991 en-US WMFSDK/9.0.0.2991_WMPlayer/9.0.0.3008 - strmtest.exe
9.0.0.3372 Windows_Server_2003 5.2.0.3790 Pentium 10 390086 1061698 rtsp
TCP - - - 389950 389950 268 268 0 0 0 0 0 0 1 1 100 216.250.117.146
robot2 1 21 - 1 file://C:\WMPub\WMRoot\encoder_ad.wmv
mms://216.250.117.140/encoder_ad.wmv encoder_ad.wmv - - 0
```

Of course, an actual log file has many entries, one for every time a piece of media was accessed.

Although the last chunk is complicated, you can see a nice key to the contents in the `#Fields:` chunk. Almost anything you want to know is in these logs—the duration of the stream, the bit rate, the codecs used, the packet loss experienced by the viewer, the number of times the viewer had to rebuffer, pauses, how long the viewer actually watched the stream, and more.

ADVERTISEMENTS

One of the most important features of a media server, from a revenue perspective, is that advertisements are supported. As much of traditional video has been supported financially through advertising, it is natural that a streaming media server has an extensive feature set relating to ads.

In fact, the types of ads that work on the Internet are different than traditional TV ads. For one thing, video on the Internet is often embedded in web pages surrounded by banner advertising, and is usually related to a web page that provides other means of interactivity with the video provider. This means that more advertising opportunities exist in online video than in traditional video, for example:

- Clickable URLs can embed in video. The characters in the video might give the users clues to click on an item in the video, or text and graphics can be overlaid to provide more explicit pitches to click through to a website.
- Banner advertising can be added in the player itself or in the web pages containing the video.
- Traditional commercials can be inserted into a video stream.
- On-demand videos can be surrounded with bumper clips before and after.
- Just like on television, video can contain product placements and other creative approaches.

BETTER TRACKING THAN OFFLINE ADVERTISING

In traditional TV systems (except in the case of modern DVR systems), ratings are tracked through statistical extrapolation, not a one-for-one log of user viewing habits. Magazines have the same problem; even if the circulation is known, it is unknown how many people read the magazine from cover to cover, and if they do, how long they looked at a particular ad. The incredible feature of streaming media advertising is that every view can be positively tracked and accounted for through the logging functions of the server. This allows for very precise billing, as well as being an advertiser's dream! Of course, sometimes it's better not to know the exact number of impressions (viewings of ads); exact numbers are usually much lower than extrapolated numbers on which the industry bases its current billing rates; however, positive, guaranteed impressions can sometimes fetch more money because the advertisers consider them more valuable.

Each system has a similar way of implementing advertising, usually with SMIL scripting and some advertising support from the player. Because most of the players are free, they already have lots of built-in advertising and media portal features. You can see some good examples by simply downloading and installing any of the big three media players.

Buzzword Translator: Advertising

Interstitial ad: An "in-between" ad.

1. A video, Flash, or animated graphic advertisement shown between two web pages or in the middle of the page. *Interstitials irritate the audience unless they are cleverly done.*

2. A traditional commercial video advertising inserted between the content video so that the viewer has to watch it. *The server allowed the viewer to fast-forward through the playlist but did not allow the skipping of interstitials.*

Preroll: An advertisement or station identification that plays before the media the viewer had requested. *The preroll was 4 seconds long and included the animated company logo and jingle.*

Bumper: Ads played before and after a video clip. *We put a bumper around all our on-demand video.*

Wrapper: A Windows Media playlist for implementing bumpers, lead-ins/intros, lead-outs/outtros, station identifications, and so on.

CPM (cost per mil) (a mil = thousand): The standard measure of how much an advertiser pays per thousand impressions (viewings) of an advertisement.

Outtro: The opposite of an intro, a video shown on the exit of other video. *They had a cute outtro at the end of all their video clips.*

Several of the most sophisticated advertising tools in the broadcast world do not exist in the standard buffet of media server features, making streaming servers less than ideal. The following sections explore these tools in depth.

AD SYNDICATION

Ad syndication allows ads to be moved around between different markets and played with ad impressions reported back for billing purposes, and it allows complex resale of advertising. Ad syndication requires advertising and content management systems, and is outside the scope of the streaming servers presented here.

REGIONAL ADVERTISING

Alternative advertising by region can be implemented in these systems, but it requires several ingredients not included in a media server. One of them is a *locality service*, a system that determines viewer location from the user's IP address. It also requires a lot of custom scripting and development, or a third-party advertiser who has already completed this development. Digital music download systems (such as Apple's iTunes) use this functionality to guarantee that music is delivered only to consumers in a particular country, as authorized in their agreements with the record companies.

Understanding Streaming Media Server URLs

A URL (Universal Resource Locator) is the line that you normally see in the Address box of a web browser. URLs aren't exclusive to web browsers; most content on the Internet can be addressed using a URL.

The URL for this content is usually just the name of the media appended to the address of the media server. For instance, if the media server was http://www. masteringinternetvideo.com, then a media file called movies.asf would be http://www.masteringinternetvideo.com/sample.mov. In most cases, the end or suffix of the URL (everything after http://www.masteringnternetvideo.com) corresponds with a directory on the web server, as shown in Figure 4-22.

Each media server can create special URLs (called *mount points* or *publishing points*) referring to a directory/folder or playlist instead of a specific piece of media, as shown in Figure 4-23. These "virtual" URLs point to an actual piece of media, but the name is whatever the viewer wants it to be. Thus, a URL like http://www.masteringinternetvideo.com/movie can point to a live broadcast of a concert being reflected off the media server, or to a playlist containing clips from a concert in a row, or simply to a specific folder or directory on the server hard drive containing media.

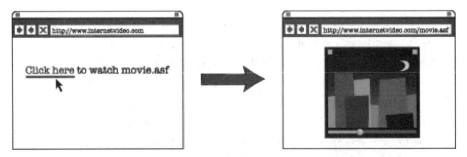

Figure 4-22   *The name of the media file is listed after the URL.*

Buzzword Translator: Special Media Server URLs

Mount point: A URL on a media server (Real, QuickTime).

Publishing point: A URL on a media server (Windows Media v9).

Station: A URL on a media server (Windows Media prior to v9).

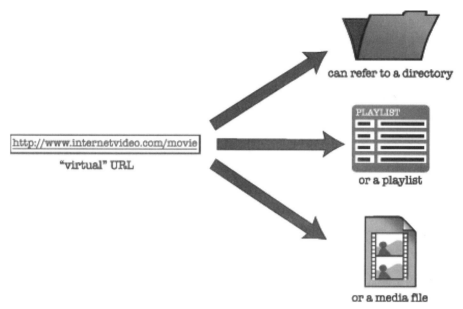

can refer to a directory

or a playlist

or a media file

Figure 4-23 *Publishing/mount points.*

Note Any of these URLs can be typed directly into a web browser. Depending on what the web browser thought it should do (depending on which players were installed and in which order and the user's configuration), the web browser might or might not launch Windows Media Player, QuickTime Player, or some other player. If the correct player was opened and then the URL was entered into its Open URL menu option, it would definitely play correctly. Thus, the trick is getting the browser to launch the right player and—an even harder task to achieve—to prompt the viewer to install the right player if he does not have it. (More on this is included in Appendix A, "A Quick List of Problems and Concise Solutions.")

CONTENT CONTROL

Streaming media servers provide the content provider with the potential to closely control and monitor media consumption. This is made possible by the the constant, two-way communication between the media server and the media player. Some of the features that media servers provide for these purposes are listed here.

KEEPING THE CONTENT ON THE SERVER

The most fundamental way in which streaming servers help control content is that they don't allow files to be downloaded. This is part of their fundamental design. Even if they cache the entire file on the hard drive, their goal is to keep the viewer from viewing it without the streaming client connecting to the streaming server, and allowing the viewing experience to be tracked, either anonymously or with identification.

DIGITAL RIGHTS MANAGEMENT

Streaming servers have also been designed with Digital Rights Management (DRM) support from the beginning. (See Chapter 7, "Video Security and Digital Rights Management.") Windows Media and Real provide DRM solutions that work with their servers.

CONTROLLING ACCESS: RESTRICTING VIEWERSHIP TO PERMITTED VIEWERS

All streaming servers have sophisticated methods of restricting who can get what content. In the case of the Windows Media server, these controls integrate with their server products, so that access to content can be controlled for anyone with an account on a Windows server (this is most relevant for controlling streaming video within a large company). The Real and QuickTime streaming servers are designed to integrate with an existing database, so that if a website already has a viewer account system, those servers can hook up to it (with some programming) and permit selective access to content.

REGION RESTRICTION

Content region restriction is a natural feature to include in streaming media servers, but none of the big three media servers provide it. Just as DVDs are region-coded, most commercial video content has licensing restrictions that restrict where it can be played and how much it costs in different countries. However, like regionally targeted advertising, it requires a separate Internet-based locality system that determines viewer location from IP address. Major content delivery networks also provide locality service, and this—combined with some custom web development—can provide a workable system.

BILLING INTEGRATION

Media servers can restrict access and integrate with billing systems for a single piece of content (such as a movie or trailer) more easily than web servers. However, a large gap exists between "integrates with" and "provides." None of the streaming servers provide an e-commerce system—that has been left to outside vendors.

SCALABILITY AND FAULT TOLERANCE

The basic issue of scalability is that a single machine can serve only several thousand viewers or listeners, and that many machines are needed to serve larger audiences. Thus, it takes 1,000 servers to serve several million viewers—this is quite expensive just for the hardware alone, and you can imagine what the hosting costs would be.

A companion issue to scalability is *fault tolerance*, or the ability to survive partial damage to the streaming system (machines failing, hard disks crashing, source video going down) without taking down the whole system. Although this section is not meant to be a full tutorial on building a fault-tolerant streaming infrastructure, it is important to point out what server features exist for creating a stable streaming setup.

> **Note**   It's worth noting that in these early days of the Internet, people are somewhat accustomed to websites going down; people hate it when their cable goes out, and people would be shocked if the broadcasting source of television ever stopped working. This is changing, however, and generally consumers expect their Internet video to work the same as their television, despite how hard that can be to achieve in practice.

REALITY OF SCALE

The reality of streaming servers is that they aren't designed to be scalable to the same extent as traditional broadcast systems, such as sateillite, cable, or television. Even the largest content delivery networks ask you to call them so they can get ready and make sure they have enough bandwidth capacity for large events. Nonetheless, live events in the tens to hundreds of thousands of viewers are a realistic goal with current technology. And on-demand streaming is less demanding (being at different times) and can handle millions of viewers for several days.

When scaling becomes an issue, there are several possible solutions:

- Give up on streaming servers; go back to web servers because they scale better, can serve more content per machine, and are easier and less costly to set up.
- Use a streaming service provider; they have generally invested a lot of money in network viewers and have already worked out some of the problems of scaling to larger audiences.
- Build your own large network using individual streaming servers; each has its own way of working in groups and can be custom-programmed to interact in more sophisticated ways.

If the third option is the choice, it can be said unequivocally that RealNetworks has the most advanced server for complex multi-server arrangements. It has had a working system (since 2000) for multiple Real media servers to automatically communicate with one another and redirect viewers between them for load balancing and optimization.

This complex intercommunication might be unnecessary for your needs, however. Unless you are deploying streaming across a complicated multi-linked company, building your own network with a variety of collocation facilities, or updating your content frequently, the automatic interconnection of the RealServers might not be necessary. A number of Windows or QuickTime servers should suffice.

HIERARCHICAL SERVER ARRANGEMENTS: LIVE BROADCAST

For many streaming configurations, a hierarchy of servers is usually the most scalable structure. This is especially true of live streams. If the goal is to build a bulletproof streaming infrastructure—one that will stay up even if several servers or even collocation facilities go down—this takes a lot of planning.

The usual arrangement for live streams is that the live stream, from either a playlist or a broadcaster, originates from a single machine. This machine is busy with encoding or producing the live stream, so it does not directly take viewer requests, and it is often safely behind a firewall anyway, away from the raw Internet. Instead, it *reflects* its stream off another media server, or even several media servers—as many as are needed to serve the intended audience. These media servers are situated outside of the firewall, or at the colocation facility, and are directly on the Internet. This hierarchy is shown in Figure 4-24.

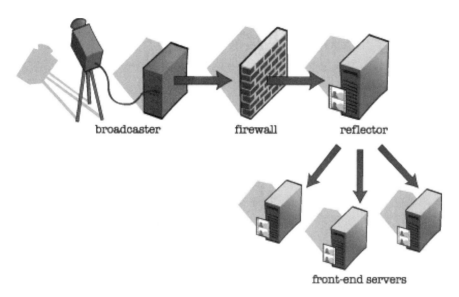

broadcaster   firewall   reflector

front-end servers

Figure 4-24   *A live broadcast server hierarchy.*

This arrangement is good; any of the front-end servers might stop working, and there might still be other servers to pick up the slack. However, the main problem is that there is only one source server! If this server crashes, is cut off, or has an interruption, the entire stream stops for all viewers. In the case of a playlist-based stream, putting the same media for the playlist on all the front-end media servers can solve this. However, for a live-encoded stream, there is only one source of the video. A solution is to live-encode the video twice with two identical machines, and have both front-end media servers.

Of the big three, only Real's servers currently support this complex redundant structure. With Windows or QuickTime, a failure of one encoding machine can be quickly repaired by switching over to the backup encoder; however, this has to be done manually, and causes an interruption. Real has built-in support for this function and other related fault-tolerance features.

CACHING SERVER HIERARCHIES

With caching, servers can be arranged in hierarchies with servers above and below them. The lowest servers in the hierarchy serve files directly to viewers. If the servers are missing files, they ask the servers higher up in the hierarchy for the missing files, and instantly start streaming the files down to the lower server, at which point the lower server *caches* the file (keeps a copy) for future requests.

In this manner, files can be distributed just to the top servers, and lower servers who actually do the serving automatically updated, with negligible delay, when the file is requested. Caching applies only to on-demand streams. This is depicted in Figure 4-25.

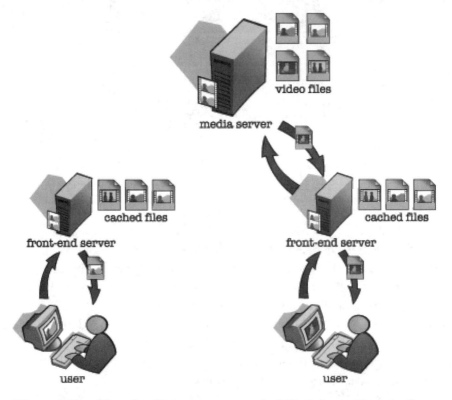

Figure 4-25 *When the client requests a cached file, it is sent from the front-end server. If the front-end server doesn't have the file, it must request it from a higher-level server.*

Real has built-in caching support in its servers. QuickTime and Windows leave these features to third-party plug-in developers, or to companies such as Content Delivery Networks (see Chapter 5).

CONTENT DELIVERY NETWORKS

As discussed in Chapter 5, CDNs are network service providers that have written their own streaming server interconnection software. They provide redundant and fail-safe server hierarchies, and bring the data closer to the viewer to reduce packet loss. They push on-demand content around to the "edges" of the network (servers that are close to the ISP where consumers get their Internet connections), and they send multiple copies of live streams for redundancy to ensure that live streams remain running. However, television-scale audiences can still overwhelm these networks. None of them are truly equipped for mainstream broadcast audiences (millions of people), as the current bandwidth costs to the customer would be astronomical.

LIMITING BANDWIDTH USE

You may have the opposite problem—the need to limit the number of viewers who can access a stream. If you only have one collocation facility, are on a budget, and need to keep your bandwidth under control, all the servers have a facility for fine-grained control of bandwidth. You can set how many viewers can connect and how much bandwidth can be used on a per-second basis. With some of the servers, you can adjust these settings for any individual piece of media.

Buzzword Translator: Scaling Up

Redundant: Using one or more backup units (of a given part of a system) to keep a system running in the event of hardware, software, or human failure, or overflow. *We had a redundant broadcast source so that we could survive a computer failure. We had three redundant servers so that we could handle spikes in traffic.*

Load balancing: In web or streaming media servers, having several machines serving the same data and spreading the clients across the different servers. *We had a load-balancing gateway routing clients to the five web servers.*

Content delivery network (CDN): A network of computers on the Internet located strategically in order to get content (media, web pages, and so on) efficiently to viewers with a minimum of delay. *We used a CDN because we wanted to serve content internationally.*

Caching: Making a local copy of data so that it can be accessed more quickly. Caching servers are servers that bring content closer to the viewer, either by keeping a copy inside a company network, or keeping a copy near the viewer on his ISP. *We put a caching proxy at the edge of our network to cut down on redundant downloads of the same video.*

Proxy: A kind of server software that obtains network data on behalf of another program. Web browsers and media players use proxies to get data safely and efficiently through firewalls in larger companies. *We installed a proxy that made streaming more efficient; unfortunately, it also blocked our connection to non-business websites.*

STREAMING SERVER DRAWBACKS

Although this chapter generally recommends the use of a streaming server, you should still be aware of some drawbacks to streaming server technology.

YOUTH

Media servers are young. Even if they have double-digit version numbers, these systems are less than 10 years old. Also, they've had a moving target all the time; computers doubled in speed every 18 months, but broadband rolled out slower than anyone had expected. As a result, obvious features (such as the video starting quickly when you click the link) have been added only recently.

UNSTABLE TERMINOLOGY

Part of this immaturity shows up in a lack of terminology convergence. In Internet video, a lot of terminology instability exists due to the rapid assimilation of terms associated with traditional broadcasting, advertising, and networking into Internet video all at once, by engineers who might not have known the terms to begin with. Add to this the marketing-driven misuse of what little terminology had been settled on, and communication becomes strained.

Each streaming system calls things by a slightly different or very different name. Sometimes the differences make sense, as the system was trying to name things that had no name before. Sometimes, however, the names are shameless marketing speak. (Think about combo-sizing at fast food chains: "go big," "power size," and "super size.") Streaming media servers, sadly, act the same way. A unique feature appeared on all the three major platforms at once, which allows playback to start instantly when a viewer clicks a link. "Fast Start," "Instant On," and "TurboPlay" are three names for comparable features on the three major media server platforms.

PSEUDO-INTEROPERABILITY

A refreshing aspect of streaming media servers is that they are actually more compatible than the players are. That is to say, several of the servers serve up their competitors' content. For instance, the Real servers can serve Windows Media and QuickTime video to those players as well as many other standard file formats, and the Windows Media Server can now serve MPEG-4 content.

Several third-party servers (both hardware- and software-based) also serve the major formats as well as their own high-quality formats.

However, this usually is a lowest-common-denominator communication because the latest and greatest client-server features are available only with a matched pair (Real Server + RealPlayer, QuickTime Streaming Server + Quick-Time Player, and so on). Over time, these new differentiating features become standardized, and cross-server support slowly develops if the feature is integrated in an industry-standard protocol.

EXPENSE

Although Microsoft and Apple provide streaming media platforms essentially for free, Real's more sophisticated server does cost money. So do hardware servers from third-party vendors. Streaming servers, being far less numerous than web servers and far less mature, tend to cost more to operate and maintain. And any service provider who manages streaming has a different set of requirements (and thus a different set of fees, sometimes higher) for providing streaming-quality bandwidth and streaming servers. Thus, there is an additional cost in using streaming as opposed to just serving video from a website. When content re-distribution is not a huge risk, many large companies choose to serve all their content as downloadable web-served media.

TECHNOLOGY MAINTENANCE AND UPDATES

Streaming servers are upgraded and modified every year, and the streaming players are constantly upgraded. Using streaming server technology can be a bit of a feature race. It's an odd thing to say, but with the relatively primitive state of Internet streaming media technology, every new version of the streaming server has "must-have" features and thus must be acquired. This upsets existing deployments whenever new versions of the server or even just the player are released.

THREE TIMES THE HEADACHES

For many sites, it is necessary to provide two or three different formats of video. Add to this the necessity to *stream* two to three different kinds of video, and you either wind up with three distinct streaming infrastructures, or pay for an all-in-one media server that doesn't provide all the features of the other two. Until a truly standard media format arises (MPEG-4 is the best hope) that can be served to whatever player the viewer might have installed, it is difficult to stream and support multiple formats while effectively minimizing cost.

MISSING FEATURES

Although the servers described in this chapter have some basic features for creating programming and inserting advertising, a mix of traditional broadcasting environment hardware and video-editing equipment might be necessary to get the result you seek. Many advanced features that are taken for granted in the tele-vision broadcasting world have yet to show up in the major Internet streaming servers, and require a more sophisticated back-end system.

SUMMARY

So, should you just upload your video to your website and serve it with a web server, or should you use a streaming media server? It depends. For the extremes, a web server can suffice: simple, low-bit rate clips that you know your audience can HTTP stream effectively, or very high-quality media that takes much longer to download than to watch but that you don't mind being copied (for example, movie trailers). For everything in between, a media server is probably better. Table 4-1 compares the merits of web and streaming servers.

Table 4-1 Comparison of Streaming and Downloading Video		
Feature	**Streaming**	**Downloading**
Client software needed.	Streaming media player corresponding to the type of media.	Web browser and streaming streaming media player.
Server software needed.	Media server software required, as well as web servers.	Only web servers needed; as simple as uploding any other web content.
Appropriate media footage.	Can be used for live events as well as archival footage.	Because of delays in preparation and uploading, not suitable for live events.

Feature	Streaming	Downloading
Audience bit rate choices.	Some servers allow multiple bit rates of same stream to be combined, and allow media server to communicate with client to determine appropriate bit rate at which to send.	Each individual bit rate must be separately stored and delivered to clients as appropriate—for example, several different links for you to choose your band width speed.
Time to playback.	User sees media streaming within seconds after initial buffering.	Usually requires entire file to be downloaded for smooth viewing. Sometimes, a "progressive download" feature can be used to watch while downloading and simulate streaming, but only if bit rate is less than the viewer's Internet connection.
Bit rate.	Must be less than the viewer's Internet speed.	Limited only by user's willingness to wait for the download.
Visual quality.	Usually less than VHS quality—often half the frame rate of normal video.	Can be VHS or DVD quality, 24–30fps.
Smoothness.	Streamed media is subject to the vagaries of Internet transmission—interruptions, delays, skips, and connection loss can occur.	After downloaded, media plays back smoothly.
Random access.	On streaming server, publisher can enable VCR controls allowing user to fast-forward and rewind within media clips. Also, user can skip tracks in media.	Media must be consumed from beginning to end because a web server serves it, but users can easily move around file once downloaded.
Location of media.	Media is kept on the stream-media server and not on the viewer's hard drive. Packets are stored either in memory or in disk cache and deleted after display.	Media is copied from web server to viewer's hard drive.

continues

Table 4-1 Comparison of Streaming and Downloading Video (continued)

Feature	Streaming	Downloading
Controlling media use.	Streaming media servers integrate DRM technology, which can be used to restrict viewing to people who have paid for content, and so on.	Downloaded content can be re-distributed by the viewer via email, or other medium to others. DRM technology can still be used to restrict content so that media players must connect to a website and verify payment before content is viewed.
Server band-width usage.	Lower bit rate content means lower bandwidth usage on server; however, client must connect to server every time he wants to see the content, using more bandwidth	Higher bit rate content in general means more bandwidth usage on server; however, the client can view content repeatedly offline after it has been downloaded.

If you've chosen to use one of the big three or four media systems, your choice of server is probably determined by the platform and codec you use. If your codec is MPEG-4 or you are supporting multiple stream formats, however, you do have more options; the Big Three servers all serve MPEG-4 in addition to their own proprietary codecs, and can even serve it to competitive clients in some cases.

The best experience for viewers is going to come from a matched server, such as Windows Media with Windows Media server. But that should not deter you from seeing if a single-server solution will do. RealServer does a good job of supporting all the media types, and there are third-party hardware servers available as well that support all the players.

Real and Microsoft are a bit ahead of QuickTime in features (for example, forward error correction), but this is because QuickTime tends to work with the standards bodies instead of racing ahead to develop its own proprietary version of a feature.

Microsoft naturally has the advantage in enterprise as it can bundle its media server for free with its enterprise server products and it's business desktop operating systems. Thus, its integration in business environments is much tighter. Microsoft also has really thought through the advertising components of its server. The latest versions of its platform have been thoroughly redesigned with a plug-in software architecture, bringing them more up to par with the sophistication of RealServer. But, Windows Media servers naturally run only on Windows servers (with some exceptions—there are some third-party harware vendors that make Windows Media compatible servers).

Apple was the latest entry into the game, but their open-source QuickTime Streaming Server (called QuickTime Streaming Server on OS X machines and *Darwin Streaming Server on Windows and Linux*) offering is quite attractive— it's free!—and it runs on all the major platforms including Windows, Macintosh, and Linux. Apple is behind on some less important features from a server stand- point, but its server is a very standards-compliant citizen. Apple's focus on the MPEG-4 standard has made their server the starting point for many MPEG-4 streaming efforts. Apple was the first to support fully Internet standard RTP streaming; it is notable that both the other vendors have converged on RTP/ RTSP as well.

Real Networks has been in the game for close to a decade and has the most sophisticated streaming environment of the major players, as that has been their exclusive focus (Apple and Microsoft also make operating systems and other software; Real writes media delivery software). This sophistication comes at a price, however, and Real charges relatively high prices for the server and very aggressively pursues a subscription fee from viewers for use of the player (they have to—they don't subsidize products through other business such as Microsoft and Apple). Downloading a free player from Real requires the user to jump through quite a few hoops on the web page, and routine upgrades to the client software guarantee that viewers are getting Real's advertising. However, Real can stream all the other media as well, and is definitely the most flexible and most cross-platform solution, running on every server system you can think of— Windows, Mac, UNIX, and Linux, and more. Real has also open-sourced almost every aspect of its platform, so that sophisticated vendors can see how every- thing is implemented and alter it as needed. (Note that open-source does not mean free of cost; the software must still be licensed.) Real's Helix server is the only server in the group that has built-in CDN features (called *System IQ*); you can build a fairly automated media distribution system with Real that makes optimal use of network resources. The other servers don't even begin to match some of Real's features for building a CDN.

Although these three companies get the most attention, they are far from the only servers that should be looked at. With the addition of Sorenson's Spark video codec, then, there are a variety of streaming servers with specialized targets (such as MPEG-4 for handhelds and mobile devices). Some very capable systems sometimes work as good as these servers, too. An example noted at the outset of the chapter is Nullsoft Video, (http://www.nullsoft.com/nsv), one of the most effective "TV on the Internet" implementations out there. Notable about Nullsoft is that, despite being owned by AOL, its technologies are generally open-source, stable, and widely used in a non-commercial capacity.

Finally, Macromedia's Flash MX media server technologies are gaining ground as a viable, competitive commercial system for multimedia delivery, on par with the big three described in this chapter. Macromedia has been in the online media delivery market, if not video streaming, for many years, and its video delivery system integrates nicely with its low-bandwidth Flash animation.

The big three servers stack up similarly for all the major streaming features, as the players are always neck-and-neck for features. Thus, the streaming experiences are about the same. The same advice given in other chapters still stands: If your content is good enough, people will download your player of choice, so choose the technology that works for you and don't fall for the myth of installed viewer base.

5

VIDEO TRANSPORT PROTOCOLS

HOW TO STREAM VIDEO OVER A NETWORK OR THE INTERNET

IN THIS CHAPTER

- How Video Travels Across the Internet
- Scalable Media Transmission
- Network Layers: A Brief Primer on Internet Protocols (and Relevant Acronyms)
- Streaming Protocols
- Streaming Through Firewalls

*I*n previous chapters, we explained video codecs, the structure of the files that contain them, and the software that serves them. Despite the best efforts of codecs and media servers, though, the quality of Internet video is still variable. To understand why, let's start by understanding some basics of how the Internet works.

How Video Travels Across the Internet

As noted in earlier chapters and as any end user would be quick to point out, viewing streaming video over the Internet is hardly a seamless experience. Streaming video suffers from hiccups, delays, drop-outs, skips, and connection loss. In this section, we explain how the Internet moves data and how this affects video playback.

It's sometimes hard to understand why the Internet has trouble moving audio and video when radio, television, and telephones do it fairly well and have existed for almost 100 years. So first let's look at the mechanisms of these traditional media.

Radio

Radio works simply because a single tower broadcasts the same signal to many receivers. Everyone listens to the same thing at the same time. All the stations are available at any time; you simply have to tune into a different frequency signal. The main barriers to radio transmission are distance; physical barriers such as hills, buildings, and tunnels that block the signal; and interference between two strong signals near each other on the dial. In terms of communication, radio is a one-way broadcast transmission.

Television

Television works much like radio, except that television broadcasting is organized into national networks. The same program is delivered to television receivers around the country by broadcasting the originating signal to branch offices, which broadcasts it out from towers (see Figure 5-1), out through cable companies, or to people with satellite dishes (see Figure 5-2). In any case, the same signal is sent to everyone at the same time—a one-way broadcast. All the channels are available at any time; there is no noticeable delay caused by changing channels. The main barriers to television reception are bent or frayed cables, badly aimed antennas or dishes, physical barriers as in radio, and interference of stations with each other.

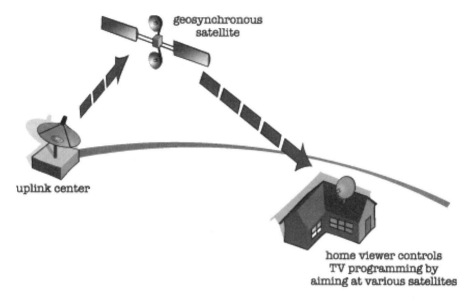

Figure 5-1 *Broadcast television delivery.*

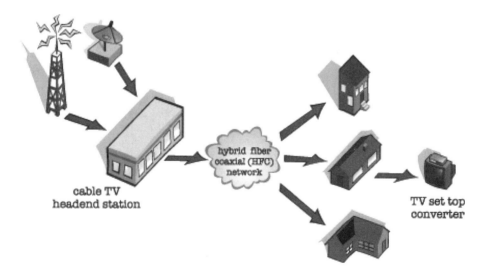

Figure 5-2 *Television broadcast via cable.*

TELEPHONE

Telephone calls use many of the same wires used by Internet. The telephone central office maintains devices called *switches* (automated versions of the classic telephone switchboard) that are used to connect the call to the next location, as shown in Figure 5-3. Telephone calls create a two-way circuit all the way from caller to receiver. The message "All circuits are busy"—usually heard only during disasters or radio call-in concert ticket giveaways—means the switch does not have any more slots in which to carry this call. The main barriers to telephone transmission are found at the beginning of the call— if there are not enough circuits to place the call. While a call is in progress, the entire route between the caller and recipient is reserved for their use only, even if there is silence and no one is talking. Telephones use what is called a *circuit-switched connection.*

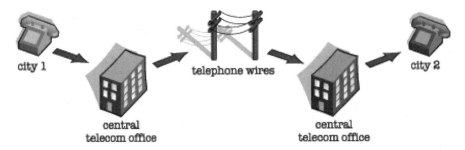

Figure 5-3 *Switched telephone circuits deliver many calls between locations.*

INTERNET BASICS

The path from a website to a web browser is different than these other systems. Conceptually, it is similar to the telephone conversation: It's a two-way conversation in which the browser asks for a document and the server sends it. Unlike the telephone call, however, there is no reserved circuit. Data, in the form of requests and responses, are organized into chunks called packets and sent between the requesting web browser and the web server.

In between the requester and the server are a series of routers. These machines route traffic between different smaller networks. Each time a packet crosses the boundary from one ISP to another, or from one kind of network to another, it goes through a router. The packets "hop" from router to router like a bucket brigade, as shown in Figure 5-4. This type of data transmission is called *packet switching*, instead of circuit switching. Internet packet switching has some attributes that make it reliable and unreliable at the same time.

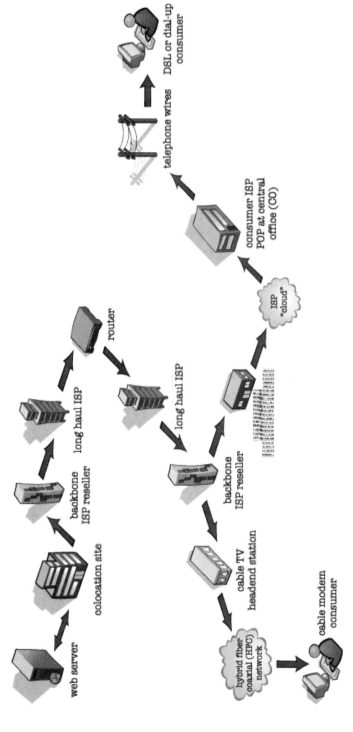

Figure 5-4 *The connection between client and server is an indirect one.*

As Figure 5-5 illustrates, the Internet is an extremely heterogeneous network, consisting of several different kinds of networks and ways of connecting networks to the Internet, as described in the next few sections.

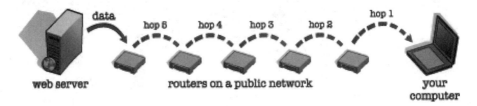

Figure 5-5 *Data transmission over the Internet is indeed a "tangled web."*

THE INTERNET BACKBONE

The Internet backbone (as much as a large, shapeless and ever-shifting cloud of networks can have a backbone!) consists of long-haul connections that carry large volumes of Internet traffic (packets) across and between continents.

PUBLIC EXCHANGE POINTS

Public exchange points exist at various points on continents and are the major nerve centers where many regional private networks, Internet providers, corporations, schools, and government divisions—large and small—converge to exchange traffic destined for other points on the Internet. You can compare these centers to major public airports, where international and domestic flights arrive 24 hours a day and trade passengers from all different airlines.

PEERING

The process of connecting a network to the Internet at one of these exchange points is called *peering*, and connecting to the backbone this way makes one a Tier-1 Internet provider. ISPs that rent their connection from a Tier-1 provider are called Tier-2 providers, and so on. The policies, prices, and agreements that cover how data is treated on these connections are as numerous as there are companies involved. This is the first source of variability for our packet switching.

PRIVATE PEERING

Peering is simply two networks connecting to each other with routers. *Public peering* occurs at large exchange points, but any two networks that find a lot of traffic flowing between them can choose to create a direct private link between the networks (called *private peering*). This reduces the cost of access through a public exchange point or other provider for all the bandwidth that travels between these two networks. It also decreases the number of intermediate connections between the networks. For instance, when several schools in the same organization link together, their inter-campus network traffic does not have to go out to the Internet at large, and is often more reliable as a result.

In this scenario, though, each school has its own connection to the Internet. What if one of the school's Internet connections went down? Would it be fair to send its traffic through the private peering connection and use another school's Internet connection? The way these kinds of questions are answered and the internal policies in this regard are another contributing factor to the variability of Internet packet switching.

INTERNET COMPLEXITY

As everything "goes digital," the distinction between cable TV wires, telephone wires, radio waves, and satellite transmission blurs. However, there are many ways to send data over these media. Internet data transmission can be complicated, leading to a variety of undesirable transmission characteristics.

PACKET LOSS

Circuit switching on the Internet is described as "best-effort," meaning that one of the routers along the way can lose a packet before it reaches its destination. In this case, the sender or receiver must somehow note that the packet was lost (perhaps by receiving the next packet and noting that it is out of context) and re-requesting the lost packet. This mechanism is fairly reliable in that two machines will usually (and eventually) figure out what went wrong and resend the missing packets. Packet loss causes audio and video to pause if the packets are eventually resent, and it causes video to pause, drop out, and skip if the packets are not resent at all. In our analogy of a public exchange point being a major airport, if it's a "foggy day" at that exchange, the part of the Internet that goes through that exchange can be slowed down (called a brownout) by the data that can't "take off."

DIFFERENT ROUTES

Not all packets in a file follow the same route to the destination computer. This is not unlike the airline's hub and spoke system: One packet might go "direct" from San Francisco to Washington; others might "transfer" in Atlanta or Chicago to get to Washington, as shown in Figure 5-6. Contributing to this issue is private peering and the variable rules and costs associated with all the choices to be made. Alternate routes can be excellent when one path between two machines goes down and a packet can use another path. It can also cause strange effects, such as when a packet is sent down a slow route, is assumed lost, is resent—and then later reappears as a duplicate packet! Audio can stutter and skip if duplicate packets are not detected and discarded. Also, some paths travel far out of the way, hopping through many more routers than necessary and causing large delays. The more "hops" or routers between two machines, the higher the chance of unexpected delays.

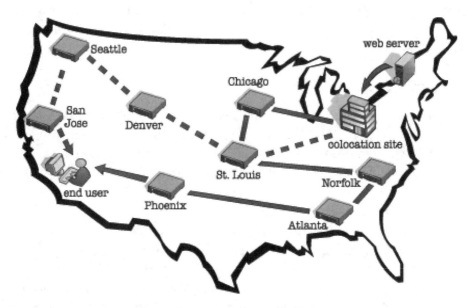

Figure 5-6   *Data can sometimes take a circuitous route to its destination.*

DELAY (LATENCY)

Because of the many different routers a packet has to go through to get from sender to receiver and because there are no reserved circuits on the Internet like there are for telephones, the delay of any given packet can be high or low, or change unexpectedly. This can be caused by a variety of factors such as:

- A router is too busy and can't keep up with traffic.
- A particular link between sender and receiver becomes saturated.
- A link goes down, causing traffic to be rerouted to a different link.

- One or more routers in between can't think fast enough.
- A firewall looks at all the packets for viruses.
- Delay is added due to the use of older technology, such as modems.
- Other downloads on a pipe cause it to delay.
- Packets are lost, resulting in resends, and other packets get bunched up behind them.

These factors make predicting how long it will take to get packets back from a server difficult. Because of varying latency, video can take a long time to start playing; fast-forward and rewind features can be slow and clunky; and video can pause, stutter, skip, and stop altogether.

BANDWIDTH VARIATION

Another factor on the Internet is the variability of bandwidth. With broadcast media, such as radio or television, as well as telephones, the bandwidth is always the same—just enough to carry the channel or the conversation. There is no wasted bandwidth; the size of the channel is just enough to carry the data. It was designed to be that way.

Because the Internet is designed to allow different computers of different speeds and different channel sizes communicate, it is possible to have bottlenecks, not just due to traffic that the size of the channel varies from sender to receiver.

The Internet link for a major website's hosting provider might be excellent. The links between the host's ISP and its branch in a particular city might be high-capacity. However, the Internet link provided by a small ISP to the end user might be very small due to oversubscription. If that Internet provider has incurred a good deal of customer growth without upgrading its own connection to the Internet backbone, the potentially high-bandwidth connection from the website host is lowered to the slowest intermediate link in the chain. In other words, the bandwidth between a website and a client is no faster than its slowest link.

> **Note** Fundamentally, the Internet is far better suited for sending web pages than real-time media because web pages are far smaller and far less sensitive to delays. There is not much difference between a one- and two-second delay in getting a web page, but a one-second pause in real-time video is unacceptable. The brute-force approach of keeping the bit rate of the video far below the maximum bandwidth of the Internet connection can be effective in getting Internet video to perform predictably.

SCALABLE MEDIA TRANSMISSION

As illustrated in technical detail later in this chapter, the Internet is primarily a one-to-one medium. The only supported connections on the Internet are between two computers—there is no concept of "broadcasting" on the Internet as a whole. In fact, the term *unicast* has been coined to describe the Internet function of sending media to just one user. Any webcast is simply many unicasts, one to each individual viewer. Each of these unicasts uses up more bandwidth at the source of the broadcast, goes through all the bottlenecks present on the path to the source of the broadcast, and uses additional processor power on the media server for that broadcast.

Since the Internet went mainstream in the mid 1990s, several major technologies have been created to address the problem of scalable media transmission (large audiences in the thousands or millions).

MULTICAST

In the mid 1990s, multicast and the Mbone (for Multimedia Backbone) were all the rage. Multicast allows every machine on the same network (using the same router) to share and receive only one copy of a live media broadcast, as shown in Figure 5-7. Basically, it could make the Internet benefit from some of the efficiencies enjoyed by traditional radio or television. And it was a standard Internet feature built into all the routers. However, the feature was optional; by default, most routers had multicasting turned off. No worries—the Mbone consisted of a technique for people to connect to the "multimedia backbone" created by this network of multicast-enabled routers. Essentially, a company that wanted to be on the Mbone, but whose ISP was not, could "tunnel" through its ISP (much like dialing into an office over a virtual private network) to the Mbone.

As any Google search on Mbone shows, the bulk of the excitement about the Mbone starts and ends in 1996. Part of the problem was the fact that at that time, a T-1 was quite expensive, broadband was hardly deployed, and multicast was a way to quickly soak up bandwidth. There was no financial incentive on the part of ISPs to enable a feature that promoted high-bandwidth applications. Though entire books were written about how Mbone could (and might have) revolutionized media delivery on the Internet, most of this did not come to fruition.

A subtle irony exists in that multimedia webcasts, such as Internet radio, are today plagued by the curse of popularity: Bandwidth cost rises as a function of audience, instead of being a large fixed cost like offline radio broadcast. A properly multimedia-enabled Internet with multicast routing can solve this. Yet, multicast as it is designed still does not address the financial accounting needs (such as usage tracking and controls) that would give ISPs the incentive to enable it. In addition, it is to a large degree an all-or-nothing proposition; a few multicast-enabled routers don't help much—it takes a majority (almost all) to make a difference.

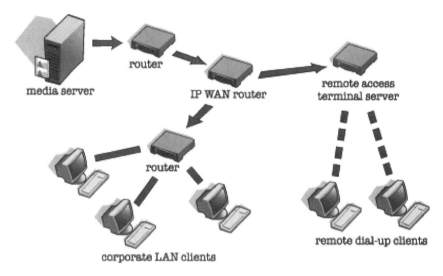

Figure 5-7 *Multicast allows multiple machines to share and receive only one copy of a live broadcast.*

Work on multicast protocols continues today, however, and they have found their niche inside corporate networks. Multicast can be used to effectively reduce the amount of bandwidth used within the corporation by live webcasts. Inside the enterprise, the relatively high bandwidth (100 to 1,000 megabits per second or 100,000 to 1,000,000Kbps) combined with the capability to control the end-to-end networking make multicast a practical choice.

Note Multicast is complicated to set up and debug and is not supported by most ISPs; quite literally, multicast has never quite been ready for prime time. However, Chapter 6, "Enterprise Multicast," describes how multicast can actually be successful within private business networks.

CONTENT DELIVERY NETWORKS

By 1997, the Internet had expanded to a large mainstream prominence. Several major, Internet-wide brownouts had people theorizing that the Internet might suddenly just stop working due to traffic growth. The scalability of the Internet for websites alone was in question, and many believed that the growth of streaming media applications could be the final blow to a functional Internet.

A large part of the problem was due to the inefficiencies in long-haul data transmission. As data traveled between major ISPs at major exchange points, bottlenecks and traffic problems prevented the data from getting through, even though there was plenty of bandwidth at the destination and source. Figure 5-8 shows how data moves from source to destination through major exchange points.

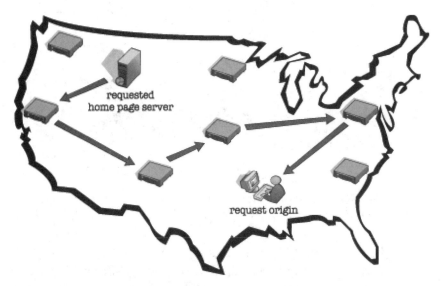

Figure 5-8 *Data takes many hops along an indirect path to get from the server to the requesting computer.*

The source of the content had a lot of bandwidth. The consumers had sufficient bandwidth to receive the content. The problem was getting the data to the "edge" of the network where the consumers were, at the dialup or broadband ISPs. One solution already in use was to host content at several different locations and direct users to the most local server. Content delivery networks (CDNs) designed a way to automate the process, and automatically distribute the content to these servers at the edge of the network. (See Chapter 4, "Internet Video Transport." for more data on CDNs).

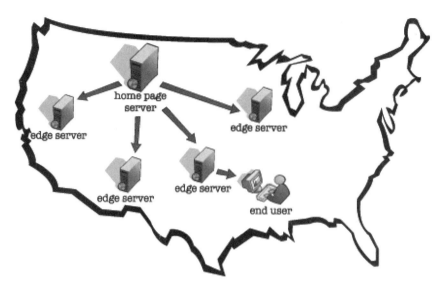

Figure 5-9 *"Edge server" scenario: content is cached at servers close to consumers.*

This solution worked fantastically for web pages and so-called static content, such as graphics and large media files. Anything that could be served from a web server benefited from this approach.

If a web server is located in New York but has viewers in London, a CDN copies the static files for that site (quite possibly beforehand) over to a local server in London. Thus, the delay in retrieving these files is low. The main HTML page might still be served from New York, but all the larger files—graphics, multimedia files, and so on—are served from a London facility from machines operated by that CDN. The source in this example would be New York, and the edge in this case would be London, as shown in Figure 5-10.

A CDN operates many servers in different places around the country or world, and thus can increase scalability as well as reduce delay. A few web servers that only have to serve HTML pages, but can offload the graphics and multimedia serving to hundreds of servers around the world, can scale to millions of users where it might have been limited to tens of thousands before. For static media, CDNs are a proven concept. For applications that permit pre-caching of content (sending the files out to edge servers before they are requested) before demand hits, CDNs are a good solution.

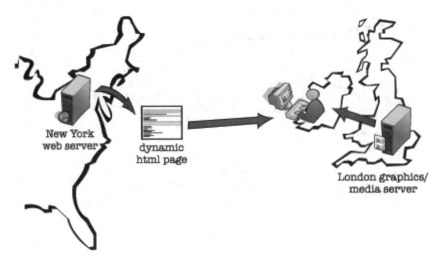

Figure 5-10 *HTML served from New York; graphics and media files served from a local server in London.*

CDNs have failed, however, to adequately address the needs of real-time media. Radio stations, live video webcasts, and similar applications all have similar scaling issues, but they do not succumb to the same CDN approach.

To distribute real-time audio or video to thousands or millions of consumers via edge servers, it is necessary to get the media file to those edge servers in real-time. As mentioned earlier, packet loss and delays inhibit this. If the stream is being generated now (as with a live concert) and packets are lost on the way to an edge server, everyone connected to that edge server experiences that packet loss.

Some CDNs try to mitigate this by sending the stream to the edge servers multiple times over different paths (in the hopes that one of the streams arrives intact). Other CDNs have explored going around the Internet and using satellites to beam the show to each CDN edge server—a good idea in theory, but quite expensive in reality. The high-profile live webcasts of concerts and events to mainstream audiences using CDN technologies have ranged from spectacular failures to qualified successes. And even the most prominent CDNs have had to repeatedly reconfigure their live 24/7 streaming audio deployments to make them stable and functional.

It would seem that CDNs are challenged only by live media streams and can deliver on-demand and downloaded media just fine. There is more to the problem than just getting the content from the server to the edge, however; even with edge networking, there are network barriers between the edge server and the client.

By using a CDN, web pages seem fast because they are small and because it doesn't matter to the user whether a static page is downloaded in 1 or 2 seconds. Audio and video are not so forgiving. Even for non-live streams, packet loss between the edge server and the client can still get in the way of media delivery.

The term last mile has been coined to describe the part of the network that connects the end user with the Internet. As shown in Figure 5-11, the last mile comprises the dial-up modem, cable modem, DSL, or wireless access between the end user, up to the ISP central office, and up to the source of the ISP's Internet connectivity.

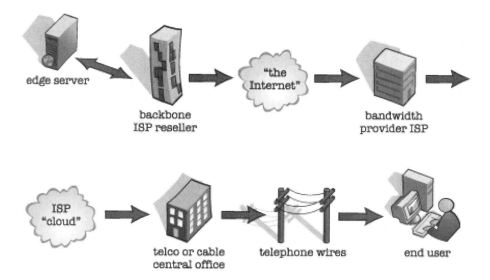

edge server

backbone
ISP reseller

"the
Internet"

bandwidth
provider ISP

ISP
"cloud"

telco or cable
central office

telephone wires

end user

Figure 5-11 *The "last mile."*

You can see that there are several points of failure between the edge server and the consumer, whether DSL or cable modem or dialup. In many cases, a shared "cloud" exists where frames (packets) are sent from the local building where wires run to the source of the ISP's bandwidth. These clouds are often shared between several competing ISPs and can actually bottleneck the traffic flowing from the consumer to the Internet. For instance, a DSL modem connection might be capable of 1.5 megabits per second (1500Kbps)of data transfer, but during a "stormy" peak period the cloud can carry only 200Kbps of traffic down to the user reliably. And as a connection is only as fast as its slowest intermediate link, traffic between any two points (say, the edge node and the backbone ISP) can similarly affect delivery of real-time media.

CDNs definitely have a place in the content delivery puzzle, but moving real-time media over a nonreal–time Internet continues to challenge Internet infrastructure builders.

DISTRIBUTED OR PEER-TO-PEER (P2P) NETWORKING

When consumers first started using the Internet, a marked distinction existed between servers and clients. Servers were Unix-based workstations; clients were slow PCs connected via modem. Today, the world is radically different. Servers are off-the-shelf PCs running a variety of operating systems including Windows, Linux, and Mac OS X. Users have broadband cable and DSL connections on fast computers that they leave running all the time. Peer-to-Peer (P2P) is a networking paradigm that exploits the new reality that users are no longer second-class citizens. The term *peer* (not to be confused with network peering in an earlier section) describes a machine on a network capable of serving as well as consuming content.

P2P networking can be used for a variety of tasks, obviously including music sharing, but we are interested in media delivery. P2P uses the consumers of content as servers, and does it in an automatic way: Peers just start finding other peers that have the appropriate content, instead of having to go to the source media server.

The complicated part of using peer networking is that it adds unreliability and randomness to an already unreliable and error-prone problem—real-time media delivery. P2P has excelled when it has transmitted media files because everyone who downloads a file instantly becomes another source, and (assuming users leave their machines running) new seekers of a given file can get it from previous users of the file, as shown in Figure 5-12.

P2P generally provides a cost savings because it offloads bandwidth demands to users. More interesting for our purposes is the fact that P2P networking can also provide increased scalability like a CDN because the peers are essentially many small edge nodes.

Different P2P approaches to content delivery have been used to solve a variety of different content delivery problems. The most famous use of P2P involves reducing bandwidth costs for on-demand audio or video downloads (Napster). Another popular use of P2P techniques has been efficiently delivering live broadcasts on the public Internet or within a corporate intranet in a manner similar to multicasting but implemented in software.

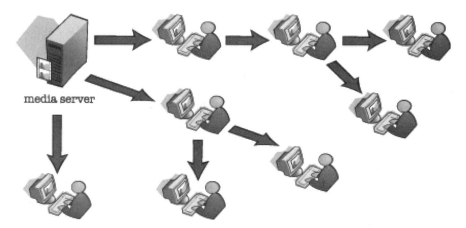

Figure 5-12 *P2P media delivery creates a pyramid effect, whereby new users obtain content from other users rather than a single server.*

Sometimes P2P networks are just considered an extension of CDN technology with more lower bandwidth nodes. Other times, P2P networks are considered a more traditional, Internet-like way to balance the use of resources (bandwidth, connectivity, and CPU time) on the Internet.

The Stigma of P2P Media Distribution

Whereas CDNs have existed since the late 1990s and are an established and respected way to deliver content reliably, P2P technologies carry a sort of stigma because of their extensive use in software and music piracy applications. However, it is an undeniable fact that P2P networks represent a substantial portion of Internet traffic, including audio and video delivery. Thus, while mainstream media publishers and vendors may be reluctant to consider P2P technology, adult content distributors, Internet advertisers, and video game publishers are already experimenting with and using P2P media distribution.

Many well-funded P2P technology companies avoid using the term P2P altogether in their pursuit of the media distribution market. They use terms such as outer edge networking, grid, mesh, and distributed downloads to re-brand their techniques and avoid controversial connotations of P2P.

As with CDNs, P2P networks are not designed to interoperate. Just as each CDN does things a bit differently and creates their own proprietary delivery network, P2P vendors create their own secure private P2P networks for media delivery.

One of the major problems (not a transport problem) of P2P is that putting transient or permanent copies of media all over the Internet is often not the desired effect, especially when the media is expensive to create as in music and video. Aside from the obvious legal problems created by applications that employ P2P to share files freely and with anyone, the various closed and secure P2P applications still create ephemeral partial copies of media all over the Internet. Content providers would love to have the best of both worlds—the tremendous cost savings of P2P delivery along with the tremendous centralized control available with traditional client server and CDN approaches. P2P solutions targeting large content providers have done their best to provide encryption, file fragmentation, security, control, and to generally make P2P solutions look exactly like their CDN counterparts, simply at a tremendously lower price point and a potentially deeper level of network efficiency.

> **Note**   If your content is popular and in high demand, you can actually count on the end users to spend *their own money* to distribute it for you, if you are unconcerned about controlling or tracking who gets it. It has been remarked that it costs money to distribute popular media in the offline world, but it costs money to prevent popular media from being distributed online.

NETWORK LAYERS: A BRIEF PRIMER ON INTERNET PROTOCOLS (AND RELEVANT ACRONYMS)

Networking is often described in terms of layers. This concept of layered protocols is exciting and important to computer scientists, but might not be as interesting to the reader. Nonetheless, it is useful to know about the many layers of software that allow the Internet to function.

> **Note**   Many other fine books do a more thorough job explaining the different protocols used in networking and how they stack on top of one another. However, this section aims to give just enough coverage of this topic to help you understand the protocols relevant to Internet video.

You have probably encountered the terms http and TCP/IP. These are protocols (networking languages spoken between computers). This section introduces you to a few other relevant protocols and explains how they fit together.

PHYSICAL LAYER

Conceptually, you know that there is a physical layer (copper wires, telephone lines, cable, fiber optic, and so on), the hardware that actually carries the proverbial 1s and 0s from one computer to another.

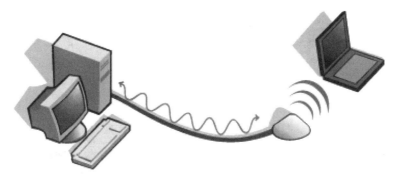

Figure 5-13   *Internet hardware layer.*

DATA LINK LAYER

The next layer up is a data link layer, the language appropriate for that hardware—Asynchronous Transfer Mode (AT) for fiber and copper wires, Data Over Cable Service Interface Specification (DOCSIS) for cable modems, and so on. You can obtain Internet access so many different ways including wireless (WiFi, 802.11). The language of all these transports are at this data link layer. Here, almost every piece of hardware—from wireless to optical to TV cable, telephone, or satellite—has its own special "language" with which it intercommunicates.

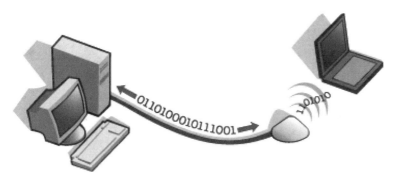

Figure 5-14   *Data link layer.*

NETWORK LAYER

The next layer up is the network layer. This is where you find IP, the Internet Protocol, the basic language used between two computers on the Internet. You've heard of IP addresses; this layer is all about sending packets from one address to another address. And, this is the layer where IP has become the lingua franca of hundreds of millions of computer devices.

In IP, a packet is a chunk of information that has its own source and destination IP addresses, a size, and some data inside it. They range in size from around 34 bytes (characters) to a few kilobytes.

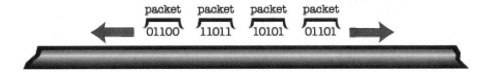

Figure 5-15 *Packets are sent over IP.*

Machines on the Internet are sometimes called hosts. Whenever a host needs to send a packet, it sends it to the nearest router. Your ISP provides the router that routes the packets sent by your host (machine) to other hosts on the Internet.

Sometimes routers go down or the links they control go down, and traffic has to be re-routed through other paths, as shown in Figure 5-16. This is somewhat analogous to freeway traffic; when a normally high-volume freeway becomes clogged, people take alternative routes or have to slowly make it through the congested freeway.

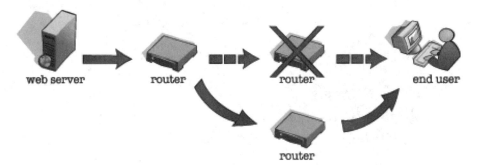

Figure 5-16 *Traffic gets re-routed when one path is too busy or unavailable.*

> **Note** If a router is too busy and there is too much traffic going through it, it has every right to simply throw packets away, as shown in Figure 5-17. This is what's referred to as *packet loss.* You will hear a lot about this occurrence in this chapter, and it is the cause of most difficulty when delivering video over the Internet. Unfortunately, it is not a phenomenon that will go away with time. It is the nature of the Internet to lose packets. Tech-niques exist to mitigate it, however, which is one of the major pur-poses of streaming protocols.

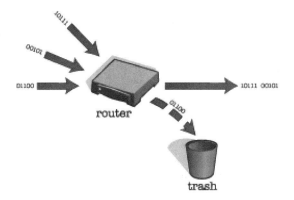

Figure 5-17 *When a router is too busy, packets can be lost or discarded.*

TRANSPORT LAYER

The next layer up is called the transport layer. At the network layer, IP controls the movement of packets around the network, and an IP address identifies a particular machine on the Internet. Here at the transport layer, TCP and UDP provide different kinds of information delivery.

This is the layer where port numbers are used to identify what the hosts are talking about. You can think of port numbers as a sort of "channel" on a computer, as shown in Figure 5-18. For instance, the port number 80 is usually used for web pages. So the transport layer allows you instead of just, "Send a packet to the machine at 216.250.117.130," to say, "Send a packet to the email channel (port 25) on the machine at 216.250.117.130."

> **Note** You might see port numbers in URLs after a colon, such as http://www.masteringinternetvideo.com:8080. This means that web services are located on a different port on this machine.

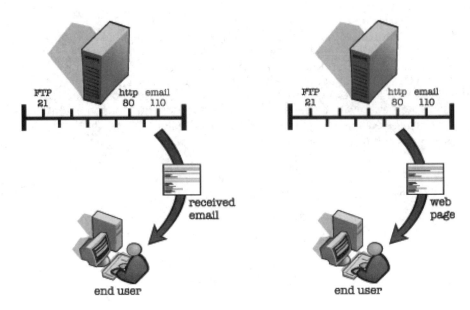

Figure 5-18 *Port numbers indicate which Internet protocol is used.*

There are 65,536 ports, and many of them are well established with specific uses, such as streaming media (554, 7070), web service (80, 8080), file service (21 and 23), network administration (161), remote access (3389), online games (666), and time service (123), to name a few.

TRANSMISSION CONTROL PROTOCOL (TCP)

TCP is the dominant transmission protocol. It is considered a self-healing protocol in that it detects errors and resends packets that were damaged or dropped because of network transmission. It also numbers packets, so that an application can identify that it received packets 1, 2, 4, and 5, but not packet 3. TCP also performs a function called *flow control,* which makes sure the sender slows down if the receiver (or the intervening connection) can't handle the speed.

All this makes TCP a high-quality protocol; you are virtually guaranteed to get all the data—eventually. But there's a price for the benefits of error detection, automatic resending, and flow control—speed. When traffic is high and connections are swamped with data, causing packet loss, TCP sends data more slowly and has to resend a lot of packets. The "World Wide Wait" is the natural outcome of TCP's high-reliability, potentially high-delay architecture. Of course, there are times when there's so much packet loss that even TCP can't overcome it. That's when you'll see the message, "A connection failure has occurred."

USER DATAGRAM PROTOCOL (UDP)

TCP is considered a reliable protocol, in that it's architected to reliably deliver the data. But reliability isn't always the name of the game. In some cases, a lightweight approach is preferable. User Datagram Protocol (UDP) implements an efficient but not entirely reliable delivery mechanism. It is a lean protocol that doesn't add many features on top of IP. Hosts send datagrams, which are basically IP packets with a destination host IP address and port number. UDP also includes checksumming—a way to tell if the packet was received intact or was damaged in transmission. You can see a conceptual comparison of TCP and UDP in Figure 5-19.

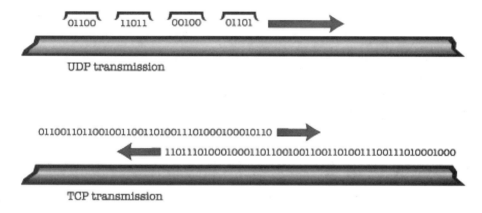

Figure 5-19   *UDP uses datagrams, whereas TCP uses two-way data channels.*

UDP leaves it up to the application to negotiate a resend of a dropped or damaged packet. Unlike UDP, TCP doesn't assume that dropped packets should be automatically resent. This has obvious advantages for video: In many cases, it's preferable to just skip a missing packet and move onto the next chunk of data. It's better than coming to a standstill, waiting to see if the Internet will manage to deliver that packet on the next attempt. On the other hand, UDP has no built-in packet ordering, so the application also has to put sequence numbers inside the datagrams it sends. Applications have to do their own accounting to figure out if a packet has been dropped.

From a delivery perspective, TCP operates like certified mail delivered by slow, thorough postal workers; you'll always get your mail eventually, and you'll be informed if there was a problem or delay. UDP operates like postcards delivered by fast, sloppy postal workers; they deliver the mail quickly but they might lose your mail as well, and unless you've numbered the postcards, you'll never know.

From a programming perspective, think of UDP and TCP like manual and automatic transmissions. It's a lot harder to drive a stick shift, but you have potentially more control over speed, acceleration, and fuel economy. It's harder to write UDP applications because the programmer has to address issues that TCP takes care of for you—things like handling dropped packets and flow control—but it gives you more control over exactly how these problems are handled. Automatics are easier to drive, but they don't always change gears when you want them to and don't give the best performance or economy possible from the engine. Like driving an automatic, TCP is much simpler to program for, but when the delays get out of hand, there's not much you can do to improve the situation.

To get a feel for how multimedia transmission sounds with unreliable packets, think about mobile phones. While making a call, the audio is constantly connected, but sometimes the signal gets worse and you can't hear anything for a while—and sometimes you lose the connection. But, when you do hear the call, it works pretty well— you hear the other party in real time and they hear you. Though mobile phones don't operate over TCP/IP (at least not yet), the protocols they use are similar to UDP.

APPLICATION LAYER

All the other Internet protocols used by applications are built upon the transport layer protocols. These protocols make up the application layer. The best known of these is of course HTTP (Hypertext Transfer Protocol). Other familiar protocols are FTP (File Transfer Protocol, ports 21 and 23) and SMTP (Simple Mail Transport Protocol.) POP3 (Post Office Protocol, version 3) is here too. All these protocols use TCP as its transport, and each performs the same basic function: connect, send data, receive data, and disconnect.

Perhaps as a more comprehensible analogy, IP can be likened to letters; TCP and UDP are made up of many IP packets and can be likened to words; and higher level protocols assemble these words into more complex sentences, paragraphs, pages, and so on. Figure 5-20 illustrates this concept.

Although the applications that most users interact with are built on TCP, several important applications and protocols are built on UDP. Perhaps the most important is the Domain Name System, the network of servers that translate domain names into IP addresses. When you type in a new URL into a web browser, the first thing the computer does is send a UDP packet to a DNS server asking to resolve the domain name you entered to an IP address. This is an ideal application for UDP in that the request can be encapsulated into a single packet.

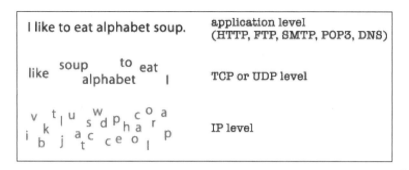

Figure 5-20 *Application protocols run over TCP or UDP, which run over IP.*

For networking programmers and streaming system designers, UDP is the preferred protocol for delivering streaming video. UDP has many advantages over TCP for delivering video including the following:

- **Delay**: If a packet is dropped in UDP, the server can just keep sending UDP packets to the receiver. A single dropped packet is probably only a frame or two of video, and the video player can just keep going. When a packet is lost in TCP, TCP then stops all sending and tries to fetch the packet again. This causes a phenomenon called "*jitter*," which results in uneven timing and delays in the data.

- **Flow control**: Unlike TCP, UDP has no built-in flow control. TCP's flow control makes it automatically slow down when the receiver can't accept the data at the speed it is sent. However, it is often not the receiver that can't accept the data, but some temporary condition on the network. Only UDP can keep sending data at a constant pace, independent of what the network does.

- **Low overhead**: UDP is a simple protocol; it essentially puts the data in an envelope, stamps it, and sends it. All the hard work is left for the application. TCP has an elaborate protocol for making sure the packet is delivered. similar to registered mail with signatures and a return mailer. As a result, there is more paperwork, so to speak; this overhead increases delays and affects the amount of data that is delivered.

STREAMING PROTOCOLS

In the previous section, we looked at the infrastructure of the Internet, starting with the physical layer and working our way up to the application layer where web protocols such as HTTP and video streaming protocols exist. We spent a good deal of time differentiating the two major transmission protocols: TCP and UDP. HTTP, the Web protocol, is based on TCP, and is optimized for retrieving files. It has commands for getting files, checking the date and size of files, posting data from a web form, and getting portions of files.

HTTP does not, however, have any concept of real-time transfer in it. HTTP takes as long as it takes. And in HTTP, the client and server take turns talking; no bi-directional chatter is allowed.

As we discussed earlier, UDP—not TCP—is the preferred transmission protocol for real-time streaming because it is not troubled by (or even aware of) dropped packets. UDP can send packets at a constant rate, regardless of network congestion or the application's ability to receive them. Now we must consider the features of a streaming media protocol built on UDP. Such protocols have to perform a series of tasks:

- **Setup**. Providing start, stop, fast-forward, rewind, and track skip commands.
- **Transport**. Providing a means to deliver multiple streams of media, (possibly) detecting missing packets.
- **Synchronization**. Providing a means to synch up different media streams into a shared time-base in real-time, and re-sequencing out-of-order packets.
- **Quality monitoring**, Providing a means to report back to the server conditions like packet loss and client playback quality.

REAL-TIME TRANSPORT PROTOCOL (RTP)

The Internet Engineering Task Force (IETF—see Chapter 8, "Internet Video Standards") has standardized a set of protocols for video delivery. The Real-time Transport Protocol (RTP) provides all the transport and synchronization features listed in the previous section. RTP is spoken between a media server and a media player application. RTP provides the actual data transfer—for example, the audio and video come down from the media server as two different streams over the RTP protocol. RTP usually runs over UDP, but it can run over TCP as well, and it can actually run over other non-Internet transports systems. It takes care of packet timing; it doesn't actually ensure real-time delivery, but it wraps the different frames of audio and video with enough timing information so they can be synchronized in real time on the receiving end. RTP is also the standard way to deliver media over UDP on multicast networks.

Another protocol in the RTP specification, RTCP (Real-Time Control Protocol), couples with RTP to provide a control channel that's useful for quality monitoring. Servers send RTCP packets down to all the clients; clients send RTCP packets back periodically (for example, every 5 seconds) to let the server know the quality of the stream it receives. The server then might throttle down the quality of the stream, if needed.

In late 1996, the Real-Time Streaming Protocol (RTSP) provided the setup features for video delivery. RTSP essentially provides the VCR controls (play, stop, fast-forward, and rewind) for a streaming media server. The protocol is modeled somewhat after HTTP because it was intended to be as good for streaming media as HTTP had been for web pages. RTSP can work in conjunction with RTP; RTSP sets up the connection and then RTP is used to deliver the data. RealNetworks and Netscape both worked on the specification of this protocol. RealNetworks then switched to RTSP for its transport setup, deprecating its earlier PNM (Progressive Networks Media) and PNA (Progressive Networks Audio) transport protocols.

MICROSOFT MEDIA SERVER PROTOCOL (MMS)

In the late 1990s, Microsoft created its own set of protocols for media delivery. Although they already used RTP in their NetMeeting conferencing application, Microsoft had not implemented RTSP in any products.

Microsoft created the MMS (Multimedia Server) protocol, which integrated most of the features of RTP, RTCP, and RTSP but removed some of the pedantic features of RTP. To reach the broadest possible audience, it designed their protocol with several different versions, each going over a more restricted kind of network:

- MMSU goes over UDP for the most efficient delivery.
- MMST goes over TCP for networks that do not permit UDP traffic.
- HTTP carries the MMS protocol over HTTP for networks that allow only HTTP traffic due to firewalls.

Falling back to less restricted protocols until the audio or video starts working is a common approach, as shown in Figure 5-21.

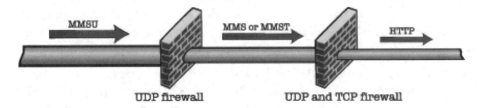

Figure 5-22 *Microsoft's "falling back" system.*

The MMS protocol provides the setup, transport, synchronization, and quality monitoring, and has additional capabilities for transmitting digital rights management (DRM) information and requesting licenses from the server.

Delightfully, Microsoft also supports the more standard RTSP/RTP protocols. RealNetworks, Apple, and Microsoft have all implemented streaming media systems that use the RTP and RTSP specifications, and each of their media servers and players can use RTP as a protocol for media transport.

RealNetworks was the first to have a full RTSP/RTP system (circa 1998) in its RealMedia G2 product. Apple adopted RTSP/RTP for the open-source Darwin Streaming Server in 2000 for delivery of QuickTime v4.0. Finally, Microsoft implemented RTSP/RTP support in Windows Media version 9 in late 2002, and is heading in the direction of fully standardizing on RTSP/RTP as well.

SHOUTCAST/ICECAST PROTOCOL (ICY)

The Shoutcast/Icecast streaming protocols began in 1998 as a simple hack to stream MP3 radio stations. A company called Nullsoft (now part of AOL), using a slightly customized version of the HTTP protocol (called the ICY protocol, with a URL like icy://www.masteringinternetvideo.com:8200), created the Shoutcast server, which can send or receive streamed MP3 or pretty much any streamable audio or video codec.

The first version of the protocol was so simple it consisted of merely MP3s shoved one after another. Later versions of the protocol added support for sending track names, titles, and more, along with the songs and having the client players display them. Finally, very stable video streaming features were added.

An explosion of different players that can play these streams as well as a variety of services that could reflect the streams resulted in the rapid improvement and de facto standardization of the Shoutcast protocol. In fact, there are more players for Shoutcast MP3 streams than any other kind of player. Every streaming MP3 player on the market—including the big three media players as well as Apple's iTunes—plays Shoutcast audio streams. Looked at it in this light: Shout-cast is in some ways the most cross-platform, interoperable protocol for streaming audio. Currently, however, the video playback is limited to WinAmp and other NSV (Nullsoft Video) players.

STREAMING THROUGH FIREWALLS

RTP and RTSP are Internet standard protocols in wide use for transport of real-time video. They usually run on top of UDP. However, for many different reasons, UDP is not always an available transport option. One of the major reasons is that many corporate firewalls are designed to block it, on the assumption that allowing it would promote the flooding of the network with high-bandwidth media. In general, UDP is understandably associated with bandwidth-intensive Internet applications, such as Internet telephony, streaming audio, streaming video, and video games. And understandably, corporations trying to prevent nonwork–related web browsing find it simpler to just turn off all UDP traffic at the firewall and internalize any services (such as DNS) that depend on it.

In the late 1990s, each major streaming vendor had systems that worked over UDP and can work (with impaired performance) over TCP. Corporations were beginning to restrict their networks so heavily, however, that even general-purpose TCP would not work; only TCP traffic on port 80 (the normal port for Web traffic) would work. More restrictive proxy firewalls have made it so that often you can't even use TCP—only HTTP traffic is allowed, as shown in Figure 5-22.

Would this development be the end of streaming media? Obviously not, but what was the solution? Enter a new concept in all these layers: Protocol encapsulation.

HTTP is a request-response protocol; the client says GET /index.html, and the server responds by sending the requested file. This certainly isn't designed to be a stay-on-for-hours protocol, but HTTP does have a feature whereby the same HTTP connection can be kept open and used. This was designed for scenarios in which the user receives multiple files from the same website.

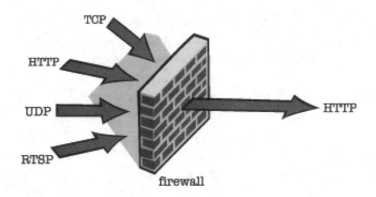

Figure 5-22 *Firewalls block all traffic except HTTP.*

Corporate Protocol Oppression

In response to this "only-HTTP" world created by corporate IT managers, developers had to come up with a way to deliver Internet video into these networks. A technique of *tunneling* transport protocols within HTTP was developed. With tunneling, all the normal packets that would be sent via UDP are constructed just as they normally would be, but then they are sent over HTTP connections. Figure 5-23 illustrates how this works.

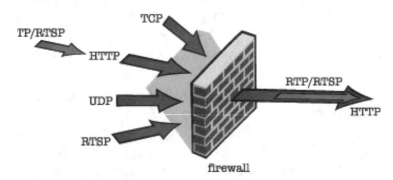

Figure 5-23 *RTSP/RTP sneaks through the firewall by being encapsulated in HTTP.*

In essence, the media server pretends to send large web pages in order to trick the corporate firewall into letting the video through!

Looks pretty inefficient, huh? Well, it is. And it's state of the art. However, the brute-force march of progress constantly upgrades the bandwidth and connectivity of the world, the speed of the routers on the Internet, and so on. Thus, structures like this somehow work. Remember, if there is no packet loss and the bandwidth between server and client has more than enough capacity, the video just works.

SUMMARY

The most important things to understand about Internet delivery of video content are:

- Delivery of video or audio over the Internet is far more complex than traditional systems such as television, radio, or telephone.

- The architecture of the Internet makes it likely that video will drop out, pause, or stutter.

- UDP, not TCP, are the transport protocols of choice. Unfortunately, many corporate networks block all UDP traffic, and some block all traffic except HTTP. Multimedia protocols are forced to "tunnel" through firewalls by appearing as HTTP traffic.

- The major streaming media protocols are the RTP family and Microsoft's MMS protocol.

- While CDNs have had success in local caching of Web pages, they have been hard-pressed to improve delivery of real-time streaming media. More radical infrastructure choices, such as P2P networks, show some potential here.

6

ENTERPRISE MULTICAST

HOW TO EFFICIENTLY BROADCAST
VIDEO IN THE ENTERPRISE

IN THIS CHAPTER

- Multicast Simplified
- Multicast Complicated
- Multicast Summarized

*I*n Chapter 5, "Video Transport Protocols," we described multicast in relation to other networking protocols and commented on its unsuitability for global Internet broadcasting. Multicast, however, is used routinely and profitably as a tool within medium- to large-sized organizations. Although it might not be ready for "prime time," multicast technology is ready for business.

This chapter has two parts. The first part contains a brief history and simplified overview of multicast technology, for conceptual understanding. The second part quickly and succinctly defines the multitude of confusing terms encountered in studying multicast.

MULTICAST SIMPLIFIED

The Internet is a large grid of interconnected computers, networks, and subnet-works. Although many home users have only one path to the Internet, most large organizations have multiple links to the Internet as well as other organizations and networks. The bandwidth, cost, and quality of these different connections vary tremendously. Thus, when sending information, there is always a choice to be made about which path to use. These decisions are made by *routers*.

Multicasting is a router-based technology that has the potential to enable efficient, wide-scale Internet broadcasting; however, to realize this potential would require the cooperation of almost every single network operator on the Internet. In practice, multicast finds commercial use in medium- to large-sized businesses and organizations. Although every router on the Internet includes some version of multicast protocols (required to be compliant with Internet standards), almost none of them activate this feature.

Multicast solves the problem of sending redundant and unnecessary copies of the same information over a single Internet link. As illustrated in Chapter 4, "Streaming Media Server Software," sending even one extra copy of the same information into a company is inefficient (and costly), and every additional consumer of duplicated information compounds the offense.

EXAMPLE: CEO VIDEO BROADCAST

Large organizations with multiple locations often have their own dedicated inter-branch network links, independent of the Internet. These branches are intercon-nected with large bandwidth pipes running TCP/IP with routers on both ends of the connection. Thus, these companies have mini-Internets of their own.

Let's look at a hypothetical company called Egotrip Corporation with the following network structure. Egotrip has many branches and redundant links between mul-tiple offices for different reasons. All the regional branches have a direct link with the headquarters; they also each have direct links with the two largest warehouses. The regional branch offices have direct connections to most of the sub-branches in their region. Finally, every regional branch has multiple direct local connections to the Internet, and each smaller sub-branch has a single Internet connection. A few of the sub-branches do not have dedicated links to their regional branch; they have only an Internet connection, and connect to their regional branch through an encrypted link carried over the normal Internet. Figure 6-1 shows Egotrip's network structure.

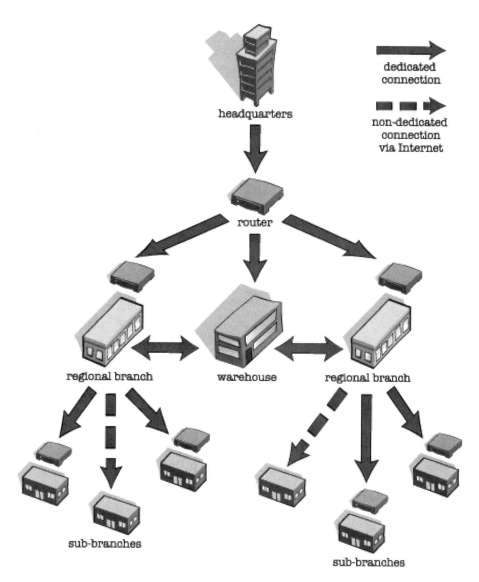

Figure 6-1 *The corporation has redundant links between multiple offices.*

If Egotrip's CEO wants to routinely address 17,000 workers residing in all the offices across the continent, one solution would be to set up a complex system of satellite delivery, and ask every branch office to install a satellite receiver. Although this solution provides high-quality video, it does not leverage the company's existing *network infrastructure* (or how the network is set up).

Egotrip could naively use video broadcast without multicast, but it would quickly find that its network would be flooded. For one thing, the CEO would probably be broadcasting from the headquarters. So, all the branch offices with their dedicated links to the main office would have fast access to the video stream. However, every single viewer at a branch office would receive a redundant copy of the same stream, as shown in Figure 6-2.

If the video were broadcast at DVD quality (which might be considered overkill for a CEO speech to workers but possibly not to external viewers), the first several users to connect would fill the entire pipe from headquarters. When viewers from sub-branches connected to the stream, they would go through their connection to regional branches to get to the stream. However, this would not only help clog the pipe from headquarters to the branch, but also to clog the connection from the regional branch to the sub-branch. In short, the video would be too big and clog every connection. Only a few hundred—and perhaps only a few dozen—viewers would see the content, which is a far cry from the intended audience of 17,000.

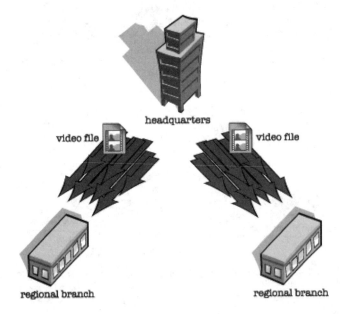

Figure 6-2 *Redundant copies of a broadcast will clog the network.*

So how would Egotrip *optimally* leverage its networking infrastructure? Because Egotrip owns and operates all the routers in its entire company, it can activate the multicast feature in all the routers. Then, using the appropriate multicast techniques and protocols (of which there are several), Egotrip could send the video in such a way that only *one* copy traveled across every network link.

EXAMPLE: STOCK TICKER

As a concrete example of low-bandwidth multicast information, take stock quotes. A stock ticker can be found on many financial news channels running along the bottom of the screen. Of course, in large brokerage companies, hundreds or thousands of employees cannot each have their own television set. A natural solution is to have all their PCs receive the stock ticker tape in real time over the network.

By using standard Internet protocols without multicast, each of these thousands of machines would have to connect individually to the server or servers that send out this information. This causes thousands of copies of the exact same information to flood the network, as shown in Figure 6-3. With even a thin stream of data, the overhead of all those connections might make it necessary to create a dedicated network just for that information; otherwise, other types of information (such as web surfing or file transfer) would fight for network bandwidth. Or even worse, a handful of users accessing high bandwidth information such as video might choke the pipes and slow down the stock ticker. In either case, the redundant information transfer is easily solved through multicast.

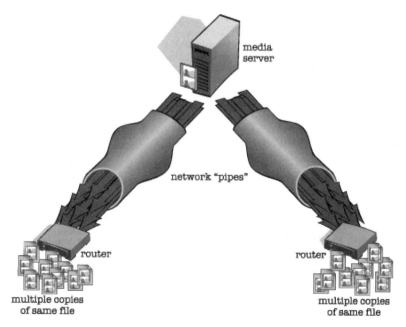

Figure 6-3 *Most standard Internet protocols fail to eliminate redundancy, which can create clogged networks.*

Single-purpose *proxy* or *relay servers* are routinely developed as a solution to this type of situation. Special application software can be developed that runs on each of these networks, grabs only one copy of the stock ticker information from the source, and then broadcasts it within the local area network. In this manner, only one copy of the data passes through the relatively narrow Internet connection, but many copies travel through the high-speed internal network, as shown in Figure 6-4. However, if each of these branches consists of even more sub-branches (as in a large multi-story building with separate networks for different departments), a relay must be installed and run for each subnetwork. Also, if there are multiple different kinds of broadcast information, a different proxy application has to be developed for each.

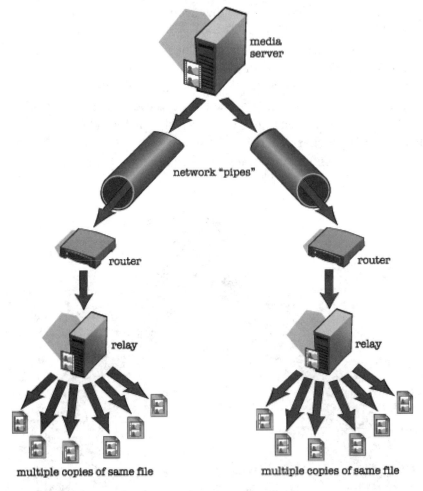

Figure 6-4 *Proxies (relay computers) can distribute multiple copies of a file through the local area network, preventing an overloaded Internet connection.*

This business of installing, configuring, and maintaining software relays is inefficient from the perspective that routers are already responsible for routing network
information to the correct location, and that these routers already contain the software needed to use multicasting. In essence, multicast-activated routers already have
the capability to efficiently relay any type of information, as shown in Figure 6-5.

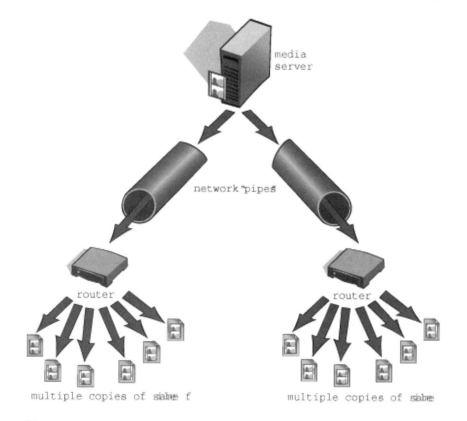

Figure 6-5 *A multicast-activated router can be used instead of a relay server,*
which achieves the same network efficiency.

MULTICAST CONCEPTS

Multicast is very simple. It really involves just two basic functions:

- **Joining the multicast group**: Computers must notify their router that
  they want to join the group of machines receiving a particular multicast
  data stream at the same time.

- **Creating an efficient broadcast tree**: Routers must work together to
  create an efficient delivery path (called a *tree*) for routing the multicast
  data stream to all the members of that group.

That's all multicast is. A computer joins the group of machines receiving the multi-cast by sending a *join message* to the source of the multicast. All the routers along the way between the intended recipient and the source see this command, and note that they should forward this particular multicast to the router from which they received the join message. This sequence of events is depicted in Figure 6-6.

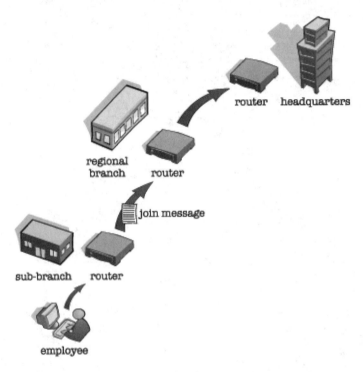

Figure 6-6 *The join packet flows up through the routers to headquarters.*

Now, each router along that path is essentially "subscribed" to the multicast. The multicast data starts flowing down to the computer that requested it, across the routers. The real gains come when subsequent users join the group and connect to the data stream. In our example, if a client from a different sub-branch to that regional branch tries to connect, the client computer sends the join and receives the packets from the already connected regional branch, as shown in Figure 6-7.

Anyone connecting from the regional branch taps into the stream that is already passing through the regional branch router, as shown in Figure 6-8.

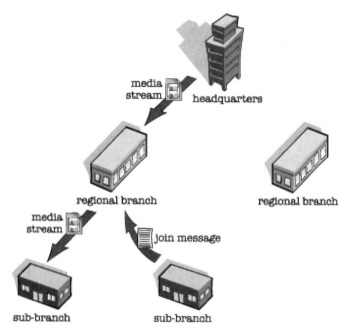

Figure 6-7   *New sub-branches that want to receive the broadcast must send a join message to their regional branch office.*

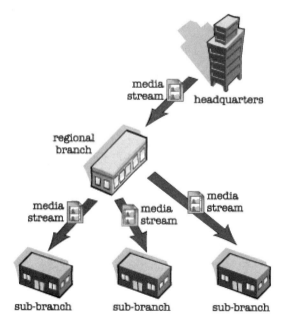

Figure 6-8   *Multiple sub-branches can tap into the existing stream from the regional branch.*

When computers want to drop off the broadcast, they send a *leave message* to their local router. When the router sees this message, it knows that it might not need to get the stream anymore, as shown in Figure 6-9.

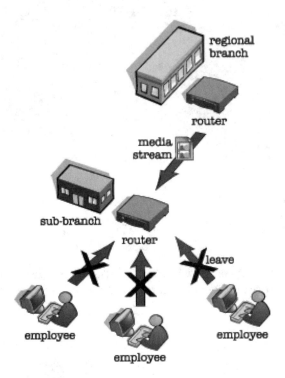

Figure 6-9 *Users send a leave message when they disconnect from a broadcast.*

When the last computer on the network leaves, the router asks the router above it in the tree to stop sending it data, as shown in Figure 6-10.

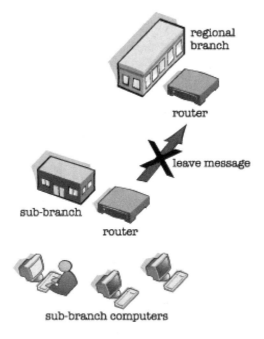

regional
branch

router

leave message

sub-branch

router

sub-branch computers

Figure 6-10   *A router with no more listeners disconnects itself from the media stream.*

BANDWIDTH CONTROL

If this great facility for occasional CEO broadcasts is suddenly adapted to run constantly cycling training videos to create several "Egotrip TV" channels or to provide broadcast television over the network for all the offices, bandwidth needs can still clog all the bandwidth, even if efficiently used.

Systems exist that work in conjunction with multicast to ensure *quality of service*, or QoS. These services, like multicast, require the ability and cooperation of the routers in reserving bandwidth for different uses. The routers can be configured to set limits on multicast bandwidth use, and to make sure that streaming video traffic does not interfere with other applications (such as email, computer inventory systems, and credit card processing).

ASSUMPTIONS MADE

If you understand the description in the previous section, you understand multicast. The simplified and slightly idealized example makes the following assumptions about the Egotrip Corporation:

- The routers used in all these locations run the same version of multicast protocols, and the company's IT staff enabled the multicast features in these routers.

- Besides the routers, the network devices to which all the computers connect (called *switches*) are multicast-capable and enabled.

- The routers themselves are properly configured—meaning, the network connections between offices perform adequately.

- We mentioned that some of the sub-branches are not connected via dedicated connections, but connect to their regional branches using *virtual private networks* (VPN). VPNs run over normal Internet connections (like home DSL or cable modem), but keep the data private through encryption. VPNs then are "virtual" because they are part of the Internet; they aren't a leased line directly between the office and that household, for instance. We assumed that the VPN knows how to pass multicast messages down to these sub-branch offices.

- In our example, the content came from a single source, which was conveniently located at the center of the whole network (the headquarters). If the broadcasts originated from a branch office or sub-branch, the router intercommunication needs to create an optimal delivery network.

- In our example, the CEO broadcasted to 17,000 employees across most of the company. The distribution of viewers was *dense,* meaning that most of the routers in the company needed to receive the stream.

MULTICAST COMPLICATED

Internet multicast originated in the mid-1980s, and has been an area of intense ongoing academic research since that time. Many additions and improvements to multicast protocols are proposed all the time, and most do not make it into the ever-evolving standards. In addition, many of the techniques used by these protocols have obscure and pedantic names and abbreviations. Because of this academic heritage, multicast uses far more than its fair share of acronyms.

This section briefly categorizes and defines a number of common multicast terms.

MULTICAST

As stated in the previous section, multicast boils down to two activities:

- Joining the multicast group.
- Creating an efficient broadcast tree.
- Multicast requires that routers implement special software to perform these functions.

GROUP MEMBERSHIP

Several versions of the protocols for joining the multicast evolved over the years, and developments are ongoing in this area. The basic protocol for joining multicasts is called the *Internet Group Management Protocol* (IGMP). Three versions of this protocol currently exist:

- Version 1 has only the join message.
- Version 2 adds the leave message.
- Version 3 adds the ability for clients to "tune in" to a particular data stream when many are sent to a single group, and filter out all the other sources (for applications such as Internet TV).

Multicast Listener Discovery (MLD) achieves the same goal as IGMP, but is a part of IPv6, the newest version of the Internet Protocol (IP).

To simplify things, two more acronyms were developed. These and other similar protocols are referred to as *Group Membership Protocols* (GMP). IGMP v3 and MLD v2 are also referred to as *Source Filtering Group Membership Proto-cols* (SFGMPs).

MULTICAST ADDRESSES

Internet addresses, or technically IP addresses—the means by which computers on the Internet are identified—consist of four numbers between 0 and 255, usually separated by periods, such as 216.250.117.130. These addresses are categorized into five classes, A through E, depending on the first number in the address (see Table 6-1).

Table 6-1 Classes of IP Addresses	
Class Name	**Address**
Class A	1–126
Class B	128–191
Class C	192–223
Class D	224–239
Class E	240–255

All the addresses in Class D are reserved for multicast. No single machine can have an IP address starting with a number between 224 and 239. These addresses are used to identify multicast *groups*, collections of machines that have indicated their desire to receive a particular broadcast. In recent terminology when multicast is being used to broadcast video or audio to an audience, these groups are sometimes called *channels*.

The actual machines that receive the multicast or send the multicast have individual IP addresses from the A, B, or C range. These machines are often called *hosts*, the traditional term for a machine connected to the Internet that can both send and receive information. Currently, Class E addresses are not used and are reserved for future use.

CREATING AN EFFICIENT TREE

The real comparison between different multicast protocols (and the reason so many are dreamed up) is how they create an efficient tree. An *efficient tree* is roughly defined as minimizing the network distance, or number of routers, between the source and the receiver. Because the most efficient tree may not be the cheapest tree, the most reliable tree, or the tree with the best bandwidth, many different approaches attempt to balance these factors.

As already described in this chapter, a tree is simply a hierarchical system of routers and computers that has no loops (the data doesn't loop back to the source) and allows efficient multicasting of a data to all interested receivers.

A *source tree* or *shortest path tree* is a tree with the source machine sending the data at its root. The *root* is the router from which all data flows. This source machine directly sends data to its nearest router, which sends the data through the shortest path (through various routers) to all receivers, as shown in Figure 6-11.

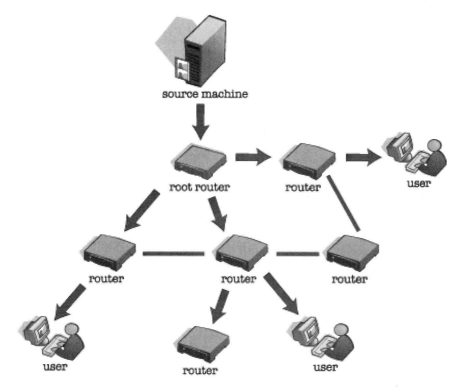

Figure 6-11 *A source tree.*

A *shared tree* is a tree where the root router is somewhere in the center of the tree, and multiple senders send their data up to the root, from which data then flows down (through various routers) to all receivers, as shown in Figure 6-12.

There are many different ways to build source and shared trees. The Internet community at large resisted many of these methods because almost all of them require additional work or bandwidth utilization on networks that aren't sending or receiving the multicast data. Thus, different methods have been developed in an attempt to minimize the global impact on non-participants in the multicast, while still providing efficient multicast. Many of these approaches required the creation of shared trees with designated shared root routers.

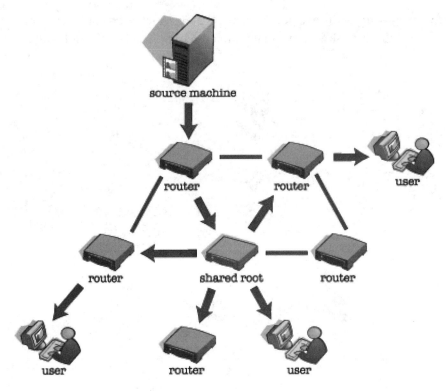

Figure 6-12 *A shared tree.*

SOURCE, GROUP (S,G) COMBINATIONS

You will often see the notation (S,G) in the technical multicast literature. *S* stands for the IP address of the source of the multicast information, a Class A, B, or C address. *G* stands for the group IP address, a Class D address. An (S,G) pair would be stored in a *link state table* in a router, and would indicate that a particular machine wanted to receive data from the source S in the multicast group G. An (S,G) pair would also mean that there was a specific *source tree* rooted at that source.

You might also see (*,G) in the same discussions. The asterisk means "anyone" or "all" and is stored in the same link state table, indicating that a machine wants to receive data from any (*) source in the multicast group G. (*,G) also describes a shared tree with a central meeting point.

MULTIPLE SOURCES VERSUS SINGLE SOURCE

A good example of many-to-many multicast is multi-party video conferencing, which requires everyone to be both a broadcaster and a receiver, and has the same number of receivers as senders.

The more usual example of one-to-many multicast is Internet radio or broadcast TV, where a single broadcast goes out to many different users.

Although multicast originally supported the many-to-many in all cases, this was inherently insecure as designed. Because any machine on the Internet can potentially send to a specified group address (just as anyone can send to any single address), a malicious or mistaken user could start sending to a group address. If, however, this group address was already being received by millions of machines (perhaps a large football game was being video-broadcast), every single machine would also start receiving this broadcast as well.

Attempts to solve this have resulted in a *Single-Source Multicast* (SSM) model that eliminates unintended senders. Instead of receiving from a group address G, receivers *subscribe* to a combination source-group (S,G). They receive only what the designated sources send. In SSM, they have also changed the terminology to fit with video broadcasting. Receivers are now *subscribers;* join and leave messages are now *subscribe* and *unsubscribe;* and groups are replaced with a combination of source and group called a *channel.*

DIFFERENT MULTICAST ALGORITHMS

Multicast protocols can be used for more than unidirectional broadcasts. They can be categorized by two main factors:

- **Flows**: Whether there is one source (*single source multicast, one-to-many)* or whether everyone in the group can send (*many-to-many*).
- **Density**: Whether most of the computers on the network will want the multicast (*dense mode*) or whether a relatively small number of computers will want it (*sparse mode multicast*).

DENSE MODE

Our earlier CEO broadcast example is a good example of dense mode multicasting. Just about everyone in the company wanted to watch the broadcast, so the system could have operated a little more quickly by simply flooding the video to all the routers, and having routers without any viewers specifically ask the parent router to stop sending, or *prune* that router, as shown in Figure 6-13. Dense mode protocols make sense only inside a private network, and even then, only when a majority of the computers on the network receive the multicast.

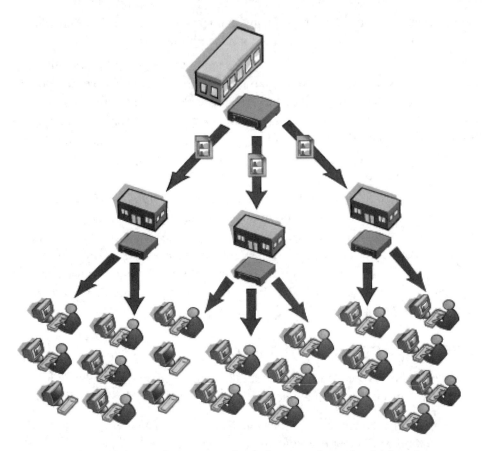

Figure 6-13 *In dense mode, most people on the network receive the broadcast.*

Distance Vector Multicast Routing Protocol (DVMRP) is the oldest multicast protocol and is dense-mode. *Distance vectors* are measurements of how many routers are between the source and the destination. This protocol minimizes these distance vectors (between routers) of the multicast tree.

Multicast Extensions to Open Shortest Path First (MOSPF) is another dense-mode multicast protocol. It is based on a routing technique that simply chooses the next shortest unused path (between routers) when building a multicast tree.

Protocol Independent Multicast–Dense Mode (PIM-DM) is the latest dense-mode protocol and is being actively developed and supported. It is *protocol independent* because it does not rely on a particular type of routing protocol and simply uses the paths determined by the existing routers.

SPARSE MODE

Sparse mode multicasting, shown in Figure 6-14, is required to multicast on the broad Internet, where most people are not aware of and will not be seeking the broadcast. It would be foolish to use a dense-mode protocol that automatically sends the data to every machine on the Internet, requiring each to then say, "Hey I didn't want this broadcast."

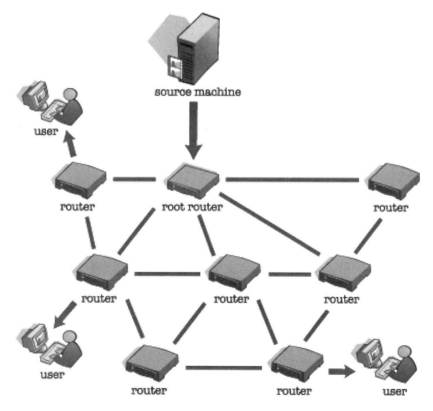

Figure 6-14 *Sparse mode is best for large networks, where a fewer number of people tune in to the broadcast.*

The alternative is to have a central router to which every machine connects, in order to communicate their intention to receive the broadcast. Then, once they communicate, they can work out a more optimal distribution tree. Like dense mode, there are several of these *center-based tree* sparse mode protocols:

- *Core-based trees* (CBT) is a simple sparse mode protocol. New group members send join messages to a designated core router. Any routers that the join message passes along the way also begin to relay the multicast. This builds up a tree as the packets move to the core. The choice of core router location is important because the broadcast tree is rooted at the core.

- *Border Gateway Multicast Protocol* (BGMP) is another sparse mode protocol that designates a domain (for example, masteringinternetvideo.com) as the central coordination point instead of a specific core router. This allows any router around that domain to serve as the core router, and reduces the dependency on a single router.

- *Protocol Independent Multicast-Sparse Mode* (PIM-SM) is the most standard sparse mode protocol. In PIM-SM, shown in Figure 6-15, the central router is called a *Rendezvous Point (RP)*. The benefit of PIM-SM is that once all the hosts are connected via a shared tree to the root or RP, they can switch over to a more efficient shortest path source-tree, if all the routers support PIM-SM.

PIM-SM is compatible with PIM-DM, and they can work together in a configuration where dense-mode is used within a private network environment, and then PIM-SM is used to connect them in a broader scale.

The PIM protocols are the most current and accepted form of multicast, but backwards compatibility with older equipment requires most routers to support the entire set of protocols described here. New installations will probably use PIM-SM. Multicast is continually researched and debated, so sooner or later PIM will be replaced as well.

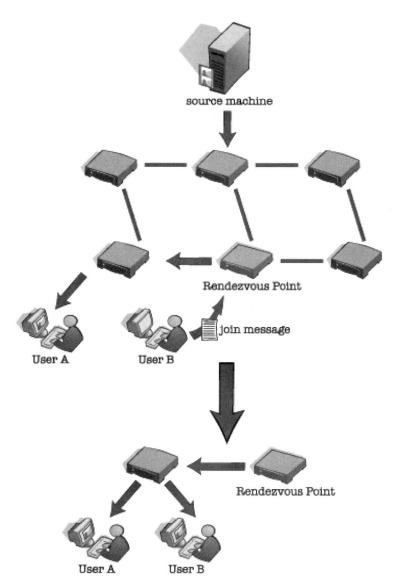

source machine

Rendezvous Point

join message

User A   User B

Rendezvous Point

User A   User B

Figure 6-15 *PIM-SM cuts out the middleman. User B sends a join message to the Rendezvous Point, and then connects with his local router to receive the broadcast.*

INTERNET PROTOCOL VERSION 6

Internet Protocol version 6 (IPv6) is often discussed in conjunction with multicast. IPv6 is the newest version of the Internet Protocol, the protocol on which the entire Internet runs. Probably the most easily understood aspect of the new protocol is that addresses will go from four sets of numbers (216.250.117.130) to eight sets of letters and numbers (2023:0000:13AF:0000:0000:09C0:522C:250D).

At this writing, the transfer from the old version of the protocol (IPv4) to the new one is in its very beginning stages. The largest networks running IPv6 already are academic institutions that are trying it out to see if it works well enough. In conjunction with this, they also experiment with the newest versions of multicast protocols.

The new Internet protocol has many other new features, including multicast addressing. Thus, in newer literature on multicast you will also run into discussions of IPv6 and descriptions of how different features in multicast work on IPv6 versus IPv4. Most of this data won't be relevant for several years unless you use IPv6 in your network or plan to in the near future.

MULTIMEDIA BACKBONE

Most of the Internet is still not multicast-enabled, because the multicast protocols have never been quite ready for global deployment. Multicast broadcasts currently stop at the edge of the network from which they originate. Each of these multicast-enabled networks is a sort of *island*, unable to multicast beyond its boundaries.

The *Multimedia Backbone* (Mbone) is a large group of multicast-enabled networks connected to the public Internet, connected together by special software that links these networks through *tunnels*, as shown in Figure 6-16.

Since Mbone's inception, in order to participate in the various video broadcasts and other multicast applications that run on the Mbone, a *tunnel* to the Mbone needs to be set up. Special applications (like the proxies or relays mentioned in the first section) can connect different multicast networks and tunnel the multicast data from the one multicast network to the next.

The Mbone is more of a research and development laboratory for multicast technologies than a viable means of commercial distribution. The groups that standardize the protocols for the Internet continue to research and develop multicast technologies suitable for broad Internet deployment and use, and it is possible (and hoped) that globally functional and enabled Internet multicast will be a feature of IPv6.

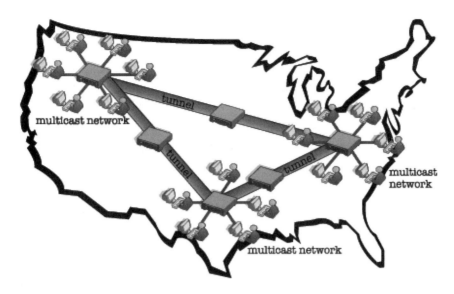

Figure 6-16 *The Mbone is made up of many linked multicast networks.*

ROUTERS AND SWITCHES

Although routers are essentially the nerve centers of the Internet, switches and hubs are the devices that tie all the computers together.

A *hub* is a simple device that connects to each computer, router, printer, or other network device, and combines them into one large network, as shown in Figure 6-17. Hubs are not used that often any more, having been replaced by switches. A *switch* is a more sophisticated form of hub that more efficiently moves the data between machines, making sure they receive only data they explicitly requested.

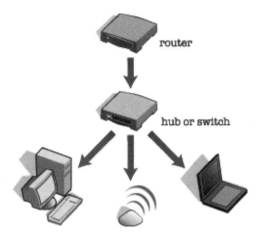

Figure 6-17 *Hubs or switches connect devices on a local network.*

Although routers need to understand multicast in order for it to work at all, so do switches. *IGMP snooping* occurs when a switch has to look at all the IGMP packets that flow by it, in order to figure out which machines are trying to join a multicast group. Because these messages were designed and directed at a router, the switch has to "snoop" and read *every single* packet as it goes by.

If it does not support this, the switch will inadvertently filter out any multicast traffic and will not forward it to the machine that requested it, even if the router was sending it. This eavesdropping requirement means that switches might have to be upgraded to be multicast-capable, and that even slower multicast-enabled switches can become overwhelmed by too many packets if a lot of high-bandwidth multicasting is going on.

Devices, such as routers and switches, usually support every standard multicast protocol, even though manufacturers no longer recommend using the older protocols for security or efficiency reasons. For a completely new multicast deployment in a large private network, the older protocols aren't needed and can be disabled. If you need to interconnect several existing multicast networks or link in with external multicast networks or the Mbone, you might need to use these older protocols.

Because of the different multicast versions and the demands they put on switches as well as routers, it might be necessary to upgrade or reconfigure every device on a network to fully deploy multicast.

QUALITY OF SERVICE

QoS describes any technologies that guarantee a certain behavior on the network, such as reserved bandwidth. You rarely pick up the phone and say, "Wow, the phone network sure is slow tonight," yet this is a routine occurrence on the Internet. Telephones almost always work because enough bandwidth was reserved for your telephone call.

Low-cost Internet providers don't usually guarantee any particular performance characteristics of their connections; they usually don't even guarantee how often the network will be up. However, business applications require a specific level of service quality, and on private or dedicated network links, special hardware and software can guarantee specific characteristics, such as maximum delay, minimum available bandwidth, and so on.

There are several approaches to providing QoS, and most require the cooperation of the routers just as multicast does. The high bandwidth demands of streaming video applications often require a simultaneous implementation of bandwidth restrictions to ensure that multicast doesn't adversely affect other important bandwidth uses, such as email.

If you begin to see other sets of unfamiliar acronyms interspersed frequently with "QoS," a good guess is that they are discussing protocols for establishing and describing QoS parameters. A broadcasting program might ask, "Can I use this much bandwidth?" via some QoS protocol and the router would answer yes or no.

While the public Internet has very little to offer in terms of bandwidth guarantees and quality of service, enterprise networks can be configured to prioritize between different classes of network use. This is called *traffic shaping.* Like multicast, these features are provided by the routers and to really implement effective QoS requires end-to-end reconfiguration. However, when all the routers within an enterprise speak the same language and are configured correctly, bandwidth can be guaranteed for critical business functions.

Often QoS in the form of traffic shaping is used to *prevent* possibly superfluous applications (such as casual Internet video consumption) from adversely affecting those applications considered more important (such as email, backups, accounting, and inventory), as shown in Figure 6-18.

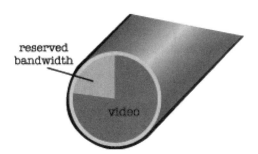

reserved
bandwidth

video

Figure 6-18   *QoS reserves a portion of bandwidth for important business traffic.*

In many cases, however, the QoS functionality exists to guarantee that the video is delivered without skips and interruptions, as shown in Figure 6-19. On many networks, such network guarantees are essential to providing any usable high-definition digital video, via multicast protocols or not.

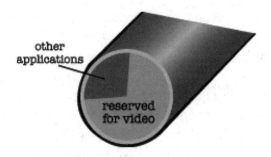

Figure 6-19 *QoS can also reserve band-width for video delivery despite heavy competing network traffic.*

End devices (such as the viewing computer) use a network protocol called Resource Reservation Protocol (RSVP) to request network performance guarantees (such as maximum delay or a minimum bandwidth). If such requests are granted by the system (as configured by system administrators), the entire network chain of routers between itself and the source of the content will work together to provide this level of service. RSVP builds up a guaranteed service channel through a series of routers in much the same way that multicast trees are built, and then guarantees the bandwidth like the circuit switching model used by telephone networks (and discussed in Chapter 5, "Video Transport Protocols").

According to the RSVP documentation of Cisco Systems (the largest provider of routers), there are three main classes of data delivery guarantees, as shown in Figure 6-20:

- Best-effort delivery
- Bit-rate sensitive delivery
- Delay-sensitive delivery

Best-effort delivery is the only kind of data transport the public Internet provides. Routers do "the best they can", but if they run out of memory, bandwidth, or have other more important data to transfer, routers have the prerogative to simply discard data packets.

Bit-rate sensitive delivery is key to applications that operate at a fixed bit rate and are sensitive to packet loss. Certain video conferencing protocols work well with this delivery profile because they were originally designed for fixed-bandwidth, highly reliable data networks (such as leased lines between two locations).

This QoS profile most closely approximates the service model of the circuit-switched telephone network. (See Chapter 5 for more information on different types of network.)

Delay-sensitive delivery is appropriate for variable-bitrate video codecs that nonetheless depend on timely delivery of key frames in order to reproduce an intelligible picture on the viewing end of the network connection. This class of delivery prioritizes the flow of data so that packets of this class are sent quickly, even if some packets are lost. Most of the codecs used for Internet video (such as H.263, MPEG, and all the proprietary algorithms in the same codec family) deal better with a steady stream and a little packet loss, than with choppy but lossless data. (See Chapter 2, "Video Compression," for a discussion of these codecs.)

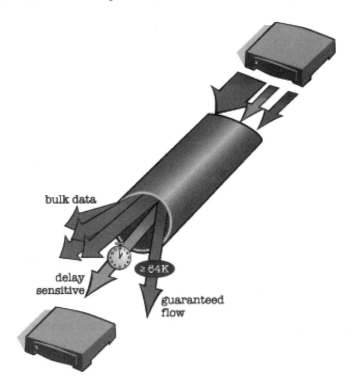

Figure 6-20   *QoS depends on the router to prioritize different classes of data traffic. Bulk data is made to wait its turn, delay-sensitive data is sent on a predictable schedule, and guaranteed flow data is allocated steady bandwidth.*

Implementing QoS within an enterprise requires end-to-end deployment of compatible QoS-aware routing and networking equipment. Thus, it is ultimately a company's router vendor who establishes the costs of enabling QoS in its network.

RELIABLE MULTICAST

Chapter 4, "Streaming Server Software," defined the two main protocols that run on top of IP: TCP and UDP. Most multicast protocols use UDP because TCP is designed to be a one-to-one connection between two machines, whereas UDP carries a discrete packet of information to a specific destination and is thus more easily duplicated to all multicast group listeners.

The liability of this choice is that UDP packets (by design) can get lost on the way or come out of order due to overloaded routers, delays, alternate network routes, and so on. Even though video broadcasts are resilient in the face of some packet loss, the cumulative effect of packet loss as a signal travels through a network can cause unacceptable glitches, pauses, and disconnections in the video at the receiving end.

Two basic solutions exist to this problem:

- Number the packets so that when a receiver notes a missing packet, he can request that it be resent directly to him. Note that this solution has tremendous scaling implications; too much packet loss would result in every single receiver asking the server for a resend, defeating the efficiency of multicast for broad delivery.
- Send the data *redundantly*, that is, with extra data so that missing pieces can be repaired on the receiving end without having the information resent. This can add significant bandwidth overhead (meaning, it increases the packet size to send error-correcting information), but it avoids the network overhead of having the multicast source swarmed with packet-deprived receivers. (For more on this approach, see the section on "forward error correction" in Chapter 4.)

Debates have existed since the birth of multicast about the ideal way to implement reliable multicast, and no single solution has ever emerged as "the" solution. You may encounter proprietary reliable multicast solutions that work with one set of vendor hardware, but in general multicast is "unreliable" in the sense that network applications (such as video players) need to deal with the possibility of missing or receiving out-of-order data packets.

In a controlled corporate network running multicast over dedicated high-speed links, packet loss is far less an issue. Reliable multicast does, however, become relevant for the new class of video applications that multicast over wireless and mobile networks.

MULTICAST SUMMARIZED

This chapter has covered most of the key concepts relating to multicast. You will undoubtedly encounter far more acronyms than have been presented here when you read the product documentation. However, many of these are merely vendor-specific extensions to standard multicast.

When you encounter completely unknown terms relating to multicast, you now have a few buckets in which to attempt to categorize them:

- Is it a new or improved group management protocol?
- Is it a new method of forming optimal trees?
- Is it a protocol to allow devices, such as hubs or routers, to participate in multicast?
- Is it an application that runs on top of multicast?
- Is it a technology that assists or accompanies multicast, such as bandwidth control (QoS), IPv6, or something else?
- Is it a research paper, a master's or Ph.D. thesis that *proposes* an extension, enhancement, or modification of multicast technology (and a new set of acronyms), but has not actually been implemented?

If you still can't make sense of your multicast documentation or manuals, try searching for any undefined terms in the Google.com search engine. More often than not, you will find a straightforward definition in simple language somewhere. Good luck with your multicasts!

7

VIDEO SECURITY AND DIGITAL RIGHTS MANAGEMENT (DRM)

HOW TO CONTROL YOUR INTERNET VIDEO DISTRIBUTION

IN THIS CHAPTER

- The Hope of Digital Rights Management
- A Tale of Two Consumers…or How to Feel Like You Are Protecting Content When You Are Not
- DRM Conceptual Ingredients
- Under the DRM Hood: Encryption Technology
- Encryption Concepts
- Tools in the Encryption Toolbox
- Truly Effective DRM

*S*o far we have discussed the various technical aspects of compressing, encoding, and distributing video. But we have not yet dealt with an even more fundamental question: Should you distribute your video online? Movie industry figures often comment that they have watched the experience of the music industry with Napster and its successors and they are determined not to find themselves in a similar predicament. When a movie studio invests $50 million in the production and marketing of a film, it wants to be quite sure the work is not going to be passed around Kazaa and BitTorrent like so many MP3s.

The Hope of Digital Rights Management

The sheer file size of a feature length movie (which can range up to several giga-bytes), coupled with the unreliability of P2P users' connections, initially limited the odds that more than a few dedicated pirates would watch a movie online rather than enjoy the high-resolution of a DVD. That has changed. Downloading a full, high-resolution movie today on a fast broadband connection now takes a matter of minutes.

Not all of the people reading this book, however, want to distribute a feature length movie for a major studio. Perhaps you are an entrepreneur who has created a new kid's series. You have no contract with Nickelodeon, but you'd like to sell the shows to families over the Internet. You're not expecting to quit your day job from your Internet TV show, but at the same time, if your shows do turn out to be popular, you want to be paid.

Or perhaps you have a series of films that are extremely valuable to a select business audience. Businesses pay a lot of money for your videos, and you'd like to be able to deliver online so you can deliver to a bigger audience and decrease your turnaround time.

Or perhaps your company just wants to make sure that footage of your CEO's cheerleading speech doesn't wind up as fodder for an Internet joke (Steve Ballmer's "developers, developers, developers" speech comes to mind).

In all these cases, we're looking at the field of *digital rights management* (DRM), the ability to charge for content and restrict the use of your content.

This sounds simple in principle. However, foolproof DRM can be difficult to implement.

One example of a compromised DRM system is the copy protection in DVD players. Around October 1999, one of the companies that knew the secret pass-words for the Content Scrambling System (CSS) used on DVDs accidentally leaked the information. The security of DVD copy protection relied on all the participating companies keeping that information secret, and once it was out, all DVDs could have the video "ripped" into the computers like audio CDs using a program called De-CSS.

Another example is the first two versions of Microsoft's online content security software. MS DRM version 1 and MS DRM version 2 were analyzed by computer programmers and found to be vulnerable to attack in 1999 and 2001, respectively. In slang terminology, this *cracking* of the two systems meant that content pro-tected by these methods could be extracted with special software written for that purpose. Subsequent Microsoft DRM solutions have taken a more "big picture" approach to the problem and have plugged some of the holes that that allowed these earlier systems to be compromised, but the difficulty in making an unbreakable system remains.

Why is so DRM so difficult to make secure? The main reason why is the kind of control that is sought requires the cooperation of every network and device in the system. In computer encryption, a chain really is only as strong as its weakest link, and a single poorly secured piece of software or network equipment can compromise the security of the whole system. And encryption is only part of the picture. As you will see, encryption usually assumes that both parties can keep the data secret from prying eyes, but in DRM, the content provider gives data to a user and tries to prevent the user from sharing that content in un-authorized ways. Even if it were possible to absolutely guarantee the video security, such measures might be self-defeating if the system is so complicated or so restric-tive that end users won't jump through the hoops necessary to get the content.

To understand the challenges of absolute copy protection, we take you now to Los Angeles where Mickey, a content producer, strives to implement DRM solutions, and Joe, a movie fan, and his friend look for work-arounds. It was the freest of times; it was the least secure of times.

A TALE OF TWO CONSUMERS...OR HOW TO FEEL LIKE YOU ARE PROTECTING CONTENT WHEN YOU ARE NOT

SCENE ONE

INT. HIGH RISE OFFICE BUILDING BOARDROOM
A well-appointed high-rise conference room. At the table sit STU-DIO EXECUTIVES in expensive suits, jackets off, no ties. At one end of the table sits MICKEY, the only computer guy in the room.

                              MICKEY
            I put the video files on a web page protected
            by a password e-commerce site. Now users have
            to pay for them before they watch them.

JACK'S ROOM - AFTERNOON

Jack sits at his computer in a cramped, tangled-wire room with a huge computer monitor and a widescreen HDTV next to it. A brown leather sofa sits 4 feet from the TV. Jack is surfing a website, pulls out his credit card, types in his numbers, and then turns on his widescreen television. We briefly see the same movie playing on the TV and the computer. Jack bursts out laughing uncontrollably. Jack picks up his cell phone and calls Joe.

JACK

(to JOE'S voice mail)

Hey man, this is Jack, I bought this movie and it's freaking hilarious, I emailed it to you. Catch you later.

JOE'S ROOM - SUBURBS - LATER THAT EVENING

Joe's immaculately organized and well lit home office contains a small desk in the corner where the computer's dust cover has been removed so that Joe can log on to check his email. After retrieving the email, he clicks the video file, and it begins to play a Michael-Moore-esque collection of unflattering quotes of the president. JOE watches through, chuckles, and then shuts down his computer and puts the dust cover on.

JOE

(to himself)

Heh, that was funny.

Hack #1: Password Protection

Passwording the site, but not securing the content fails because the content can be downloaded and then redistributed by the first person who pays for the content and downloads it, as shown in Figure 7-1.

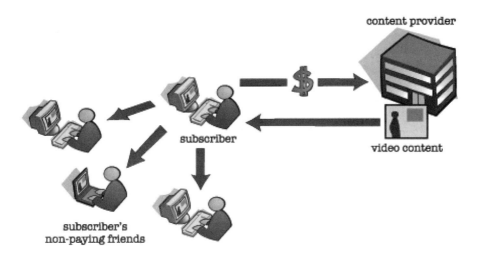

Figure 7-1 *A subscriber can pay once for content, then share it with his non-paying friends.*

SCENE 2

MICKEY stands presiding over the conference table, commanding the rapt attention of a group of men in suits.

                              MICKEY
            ... so what I've installed is a streaming media
            server. Now, we are streaming the video files to
            the user *after* they pay for the content. With
            this technology, the files are never stored on
            the user's hard drive. Each user has to pay for
            the content before they watch it. And because
            of the streaming server, the user can't save the
            files to disk, and he has to come back to our
            site to view it, which means more community ...

INTERCUT JACK AT HIS COMPUTER/JOE AT WORK ON A LAPTOP

> JACK
>
> (to Joe on his cell phone)

Man, this is so bogus! You have to keep coming back to this site to watch this movie… You have to be connected to the Internet any time you want to watch it.

> JOE

What I'd really like to do, if this is possible, Jack, is watch it while I'm on the airplane. I'm going to be flying to Buffalo and the business class has a power adapter for my laptop.

> JACK

I can do it, but I have to get a special program that saves it to disk. I will email it to you if I can get it to work.

> JOE

Thanks a lot. Ok I have to get back to work.

Hack #2: Stream Recorders

The hack: Programs have been written that save streaming Windows Media, RealMedia, and QuickTime media to disk. Streaming media is supposed to be broken only into small data packets, sent over the Internet, and then played back by the media player on the screen, never going on the hard disk.

However, it is a fairly straightforward exercise for an experienced programmer to write a program that takes the network packets that are sent, and assembles them into a file that can be stored on disk and played back later, as shown in Figure 7-2. This is analogous to a VCR that simply records a show on TV.

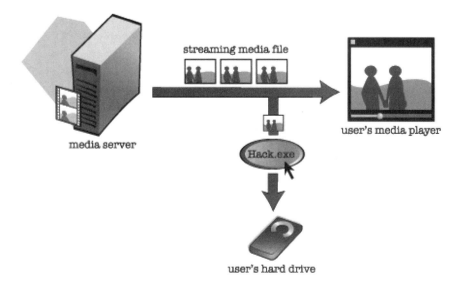

Figure 7-2 *The user can run a hack program that saves a streamed file to his hard disk.*

SCENE 3

OPEN ON MICKEY AND EXECS IN BOARDROOM

A reduced number of EXECS sits in the board room listening to Mickey. Two of the execs are having a side conversation. Mickey has a laptop open on the table with some of the studio's movies on a website that says, VIDEO ON DEMAND. He is exasperated.

                         MICKEY
        We need to license DRM. We need to use Microsoft's
        DRM. That way, users need a strong encryption key
        to watch the movie. Instead of streaming the
        file, they can download it; but, it's locked with
        DRM. So if they email it to their friend, their
        friend will have to pay for it too.

CUT TO: JOE AND JACK AT A STARBUCKS

Both Joe and Jack have laptops with wireless cards. Jack is drinking an ice blended drink with a straw and Joe is sipping a latte.

> JOE
>
> Jack, I wanted to tell you that I tried that movie you sent me, but it wouldn't play. I wrote down what it said…

JOE opens a day planner and opens it to a bookmarked page.

> JOE
>
> It said it was "downloading DRM components," and then it brought me to a website and wouldn't play unless I entered my credit card information. I thought you already paid for the movie. I don't understand why you can't just copy it over to my...

> JACK
> (interrupting)
>
> I totally know what it is; they want everyone to pay for it individually. I'll download the crack for the latest DRM and send you the file. Hang tight.

JACK types busily.

> JACK
> (smiling)
>
> Here ya go.

JOE clicks around slowly and methodically until a movie goes full screen on his computer and the opening sequence for THX sound starts to play.

JOE

Well, that's remarkable. I don't know how you
do it!

Hack #3: DRM Crack Programs

Even though Jack sent Joe the downloaded movie file, Joe couldn't play it because the DRM system couldn't identify him as an authorized user (which of course he is not). As you will see later in the chapter, some DRM systems send two separate files: the media itself, locked, and a separate "key" file, which is sent after you have been authenticated as a paying customer. Originally, Jack sent Joe the content but not the key. However, because the key is now on the computer, a knowledgeable programmer can—with effort—extract the key.

The only thing preventing the key's use is *"security by obscurity."* This is analogous to putting a key to your house in a "hide-a-key" box or putting it under the mat. In this case, the key file is hidden in an obscure location on the user's hard disk. This works fine when the user doesn't know where the key is, but when the key location is discovered, the security is utterly defeated, as shown in Figure 7-3. Because everyone has the same encrypted copy of the media file, software can be written to allow anyone who gets the file to also play it using the pilfered key.

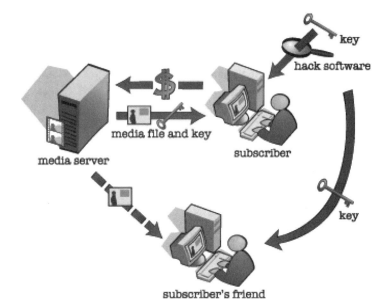

Figure 7-3 *The subscriber runs hack software to find the hidden key file. He then shares the key with his friend, who can download and watch the media file without paying for it.*

SCENE 4

INT. BOARDROOM MICKEY MEETING WITH EXECS.

> MICKEY
>
> We aren't getting the viewer numbers we wanted, and
> we think it may be due to content piracy. We've con-
> tracted a firm that creates special hardware that
> encrypts the movie on-the-fly. See, with the last ver-
> sion, there was one key for the movie, and once you
> cracked that key, anyone could open the video. With
> this new hardware, the movie is encrypted for that
> user and that machine only. It costs a bit more and
> requires more server hardware, but we think it will
> solve our piracy problems.

EXECS look blankly at MICKEY.

CUT TO: JACK IN HIS COMPUTER ROOM

> JACK
>
> I don't really know how to get it for you, Joe. They
> changed the encryption and it's got all this new third-
> party stuff... it's not Microsoft encryption anymore;
> it's some weird company I have never heard of. In any
> event, I can't find a crack for it in Google. Gimme a
> couple of days, though. I'll figure it out.

JACK hangs up and brings up google on his screen.

COMPUTER SCREEN

JACK types in various search terms on the screen. We see keywords
being entered into google's search box. Jack types:

> screen capture

A page of results comes up. No obvious winners. Jack continues to type:

>VIDEO HACK

A page of results comes up. None seem interesting.

JACK types:

>VIDEO HACK
>SCREEN GRAB
>DRM WORKAROUND

A page of results comes up, and Jack clicks a link half way down the page.

JACK'S ROOM - JACK'S FACE

>JACK
>(grinning, to himself)
>Oh, here it is! Wow this is awesome.

We see a program installing, with Jack clicking NEXT, NEXT, NEXT. Finally, we see a movie playing full screen. Jack picks up the phone and dials.

INTERCUT JACK AT HIS COMPUTER/JOE IN HIS CAR ON HANDS FREE

>JOE
>(watching the road)
>Hello, Jack.

                    JACK

Hey, Joe! I just found this awesome program.
Basically, it emulates a video card, but it
saves all the video directly to disk. It's
totally cool! I think it will help with a lot
of these movies. I'll send you the latest three
after I watch 'em.

                    JOE

Well that's really thoughtful. Thanks for doing
that again…

                    JACK

Oh, no biggie, I just downloaded the right program. There's this Linux hacker in Norway you
should really be thanking.

Hack #4: Fake Video Card

A chain is only as strong as its weakest link, and in defeating DRM, the weakest link is the user's own machine. Even if the media player respects every restriction on the content being displayed, as soon as it leaves the player and is rendered to a screen, the DRM rights control chain can be broken.

Encrypting the content for each individual user prevents the problem of people sending content to each other because they can't just download an encryption crack from someone else — the content was encrypted for their machine only, and the decryption keys are probably well hidden on their machine.

The way to get around all this complicated nonsense is simply to accept some content degradation, and capture the data after it leaves the well-encrypted DRM chain of the media player, as shown in Figure 7-4.

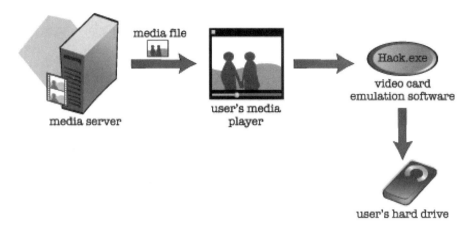

Figure 7-4 *Hack software captures the media from the user's media player by pretending to be a real video card installed in the system, and then saves the video to the hard disk.*

Even if the media player and Windows OS wise up to this hack and blacklist any video card that doesn't play ball with DRM, there's still a solution in the analog domain, called a VCR.

SCENE 5

INT. HIGHRISE BOARDROOM WITH EXECS

                    EXEC #1
    Look, Mick, we're getting real tired of excuses.

                    EXEC #2
    We've been pouring money into these online con-
    tent trials for a year and a half now and you
    only have two thousand subscribers.

                    EXEC #1
    I don't care if you say that broadband is a real
    market. Why can't you show us real subscriber
    numbers?

MICKEY

(coming on strong)

We think the low numbers are due to piracy. But there's a solution. Microsoft has been listening to it's customers and they've created a new security system that plugs some of the holes of the old system. The new Media player plays back only on video cards that have been approved by Microsoft, which means they have to enforce copy protection or they can't play back.

EXEC #3

Look. We've lobbied Congress through our standard channels to create a bill that allows us to crash the computers of these damned hackers. But until then, we don't want to put any more content out there if it's just going to get compromised.

EXEC #4

(to EXEC #3)

Dammmit, it's already illegal, and MPAAs on the case; there's just no market.

EXEC #2

Did you ever stop to think about the fact that I can go into any store and get a big screen TV for less than $1000, and it fills my whole wall? Or I can buy a gigahertz computer that I can barely get out of the store with before it's obsolete and has a little screen that nobody wants to watch anything on...

EXEC #1

Mick, we're seriously considering sticking to teasers and trailers online.

MICKEY
(considering his options)

All our studies show that there are 200 million broadband users out there. You all know I'm a big believer in broadband rollout and broadband customers are the future of entertainment consumption. They would be happy to pay $4 a movie if they knew they could get all the new releases. I honestly believe that 99 percent of our sales are cannibalized by file-sharing networks. If we can get the content protected, this can work.

EXEC #1

Mick, you don't have a lot of options here. We don't have a lot of options here. What we're going to do is...

INTERCUT JACK AT HIS COMPUTER/JOE IN LINE AT BANK

JACK

Yeah, it's actually really cool.

See, they did this thing to make it not play back with the vid card hack I used last time.

So first I'm thinking, what am I gonna have to do, point a video camera at the screen? And then I think, wow, that would actually work.

So I said, hell with it, and I popped in a tape and taped it. It's was a bit grainy, but it worked.

I had a DV camera so I thought about looping it back into the firewire port on the back but then the CPU couldn't handle playback and recording of DV because it's a different program, but the video capture card did it perfectly and then I—

JOE

Can you hold on a second? I'm up to the teller.

(to teller)

Yes I need to deposit these checks into the
account ending in 3238, but the other ones are
supposed to go in 4485.

Hack #5: Exploiting Video Outputs

Even though the code-level security prevents Jack from grabbing the video from
his video card, he can use his PC's video outport to route the content to an analog device and re-digitize the analog. Usually, commercially-authored VHS tapes
are protected by a form of analog scrambling called *Macrovision*, which allows
TV watching but prevents copying. However, there's no copy protection on recordings you make yourself. It's bit of extra labor, but for Jack, it's all in a day's work.
Figure 7-5 shows Jack's setup; Figure 7-6 shows how to connect a VCR to a PC
with a TV capture card.

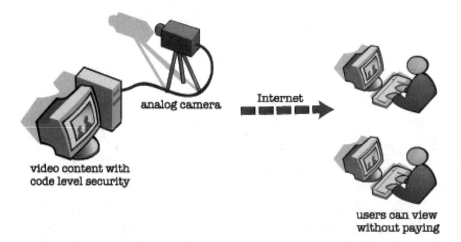

Figure 7-5 *By using an analog device to capture the video from his
computer, the user can then redistribute it to non-paying friends.*

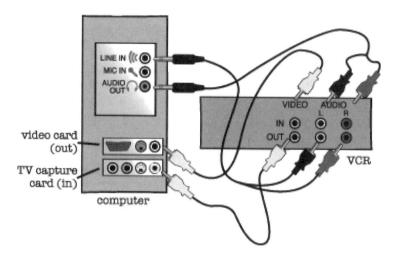

Figure 7-6   *Configuration for Hack #5.*

SCENE 6

INT. MICKEY'S OFFICE

MICKEY'S office has not been seen before. It's a private office, but the décor is cheap and the shelf on the wall is a mix of kitchy movie toys and shiny, empty boxes for expensive software.

                         EXEC
      Needless to say, we're pulling the plug on your
      online video initiative.

                         MICKEY
      What about the department?

EXEC

We're signing a deal with one of the video-on-demand cable systems on a trial basis. They're in a market that has had a very high uptake on digital cable and we're going to market it through Sid's group. Most of your group will be reassigned to the web division.

MICKEY

(glowering, near tears)

This is total BS. We know why we can't get the numbers; the reason the piracy is happening is that vid cards allow a TV out feature. Kids are piping the signal back into their computer and pirating it.

We found 18 out of the 20 newest titles up on the file-sharing networks within 24 hours of release.

EXEC

(in a formal tone of voice)

It really doesn't matter at this point, and I don't agree with your perception of the issues.

MICKEY

(ignoring Exec and continuing his rant)

We've found out how to disable this, but there's an unfortunate sideeffect that people cannot watch the movies on their TV screens, only their computer screens.

Exec gets extremely impatient and makes a motion of a talking puppet with his hand. Mickey is in strong denial of reality and Exec is tired of the conversation, but he has to "hear Mickey out" as a formality for some human resources dispute avoidance provisions before he can reassign him.

>   EXEC
>   (losing it)
>
> Mick, I'm sick of this! You've spent enough of
> our department's money on this experiment. You
> got to play with your toys; party's over.
>
> We're also reassigning you to the web properties
> division under Carole. You can work with the web
> team on all the TV properties and a few of the
> boilerplate movie sites.
>
> Maybe rubbing elbows with marketing for a while
> will teach you how to build a subscriber base.

CUT TO: JOE AND JACK AT A BAR

Bar is trendy blue and lit with strong solid-colored blue walls.
Frosted glass abounds in a room lit by seemingly hundreds of tiny
wire-hung track lights.

>   JOE
>
> You're saying they've pulled the video-on-demand
> section? Completely?

>   JACK
>
> Yeah, they cancelled it because of low subscriber
> numbers. I guess they only had like 2,000 sub-
> scribers and they needed 100,000 to be prof-
> itable.

>   JOE
>
> But it's so hard to access! How would they ever
> get that many subscribers? I mean, I always had
> to call you just to figure out how to get the
> things. If I didn't know a computer guy, I
> wouldn't be able to use the thing.

JACK

Yeah, they did make it kind of inconvenient. But
it was cool to watch what you wanted when you
wanted it. They said the system also had a lot
of piracy. But it's not like I uploaded them to
Kazaa or anything. I mean, I used to tape
"Friends" for you; in my opinion, it's the same
thing. If I pay for something, I should be able
to do what I want with it, within reason.

JOE

I don't see why not. You paid to see the
movies.

JACK

Yeah. Whatever. Oh well, someday they'll figure
that stuff out. I'm just tired of cool stuff
going away.

JOE

I know what you mean. Napster was so good. I
found stuff on there I've never found again. Old
stuff, obscure stuff. I can't find any of that
on those other programs you sent me and you
know I won't touch them any more.

JACK

I still can't believe your virus came from that
app I sent you. I use them all the time and
I've never had any trouble.

SCENE 7

EXT. RESTAURANT PATIO

Mexican restaurant near the beach has a large, external fountain bubbling water and a large number of waiters standing around waiting for the lunch hour to start. Joe and Jack are there early for brunch and both wearing sunglasses because of the very bright sun.

JOE

So then I told her we have to save up some more before I'm going to invest that much money in an entirely new system.

JACK

Makes sense.

JOE

Oh I've been meaning to ask you; have you tried NetFlix?

JOE

No, but I know somebody who has and they swear by it. (pause) Do you have a recent model TiVo?

JOE

Yeah, we just bought a new one for the bedroom. It says you can network them now or something, but I can't figure out how. I keep recording shows in the living room and wanting to finish watching them in the bedroom…

JACK

I totally know how to solve that!

JOE

Really? how?

JACK

I went to this website and found out how you
can copy the files directly onto a computer with
no generation loss, and burn them to DVD...

FADE TO BLACK and ROLL CREDITS

DRM CONCEPTUAL INGREDIENTS

In the previous screenplay, you learned about some of the pitfalls of DRM. At least you know that the hacks are out there, but surely some of the DRM solutions out there on the marketplace offer the right level of security, don't they? To answer that question, let's understand conceptually what DRM solutions need to offer.

All DRM systems for digital media have several basic elements:

- A concept of some sort of digital object, such as a movie, a song, or a document.
- A concept of different rules about how that object can be viewed, consumed, or manipulated.
- Software and hardware devices that enforce the rules.
- End users who consume the digital objects.

Figure 7-7 illustrates part of a media supply chain and the various devices that have to cooperate.

Note that DRM does not necessarily imply a seller and buyer; it merely involves enforcing rules about digital objects. But it turns out that "merely enforcing rules about digital objects" is easier said than done. A DRM system can work only when *all*, not some, devices in a content delivery chain enforce the rules. This is why DRM is such a difficult proposition—it requires the cooperation of a multitude of devices, the so-called "media value chain," any one of which can potentially break the entire security of the system.

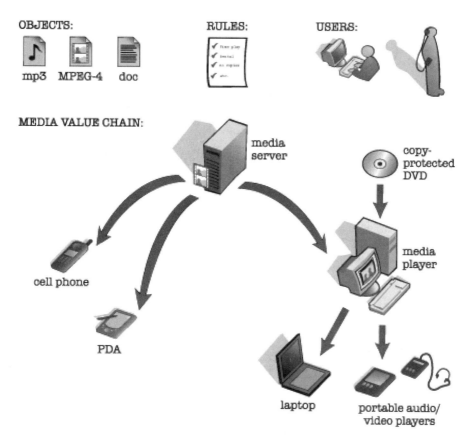

Figure 7-7 *The basic elements of a DRM system.*

THE MP3 EXPERIENCE

One way to understand the challenges is to look at where DRM has failed. MP3 is a fantastically successful file format that has evaded DRM protection. Why? Consider these facts about MP3:

- MP3 is a digital object that can be created from any CD or other audio source.
- MP3 does not contain any rules within its file as to how it should be used.
- Almost all MP3 devices and most MP3 software has no concept of limitations on MP3 and allow it to be manipulated, copied, and more, without limits.
- MP3 has many avid consumers.

To make an effective DRM system, then, we must:

- Create a new digital object that does not work with existing, ruleless software and devices. This can be an existing format, such as MP3, simply presented in an incompatible format.
- Create an effective language or standard for expressing the different rules about how the content can be used. This method of rule expression needs to be flexible enough to support the myriad of business models and rules that companies can come up with (pay-per-view, subscription, purchase, time-limited rental, licensing, resale, and so on) while being enforceable by a cooperating computer program or hardware device.
- Create a complete, rule-enforcing media delivery chain, ensuring that every link in the chain between seller and consumer (assuming you can trust suppliers and distributors without DRM) will enforce these rules. For this to work, you need new media server software at the ISP, new media player software, and new hardware devices (unless existing software and hardware can be upgraded).
- Find users who will upgrade/switch/replace their existing media consumption software and hardware devices with new rule-obeying versions.

Does this sound difficult? This evolution is in progress right now. And in some ways, it's not new. In other parts of the computer industry, consortia of computer vendors have traditionally worked together to enforce copy protection, and in the hardware world, this was easy to enforce. Macrovision has made VCR-to-VCR copying difficult for years; double-deck VCRs didn't arrive until it no longer mattered.

Whereas the entertainment industry has deep ties and control over consumer electronics for media, the computer industry has not been so agreeable to adding expensive and mandatory copy protection to every computer and computer-connected device in existence.

Case in point: DVD burners. A DVD is just a high-capacity format with a single compelling use: storing large amounts of data on a single disk. But the fact that the movie industry has adopted DVDs as the platform of choice for consumer sales and that there are compelling non-infringing consumer uses of the format (long-playing music collections, hard disk backup, home movie distribution) means that DVD-based copy protection is not adequate to prevent the (legal or illegal) copying of copyright content, as shown in Figure 7-8.

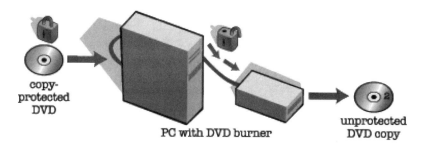

copy-
protected
DVD

PC with DVD burner

unprotected
DVD copy

Figure 7-8 *DVDs were secure until personal computers and DVD burners entered the picture.*

MPEG-21 is an MPEG sub-group that is working on standardizing rights definition and enforcement for MPEG media. The challenge faced by the MPEG-21 group is not so much a technical one but a political one: Getting a majority of vendors to agree upon a common rights definition language and enforcement system, and then ensuring that it is adopted.

Any DRM system must include these high-level pieces. After we achieve an ideal arrangement of well-expressed rules and dutifully obedient devices, however, we must still deal with a technical problem. One critical part of the media value chain—end users—might try to work around the system. This puts DRM in the interesting position of trying to securely deliver data to users on the one hand, and trying to stop these users from breaking the security and subverting the rules on the other.

> **Note** MPEG-21 is not a successor to MPEG-4; MPEG-21 is the numerical designation of the groups. There is also an MPEG-7 group that is standardizing content descriptions for searching and copyright. The in-order numbering scheme seems to have ended.

UNDER THE DRM HOOD: ENCRYPTION TECHNOLOGY

Microsoft's website contains a page with this innocuous sounding sentence:

> When a consumer acquires an encrypted digital media file from a website, he or she must also acquire a license that contains a key to unlock the file before the content can be played (http://www. microsoft. com/windows/windowsmedia/howto/articles/drmarchitecture.aspx).

We spend much of the rest of this chapter exploring what is meant by the concepts in this sentence.

In most scenarios, when you download a movie you are entering into a limited contract, much as when you buy a ticket to a movie theater. That ticket grants you the right to enter the theater and watch the movie during a specified showing—not all day long, and not with a video camera in your jacket. It's a contract, and it's enforced by the ushers who can kick you out if they notice you sneaking into a movie you didn't pay for. Likewise, downloading a movie is a contract granting you the right to watch the movie under certain restrictions. In Internet movie viewing, the usher is DRM, but of course the usher can't see what you're doing at home, which makes the job of policing user behavior particularly difficult.

So what are the rules? In the theater, as we've said, you watch one movie at a specified time, you can't videotape the movie while you're sitting there, and you have to buy the theater's absurd prices for popcorn and soda. Here are some possible rules for online viewing:

- Single viewing
- Single viewing within limited time frame
- Unlimited viewing on the computer used to purchase the movie
- Limited copying to other devices
- Unlimited copying to other devices
- No right to copy

So by paying money, or otherwise agreeing to some terms, "the consumer acquires an encrypted media file" (we talk about the nature of this encryption in the next section) and a "license that contains a key to unlock the file." The license contains the rules that the user previously agreed to. As for that key, we discuss keys in depth in the section, "Tools in the Encryption Toolbox."

The whole essence of DRM is contained in these two concepts: the encrypted media file and the key that unlocks the file (see Figure 7-9). Underlying these simple concepts is some fairly sophisticated computer science. You can't really evaluate DRM claims or have confidence in the security of your content unless you understand how encryption is applied.

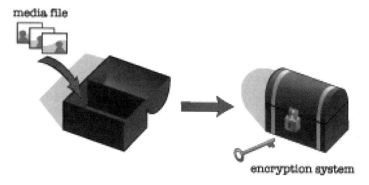

Figure 7-9 *Encryption.*

ENCRYPTION OVERVIEW

Encryption is the world of spies and secret messages, intelligence, and counter-intelligence. Although DRM's realm of content delivery and secure transactions is more prosaic, it does have a cloak-and-dagger heritage. Encryption, in its many forms, can be described simply as the locking of data with a password. Encryption makes data unreadable until it is decrypted or unlocked with a digital password called a *key*.

The point of locking the data is to make the message secure. Headquarters wants to be sure that an enemy who intercepts a message sent to an agent won't be able to read it. So the message is encrypted with a special code, or key, which lets the agent unlock the message but not the enemy. If the enemy wants to read the message, they need to steal the key from the agent or analyze the message well enough that they can figure out the key.

Thieves generally do not "break" locks. They pick them, or they go through a window. The same analogy holds for encryption. Breaking an encryption system altogether would be to find some weakness that renders it weak or useless for all systems that use it. For widely trusted encryption systems (used by finance, the military, and so on), this is unlikely; the systems have been designed and attacked by the equivalent of master locksmiths for decades and have withstood the attacks.

What *can* be broken, though, are short passwords. They are much more vulnerable to being picked because they can be quickly guessed. Computers can try every conceivable combination of bits to guess the password very quickly. A password that is 4, 8, or 16 bits in length is far too short to provide security. What is needed are very long keys used in such a way that it takes a computer some time to try each one. If it takes a computer only a fraction of a second to make one guess at a key, but there are trillions of possible keys, it still will take perhaps hundreds or thousands of years for that computer to try all the possibilities.

Encryption technology gets weaker as computers become faster, but not that much weaker. Older encryption standards lasted for decades before it was even possible to build a machine that could guess all the keys in a lifetime. Now, modern computers can crack some of the oldest standards, and even newer standards with short key lengths are weak enough to cause concern. Thus, better encryption standards and longer keys continue to be developed.

Two measurements involved in assessing encryption vulnerability are time to crack, and cost to crack it. If, 10 years ago, it took a $10 million machine to crack a key in less than a few hundred years, that same key might be crackable by a $10,000 machine today. The number of people who could afford to crack your key has risen exponentially; so has the risk of compromise.

USING ENCRYPTION IN DRM

All DRM systems look something like the system shown in Figure 7-10.

How is encryption used to implement DRM?

1. The content (movies, music, and so on) is encrypted with a key and served from a streaming media server or an HTTP server. This involves a fast encryption technique (called symmetric encryption), because content is generally large and it takes a computer time to decrypt it.

2. When a user purchases the content, the encrypted file is downloaded to her machine.

3. In order to watch the movie, she must get the key that will decrypt the file. This is sometimes called acquiring a license because the user is agreeing to some terms of use (by clicking "I Agree") in order to purchase the content.

4. After the key is downloaded, the client software decrypts the movie and begins to play it.

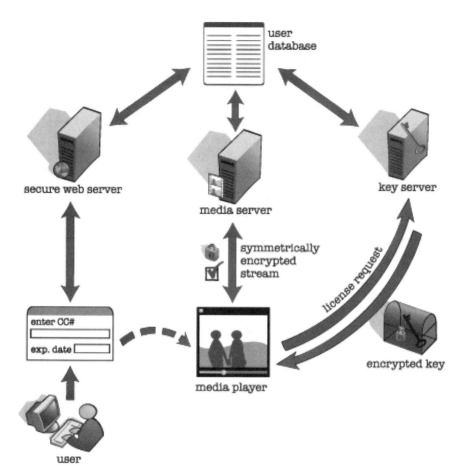

Figure 7-10 *An idealized DRM system.*

DRM and its Impact on Fair Use

The concept of licensing instead of outright sale is critical to the acceptance of DRM. If you sold the consumer your content, there would be no question of their fair use rights to make backup copies, watch it on other devices, and so on—copyright law would be the only restriction. DRM, combined with licensing click-throughs, gives content owners the ability to constrain activities that would otherwise be allowed under copyright law, such as "fair uses."

Licensing is not required to make piracy illegal; piracy is already outlawed (check the FBI warning at the beginning of any videotape or DVD). DRM is used in an attempt to stop illegal activities *before* they occur under the theory that pirated content would soon spawn all over the Internet and that serious financial damage would be done to the content owner, which is a reasonable concern.

One risk of DRM is that in the quest to protect content, the content owners prevent many legal uses of information granted by copyright law. Eventually, DRM technology, combined with content licensing will effectively put media distribution companies, instead of lawmakers, in charge of public rights to media. It is a subject of much debate whether this is a good thing.

Because the file is usually encrypted only once, the same key works for any user. Thus, that key needs to be protected from users like Jack (in our movie earlier in the chapter) who are too happy to pay once and share the key with everyone.

In order to make sure Jack doesn't give the encryption key to anyone, it is retrieved only as needed from a secure Internet media server and is sent directly to the consumer's secure media player. Both the server and the player are obedient participants in the system, and must understand the encryption used. They also understand the rules that accompany the content and are able to enforce them (such as limits on copying). To do this safely without threat of compromise, the key itself is encrypted using a different password for each consumer of the content.

To be clear, in this example the content is encrypted only once: The same key works for everyone. The key itself is encrypted separately for every user. As an analogy, consider real estate combination key lock boxes that have a key to the house inside. Each user has his own key lock box combination, but the key inside (to the house) is the same.

How DRM Is Compromised

For maximum security, this decryption key is ideally stored only on the media server and retrieved whenever the user wants to play the content. The key itself is carefully transferred between the streaming server (which has presumably not been hacked) over the Internet to the client software (which hopefully has not been hacked), which carefully looks at the key, keeps it in computer memory (without writing to the hard disk), and uses it immediately to decrypt the video file. When the user is finished watching, the key is erased from computer memory so there is no trace, and the still-encrypted file remains on the user's hard drive. Each time the user wants to watch the video, he has to re-download the key, and thus their credentials (right to watch the movie and payment status) are re-verified, as shown in Figure 7-11.

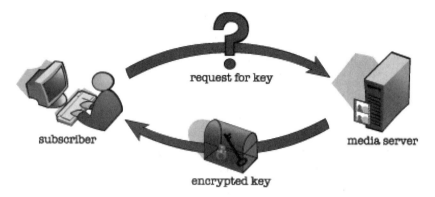

Figure 7-11 *Each time the subscriber wishes to access the media, he must request a key and wait for it to download.*

Most users want to play the content even if they are not connected to the Internet, however, so the *license* (the decryption key and rules about the content) must be stored securely on the user's machine, as shown in Figure 7-12.

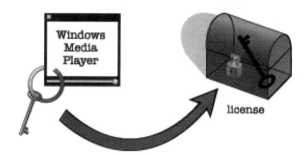

Figure 7-12 *The media player has a key to unlock the license, which contains the key to unlock the media.*

The license is usually stored by the media player program somewhere on the user's computer, in such a way that it is (hopefully) not practical to try to copy it to another computer. The key is usually encrypted so that it works only on that computer for that user.

Unfortunately—and this is the weak link in current encryption systems—the key is on the computer! No matter how obscure it may be, if everything that is needed to play the content is on the computer, it is potentially discoverable. DRM systems generally do not fail because the encryption ceases to function; they fail because one of the many pieces in the chain of control is compromised. Just as a yellow sticky note with a password stuck to the monitor can make it very easy to compromise a system, having the encryption keys somewhere on the computer is close to having no encryption at all.

If the device that received the keys is not a personal computer but a non-programmable entertainment device, this system would be a lot stronger. "Any code made by man can be broken by man," as the saying goes, but your average consumer is not going to break out their soldering iron and electronic test equipment to analyze a piece of hardware. And even if he did and extracted the key that unlocks the content, how would other consumers use the key in their non-programmable hardware media playback devices?

Computers, however, are agreeable when it comes to user requests. This is the reason why initiatives exist to make certain sections of a computer inaccessible to the user. These sections are where only special software—software approved by a manufacturer consortium—is obeyed. Such a scheme can work because it would be implemented in hardware, which is hard to tamper with—not software, which is eminently hackable. Theoretically, hardware is also hackable, but the number of people with the skill and will to do hardware hacking is much lower than the vast numbers of programmers willing to spend a weekend analyzing the latest media DRM.

So far, this discussion involves a high-level explanation of what encryption is; we have overlooked most of the details. The next section goes over DRM in more detail.

Encryption Concepts

DRM consists of the capability of a content producer to specify conditions for the use of content, and the capability to enforce those conditions. Enforcement is the purview of encryption technology, so we spend some time explaining encryption technology.

Following are some possible conditions:

- Allow the user to watch a movie just one time.
- Permit unlimited viewings on one machine but no copies.
- Allow copying between PCs but not to other devices.

To enforce any of these conditions, DRM systems invoke a type of encryption scheme to allow a given legitimate user access to the content, but prevent unauthorized uses. Encryption, of course, is the science of encoding a message that can be read by the intended user but not by others. At a basic level, encryption involves transforming original content into encrypted (unreadable) content by the application of some set of rules.

SIMPLE ENCRYPTION ALGORITHM

For a truly basic example, consider an encryption system that simply offsets the alphabet by 13 letters, such as:
    A=N, B=O, Z=M
The original message follows:
    FOUR SCORE AND SEVEN YEARS AGO
It is encrypted as follows:
    SBHE FPBER NAQ FRIRA LRNEF NTB

When someone figures out the rule, either by guesswork (not difficult in this case) or spy work, the encryption is compromised. Even if the algorithm were much more sophisticated than this, the problem remains: If the algorithm is compromised, all bets are off. This algorithm is about as secure as a safe with only one combination—once the secret is out, it's not a safe.

A way to improve upon this is to use a key, or a string of text or bytes that you scramble with the original message in some way. In what way, you ask? That's defined in the algorithm, the way the encryption "lock" works. Thus, if the algorithm is exposed—and in fact, it's considered advantageous for the algorithm to be public—the message is not compromised. This can be compared to a safe manufacturer being so confident in its safe, the company publishes the blueprints and challenges people to crack it. To decode the message, you have to possess the key.

Again, take a simple example. Imagine the following simple encryption system:

1. Each letter of the alphabet is assigned a number from 1 to 26—A=1, B=2, and so on.

2. To encrypt, add the first plaintext (original message) character to the first key character, the second plaintext character to the second, and so on, wrapping around with the key.

3. To decrypt, subtract the first key character from the first encrypted character, and continue doing so.

Here is the original message:
FOUR SCORE AND SEVEN YEARS AGO

Here is the key:
YIRNTNQP

For the first character, F=6 and Y=25. So the encrypted character is 31 or E (on the second pass through the alphabet, A=27, and so on). When you get to the end of the key, you repeat it. Continuing like this, the encrypted message is:
EXMF GTEQN OHR IDEWB MVQQB OAC

Thus, although someone might have the encrypted message and the algorithm may be public, the code is still unbreakable unless you know the key, right? Not quite. Given the simple algorithm and the short key, how long would it take a computer to run through all the possibilities of our encrypted message? Not long. In addition, the pattern of spaces in the message lets the cracker program work on guessing single words at a time, a strong hint. After the key has been discovered, all future messages encrypted with that key are compromised.

TOOLS IN THE ENCRYPTION TOOLBOX

Implementing a robust and crack-resistant data security system requires the use of a variety of encryption techniques. Different problems can be solved in a complete solution, such as locking the data, getting keys to the users safely, changing the locks from time to time, and even knowing when to change the locks. This section describes the various tools involved in building a DRM system or any secure data delivery solution.

ONE-TIME PAD

The ideal situation from a no-one-will-ever-guess-the-key perspective would be to use the key only once, and to have the key larger than the text that you want to encode (so that it doesn't repeat and possibly leave clues). This is called a one-time pad (shown in Figure 7-13), and is an ideal form of encryption, although not necessarily practical for gigabyte-size movies.

If both parties use a long key, change every single character in the message in an unpredictable way, and throw away the password after it is used (and move onto a new one), intercepting the message serves no good. But arranging this idealized situation can be difficult.

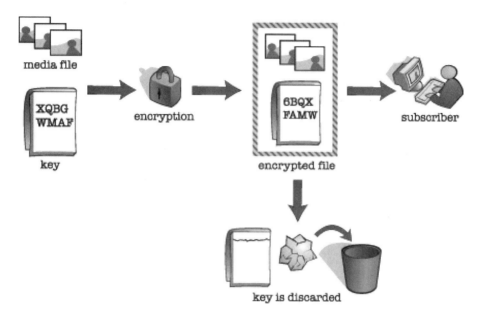

Figure 7-13 *With a one-time pad, a large encryption key is used once and never again. The strength relies in how secretly the pad was conveyed to the recipient beforehand.*

SYMMETRIC ENCRYPTION

Although the illustrations in this chapter have been based on readable characters, computers work in the binary world. Let's take a more real-world example: a two-hour long video. That's a lot of data. In computer encryption, we take a key of a certain number of bits, say 64 bits, and scramble those bits with the same number of bits from the original content. We then repeat the process on each 64-bit chunk of plaintext.

This is called *symmetric encryption* because the same key is used to lock and to unlock the message. Figure out the key, and you have the message and all other messages encoded with the key. If the algorithm is strong, the "enemy" won't be able to figure out your key simply by analyzing it.

How does symmetric encryption work? There are many different ways to scramble up data. In all symmetric encryption, the key is combined with the data, or used as input to a scrambling procedure. In good encryption systems, the strength of the system depends on the length of the key and not the complexity of the scrambling. In practice, the scrambling approach is publicly known, but is designed so that it gives no clues or shortcuts to figuring out what the key is. In our safecracking analogy, a strong algorithm is like a safe without many weaknesses—you can't hook a stethoscope up to the front and listen for the tumblers to fall; you simply have to try all the combinations or you aren't getting into that safe.

Following is a description of the *Data Encryption Standard* (DES), an algorithm developed by IBM, evaluated by the National Security Agency, and adopted as a federal standard in 1976:

> DES operates on a 64-bit block of plaintext. After an initial permutation, the block is broken into a right half and a left half, each 32 bits long. Then there are 16 rounds of identical operations... in which the data is combined with the key. After the sixteenth round, the right and left halves are joined and a final permutation (the inverse of the initial permutation) finishes off the algorithm.
> —*Applied Cryptography* by Bruce Schneier (©1995, John Wiley & Sons)

Because the algorithm itself is very unlikely to be broken, the only way to attack a message is through brute-force, or attempting to guess every possible key. If the key is too short, computers can break it in a reasonable amount of time. The ultimate line of defense is having a long key. DES uses a 56-bit key. In other words there are 2^{56} possible keys. That is seemingly a big number, but a specialized machine that cost $1 million in 1995 can crack DES in 3½ hours. Moore's Law, (that computers double in power every 18 months)suggests instead that a $10,000 machine in 2005 could do it in the same amount of time. Time to solve 112-bit keys, by comparison, are measured in thousands of years.

Schneier on Algorithms

"If the strength of your new cryptosystem relies on the fact that the attacker does not know the algorithm's inner workings, you're sunk. If you believe that keeping the algorithm's insides secret improves the security of your cryptosystem more than letting the academic community analyze it, you're wrong. And if you think that someone won't disassemble your code and reverse-engineer your algorithm, you're naïve."

—*Applied Cryptography* by Bruce Schneier (©1996, John Wiley & Sons)

ASYMMETRIC ENCRYPTION

As we've seen, virtually foolproof symmetric encryption is possible. You can encrypt your content in such a way that the coding is not broken by any known technology: That is, your video is theoretically secure. You can encrypt it so the key can never be broken, and if humans leak it, it will not be compromised.

But this raises the question, "How do you give the key to the legitimate user without exposing it to private eyes?" This is where we turn to *asymmetric* or *public key* encryption.

Asymmetric encryption involves a pair of matched keys: one key to lock and another key to unlock the data. Usually both keys can lock and unlock; Key A can unlock only things locked with Key B, and Key B can unlock only things locked with Key A.

Asymmetric encryption is best used for authentication and the initial *handshake—* starting the conversation with the media server and exchanging information securely. The key used to lock the data is kept private (the *private key*), and the unlocking key is made public (the *public key*). This is a great way to ensure that only the person who had the private key can encrypt the message, as shown in Figure 7-14.

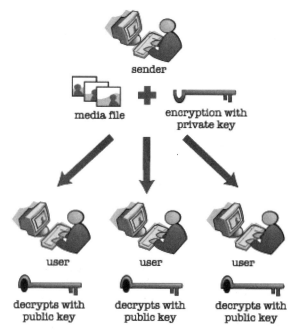

Figure 7-14 *If you encrypt with a private key, anyone can decrypt with a public key—but only the holder of the private key could have sent it.*

And it works both ways; things that are locked with the public key can *only* be unlocked with the private key. This allows people to send messages to someone with the guarantee that only the receiver can read them, assuming that the person hasn't shared his private key with anyone.

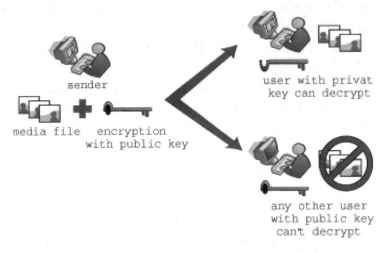

Figure 7-15 *If you encrypt with a public key, only the holder of the private key can decrypt.*

Asymmetric encryption solves the problem of getting the key to the recipient. However, this procedure becomes more interesting when both parties have a private and public key (for a total of four keys), as shown in Figure 7-16.

If someone wants to send a message to someone else, he encrypts it with his own private key and then the recipient's public key. This does two things:

- It makes sure that only the recipient can decrypt it first (with his private key).
- It guarantees that only the sender could have sent it (by decrypting it with the sender's public key).

Inside Public-Key Encryption

The technology behind public-key encryption involves hard math problems. By using really large numbers, a variety of mathematical problems or functions would take computers years to solve. The keys provide those large numbers, and then a particular asymmetric encryption system uses a particular hard math problem. One example is large prime numbers; the algorithm generates a pair of large prime numbers (numbers divisible by only themselves and the number 1), which are then factored together. You then use this pair of numbers to generate the private and public keys.

There are many "hard problems" to choose from—for example, another approach involves the mathematics of elliptical curves (ovals). In any event, each of these mathematical functions scrambles the message, using the large keys, and the only way to get the message is to guess the key. To guess the key requires solving the hard problem, and the hard problem is designed to take a fast computer many years to solve. And in the same way as symmetric encryption, the longer the key, the harder it is to solve the problem.

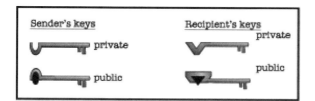

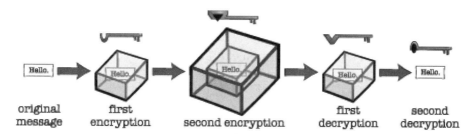

Figure 7-16 *Four-key encryption and authentication.*

HASHING: ONE-WAY ENCRYPTION

Hashing is a special form of one-way encryption that is used for passwords. It is another basic building bock used in DRM and computer authentication systems in general.

What we mean by "one-way" is that you can't undo it—the data that is hashed cannot be unhashed. Hashing "hashes up" a password in a predictable but irreversible way. What comes out of a hash is a new scrambled string. When someone enters a password to, say, get their email, the password is hashed, or turned into a longer string of characters. For instance, one possible hash of the word password is $1$0ZX5WIpr$HbsZvyyyeltL95mVikp831.

Now, $1$0ZX5WIpr$HbsZvyyyeltL95mVikp831 cannot be turned back into password, but hashing the word "password" always results in that same string if the same hashing technique is used. Thus, when the user types in his password, the hash of the password is compared to the stored password-hash. If they match, the user is let in. Note that in this case, the hash is larger than the password.

Hashes are used to avoid storing passwords in *plaintext*—that is, in clearly readable text. That is why most systems cannot tell you your password if you forget it; they can only have you create a new one. They don't know your password; they only know a hash of your password, from which they can't retrieve your password.

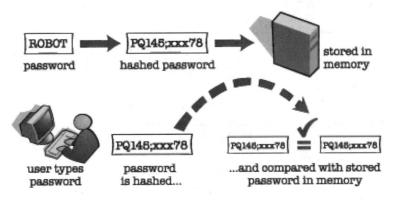

Figure 7-17 *Hashing encryption is used to securely store passwords.*

Another common use of hashing is to create what is called a signature (also called a fingerprint or a digest) for a file. This is a small file that can be used to uniquely identify a much larger file. For instance, many file-sharing programs use hashes to check whether a file has been successfully downloaded. Thus, hashes are a form of checksum as described in earlier chapters. These hashes are much smaller than the file. Instead of comparing the entire file, they simply compare the two hashes.

> **Note** Common acronyms you may encounter for hashing systems are *MD5* (for "message digest") and *SHA1* (for "secure hashing"). MD5 is still used by web servers and browsers to hash identify content. SHA-1 is more resistant to spoofing than MD5 and has replaced MD5 in many applications.

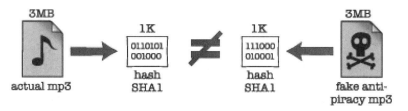

Figure 7-18 *Hashes can also be used to checksum the integrity of a file.*

KEY MANAGEMENT AND REVOCATION

In DRM systems, the software possesses the keys, not the user. The encryption is all going on behind the scenes. Usually what happens is that video is encrypted with a symmetric key, but the symmetric key is sent to the user via a small conversation using asymmetric encryption. The symmetric key remains encrypted on the user's hard drive or in memory, and the media player uses its own private key and the media server public key to decrypt it. The media player might have its own unique decryption key for that particular user. The asymmetric keys take care of all the questions in a typical transaction:

"Are you really the media server?"
"Are you really who you say you are, Joe User?"
"Have you paid for the content?"
"Yes I have, here's my receipt."
"Okay, here's the symmetric key to decode the movie."

Because symmetric keys are much faster to decrypt, they are used for the bulk of the data: the large movie file the user wants to watch. And the hash or checksum is used to verify the integrity of the whole file that is downloaded.

Because of all these keys, key management becomes an important part of any DRM system. In the case of Internet-based video distribution, some of the keys are usually stored securely by the media server or (in the case of some third-party systems) on a separate website with client software to communicate with that website.

Sometimes, it is necessary to revoke a key that has been granted—say, to remove Bill's ability to obtain content when he cancels his subscription, or even prevent him from continuing to view content he has already downloaded, as depicted in Figure 7-19. Systems vary in the way they implement this, but most media DRM systems are centralized, so there's not a lot of worry of "checks crossing in the mail." This is simple when the key is on the server.

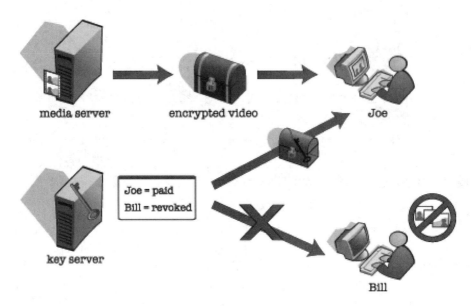

media server   encrypted video   Joe

Joe = paid
Bill = revoked

key server

Bill

Figure 7-19 *Key revocation prevents a non-paying user from accessing the secure media.*

This approach of granting and revoking server-stored keys helps prevent situations where the content is copied from user to user. Because the movie's symmetric key is locked inside an asymmetric key for that user only, if the locks are changed for that user, the user cannot get the key to the movie.

When the key is in the client, however, *key revocation* (changing the locks) can become trickier. For instance, a media player might have several private keys built into it. If those keys are compromised (for instance, discovered and published on the Internet), all the media players on the Internet might want to update their keys to new ones that haven't been made public. So they go to some sort of key server, find out what keys not to use any more and not to accept, and then download new private keys, which must be done securely as well (so they aren't altered in transit).

DIGITAL SIGNATURES

Digital signatures are built using hashes and asymmetric encryption. If you have a chunk of data that you want to send unencrypted, but you want the recipient to know for certain that it came from you, you do the following:

1. Hash the chunk of data, creating a digital fingerprint.
2. Encrypt the hash using your private key.
3. Send the chunk of data (such as a picture) along with the encrypted hash. The recipient receives the chunk of data, and hashes it using the same technique. The recipient then decrypts the encrypted hash received, using the public key of the person it assumes sent it. If the hashes match, then only a person with the private key corresponding to the public key used could be the sender.
4. In this way, hashes and encryption are used to verify identity. Note that this scheme depends on trusting that the public key really matches the sender (it is assumed that the public key of the sender was correctly received and verified in earlier conversations).

CERTIFICATE (KEY) AUTHORITIES

Just like a government or a bank serves as a trusted third party to verify identity in business and financial transactions, Internet systems often use a designated third party for digital signature and key exchange. In the case of web browsers, several companies have public keys built in to most web browsers. These companies (such as Thawte or Verisign) digitally sign other companies' public keys. These public keys are called certificates when they are presented to a user for acceptance by a web browser.

Thus, a chain of trust and security is created; your web browser trusts Verisign (the browser knows Verisign public keys and implicitly agrees that it is a trustworthy company), Verisign then securely sends (digitally sign) the certificate for Company XYZ, and now your web browser can trust encrypted messages from Company XYZ. (A whimsical certificate is depicted in Figure 7-20.)

Finally, the web browser connects to a URL, such as https://www.companyXYZ.com. Company XYZ's web server encrypts a temporary session key for symmetric encryption of that session's conversation (such as completing an online purchase). Because symmetric encryption is faster for the large amounts of data, the session key is used to encrypt all the secure web pages instead of Company XYZ's private key.

Figure 7-20 *The browser trusts Verisign.com, and can communicate securely with Verisign. Verisign vouches for Company XYZ and now the browser can securely communicate with CompanyXYZ.com.*

UPDATABILITY

Simply stated, a software-only video DRM system that stores keys locally will eventually be hacked. The only insurance against this is the ability to patch and update all the existing and deployed compromised (or still compromisable) clients to repair the faults. The location of the locally stored keys could have been discovered; a way of disabling the checking with a central authority might have been devised. As long as the system is designed to shut down and refuse service to any older, non-upgraded media player when it attempts to acquire more content, the system is still workable.

COMBINING IT ALL

What rights are DRM systems trying to manage? Not just "you're allowed" or "you're not allowed." DRM systems typically try to manage price, length of time, number of copies, copying to other devices, and license revocation. There's a lot there, so let's break it down into several business processes:

- The transaction. Communicating the terms of the license and collecting money.

- Delivering the content. Securely transmitting the content.
- Unlocking the content. Basically, providing the key to unlock the content under the agreed-upon license.
- Turning off access. When the agreed-upon usage has expired, it's time to find a way to turn off access.
- Revoking the key. If the rules are violated, access must be disabled after the fact.

The financial transaction is not our concern here; a secure mechanism (`https://`, provided by a certificate authority as discussed earlier) allows for credit card processing or other payment methods. Figure 7-21 repeats our diagram of an idealized DRM system.

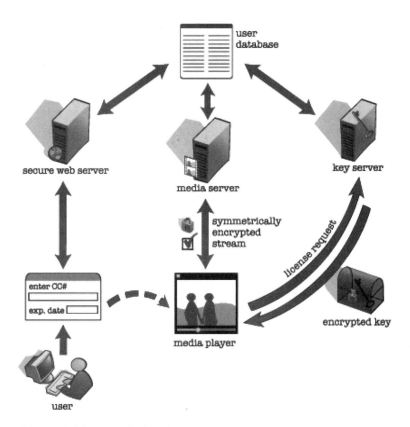

Figure 7-21 *An idealized DRM system.*

The building blocks that commonly provide for these processes are:

- Rights description protocol, language, and standard software that obeys these rules.
- Key exchange, a centralized authority to say yes or no.
- Symmetric encryption piece for content.
- Asymmetric for bootstrapping the connection.

DRM technology has to be integrated into the content itself as well as into the encoding and playback system used. This is because it has to be locked, transported securely, and unlocked (with some sort of verification of rights) before it is watched.

For both streams and downloads, decryption occurs at the point that the content is viewed. For streams, that is immediate, and the license needs to be already there or acquired at the point the content is watched, as shown in Figure 7-22.

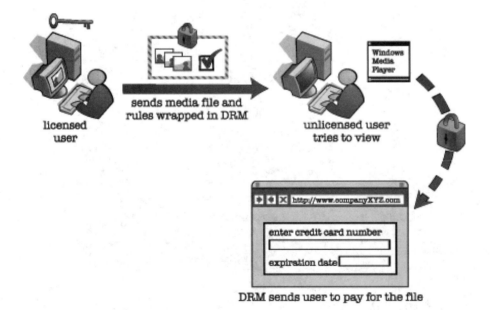

Figure 7-22 *A DRM-wrapped file forces would-be viewers to purchase a license before they can access the file.*

For downloads, the license does not need to be activated until the file is clicked for the first time. This allows download-based DRM to trigger an interaction (such as launching a web page where they user can pay for the content) in order to acquire a license. Downloadable media files can then be wrapped in DRM and traded freely because when they reach another computer, that computer (which lacks a license) needs to acquire one, repeating the procedure.

The example of a just-in-time (JIT) license acquisition for downloads is only one example business model, and although it is popular with content providers, there are many other ways to deploy and license content. The point is, these same DRM building blocks are used to implement rules in any media chain.

TRULY EFFECTIVE DRM

The fundamental difference between encryption techniques and DRM challenges is the trusted parties. In usual encryption scenarios, the end users are assumed trustworthy and a malicious third party is assumed to be the threat that the user needs to defend against. In contrast, DRM assumes that only the devices are trustworthy, and that the users are the potentially malicious interlopers. This is why DRM cannot depend on encryption technology alone—it is only one technical component of a complete DRM solution. Vendors that brag about the strength or complexity of their encryption are saying little about the robustness of their DRM.

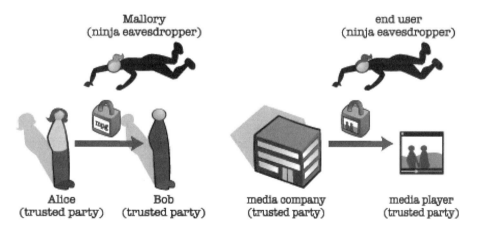

Figure 7-23 *Encryption assumes trustworthy end users and a malicious third party. DRM assumes that only the devices are trustworthy, and any user is potentially malicious.*

HARDWARE SOLUTIONS

Despite the difficulties described in this chapter, effective DRM is not completely impossible. If some sort of hardware or controlled environment is involved, it is certainly workable. Some of the more effective DRM technologies for video include:

- Cable TV/descramblers. Although there is a gray market of black boxes, cable box descramblers, and more, DRM keeps most consumers from paying for access to digital video.

- Digital Satellite Systems (DSS) and other dish networks. These involve hardware and continually changing access keys, and are even more annoyingly secure than cable boxes.

- Digital cable video-on-demand systems. Digital cable systems that offer VOD store the video on the server, and only stream it to boxes when it is ordered. The box is closed, runs proprietary software, contains proprietary hardware, has its software routinely updated by the cable company, and shuts down completely to a useless rock if it doesn't receive its okay to watch from the central server.

- Encrypt for each person. Newer DRM systems do not simply encrypt the content once but encrypt it for each user who downloads the content, so that only that user with his keys can decrypt the content. To pirate the content, it is necessary to disentangle the user's specific encryption code from the file, and then do this for each individual piece of media. Additionally, because the decrypted song or movie can still have some user fingerprints in it, the incentive to wildly share the content is greatly reduced, as they may be more provably liable for the copyright infringement.

- Hardware "dongles." Many software companies use plug-in hardware devices (called dongles) that connect to some port on the computer, and the content (the software) will not operate without the secret code in that specific dongle. For high-end software costing many thousands of dollars, this is practical and somewhat effective, but it is too annoying for large numbers of general users to accept.

- "Trusted computing" and other such initiatives. Although we do not cover any specific plans in depth, it should be clear that the key to maximum security is a cooperating piece of hardware that enforces DRM rules. The holy grail of computer-based DRM is to run code on computer hardware such that users cannot look at or change how the code runs. An industry-wide movement is creating a part of all consumer PCs that is impervious to user manipulation and that permits reliable encrypted communication as well as guaranteed untampered software execution. If and when such initiatives come to fruition, the building blocks of an extremely robust and hack-proof computer DRM system will finally be available. (Search for "trusted computing" in Google to learn more about the pros, cons, and current standards groups working on these issues.)

These DRM systems work. Software-based DRM systems simply don't offer foolproof rights management. Software is hacked. Hardware requires them to break the law or violate their agreement, which by definition a small minority does. Software requires only a small minority to break the agreement or license in order for the majority to enjoy the benefits with little or no effort. When this is coupled with a system that reduces traditional rights instead of increasing them (as digital can technologically do), then it becomes a point of moral righteousness (or, the behavior of music consumers).

Conceptually, digital should be more open than analog, not less. This creates a climate where software developers who defeat DRM are sometimes characterized as heroes who liberate the content from oppressive content holders, whereas those who produce and sell cable descramblers are still viewed as somewhere between unethical and criminal. On the other hand, these moral arguments don't take into account the reduced revenues of digital distribution as compared to its analog counterparts.

This "Robin Hood" attitude towards content providers shows how important it is to implement a *reasonable* and user-friendly DRM solution if it is to be effective.

GUIDELINES FOR EFFECTIVE DRM

When evaluating DRM technologies for use in protecting content online, here's some final advice:

- Use well-tested systems with a deployed base. Use a DRM system that has worked in practice—under attack by consumers.
- Use updatable systems. If the system relies on software alone, it is inherently hackable, no matter what promises are made. If it can be updated, however, the vendor can perhaps keep up with the hacks by requiring new versions of the software to access content and, better yet, seamlessly upgrading this software without user intervention.

- Look at and talk to existing customers. Although this advice is fairly generic, looking at what content other people have felt safe enough to put on the Internet will give you insight into the level of trust you should put in it. And if you can't find anyone else who has used the software, then use a well-tested system (see the first bullet).

- Keep the family jewels offline. Whatever you put online, don't put up anything that, if bootlegged, *would destroy your business.* Don't put your DVD-quality full-length movies online if you feel that it will cannibalize your DVD sales because everyone who really wants that content can quickly get it. If you can tolerate the risk, by all means experiment. But in general, put lower-quality material on the Web so that the offline media versions are still attractive. That said, you might be highly overestimating the impact of content piracy on your business, and reactionary fear should not overshadow your sober analysis of where the technology ultimately takes your market and business.

- Test so-called "better mouse traps" with good cheese. A vendor stating that its system has been "deployed for years" or "worked with tens of thousands of pieces of content" is no good if it hasn't been tested with good content. Look for a system that has been tested with high-value content that many people actually want, and use that as a benchmark for whether the DRM system can survive the notoriety.

- Evaluate DRM solutions as a whole system, of which encryption technology and security products are only one component. There are so many low-tech ways to compromise security. Many of the movies that are uploaded to the Internet were leaked for personal use by people internal to the studio or post-production organizations. DRM accomplishes nothing if the entire chain of people securing the content cannot be trusted.

"SAFE" ONLINE DISTRIBUTION MODELS

Here are some possible strategies for delivering online content without risking your revenue model:

- Distribute low-quality versions with moderate protection but no encryption (such as streaming without allowing save to disk).

- Distribute high-quality versions with lockbox encryption. Allow redistribution because the content has to be unlocked on every machine or device.

- Distribute only teaser, filler, or "exclusive" content that is not provided on other media channels. Use it to promote the sale or consumption of other similar or related media.
- Distribute a small subset of the high-quality media that is unlocked; use it to advertise a greater body of media that is locked with stronger encryption.

The resulting effect is that copy protection needs to be just sufficient to make it difficult for the majority of the people to circumvent it, and that any circumvention requires deliberate and clearly infringing action.

SUMMARY

It can be difficult to fully appreciate how secure DRM systems are without studying the complicated mathematics used to create symmetric and asymmetric keys. The main thing to know is that several different kinds of encryption are used for different parts of the DRM system, and that DRM involves all the elements of the system (the server, the transport, the media, and the client playback application) in order to be as secure as possible.

It is important to know the basics of what is occurring with any DRM solution are the same between systems—the same technical building blocks are used. DRM systems are far too new and varied to be called *commodity technology* (the term for relatively undifferentiated products that can be purchased from many vendors for a low price). Nonetheless, choosing the right DRM system can involve political, partnership, and trust decisions more than it depends upon substantial technical differences.

8

INTERNET VIDEO STANDARDS

SOME COMMENTS ON THE STANDARDS THAT SHAPE THE INTERNET VIDEO INDUSTRY

IN THIS CHAPTER

- A Nonstandard World
- The Two Types of Standards
- The Browser Wars
- Standards Organizations Relevant to Internet Video
- Creating MPEG Standards
- Some Final Notes

In this book, we thoroughly explored the topic of Internet video, using a sort of "video assembly line" as the framework. We covered capturing the video, getting into the computer, compressing it, uploading it to a server, transporting it across networks, and securing it along that path. And we've presented many methods, some widely known, some obscure, for doing each of these steps.

The plan of this book has been to cover the breadth of the techniques in use for Internet video, distilling them to their basics, so that the reader would then have a large context in which to evaluate both current and future tools. Whether possible or not, the plan was to make the reader an immediate expert on Internet video, and then leave it up to them to decide what tools they wanted to use.

This chapter has two goals. The first goal is to briefly outline the major organizations that influence Internet video standards. The second goal is to cap your reader's newfound expertise and wisdom by conveying a sense of the realities of the technology standardization process.

A NONSTANDARD WORLD

Imagine, if you will, a world in which technology is always improving; where companies are absolutely free to innovate without being burdened by the onerous pressures of backwards compatibility. Imagine a world in which the state of the art can always be realized, without the reactionary pressure of slow-moving, politically motivated standards organizations destroying the spirit of creativity.

Imagine a world where nothing is compatible with anything else.

Jack: "Can you guys fax me that report?"

Fred: "Um ... What kind of fax machine do you have?"

Jack: "Sony. We also have a Panasonic."

Fred: "Nope, we only have a Toshiba fax. That's what our headquarter uses. Sorry."

Megan: "Hey, have you seen the new show on HBO?"

Lin: "No... We don't have the right kind of TV."

Megan: "You don't have an HBO TV?"

Lin: "No, after buying the ABC/Disney TV and the Nickelodeon TV for the kids, we're over budget this year for TVs and frankly, we're out of space!"

Hooman: "That's so thoughtful... They got us a toaster."

Dora: "Where did they buy it?"

Hooman: "Looks like... Nevada. Darn it, wrong voltage. We'll have to trade it in for a California model. The adapters don't work for toasters."

Chuck: "I left you a voice mail. Didn't you get it?"

Rajid: "Sorry, Chuck! I wondered who that was from! I think it's because we use different phone companies, but your message didn't come through. It said, 'Missing audio subsystem' and I didn't know what else to do."

Can you even imagine such a world?

Rebecca: "Hey I'm taking Professor Abdul's class and he wants me to download these videos. I just can't seem to play them back."

Tech Support: "What speed is your computer?"

Rebecca: "It's a few years old… It's a 7.5GHz."

Tech Support: "That should be enough. It requires only a 5GHz CPU to play those videos. What OS are you using?"

Rebecca: "I recently upgraded it. I don't know… I'm not an expert in this stuff."

Tech Support: "I think I know what your problem is. You're running the latest operating system. There's no player for those videos that run on the new OS."

Rebecca: "I don't understand. Shouldn't the newest software play all the older videos?"

Tech Support: "Yes, but when the company that made that video standard went out of business, their player became an orphan. All operating systems that shipped in the last two years dropped support of the old video drivers used by the player because they wanted to get everyone on the new video standard. There aren't a lot of options open. You could downgrade your OS… Um, no, that wouldn't work, because you can't get on the university network that way. Hmm… I guess you'll have to go to East Quad where we have the older computer lab."

Perhaps in some future time:

Joe: "Hey, you have to check out these video clips. They are hilarious!"

Friend: "I already tried. I couldn't play them."

Joe: "Oh, I forgot. You're using Windows. They only play back on Palm OS, Linux, Mac OS, and fourth-generation cell phones. Bummer for you."

THE TWO TYPES OF STANDARDS

As illustrated in previous chapters, *standards* are agreements between large numbers of people or companies about how specific technology should be implemented. A major goal of standards is *interoperability,* by which products are developed independently by different companies to work together. When a specific implementation of a technology (in the form of hardware or software) works according to a well-specified standard, it is said to be *compliant* to the standard. DVDs are examples of standard media; they play back in any compliant DVD player.

Sometimes a standard has to be added to or improved. When these additions are done in such a way that a product built on the improved standard can continue to work with products based on the earlier standard, the standard and new products are said to be *backward-compatible*. Almost all DVD players (which use MPEG-2 video) also play VCDs (Video CDs), which use MPEG-1 video and are popular in Asia because they were designed to be backward-compatible.

Standards come about in two ways: formally or informally. With formal methods, groups of people appoint themselves (or are appointed by other bodies that have appointed themselves, or perhaps by governments) as the *standard bearers*. These groups of people, by committee or royal decree, with careful deliberation or not, declare that technology is implemented or used in a specific way in their area of authority. Examples of this are the metric system, television, unleaded gasoline, wall power outlets, and fax machines. Each of these technologies are deliberated and standardized. And for some of these, there can be formal legal or other penalties for using a different system.

Proprietary Versus Standard

You will often see the term *standard* used in contrast with the word *proprietary*. In these sorts of discussions, "standard" is often held up to be a nobler, more righteous approach to technology, while "proprietary" has the connotation of being a capricious and even off-the-cuff technology, beholden to one large, evil corporation.

Proprietary basically just means "owned," as in owned by one company, but there are thousands upon thousands of so-called "proprietary" standards that are high quality, fairly priced, have not changed in years, and have enabled the growth of industries. Similarly, there are many examples of standards organizations being formed, talking a lot, and accomplishing next to nothing, while single ividuals or groups picked up the ball, ran with it, and created technology that changed the industry or the world.

The political overtones of these terms, and the terms themselves, should be ignored and video tools should be judged on their technical and economic merits. If a "proprietary" video codec is seeking the blessing of several standards organizations, outperforms the "standard" codec, and is cheaper by a significant margin to license, which one would you choose?

Informal standards come about either through market dominance of one implementation of a new technology or because the industry simply goes with the first implementation that comes along. Examples of these are FM radio, gasoline-powered engines, VHS VCRs, Intel-based microprocessors, and the Windows desktop operating system. Each of these technologies defeated its competitors in one way or another and achieved *de facto* (Latin for "in fact") standard status. Even though no formal authority has said that consumers have to use one of these technologies, not going with the standard choice is rarely a workable option. In addition, not acknowledging and supporting these de facto standards prevents interoperability.

Despite any arguments made against them, standards are powerful and useful. Even if the process of getting thousands of people around the world to agree on them is painful and slow, the results tend to be better than the alternatives—a world where a few companies decide what constitutes the state of the art—or even worse, one where technology is never broadly used. Indeed, the entire world of high technology is based on the promise to users that the products you buy today will not be obsolete in two months time, that new innovations will provide backwards compatibility, and that products from different vendors will interoperate at some level. A world without standards is a world without technology customers.

Strategic Standards

In addition to the large, deliberative standards bodies, small groups of companies often form new standards committees to cooperate in specific areas. In general, when the groups are not focused on building technical standards but rather trying to specify industry interaction, a lot of noise can be made about plans and agreements that fall apart or are later abandoned. For instance, several high-profile groups have attempted to standardize the "one and true digital rights management framework," but none have succeeded as of yet.

Where MPEG has ventured into the DRM realm, for instance, MPEG–21 (to standardize digital rights description languages), it has focused on creating thorough and well-thought out *technical* solutions to the well-known requirements of DRM systems. This is in contrast to trying to "strike a deal" first and figure out the technology later.

THE BROWSER WARS

For a case study in the problems with mixing industry standards and de facto standards, we can look at the browser wars of the 1990s.

In 1992, the first web page was put up using the earliest version of HTML. The first browsers were created by academic institutions, such as the European nuclear research center (CERN) where web inventor Tim Berners-Lee worked, and the National Center for Supercomputing Applications (NCSA) at the University of Illinois at Champaign-Urbana where Marc Andreessen worked. Browsers soon became a commercial enterprise, and Andreessen helped form Netscape Communications in early 1994.

A standards body called the W3C (World Wide Web Consortium) was formed in late 1994 to foster web standards and worked hard to standardize HTML throughout the 1990s. Because HTML was a published standard, any web browser could support and correctly display the latest version of HTML, and many web browsers were developed. However, two competing browsers led the pack: Microsoft Internet Explorer (IE) and Netscape Navigator.

Netscape and Microsoft began to "freestyle" with the standard, instead of waiting for the arguably slow-moving and pedantic standards body to add more features that web designers and developers wanted. Netscape addressed the needs of these web authors by creating extensions to HTML that enabled users to center text and wrap text around pictures. Unfortunately, Microsoft *also* added similar features to its own dialect of HTML, and thus the divergence began.

Netscape and Microsoft continued to pursue different ways of accomplishing the same effect. Eventually, so many sites used both kinds of tags that the two competitors had to add each others' proprietary tags and support both tags. In practice, developers had to maintain sites according to three similar but divergent languages: HTML, Netscape HTML, and IE HTML. Smaller browser makers couldn't keep up. Often the competing browsers would support tags of the same name, but interpret and display them differently. It became extremely difficult to create sites that presented the same design to users of both programs, and born was the concept of, "Best when viewed with Browser X."

Netscape had created a way to write plug-ins for displaying a variety of multimedia content (such as Shockwave, Flash, and QuickTime, as well as myriad of long-forgotten technologies) within the browser. When Microsoft joined the browser fray, it supported Netscape plug-ins, but also developed its own architecture, ActiveX controls, for running third-party applications in a browser.

The W3C continued to standardize throughout the fight, but always in an after-the-fact manner. Eventually they managed to get the standard somewhat under control. But by the end of the decade, Microsoft was the clear winner of the browser wars. IE had become the de facto standard browser, and thus Microsoft's version of HTML became the de facto version of the language, although that version now included much syntax developed by Netscape and the W3C. Even IE's misinterpretations of Netscape-style tags became frozen in this large de facto standard.

And of course, HTML was just one of several web standards. The browser wars were fought over plug-in architectures (Netscape plug-ins versus ActiveX controls), scripting languages (Netscape's JavaScript versus Microsoft's Jscript), and full-blown client-side applications (Sun's Java versus ActiveX client-side applications and Microsoft's "Java" variant).

By 2000, users finally had a stable combination of formal and de facto standards. The standard included IE, Netscape plug-ins, JavaScript, and Java or Microsoft ActiveX controls. W3C had developed many other standards not listed here, but the fundamental building blocks of creating a web experience were pretty stable for a few years.

Around 2001, with IE now the standard browser, Microsoft made several major changes that broke countless websites. One of them was disabling Java. This broke any websites that used IE as the target browser and depended on Java as the client-side application system. This was followed by another change: removing support for Netscape plug-ins in IE. Overnight, hundreds of plug-ins were orphaned, without support by the standard web browser. Notably, the QuickTime plug-in (which allowed QuickTime video to be embedded in a web page) was broken for everyone with the newest update of IE. Apple, as well as the authors of every other Netscape-style web browser plug-in, had to quickly write a new plug-in for IE, and any web pages that used the old plug-in no longer worked. And as a result, all audio, video, and other multimedia content around the world created for these orphaned plugins was now unusable by the majority of Windows machines.

The moral of this story is that ever-shifting technologies can limit the longevity of multimedia published on the Internet, and de facto standards created and maintained by a single company cannot be counted on to preserve backwards compatibility. The story also shows the weakness of standards bodies when there is a single dominant player. After the demise of Netscape, when Microsoft chose not to support part of the standard in IE, that part of the standard effectively ceased to exist. When Microsoft added a new feature, because of the company's dominance in both browsers and operating systems, its eventual rubber stamp addition to the W3C standards was only a matter of time.

STANDARDS ORGANIZATIONS RELEVANT TO INTERNET VIDEO

There are actually many different standards groups and organizations relevant to Internet video, almost too many to count. Many of the standards organizations overlap heavily in the areas they standardize. Often, when this happens, they either work together on a joint standard, or they simply "bless" the standard created by another organization after they ensure it complies with their own standards qualifications. Some large standards organizations (such as MPEG) are just subgroups of other even larger organizations. Some standards organizations do not create or standardize new technologies; rather, they pick and choose relevant technologies from a variety of other technical groups, and declare that unique combination of elements a standard.

This section introduces you to the standards groups you are most likely to encounter in Internet video.

GENERAL PURPOSE STANDARDS ORGANIZATIONS

Several standards organizations are broad in scope and have been around for almost a century:

- *ISO*, the International Organization for Standardization, is the largest international body. ISO creates standards of everything from units of measurement to country codes to freight container dimensions.
- *IEC*, the International Electrotechnical Commission, is another large international standards body specifically for electronics-related standards, which overlaps and cooperates with ISO. ISO and IEC are independent of governments, but governments adopt many of their standards.
- *ITU,* the International Telecommunication Union, is part of the United Nations and forms worldwide telecommunication (ITU-T) and radio communication (ITU-R) standards. The H.xxx standards, such as the H.263 video codec, are ITU-T standards.

ISO and IEC often work together with joint committees on standards. They have formed a special Joint Technical Committee that works on standards related to information technology. Because of the tremendous overlap of information technology and telecom standards efforts, this joint technical committee in turn works with the ITU on certain standards. Most countries have their own national standards organizations that ratify ISO, IEC, ITU and other international standards in that specific country. In the United States, *ANSI* (American National Standards Organization) acts in this capacity. ANSI's *BSR* (Board of Standards Review) reviews and approves standards for ANSI. Thus, when ANSI publishes an ISO standard, it's labeled BSR/ISO/IEC followed by the ISO/IEC document number.

INTERNET STANDARDS ORGANIZATIONS

IETF, the Internet Engineering Task Force, has formalized Internet communication protocols since 1986. The IETF documents many of the Internet standards, such as TCP, UDP, RTSP, RTP, and more through the creation of *RFCs* (Requests for Comments). W3C, the World Wide Web Consortium, standardizes many of the protocols and technologies for delivering web pages, such as HTML and XML.

VIDEO STANDARDS ORGANIZATIONS: **MPEG**

One of the most important technical standards organization for Internet video is MPEG. The Moving Picture Experts Group, *MPEG*, was formed in the late 1980s as a working grooup of ISO to develop international digital video standards, well before the consumer Internet and the Web emerged, and it has been enormously successful with MPEG-1 and MPEG-2. Just about every second of video on television, cable, or satellite TV has been converted into MPEG-2 video at some point in the process of getting to the screen. While MPEG-1 was popular in early CD-based multimedia, such as CD-interactive, it is best known for the revolutionary MP3 audio codec. Not to be confused with MP3, MPEG-3 development was abandoned because MPEG-2 worked better than expected for HDTV and achieved the goals of MPEG-3.

The MPEG-4 group started in 1993 as a group focused on low bit rate (less than 1000 kilobits per second) coding of audio and video. At this time, no consumer Internet existed, and television was the only broadly deployed consumer video device. Anticipating a large number of low bit-rate applications, as well as the evolution of television to even higher levels of resolution and interactivity, MPEG-4 developed into a comprehensive standard for all bit rates of video, and as the state-of-the-art successor to MPEG-2.

MPEG as a standards organization is focused on the best technology and has left advocacy and licensing up to other organizations.

- The Moving Picture Experts Group (MPEG) is part of ISO and coordinates the development of multimedia technology standards. It produces many different standards, such as MPEG-1, MPEG-2, MPEG-4, MPEG-7, and MPEG-21. Industry forum (M4IF) is an advocacy and marketing organization that works to further the adoption of the latest MPEG standards.

- MPEG LA, VIA Licensing Corporation, and various other organizations handle the payment and licensing of MPEG technologies. These groups have no relationship to MPEG or ISO; they deal directly with the companies that hold patents to MPEG technology and the customers that license these technologies.

The Growth of Internet Video

Internet video—and network-delivered video in general—has already taken far longer to "take off" than most experts and forecasters had predicted. This has been blamed on a number of issues, including:

- The dot-com crash
- The slow adoption of broadband
- The lack of an effective way to bill for content on the Internet

Although "bad economy" is a tired but effective excuse for the lack of video deployment, the third reason (difficulty in billing for content) actually opens the door to a solution for the problem.

Standardizing the e-commerce environment for video can make it easier to generate profits from online media. This, in turn, stimulates capitalists to invest in online video as a business, not as a "cool" technology, and Internet video deployment increases exponentially as predicted.

MORE VIDEO STANDARDS ORGANIZATIONS

Because MPEG-4 has the potential to enable broad interoperability of video between many different consumer electronic devices, MPEG-4 is used as the basis of other industry standards as well:

- The Internet Streaming Media Alliance (ISMA) is one group that has specified the use of specific parts of the MPEG-4 standard over IP networks (the Internet), and is continuing to work on DRM specifications as well. Rather than creating the technology, ISMA is specifying the use of existing technology standards so that many different vendors' technology products can interoperate. In fact, many standards organizations simply bless another existing standard, after putting it through their own criteria for what a "good" standard is.

- The Third Generation Partnership Project (3GPP) was formed in 1998 to standardize what is considered to be the third generation of cellular communication technology. The 3G wireless networks are bringing potentially hundreds of millions of new computing devices onto the Internet, and the 3GPP standardizes how they will send and receive multimedia messages using existing video technologies, such as H.263 and MPEG-4.

- The Society of Motion Picture and Television Engineers (SMPTE) is a standards group in the field of motion imaging that has been around since the early 1900s. They have created a vast number of standards for the television and motion picture industry, as well as disseminating related ANSI standards in the USA. Many of the tape and film formats listed in Chapter 1 of this book were standardized by SMPTE. Naturally, most of the technologies related to the delivery of digital video also fall within the scope of their standardization efforts, including the standardization of video codecs.

- The DVD forum is the standards group responsible for establishing and disseminating the standards relating to Digital Versatile Disks (DVDs). While the original DVD standards specified the use of MPEG-2 to deliver standard resolution television on DVDs, the DVD Forum is also responsible for establishing which newer codecs will be used to distribute high-definition television on DVDs. In this area, any video standards the DVD Forum adopts for future DVDs will undoubtedly influence Internet video standards as well.

CREATING MPEG STANDARDS

The MPEG process works in ways the Web standardization process never did, in large part because a number of equally powerful companies all have a vested interest in the creation and adoption of standard methodologies. MPEG consists of a number of working groups, each of which focuses on a specific technology, such as audio, video, and 3D. MPEG sets a large number of goals and requirements for each version of the standard. During a several-year period, MPEG cast a net far and wide for companies that can contribute useful technology. The most advanced, state-of-the art techniques are included for consideration in the standard. Solutions are selected or newly developed if no existing technology fully addresses the requirements. Eventually they arrive on a first version of the standard. After this is accomplished, they evaluate new technologies and continue to solve emerging problems—*without invalidating or changing the original standard*—as shown in Figure 8-1.

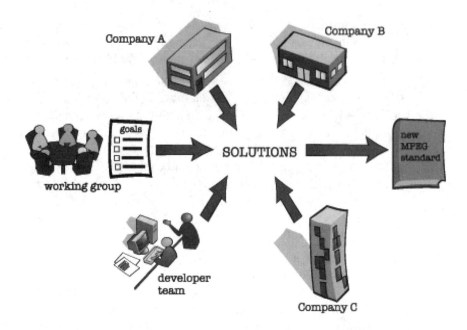

Figure 8-1 *With the efforts of many groups working in coordination, technology standards are achieved.*

MPEG's Dream Team

The members of MPEG include thousands of engineers, scientists, and academic researchers around the world. Hundreds of potentially competitive companies work together with confidence that they are better served by contributing technology to an agreed-upon standard than by striking out alone with their own proprietary technology. And MPEG establishes tight, achievable targets, and routinely meets them, which establishes confidence so that product ship dates and financial plans can be based on it.

MPEG does not own the technology; each contributing company is paid a proportion of license fees when MPEG is used. This *license pool* of technologies is managed by another group formed for the specific purpose of offering licenses to MPEG standard technology at "fair and reasonable terms and nondiscriminatory conditions." This allows any company access to the standards, and works further to even the playing field for smaller companies.

FUTURE PROOFING

When the new standard is agreed upon, the technologies that comprise it are state of the art; however, this does not make a several-years-old MPEG standard out of date. MPEG addresses *future proofing* of technology (making it equipped to handle future problems) in several ways. One way is by standardizing only the player, not the encoder. This is a key point: MPEG specifies only what a valid MPEG audio/video bitstream (data stream) is—how many frames, what bit rate, size, and computational complexity. The art of how to produce the best MPEG bitstream is left to the competing companies.

Future Proofing Without the Mess

If you ask any video aficionado, he will agree that early DVD movies from the mid 1990s are not as high quality as the encodings of today. This is because the art of encoding (and the amount of computer power that can go into encoding) has increased many times since then. Yet the same DVD players made in the mid-1990s will play back a new DVD mastered this year—with all the improved quality. As engineers became more and more familiar with the ins and outs of an MPEG-2 decoder, they learned how to squeeze more quality out of the techniques that MPEG-2 uses to reproduce video. They found ways to make the motion smoother, to create streams that were less taxing on the DVD's processor, and to pack more hours of video on the disk in the same space.

As another example, encoding broadcast-quality video into MPEG-2 in the mid-1990s required 6Mbps or more. The same quality is now achievable in one-third the bandwidth—2Mbps. Again the improvement was achieved, with no change to the playback device. It is not necessary to constantly change all the playback devices in order to improve the quality of video.

MPEG also future-proofs the standard by developing new parts and enhancements to existing parts. But all these additions are carefully designed to expand upon but not replace earlier portions. New, compliant products, in general, support newer parts of the standard while preserving compatibility with all earlier versions using the same techniques.

> **Note** MPEG-4 is a vast and imposing body of technology and will influence the evolution of Internet video for years to come. A standard this large, however, can be hard to wrap one's head around. Appendix B of this book carefully illustrates the entire current MPEG-4 standard and can serve as a helpful reference for understanding other MPEG-4 literature.

SOME FINAL NOTES

Despite the many glowing compliments paid to MPEG in this chapter, MPEG is clearly not the final word in video standards, off or on the Internet. Some of the clearly dominant players in the Internet media space are Microsoft, Real Networks, Macromedia, and Apple. All of these companies work with or utilize MPEG video in some capacity; however, each contributes its own de facto standards to the array of solutions:

- In the corporate environment, Microsoft owns the desktop. Thus, their media player is the preinstalled "TV set" that can be counted on, making it a de facto standard media player for enterprise.

- Apple has used standard MPEG-4 audio technologies (AAC) in delivering music to iPods and their iTunes application. However, they use a proprietary DRM approach (FairPlay) that only they use. Each of the competitive music delivery systems uses its own DRM system as well. It is possible that no "standard" will emerge in this particular DRM situation because only a handful of very large well-funded companies can compete in the major label music distribution business.

- RealNetworks has focused in on two major areas: delivery and subscription services. Through wide use, their delivery technologies may eventually become a de facto standard for service or transport of video. Although RealServers can transport MPEG-4 as well as RealMedia, they have no preferences, and transport other proprietary media just as well. RTSP and RTP, as discussed, are Internet standards, but not MPEG standards. They are used by Microsoft, RealNetworks, and Apple to stream video.

- Macromedia's Flash has been the de facto "rich media" standard on the Internet for many years. All online animation for entertainment and advertising, excepting natural (filmed) video, has been the virtually exclusive domain of Flash. Now, Macromedia has teamed up with Sorenson and integrates a non-MPEG video codec in its dominant flash web plugin. Many companies now standardize on Flash for all their online video. The wide availability of their Flash MX player (which is now available on most handheld computers and an increasing number of mobile phones) ensures that Flash will continue to be a de facto standard for years to come.

- Microsoft has hedged its bets remarkably in the codec business; they hold patents to some of the MPEG-4 technology, so if it takes off, they get paid; however, they have been demonstrating a very competitive, non-MPEG codec called WM9. To compete with MPEG, they've not only priced it better, but they've submitted the standard to bodies such as SMPTE and the DVD Forum. Already, many DVD players can play Windows Media in addition to MPEG-1, MPEG-2, and MPEG-4 video. Thus, the heir apparent to the DVD video standard, MPEG-4, may very well share the throne with Windows Media.

- The standardization of Windows Media technologies by standards groups generally means that the format will not suddenly change, that the standard will be available on non-discriminatory licensing terms, in a similar manner to MPEG. Although only one vendor controls the price (Microsoft), they have tended to stay competitive and even undercut the pricing of MPEG licensing. This also makes Windows Media potentially available for broad license in competitive media players, such as QuickTime player and RealPlayer, as it is a standard.

- Many of the standards bodies look primarily at technological suitability and fair pricing. To the degree that any single vendor can satisfy these two requirements, their technology is a candidate for standardization. If that vendor offers superior technology at a fairer price, it has a chance at pricing other "standard" technologies out of the game.

Truthfully, there are many ways for standards to emerge. The dominant Internet video technology of tomorrow could be a hybrid of the previous standards, but it could turn out to be a new technology that no one has even heard of today.

A

A QUICK LIST OF PROBLEMS AND CONCISE SOLUTIONS

This appendix aims to give brief and to-the-point answers to the many questions that often arise when setting up Internet video. It is divided into two parts. The first part addresses questions related to setting up an Internet video system from the ground up. It presents a high-level overview of the steps involved with specific tasks. The second part addresses specific problems you might run into while running or operating your Internet video system.

In this appendix, we categorize the common areas of trouble and provide brief solutions for each. After a problem category is known, you can also consult the full chapter on the topic (compression, transport, storage, and so on) for a more complete understanding of the issue. For each question and answer, the chapters that are relevant to that topic are listed, and can be read for deeper understanding.

PART 1: SETTING UP INTERNET VIDEO

BASICS

HOW DO I GET THE CONTENT INTO THE COMPUTER IN THE FIRST PLACE?
CHAPTER 1

- Make sure to receive the content at the highest quality possible. Preferably, you should accept data in the highest quality *digital* format possible (not an analog format such as VHS) because the more random noise there is in the video, the harder it is to compress.
- Import the data into the computer using some sort of digital interface. If you do not have access to hardware that can read the tape format, use a video conversion agency that has the correct system. Ask them to give the data to you on hard disk or DVD (but as raw, uncompressed digital video, not compressed as MPEG).
- Older high-end analog equipment, such as BetaSP cameras and decks, are comparable to consumer DV in quality and can be used if available.
- If consumer analog is the only option, use an analog capture card or DV converter. Use an S-Video cable with four pins instead of the yellow RCA video cable.

DO I NEED AN AVID OR OTHER HIGH-END VIDEO EDITING SYSTEM, OR CAN I USE THE CONSUMER-GRADE SOFTWARE THAT CAME WITH MY COMPUTER OR CAMERA?
CHAPTER 1

- The video editing capabilities that were once available only in expensive high-end hardware workstations are now available in consumer-level software and hardware.
- For a moderate investment, mid-range software approaching pro-level features on personal computers is also available.
- Obviously, the results of any tool—entry-level or high end—depend on the experience and expertise of the operator.

HOW DO I CHOOSE THE BIT RATE FOR ENCODING MY CONTENT? CHAPTERS 2 AND 4

- Choose the minimum bit rate that effectively conveys the type of content you are encoding because the bandwidth cost is (usually) the largest constraint on your video delivery.

- For downloadable content or HTTP streamed content (sent from a web server), base the bit rate on how long viewers will wait to download the video. Given that broadband download speeds range from 1–10MB per minute (based on 384Kbps to 2Mbps connections), a 30MB video clip would take between 3 and 30 minutes. Estimate your average broadband audience bandwidth, and decide accordingly.

- For streamed content, you need to choose a bit rate that fits in the lowest downstream bit rate of your audience connection speeds, plus some headroom. For example:
  - 28.8–56Kbps modems: 20–30Kbps
  - 128–384Kbps low broadband: 100–250Kbps
  - 1.5–2Mbps broadband: 300–700Kbps

  If you want to target multiple classes of viewers, target multiple bit rates using the same considerations, but use the multi-bit rate features of the codecs.

- Balancing the audio and video bit rates is also necessary. For content where the audio is very important (such as music videos), set the audio bit rate greater than 32Kbps and make it stereo, then use what remains for video. For content where the video is more important, set the audio to a tolerable low level; use most of the bandwidth for video. If the audio is spoken without any music (sports, lectures, or other entertainment), you can even use a voice-only (non-music) codec for maximum bandwidth savings and sound fidelity.

- To deliver full-length movies in a downloadable format, use codecs over approximately 500Kbps to achieve what is sometimes called VHS quality or DVD quality. Actual DVD quality is extremely high; nonetheless, with newer codecs, bit rates between 500Kbps and 1Mbps can achieve high-resolution, high-quality results. Feature-length films encoded at these bit rates range between several hundred and several thousand megabytes—approximately the size of one or two CD-ROMs.

SHOULD I DE-INTERLACE MY VIDEO?
CHAPTERS 1 AND 2

- When importing media that was designed to play back on a television set, you must de-interlace it in some way after capturing. If the video was imported from a television source (or videotape of almost any kind), then it will have either 25 (Europe) or 30 (North America) interlaced frames per second. In fact, the video contains 50 to 60 *fields* of video, each field being half the horizontal lines of a full frame. Computer screens are rarely interlaced. Interlaced video blurs motion, flickers, and creates streaking effects when played back on a non-interlaced display, even though it looks fine on a television set.
- A variety of de-interlacing approaches exists, and are of varying quality. Some tools are built into image capture and editing programs. Some additional, more sophisticated de-interlacing filters are available as third-party plug-ins to these programs.

SHOULD I DO INVERSE-TELECINE ON MY VIDEO?
CHAPTERS 1 AND 2

- Use *inverse telecine* whenever you import source material that was originally 24fps film. Because the film had frames added to get it up to 30fps (a process called *telecine*), dropping it down to 24fps eliminates redundancy, lowers the frame rate necessary for encoding, makes it compress more effectively, and looks better.

HOW CAN I EXTRACT STILL FRAMES FROM MY MOVIE?
CHAPTERS 1 AND 2

- If you have the actual file (and aren't streaming it off the Internet), extracting a still frame should be as easy as opening the file in a video editing application that opens that format.
- Sometimes, in the case of Digital Rights Management (DRM) protected video or video in proprietary formats, the editing tools are either expensive or unavailable. In this case, a workaround is to expand the video player to the desired size, pause it, and use the screen capture features of the operating system. These usually create a high-resolution, uncompressed image file of the whole screen, which can then be cropped and worked with in still image editing programs.

HOW DO I TRANSLATE VIDEO BETWEEN FORMAT X AND FORMAT Y?
CHAPTER 2

- If the video in Format X is already highly compressed, you are better served getting the original source (at a higher resolution and frame rate), and compressing it directly into Format Y from the high-resolution version.

- If you have a flexible, multi-format encoding program, simply use the program to select the source video in Format X and the destination format as Y.

- If you have only the tools for each of the two formats and the video in Format X is high enough quality already (or a higher resolution version is unavailable), then use the tools for working with Format X to export it into a raw (uncompressed), high-resolution format. Then use tools for compressing into Format Y and use the uncompressed version as a source.

- If you are translating video within the same family of codecs (for example, MPEG-2 to MPEG-4), it is possible that the transcoder exists. If available, use that.

- If you have a large number of such conversions to make, you have two options. Most proprietary codec vendors provide tools to convert to their format, in large batches. For more general conversions between competing file formats where no such tool exists, there are a number of third-party tools that can be programmed to convert large batches of media from one format to another.

WHERE CAN I FIND OUT WHAT APPLICATIONS INPUT AND OUTPUT THE FORMATS I WANT?
CHAPTERS 2 AND 4

- This requires a bit of web sleuthing. The key to answering these types of questions is determined not only by the vendor, but by what generation or version number of its codecs and streaming media system the format is a part of. First, determine which vendor makes the format you want to use. Then determine through that vendor's support site which version of its software worked with or produced that format.

- Third-party conversion tool vendors usually give comprehensive lists of the different formats they support. This list usually consists of only the latest version of the proprietary vendor codecs that the vendor doesn't fully support.

- Some vendors stop supporting earlier versions of their media, or they intentionally make them incompatible. Just because a program claims that it works with Media X, it does not mean that it still works with Media X. You need to determine which version of Media X it supports.

WILL I REDUCE THE QUALITY OF THE VIDEO BY TRANSLATING IT FROM FORMAT X TO FORMAT Y? CHAPTER 2

There are two ways to interpret this question:

- If the content is compressed in Format X and then translated into Format Y without using the original source, the content will almost always be worse (similar to making a copy of a copy of a VHS tape).

- If the content is compressed in Format X and then the *original* is re-compressed into a different format (Y) at the same bit rate, then the question "Will it be worse?" depends on whether the codecs are more efficient at that bit rate.

  A good rule of thumb is that the newer codec will almost always be better at the same bit rate. This does *not* mean that you should always use the latest codec; it simply means that, in general, the latest codec tends to be the best because the increasing speed of computers permits more advanced compression techniques.

CAN I USE OPEN-SOURCE TOOLS TO WORK WITH VIDEO? ALL CHAPTERS

- There are a wide variety of video editing, capture, and conversion tools available on open source platforms, especially Linux. In fact, open-source tools usually have far more features than consumer software (rivaling some of the professional tools), and only after several years do the consumer software packages catch up with professional and open-source tools.

- Open-source tools have led the way in such areas as MPEG-4 encoding, format conversion, DVD video extraction, conversion of DVDs to video CDs, compression of full-length movies to MPEG formats, advanced MPEG-2 format conversion, audio conversion, digital video splicing, and video capture, to name a few.

- A software developer who becomes interested in video projects can literally "take matters into his own hands," and develop software tools to achieve his purposes if none exist. When a developer makes this tool available for others, the software grows in popularity and functionality.

SCENARIOS

HOW DO I SERVE VIDEO FROM A WEB SERVER?
CHAPTER 4

1. Upload the video to the web server, just like any other file, such as an HTML, JPEG, or GIF file.
2. Insert the URL of the uploaded link into a web page, or email it to recipient.
3. For better integration, learn specific HTML tags for linking to that kind of media and invoking the correct player that is provided on the help site of the video format you choose.

HOW DO I STREAM VIDEO FROM A WEB PAGE?
CHAPTERS 3 AND 4

1. If you operate the server from which you want to stream, install streaming media server software on that server.
2. If you do not operate your own server and your web hosting provider does not provide streaming, find a streaming media hosting provider. You will not have to switch your web-hosting provider.
3. Upload your content to the streaming hosting provider.
4. Get the URLs of the hosted streams from the hosting provider.
5. Present the URLs on your website, using the correct HTML for linking to that type of media from a web page. (This information is easily located on the support or frequently asked questions area of the streaming media vendor's website. For more data on index files and web embedding, see Chapter 3, "Video Storage File Formats.")

HOW DO I MAKE A DOWNLOADABLE MOVIE TRAILER?
CHAPTERS 1–6

1. Capture the content into the computer at a high resolution.

2. Compress the content in its native aspect ratio using any of the tools available, emphasizing good audio and aiming for smooth, high-resolution video.

3. Decide how long viewers can wait for the movie to download. Given that broadband download speeds range from 1–10MB per minute (based on 384Kbps–2Mbps connections), a 30MB trailer would take between 3 and 30 minutes. Estimate your average broadband audience bandwidth and decide accordingly.

4. Store the content in a downloadable file format—for example, only a single bit rate in the file, not for streaming.

5. Host the file on a high-bandwidth web server, hosting service, or Content Delivery Network (CDN).

HOW DO I CREATE A VIDEO WEBLOG?
CHAPTER 4

- Establish what "blogging" software you are going to use. A variety of sites exist that will host your blog for you, or you can install and run blogging software on your own server.

- Capture video clips using the video capture system you have. You can use a webcam and a microphone plugged into your computer, or you can record your source video with a DV camera and import it in to your computer.

- Edit the video clips down to the minimum length possible.

- Decide at what quality you want to encode the blogs. If the content is short-form but needs to be of very high visual quality, approach it as you would when creating a downloadable movie trailer, and estimate the quality, length, and tolerable wait for your audience. Offer the clips as progressive download (HTTP streamed) video in the 500+Kbps range.

- If the visual quality is not the main aspect of the clips, but the motion and the audio are the emphasis, and you want people to watch the clips instantly without waiting for a download, encode the clips in a lower format, such as 150Kbps–300Kbps, and host them on a streaming server.

- On the main blog page that lists all your blogs in order, provide links to the media player you have for content delivery. Now, to create a video blog, follow these steps:

    1. Capture the content.
    2. Edit the content to the correct length.
    3. Compress the content to the correct size and media format.
    4. Upload it to the media server or web server, noting the URL in the process.
    5. Edit the text portion of the blog as normal.
    6. Insert <object> and <embed> tags to embed the video in the appropriate place in the blog itself. (The correct tags vary and are described on the help site of the corresponding media player.)

HOW DO I SERVE MY CONTENT IN MULTIPLE FORMATS?
CHAPTER 2

- Encode your content in each bit rate needed in each format. For example, if you have three bit rates (40K, 100K, 500K) and three formats (Windows Media, QuickTime, Real), then you would encode nine versions of the video. The process for encoding the video as well as creating the web pages that link to this video can be automated with scriptable content preparation and encoding tools.
- Use a just-in-time encoding system and create only one high-resolution version of all the content. These hardware-based systems automatically encode the content to the correct bit rate and format on demand.

HOW DO I WEBCAST A LIVE EVENT?
CHAPTERS 1, 4, AND 6

- Provide (ahead of time) broadband connectivity to the locale of the event. Ensure that the uplink/upload speed of the broadband is enough to carry the resolution of video desired. In general, a T-1 (1,544Kbps) is sufficient for a high-resolution stream. If the successful broadcast is financially critical, provide a backup broadcasting solution as well (such as traditional video satellite link to another location from where it can be webcast redundantly). Try to estimate how many viewers will see the webcast. A hugely popular program can be a victim of its own success without sufficient bandwidth.

- Use a streaming service provider with experience in live events and sufficient bandwidth to handle the expected load.

- Capture and encode the live stream in real time at the site of the event using the highest CPU speed you can afford, along with the appropriate encoding software.

- Webcast at the lowest resolution that successfully conveys the event. If multiple bit rates are supported, realize that most people try to get the highest bit rate.

- Use multiple redundant encoding machines, each with its own capture card if possible.

- Do not assume you can predict the audience size unless you have actually completed such events in the past. At least consult with someone who has accomplished a similar webcast.

- If any special client software needs to be distributed, or if a new version of the media player is used, have viewers register for the event beforehand. In this registration, have them view a test stream as a pre-flight check. This spreads bandwidth use over the times *before* the event is in place and increases the number of viewers who will view it successfully.

HOW DO I PUT UP A RADIO STATION ON THE INTERNET? CHAPTER 6

- Ensure that the legal rights to the content are understood and acquired, and that the structure of the organization (profit and nonprofit, for example) is appropriate to the type of use.

- For online radio, MP3 streaming is preferred over proprietary streaming formats.

- If a terrestrial radio station re-broadcasts a program on the web, then use an encoder that live-encodes it into the appropriate streaming format.

- If a computer-generated playlist is the source, simply encode all songs on the playlist into the appropriate format and bit rate to be streamed. Use software to broadcast the playlist as if it were a live broadcast.

- Beam the encoded stream to your own high-bandwidth server that runs stream reflection software.

- Alternatively, beam the stream to a radio streaming service. Several providers focus exclusively on radio station aggregation and rebroadcast.

HOW DO I PUT UP A 24/7 INTERNET TV STATION?
CHAPTERS 1, 4, AND 6

- Determine the average watching time per viewer, and the average number of simultaneous viewers. Use this information to determine the total bandwidth needed. Use peak traffic periods to determine the largest instantaneous bandwidth needed.

- Choose a format(s) in which to encode the content. Do not be captive to what the viewer has installed. If the content is worth watching, the viewer will download another codec or player.

- Find the codec that provides a version of the intended content at the lowest possible bit rate that can be comfortably viewed.

- Adjust the balance of audio and video so that the audio is of good quality. Good quality audio can make low bit rate video more effective.

- If the content is existing television programming being repurposed for online, acquire the video signal at the highest quality possible. Ideally, get the digital signal or broadcast-quality signal directly from the studio and encode it for Internet there. Encode from S-video output of a receiver unit as a last resort.

- Use a real-time hardware encoder or a high-speed software encoder to create the stream.

- Run multiple redundant encoders at different sites, depending on the reliability needed.

- If the content is pre-recorded content that is assembled into a playlist, spend as much time encoding to get the smallest but highest quality signal.

- Beam all encoded streams to a reflector—either a streaming service provider, CDN, or your own high-bandwidth and high-reliability Internet server running media server software.

HOW DO I PUT A HUGE LIBRARY OF CONTENT ONLINE?
CHAPTERS 1–2 AND 7–8

- Ensure that the source content is in a high-quality, uncompressed, or lightly compressed digital video format.

- Establish how strict content control must be: Can viewers download a copy of the content on their hard drive, or should the content be streamed only? Must they pay for the content before they view it?

- Choose a media delivery system based on the strictest content control needed. If advanced DRM is needed, choose a media format with tightly integrated DRM, or for which a comprehensive DRM solution is available.

- If tight content control is not a concern, then the video content can be made available through standard web application development methods; web serving suffices.

- If the goal is to encode the content only once, choose a less proprietary media format of sufficient quality that can be used for a long time.

- Use an automated encoding system that works continually on the content library and compresses it in large batches. Hardware-based encoding systems generally provide faster encoding. These systems are usually provided by third parties.

SHOULD I STANDARDIZE ON MPEG-1, MPEG-2, OR MPEG-4 AS A NEUTRAL HIGH-RESOLUTION STORAGE FORMAT?
CHAPTERS 2 AND 8

- For a high-resolution storage format, MPEG-2 or MPEG-4 is the best choice. The goal is to have a broadcast-quality format, and MPEG-1 is considered VHS quality—approximately the quality of VHS videotapes.

- Almost all video viewed on television—via terrestrial broadcast, satellite, or cable—is encoded in high-resolution MPEG-2. If the video is broadcast or published to DVD, the usual approach is to create archival and master recordings in a higher-resolution MPEG-2 (called *Studio Profile*) from the start, and then reduce it to lower bit rate MPEG-2 for DVD or broadcast.

- MPEG-4 is the emerging successor to MPEG-2 and has a more efficient compressor, resulting in smaller file sizes at the same quality. If the video is primarily going to be used in computer streaming scenarios, MPEG-4 is the best choice. In time, MPEG-4 broadcast support will be as prevalent as

MPEG-2, and some DVD players already support MPEG-4 video on CD and DVD media.

- As an archival format (meaning, a format from which all lower resolution formats are made), a non-MPEG codec, such as DV or motion JPEG, might be better. These codecs compress lightly and are more readily edited. MPEG codecs (and proprietary delivery codecs) are more appropriate when the editing has been completed and the video is in its final form for delivery.

HOW DO I IMPLEMENT VIEWER-DEFINED PLAYLISTS?
CHAPTERS 4 AND 6

- Ensure that licensing terms for the content are understood because they often become more expensive when interactive access to content is allowed (such as viewer-defined radio).

- Create a web-based application that allows viewers to select the names of the content they listen to or view online. This involves server-side development and storage of viewer preferences.

- Have the web application create an index file (see Chapter 3), which contains the sequence of media URLs that the viewer has selected.

- If the media is served from a web server or a media server, client-side playlists can be used. The viewer can pause, skip songs, and more. The web application should serve the index file directly to the client media player.

- If tighter control over viewer listening is desired, use server-side playlists. The web application should serve the index file to the media server, creating a new channel for that viewer, and then direct the viewer's media player to the URL of that channel.

HOW DO I INSERT BANNER ADVERTISING IN MY STREAMS?
CHAPTERS 4 AND 6-7

- Many media players have a documented way of inserting banner advertisements into them.

- The simplest approach is to contact an online advertising provider. This type of provider has the ad inventory and tracking systems, and provides a turn-key system for inserting banner ads into the media player.

- Another approach is to install ad banner software (also called script) that runs on the web server. Then, insert the ad inventory on the web server.
- Using player-specific options, configure the media player to retrieve ads from the ad banner service or web site when it is connected to streams from that site.

HOW DO I MAKE A CUSTOM MEDIA PLAYER THAT SHOWS MY BRAND? CHAPTER 3

- Several of the major media players have several ways to put a custom skin around their player. Most can be implemented without any programming.
- Alternatively, a web-based or Flash-based client viewer interface can trigger playback using a media player that embeds in the browser page.
- A third option is to have software developers write downloadable software that embeds an existing media player within it. Viewers would download your application to view the content. The application can be as feature-rich as desired, and you can even create a "gated community" in which users can interact. Simple examples include Apple's iTunes or the original Napster app. AOL is a good example of this approach—their entire application is a media-delivery system.

HOW DO I INSERT INTERSTITIAL (IN-BETWEEN) VIDEO ADS IN MY STREAM? CHAPTERS 4 AND 6–7

- A simple option is to split up the content manually, put commercials where appropriate, and then recombine into one stream before compressing.
- Another approach is to split content at commercial boundaries and then use server-side playlists to combine the video.
- A more sophisticated approach is to get a syndication system that can actually vary the placement of the inserted ads depending on viewer-specific information, such as locale or demographic data about the viewer.

HOW DO I INSERT DIFFERENT ADS DEPENDING ON VIEWER REGION, OR CREATE TARGETED ADS DEPENDING ON THE TYPE OF VIEWER? CHAPTERS 4 AND 7

- The simplest method of targeting advertising is to provide media only to people who have registered and filled out a demographic survey. Then, through cookies or customized session keys, the web application can provide them with customized playlists and advertising.

- Some media players have a unique identifier enabled. Viewers generally try to disable these because they don't want to be tracked, but these can be used in conjunction with the aforementioned registration features to map a media browser to the demographics of the viewer.

- Another approach that does not require interviewing the viewer is to use a *locality service,* which maps IP addresses to physical locations with reasonable accuracy. (Online music services use these to restrict purchases to specific areas.) This type of service is available from CDNs as well as independent vendors.

HOW DO I DISTRIBUTE CONTENT IN A FORMAT THAT CAN'T BE VIEWED WITHOUT PAYING? CHAPTER 7

- Use a "lock box" DRM wrapper solution. Several vendors make systems that wrap media along with a player and an online e-commerce system. If a viewer copies content to another viewer via email, disk, or file-sharing, the recipient's computer is authorized and he is prompted to pay.

- Stream the content in a pay-per-view situation using DRM technology. Streaming ensures that it will not be stored on the viewer's hard drive, and DRM technologies make sure that viewers have paid for content and acquired a license before they are permitted to watch it.

HOW DO I REDUCE THE COST OF STREAMING? CHAPTERS 2 AND 4–6

- Lower the bit rate of the media (use a more efficient codec, or send a lower quality or frame rate).

- Standardize on only one media bit rate.

- Standardize on only one media format.

- Share the cost of a bandwidth with another entity. For example, you can share the cost of a large bandwidth pipe and use the bandwidth at different times.

- Avoid CDNs and other value-added services. Try to make the system work with plain-vanilla bandwidth providers.

- Use web servers instead of streaming servers, and benefit from web-priced bandwidth.

- Use low-cost bulk bandwidth providers with lower-quality bandwidth, and cover up for it with the pre-buffering features present in the big three media players.

- Within an enterprise, use multicast technologies (Chapter 5).

- Use mirror sites (and present a list of alternatives), and have viewers choose the closest server. Use mirror sites that provide cheap "buckets" of gigabytes transferred, and take them off the list when they are used up.

- Stream off-hours, using bandwidth from another country in a different time zone. Or, sublease bandwidth from a company with a T-3 or greater that does not use it at night. Negotiate favorable rates as a result. You can benefit from one-off live events.

- Write or license a simple download-scheduling program. Have the recipients of the video download the content off hours, or at a slow but predictable bit rate. Push out the content ahead of time and purchase bandwidth just large enough to handle the scheduled downloads. Viewers will need to install this application in addition to their media player.

- Allow others to host content for you in exchange for providing the content near their own ads, to attract people to their site, and so on. This option can completely eliminate bandwidth costs.

- License a peer-to-peer or similarly decentralized solution. Viewers who have downloaded or viewed the content will pass it on to others using their own bandwidth. You can thus lower bandwidth cost by more than 90 percent. However, this option requires viewers to install special software in addition to their media player.

- If you are a legitimate nonprofit organization, find providers with under-utilized bandwidth who can donate it and recoup tax benefits.

- Use laws providing for such things as public access TV to provide public access broadcast bandwidth over the Internet, or access to local cable modem bandwidth.

HOW DO I INCREASE THE SCALABILITY OF MY STREAMING SYSTEM? CHAPTERS 4 AND 6

- Lower the bit rate of the media.
- Use time-shifting, download scheduling, or peer-to-peer download technologies that can provide off-hours delivery.
- Make the system web-based instead of streaming-based, and use traditional web scaling techniques that are more developed and well known.
- Design the system so that people will not try to download the content at the same time; stagger e-mail announcements of content, and don't make content available directly on the website, but through email links only.
- Use multicast wherever possible in an enterprise.
- If multiple people within enterprises go for the same content, use caching technologies on the "edge" (near the Internet connection and the firewall) of the corporate network.

HOW DO I TARGET HANDHELD PLAYERS, MOBILE PHONES, AND PDAS? CHAPTERS 2, 4, 6, AND 8

- Cell phones have not only taken over computers in terms of deployment, but they are becoming general-purpose computers themselves. Many people see the future of streaming media in handhelds. Handhelds usually have small screens and choppy, if fast, bandwidth. A reasonable lowest common denominator resolution for handhelds is around 160×100. PDAs and picture phones can view 320×200 resolution, but even then you can't depend on the CPU of these cell phones to speedily decode video of that size unless they are designed for it.
- The mobile phone industry has worked to adopt video standards for mobile phone video compatibility. *The Third Generation Partnership Project,* or 3GPP, has standardized a 3GP mobile phone video file specification, incorporating low-bit rate MPEG-4. For more information, check http://www.3gpp.org.
- MPEG-4 had low bit rate video delivery as one of its primary goals, and it's no surprise that it is the dominant emerging standard for mobile and handheld video. Sony's Clíe line of Palm-based PDAs all support and even record MPEG-4 video. The usual suspects in Internet video are also pursuing non MPEG-based handheld video approaches; PDAs that run a Microsoft operating system naturally support Windows Media technologies. At this writing, low-bit rate MPEG-4 (Simple Profile) and the 3GP standards appear to be your best bet.

PART 2: TROUBLESHOOTING INTERNET VIDEO

CONTENT PREPARATION AND CAPTURE ISSUES

I DON'T KNOW HOW TO IMPORT MY VIDEO. IT'S BEEN GIVEN TO ME ON UNFAMILIAR MEDIA.
CHAPTER 1

- Many analog and digital tape formats exist, in addition to consumer DV, DVDs, laser discs, and various film sizes. The easiest approach is to take the media to a video service bureau that can identify it and have the correct equipment to work with it.

I WANT TO IMPORT VIDEO FROM A DVD.
CHAPTER 1

- Because the DVD was created from an uncompressed digital source, locate that source instead of using the DVD.
- If the DVD is not encrypted (meaning, it was produced using consumer DVD-burning hardware), then you should be able to be import the content directly off the DVD using any software capable of importing MPEG-2 video.
- If the DVD is a professionally mastered DVD (sold in stores), the publishers of that DVD have encrypted the video and do not authorize any digital importing of the video or translation to other formats. Certain fair use of the video may be legally permissible, however. In this case, "DVD-ripper" software (De-CSS) is necessary to extract and decrypt the VOB (video object) files from the DVD. Once on the computer, these files are simply high-resolution MPEG-2 video.

MY VIDEO LOOKS BAD ON IMPORT.
CHAPTER 1

- Make sure you have the highest quality original. Don't use a copy of a copy.

- Use a well-maintained playback device for importing into the computer. Dirty read heads on a video tape player can add their own distortion to the signal, whether digital or analog.

- If the original is digital, make sure you import it digitally and do not convert it to analog in the process. Don't use an analog capture card for digitally recorded video.

- Never use USB 1.1 connections for importing video. Use DV or an analog capture board. Period.

- Use composite video (the yellow of yellow-white-red RCA cables) connections as a last resort.

- Ensure that the capturing computer is fast enough, the software is compatible and properly installed, and no other programs or software drivers are running that could affect real-time video capture.

- If you still have no luck, have a service bureau import it to a high-quality digital format, then compress from there.

MY VIDEO EDITING APPLICATION WON'T EDIT MY COMPRESSED VIDEO. CHAPTER 2

- All of the major compression techniques (such as MPEG, Windows Media, and Real) compress the video in such a way that it cannot be easily edited. This is because they produce frames of video that depend on other frames. If any of those frames are edited out, all the frames that depend on them are suddenly missing information.

- Major editable formats include DV, MJPEG (Motion JPEG), Pixlet (studio-grade Macintosh format), RAW (completely uncompressed video), and MPEG (stand-alone intraframes only). In these formats, each frame can be considered an intraframe or stand-alone keyframe. Thus, video-editing applications can easily slice up and rearrange these formats.

- To edit high-quality compressed video such as MPEG-2, it must first be converted to one of these formats. Many consumer video-editing applications work with DV. RAW video is about five times larger than DV and is generally too large to work with easily.

- To convert a file to the appropriate editable format, use the professional version of the media-editing tools from that vendor, or use a third-party format conversion tool. Choose the working format used by your video-editing software as the output format.

ENCODING AND COMPRESSION ISSUES

THE MOTION OF THE VIDEO I ENCODED IS BLURRY.
CHAPTER 2

- Use the native frame rate of the original video in encoding (for instance, don't drop 24fps film to 12fps, or keep TV at 30fps).
- Shrink the frame size and increase the frame rate.
- If the source is TV footage, look for a more sophisticated de-interlacing filter that preserves motion while making the footage progressive.
- Use a more sophisticated video codec.
- Use variable bit rate encoding and two-pass encoding. Doing so will analyze scenes in the video and allocate higher bit rates for the high-motion scenes.

GREEN BLOCKS OF COLOR APPEAR IN MY VIDEO.
CHAPTER 2

- Increase the frequency of keyframes or I-frames (intraframes). These blocks are caused by a lack of earlier reference frames, and green is substituted for the missing
- Increase the encoding bit rate.

VIDEO LOOKS BAD/TOO SLOW/TOO SMALL/TOO CHOPPY FOR MODEM VIEWERS.
CHAPTERS 2 AND 4

- No existing compression technology can transmit full-motion video at 30fps at 640×480 pixels, along with audio, using a 20–40Kbps connection. You have to make compromises in the size, frame rate, audio quality, and smoothness of the video, or the time the user must wait.
- Present the content as a high-resolution slide show (a few frames per second) with good audio.
- Present the content as smooth-motion (12–15fps), thumbnail-sized video with good audio.

- Remove audio altogether and present the content with subtitle text tracks that compress well. Use all available bandwidth for video.
- Offer modem viewers audio only.
- Encode the video at good quality and make modem users download the full file before watching.
- Eliminate modem viewers. Target only broadband viewers.
- If the application permits, deliver the video to the viewer on CD or DVD, and use the modem connection to trigger the appropriate video.

JAGGED EDGES/BLOCKINESS APPEAR IN MY VIDEO.
CHAPTER 2

- Ensure that interlaced source video is de-interlaced before encoding.
- Most modern codecs can have unwanted staircase and jagged aliasing effects because they break images into blocks and compress the blocks. Increase the bit rate of the stream so that more bits can be allocated for each frame, reducing aliasing. If removing block-based artifacts is the most important thing, you can use a different style of codec that does not use block-based compression. Some vendors have hybrid codecs that employ wavelet and other compression techniques, resulting in different artifacts than blocks. Use a codec with a deblocking filter, such as MPEG-4 AVC. Deblocking filters are designed to solve this exact problem.

THE TEXT IS ILLEGIBLE IN THE ENCODED VIDEO.
CHAPTER 2

- Send text as a separate text or subtitle track, not within the video, if the text data is important.
- Use SMIL to synchronize text with the video.
- Increase the resolution (horizontal by vertical pixels) so that the text is readable.
- Increase the size of the fonts; use bold, sans-serif fonts.
- Use a different kind of codec that reproduces text better.

I NEED TO REMOVE SUBTITLES FROM THE VIDEO.
CHAPTERS 1 AND 2

- When capturing from DVD, simply disable subtitles.
- If the subtitles don't overlay the main picture (for example, in letterbox format), crop the subtitles by setting the video capture region to the picture area and no larger. You can also simply capture the whole screen and then crop out the subtitles at the compression stage.
- If the subtitles overlay the content, use image-editing tools to edit each frame individually. If this sounds like a long and painstaking process, it is. Even so, blurry artifacts remain where the words were removed.

MEDIA FORMAT ISSUES

I WANT TO TRANSLATE FROM A PROPRIETARY FORMAT THAT I NO LONGER USE.
CHAPTERS 2–3, AND 8

- If the original (pre-compressed) content is available, use that instead. Re-encoding compressed video will most likely produce unsatisfactory results.
- If the proprietary content version is the only one available, obtain the original tools for working with that format and export it as uncompressed video.

I'VE STANDARDIZED ON A MEDIA FORMAT BUT IT DOESN'T PLAY BACK ON MY TARGET PLATFORM. WHAT DO I DO?
CHAPTERS 2 AND 8

- If the target platform is a minority desktop operating system, see if that OS can emulate an operating system that can play the content. Then, any viewers on that system might be able to play back the content with satisfactory results.
- If the target platform is a handheld, consider targeting the standards for those handhelds as well as your chosen media format. Also, talk to the vendor of your format and ask them what the solution is for targeting the platform.

- License the media format from the original vendor, or work with a third-party vendor that can "port" (adapt) the format to your target platforms. Many vendors (such as Macromedia) provide source code so that their standard can be adapted to any platform.

- Select a more standard media format, even if it doesn't have the best compression quality of all the codecs compared.

**I'M TRYING TO PRESENT MY VIDEO SO THAT THE MAXIMUM NUMBER OF VIEWERS IS ABLE TO VIEW THE CONTENT.
CHAPTERS 2, 4, AND 8**

- Target all the formats, using the correct (and different) launching approaches for each popular web browser.

- Survey your viewer base for media player preference; choose the most popular player based on survey, and focus assistance on getting all viewers to install that software.

- Choose the media player with the most flexible feature set for content creation and production. If the content is worth viewing, viewers will install the player to access the content. Do everything possible to facilitate installation of this player, such as web-based auto-installation. Create custom HTML for every different browser (Internet Explorer, Netscape, Mozilla, Safari, and so on) to ensure that they launch the correct media player.

STORAGE AND FILE FORMAT ISSUES

**I AM HAVING TROUBLE KEEPING TRACK OF THE VERSIONS OF THE DIFFERENT FORMATS.
CHAPTERS 3 AND 4**

- Use a commercial content management system instead of manually creating and managing changes to all the content. Use software that integrates into the video production workflow and that can be scripted to encode the many versions of video and distribute them.

- Reduce the number of supported formats. Standardize on a lower number of media formats and/or bit rates.

I AM TRYING TO ARCHIVE ALL THE VIDEO (24/7) FOR VARIOUS TV STATIONS. THE STORAGE REQUIREMENTS ARE IMMENSE. IN WHAT FORMAT SHOULD I STORE IT?
CHAPTERS 2–4, AND 8

- MPEG-2 is a widely deployed standard format for digital recording. Use MPEG-2 hardware encoders, and then capture the channels directly to disk at a broadcast quality bit rate.

- MPEG-4 is more compact than MPEG-2 at the same bit rates. Use a high-quality MPEG-4 compressor, preferably in hardware. Also, extra metadata, such as closed-captioning and program information, can be stored in the more flexible MPEG-4 file format.

- Try to avoid proprietary formats for something like bulk archiving, as the formats tend to change often, whereas MPEG formats are valid for many years.

- Using hardware compressors allows consistent quality while allowing the computer to focus on archiving the information.

TRANSPORT, NETWORKING, AND CONNECTION ISSUES

VIEWERS CANNOT CONNECT TO THE STREAM.
CHAPTERS 4 AND 6

- Categorize the viewers who cannot connect. Find out what player they use, where they are, and what operating system they use.

- Ensure that there are no domain name service problems. Try the URL of the media outside of the company where it is produced. Sometimes domain names work inside a company but not outside or vice versa due to misconfiguration or firewalls.

- As a test, send viewers a link with an IP address instead of the name.

- Verify that all viewers have the correct link/URL from the web page that links to the video.

- If no viewers can connect to the stream, suspect a server configuration issue (the stream is not running or it is behind a firewall).

- If some viewers cannot connect to the stream, check whether they are behind restrictive firewalls. Verify that the server is serving on port 80 for viewers who can connect only to that port.

- If all viewers after a certain time cannot connect to the stream, verify that the viewer capacity of the server (or the bandwidth of the server) has not been exceeded.

- Verify that viewers are running the correct media player, along with the correct version of the player.

- Verify that viewers have the correct codecs. Some platforms have only older versions of codecs and cannot auto-update to the new codecs without downloading a new version of the player.

- Verify that viewers have basic Internet connectivity to begin with.

- Verify that viewers are not trying to access broadband streams with modem connections.

- If DRM is used, ensure that viewers have correctly installed decryption keys through the purchase and fulfillment system.

- Verify latency between viewers and the server. High latency (for example, in transcontinental connections) can result in the system timing out, and often produces the same error results as if the server was simply not operating.

VIEWERS CAN CONNECT ONLY THROUGH PORT 80 OR VIA TCP OR HTTP.
CHAPTERS 4 AND 5

- Fifty percent or more viewers are likely to be be behind restrictive firewalls or connection sharing NAT (network address translation) devices. As a result, UDP transport (which is more efficient) and even TCP transport may be unavailable. In general, there is no workaround.

- If target viewers are behind corporate firewalls, have them configure their firewalls to be more streaming-media friendly.

- Have corporate IT staff install a streaming proxy at the edge of their network.

- Have viewers reconfigure the transport settings in the preferences of their media player. It is possible that they could have it configured more restrictively (HTTP only, port 80 only, connect through a proxy, and so on) than their connection actually allows.

CONTENT STOPS UNEXPECTEDLY AND DISCONNECTS. CHAPTERS 4 AND 6

- Check the packet loss of stream before it was disconnected. (This option is available in Info dialogs of most media players.) Too much network packet loss can cause a sudden disconnection. The only real solution is to change the route between the viewer and server—use a different hosting provider or a different viewer ISP, or wait until another time.

- If connection is over TCP or HTTP, no packet loss is visible (even if it is there). Check the latency between the viewer and the server; if it approaches 1 second (more than 500 milliseconds, i.e. half a second) or is very unstable (up and down quickly), then it is likely that a delay of more than a few seconds can occur spontaneously, which would sever the connection.

- Verify that the content is all encoded in the same way, and that interstitial advertising is online and available. It could be that a track transition caused a disconnection by being offline.

- Ensure that the viewer media player has proper codecs for all content being streamed.

PLAYER TRIES TO CONNECT FOREVER OR SAYS BUFFERING FOREVER. CHAPTERS 4 AND 6

- Often, the server is misconfigured just enough to let the player try to connect, but never enough to give it any media. Try connecting to the video with a machine on the *same* network as the server, to verify it is properly served but eliminating the variable of the Internet.

- Have a player try to connect directly to the media player source URL instead of being launched from the possibly complicated URL produced by a web publishing system.

- Reduce latency, reduce packet loss, or increase bandwidth between server and viewer by switching either hosting provider or client ISP.

VIEWERS IN OTHER COUNTRIES OR CONTINENTS CANNOT SEE MY CONTENT. CHAPTER 4

- Locate a streaming media server in every continent where you intend to have an audience.

- Contract with a streaming service provider or CDN provider who will distribute your content on any continent where you have an audience.
- Switch to download-based content instead of stream-based, and make your content freely distributable, but put identifying information, ads, and so on (including URLs) within the stream. Specify simple license terms that permit other sites to copy the content to their site. If it is worth watching, other sites will mirror the content, yet clicking on the video will bring viewers to your site.

COMPATIBILITY ISSUES

THE VIDEO IS MISSING, BUT THE AUDIO STILL PLAYS.
CHAPTERS 2 AND 3

- This is a common occurrence when viewers have an earlier version of a player but lack the correct codecs. Check first to see if viewers have the latest player for that type of media.
- Check if the media is using a codec that does not come with the media player. Some popular video codecs have to be downloaded from the vendor's website or purchased, and then installed into the media player before it can play them. If the user is missing the video codec, the audio plays (because it is encoded in an included format), whereas the video does not. To verify this, open the stream or file, then get info in the media player menu. It will show which audio and video tracks and codecs are in the media file. If the codec is not recognized as one belonging to the player, search for the video codec name in a search engine and see who provides it.

THE AUDIO IS MISSING, BUT THE VIDEO STILL PLAYS.
CHAPTERS 2 AND 3

- Ensure that the computer has a functioning sound card by using some other audio program and hearing sound.
- Ensure that the volume is turned up in the media player.
- Use option menus to view track information on the media as it plays. It lists the codecs used by the audio and video tracks. It often says if the codec is unrecognized or unavailable.

- If the data is corrupted in some way, it might recognize the audio, but not play it back. Try playing that clip on another computer.
- If the audio plays on other computers but not this one, try playing different media with the same audio and video. If it still has no audio, you might need to update or reinstall the media playing software, as there is some glitch preventing the correct codec from working.

PLAYER SAYS THAT IT IS MISSING CODECS.
CHAPTER 2

- Make sure the player is the most recent version of that media player.
- Check to see if the content uses a third-party codec that needs to be manually installed. The site hosting the content might indicate this; otherwise, check properties on the movie tracks (in the media player menus) to view which audio and video codecs are listed.
- Visit the codec developer's website to download the missing codec. You might have to search on the codec name to identify the manufacturer.
- Some media players "hijack" the formats of other media players. For instance, Windows Media claim that it can open a MOV or MP4 file, but then claims missing codecs. Open the content with the correct media player manually instead of letting the browser or OS choose the player.
- Another solution is to reinstall the player that is supposed to play that content, or to go into its preferences and look for a selection like "Reassociate this media player with media files of type X."
- In the browser's preferences, or in the Internet control panel under Helper Application, make sure the application is associated with the format in question.

THE WRONG PLAYER IS LAUNCHING. HOW DO I GET VIDEO TO PLAY BACK IN THE PLAYER OF MY CHOICE?
CHAPTER 4

- Ensure that the right player is actually installed on the machine in question. If it isn't installed, it cannot launch.
- If it is installed, ensure that it is the latest version or at least the correct version for the media that it is trying to play.

- Ensure that the correct <embed> and <object> tags are used for the web browser that launches the player, if it is launched from the web. Each browser (Netscape, Mozilla, Safari, Internet Explorer, and so on) has its own preferred way of being told to launch a player correctly.

- If the wrong player is launching when media is opened from the hard drive (not from online), then either the correct player is not installed or another player has "hijacked" that format and told the operating system that it can play it when in fact it cannot. To solve this, reinstall the correct player or run the correct player manually and open the media from the File, Open menu.

- In the browser's preferences, or in the Internet control panel under Helper Application, make sure the application is associated with the format in question.

HOW DO I GET THE MEDIA PLAYER TO AUTOMATICALLY INSTALL? CHAPTERS 3 AND 6

- Most web browsers on Windows-based PCs have the option to automatically install a media player if it is missing. To make the right player install, put the player-specific, auto-installation HTML near or around the media link in the web page. Documentation for these features can be found on the help site of the media player in question. This might be limited by the security settings of the computer, especially on corporate networks.

INSTEAD OF LAUNCHING THE PLAYER, A SYSTEM MESSAGE SAYS, "DO YOU WANT TO OPEN OR SAVE?" CHAPTERS 4 AND 6

- This error message means that the browser does not know how to deal with this media, and is just trying to download it to disk as a large object. First, check to see if the appropriate media player is even installed. Then, re-install the correct media player. This sometimes re-sets the correct options so that the browser can identify the content.

- Ask the hosting service to correct the MIME-type information provided by their web server for the video or audio in question. It is partially the web server's responsibility to identify the content as video and correctly inform the web browser what type of video it is. If the web server is not correctly configured, it tells the browser that it is merely a large chunk of text, an "octet (byte) stream," or some other generic object, instead of video/mp4, for instance.

- Insert the correct <embed> and <object> tags in the HTML that hosts the content, as specified on the help site for the streaming media in question.

- Check the MIME associations in the web browser.

PLAYBACK QUALITY ISSUES

MEDIA DOESN'T LOOK OR SOUND GOOD ENOUGH. CHAPTERS 1–6 AND 8

- Improve the capture process. If the original content was dark, blurry, and imported from an overplayed VHS dub on an ancient VCR deck using a USB capture card and monophonic audio on a slow computer, compression only makes it worse. Get the best possible version of the content (high-quality, digital, high-resolution, bright, and first-generation) and import it using the best possible capture process (high-bandwidth, low-loss, or digital).

- Clean up the video once it is on the computer. If it was originally film content that was subsequently put onto DVD or VCR tape, you need to de-interlace it, do inverse-telecine, and then work with individual sections of the film to make sure they have proper color and brightness levels to begin with.

- Encode the content with the appropriate modern compression technique. If the content is long with many different scenes, fast and slow motion (for example, a movie), use a codec that has variable bit rate and two-pass encoding. This ensures that the correct number of bits is used to retain motion features.

- Verify that poor network conditions are not the cause of the low quality. Serve the content on a high-bandwidth hosting provider that has not overcommitted their bandwidth (sold the same bandwidth to everyone on the assumption that only a few of them use it), or use a CDN service provider that focuses on video delivery.

THE VIDEO FRAME RATE IS TOO LOW.
CHAPTERS 2 AND 4

- Reduce the resolution, but maintain the original frame rate of the video when it is compressed. By trading off size for frame rate, fast-motion footage can be transmitted with better fidelity and play back more smoothly. Note that you should always keep the frame rate either equal to or an even divisor of the original frame rate—30fps, 15fps, 7.5fps, and so on.

- Ensure that network packet loss is not the problem. Poor networks with high packet loss can result in dropped frames of video, which shows up for the viewer as reduced frame rate. Watch the video right at the source (on the same network or machine) and ensure that it has an acceptable frame rate and isn't dropping frames.

- Ensure that viewers have a fast enough computer. If the codec relies on an extremely fast processor to play back smoothly, a slower computer might be dropping frames to keep up with the video.

VIDEO SMEARS, OR IT HAS COLORED BLOCKS IN IT.
CHAPTER 2

This is usually caused by a missing keyframe. Future partial frames that depend on the key frame have no data upon which to build and show up with strange colors. The underlying causes of missing keyframes are:

- **Not enough keyframes in the source video.** The solution is to increase keyframe frequency in encoder settings.

- **Packet loss, resulting in lost keyframes**. Solutions are to reduce network packet loss or to increase keyframe frequency in encoder settings.

- **Data corruption.** Sometimes the original video is simply corrupted, perhaps during the original transfer, or even before the re-encoding—perhaps glitches from the original source. Verify that the copy on the server does not glitch when played start to finish; if blocks are still found, verify the original copy of the encoded content does not look blocky or oddly colored; verify that the source of the video, before compression, does not have the same problems.

AUDIO AND VIDEO ARE OUT OF SYNCH.
CHAPTERS 1–6

This is a difficult problem with many potential causes. If the data flows over a network, the network is suspect, but the synch error could have originated in any stage: production, editing, compression, storage, or delivery. Some steps to correct it are:

- Put a copy of the media on the hard drive of the computer on which it plays out of synch. This eliminates potential errors due to networking. If the A/V is now in synch, the error might be due to network issues. Often, audio and video are sent as separate tracks over a network, and have to be resynchronized on the receiver. This test determines if adverse network conditions are to blame.

- If the network does not seem to be the issue, get the fastest, most powerful, well-maintained computer on the fastest broadband connection available and see if the video plays correctly on that computer over a network. It can be that the first machine that had trouble did not have enough bandwidth or CPU power to keep the audio and video in synch, and it may have been a combination of CPU slowness and adverse network conditions.

- Ensure that the source material had synchronized audio and video before being compressed. Perhaps the original video was out of synch.

- Check if the capture process is throwing the A/V synch out. If you have access to the pre-compressed video, ensure that it was in synch. It might be that the data didn't make it safely into the computer before it was edited and compressed. If you have established that A/V still goes out of synch—local or networked, fast or slow machine—and that the original was in synch and the captured pre-edited version was in synch, then the synch error is probably because of slight time differences inserted during video editing.

- Audio synch drift is common when movies are converted to or from formats such as MPEG, MOV, and DivX. Often, the original A/V stream has to be *demultiplexed,* meaning the audio and video are split apart. Once this is done, synch can fall out when any editing or segmentation is performed to the file. The basic cause of these errors is that work is being done on an already compressed version of the content (MPEG, Windows Media, and so on) and that it was not intended to be an editable format. The format has to be converted back from it's highly compressed format. In the process of these conversions, frames get lost here and there. Lost frames change the frame rate, which makes video go out of synch with audio.

- In AVI and other files, the presence of bad frames can cause synch errors. Lost frames result in the video not being exactly 24fps or 30fps. If any frame is invalid (as a result of a software conversion process), it will be dropped. Dropped frames reduce the overall length of the video, causing it to gradually go out of synch with audio.

- Analog capture can also be a source of drift. Analog capture systems do not always capture audio at the precisely specified frequency. Depending on many factors including the speed of the machine, the capture card, and the software, audio and video can wind up being slightly different in length.

- One solution is to resize the audio track (using A/V editing tools) so that it is the exact same length as the video (down to precise fractions of a second). For instance, if the movie track is 1:48:19 long and the audio track winds up being 1:46:11 long after editing, the audio track can be stretched out and then pitch-corrected to be 1:48:19. This often puts the audio back in synch.

- Another solution to this sort of drift is to capture in smaller pieces (for example, 15 or 30 minutes at a time). This keeps the audio and video better synchronized at these points.

- Another solution is to use DV import with locked audio and video instead of using analog capture sources or MPEG as the source. Locked audio and video can be precisely cut and pasted without drift.

Video or sound is choppy, jittery, or stutters.
Chapters 2, 4, and 6

- A choppy video implies network trouble. Mobile phones start to sound choppy when the signal is low, which means that packets are lost. The solution lies in improving the network transport conditions with better server bandwidth or lowering the bit rate so the media travels more easily to the user.

- If the audio or video stutters, is jittery, or choppy, the viewer machine possibly is not fast enough to decode the content, or it is running too many other programs and temporarily doesn't have enough CPU to play back the file.

- Another reason for stutters or jitter can be during progressive download. If the media downloads slightly too slow for real time as it is played back, the player can keep hitting the end of the video, stop for a moment, and then restart, repeating this cycle with resulting jittery sound and video.

THE VIDEO TAKES TOO LONG TO START.
CHAPTERS 4 AND 6

- *Buffering* is the process of getting a head start on playback, and storing up several seconds of video so that momentary delays or interruptions of network data flow can be smoothed out. Buffering techniques have improved over the years in the major media players. When video takes a long time to start up, it usually indicates that the connection between the server and the viewer has a lot of delay, possibly caused by packet loss or distance. To solve this:

  1. Position servers closer to the end viewer; for instance, if the viewer is on another continent than the video server.
  2. Reduce the bit rate of media for these users. Lower bit rates require less buffering and won't be so close to the top limit of this user's bandwidth.

- Viewers can actually select the amount of buffering in most media player option/preference menus; however, setting a lower delay won't solve much if the fundamental problem is network-related. In this case, decreasing the amount of buffer speeds up the start time, but then the video is choppy and jittery.

- Long startup delays have been addressed in the recent faster starting features of the major media servers and players. Another solution to this is to simply adopt these versions of the media servers and require viewers to update to that version of the player. (These features appeared in Windows Media v9, QuickTime v6.4, and RealOne v2.)

THE AUDIO SOUNDS METALLIC AND ARTIFICIAL.
CHAPTER 2

- Increase the bit rate of the audio. For example, low MP3 bit rates (less than 32K) tend to make music muddy and create unnatural metallic sounding audio at times.

- Use a different audio codec, perhaps a more appropriate one. Voice codecs often garble music with a metallic sound, as they try to interpret it as speech.

THE AUDIO HAS POPS.
CHAPTER 2

- Check to see if other machines have pops. It can be the sound card or configuration of that machine, its speakers, or its network conditions. Too many background programs running can choke the CPU and cause it to have sound problems.

- Check to see if the codec is used at a low bit rate. Low bit rates in any codec increase unwanted artifacts.

- Check to see if the original content has pops in it. Perhaps it was affected during the recording, capturing, editing, or compression stages. Backtrack through these phases until you find a version without pops.

THE VIDEO IS TOO DARK.
CHAPTER 1

- Test the video on other computers. It might be that the monitor is old or has its brightness turned down, or that the color settings on the video card itself are out of adjustment.

- Ensure that PCs with average monitors are used to test during video production. A lot of media content is produced on Macintosh, and the *gamma* settings (color adjustments) of Macs are often much brighter than PCs. Also, a creative department, Mac or PC, might have expensive, large, and high quality monitors that give them an incorrect perspective on the average user's viewing experience.

THE ASPECT RATIO IS WRONG (VIDEO IS THE WRONG SHAPE).
CHAPTERS 1–3

- To make a long story short, computer pixels are square, but TV and movie pixels are not perfectly square but rectangular. Thus, in order to show movie video correctly on a computer screen with square pixels, the player needs to know what the *aspect ratio* (horizontal and vertical dimensions) of the image should be. Otherwise, it looks squished or too tall. These problems usually arise when dealing with broadcast formats in full resolution (720×576, 720×480) because the compression process converts everything to square pixels.

- The viewer may have simply resized the video to the wrong shape, depending on whether the player allows this. Try to get information on the media file (via a menu option) and see if the reported horizontal and vertical pixels match the shape of the display. If not, try resizing the window until the video looks correct.

- Nonstandard or loosely standardized formats, such as SVCD or XSVCD (eXtended Super Video CD), expect the content to be stretched out to the proper aspect ratio. If the information about the aspect ratio is not present, or if the content was authored using tools that did not correctly set it, the media player will render the image incorrectly. The solution is to play these formats in custom players or on DVD players designed for them.

THE VIDEO PLAYS IN THE BOTTOM-LEFT CORNER OF THE WEB BROWSER IN A SMALL BOX.
CHAPTERS 3 AND 6

- Microsoft added a media feature to version 6 of Internet Explorer that allows one to start playing music or video and have it "dock" into the corner of the web browser. The user's preference determines whether web video "pops out" in the media player or play in this docked browser window.

- If you want more control over the size and presentation of your content on the user's desktop, you need to specify exactly whether to embed Windows Media Player or to pop up the player externally. The specific HTML needed to do this is documented on the Windows Media help site.

- If you experience this problem as a viewer, you can set a preference in the web browser preferences or options menu to disable or change this behavior.

THE MEDIA PLAYER POPS UP DISTRACTING DIALOGS TO THE VIEWER BEFORE PLAYING MY CONTENT.
CHAPTERS 3 AND 6

- All the major media players have different business models. For some of them, advertising is part of their plan; to others, up-selling consumers on professional versions of the player is part of their plan. And still to others, converting customers to a content subscription model is part of the plan.

- Each of the media players is designed to quietly embed within a browser window, without showing the full media player and play content. By invoking the embedded version via HTML, much of the vendor-branded extras go away, but some dialogs still remain the first time the user launches that media player.

- Licensing or using a third-party media player is a possible solution. In some situations, you get what you pay for, and directly licensing an auto-installing, web-based streaming media player gives you full control over the user experience once the player is installed.

- Programming a standalone application is another way to get around media player vendor marketing. Although an extreme solution, software can usually use all the features of media players for free and suppress any unwanted dialog boxes, ads, and questions that the media player would otherwise pop up.

B

THE MPEG-4 STANDARD

This appendix is about MPEG-4, one of the major standards influencing Internet video and video delivery. Although the primary resource for MPEG-4 is the standard itself, these documents are thousands of pages long. Most books on MPEG-4 are either aimed at technical implementers and are too complex. This chapter is designed to present a complete and easily readable reference for the entire current MPEG-4 standard. In keeping with the style of the book, an illustration accompanies each of the standard parts.

Much of this material is available (and this chapter draws heavily on these) from the following fine sources:

- Pereira, Fernando and Touradj Ebrahimi, *The MPEG-4 Book*, Prentice Hall PTR, 2002.
- Walsh, Aaron E. and Mikaël Bourges–Sévenier, *MPEG-4 Jump Start*, Prentice Hall PTR, 2002.
- Watkinson, John, *The MPEG Handbook*, self-published through Focal Press, 2001.
- Topic, Michael, *Streaming Media Demystified, McGraw-Hill, 2002*
- The MPEG-4 Industry Forum at http://www.m4if.org.
- Leonardo Chiariglione's MPEG site at http://www.chiariglione.org/mpeg.

The MPEG-4 standard itself is the primary resource for information on MPEG-4, and it is available for purchase from the ISO. You can find this link at the following address: http://www.masteringinternetvideo.com/mpeg4/

MPEG-4 OVERVIEW

MPEG is offered as a large, comprehensive set of tools for audiovisual coding. *Coding* means the representation of audio and video in a digital form (code). And there are many, many ways to do this coding in order to achieve optimal compression.

MPEG-4 is a very large standard. No one product is likely to implement *all* of MPEG-4, so statements, such as, "We support MPEG-4," are ambiguous at best. Similarly, comparisons, such as, "Our proprietary codec is better than MPEG-4 at the same bit rate," are ambiguous, unless they tell you what part of the standard they are comparing to.

For example, in Chapter 2, "Video Compression," we described the H.263 codec. H.263 is actually part of MPEG-4, and any MPEG-4-compliant video decoder should be able to decode H.263 as well. Yet H.263 is not representative of the best quality available from MPEG-4 video, even though it is technically "MPEG-4 video."

TOOLS

A toolbox analogy is perhaps the best way to understand MPEG standards. The first seven chapters of this book are structured around a sort of video pipeline, comprising content preparation, encoding, storage, transport, service, and control.

MPEG-4 provides tools in each of these categories. MPEG-4 was originally designed to standardize only preparation, encoding, storage, and service, but has also specified some transport issues as well. MPEG-7 and MPEG-21 have gone on to provide tools for control and identification of media content.

With so many tools to choose from, MPEG has to designate specific small sets of tools in order to guarantee that different MPEG products are compatible with each other.

PARTS

MPEG standards are divided into *parts*. These parts are documents, which can include software and even hardware designs. All these parts together define the standard. Each part can be added to over time or have small typos corrected, but cannot be substantially changed—thus, products that were compliant several years ago, are always compliant. So, for each part there are multiple versions— Part 1 v2, Part 1 v3—each *added* to the existing Part 1 v1. Entirely new parts can be added if the MPEG group thinks it is warranted—for example, if technology has improved enough that it is worthwhile to add new features to the standard that are not simply revisions of one of the existing parts. There are 17 parts to MPEG-4 as of summer 2004; the bulk of this chapter describes each of them.

PROFILES

Because MPEG solves so many different problems and offers so many different tools, only a small subset of the tools is used for any particular application. For instance, Apple Computer's iPod supports not only MP3 but also Advanced Audio Codec (AAC) audio, specified in MPEG-4 Part 3 (Audio). The iPod does not play back video, so obviously it should not be required to implement video tools in order to be compliant.

Thus, MPEG has a concept of *profiles*, which are subsets of tools from the entire set. For instance, one can choose from only natural video encoding tools for video captured with a camera, or only synthetic 3D video tools for creating artificial scenes with 3D models, or a combination of both. Each of these is described by a different profile, as depicted in Figure B-1, and if many handheld devices used a particular profile, then they could all share the same MPEG-4 content created for that profile. There are many profiles within each part of the standard. In practice, other standards groups (such as H.263), in making their use more prevalent, have blessed several profiles. Profiles apply only to certain parts of the standard, mainly the visual, audio, and system parts.

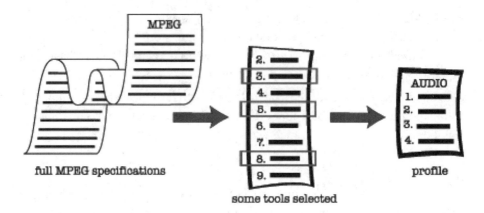

Figure B-1   *A profile is a subset of tools taken from the full MPEG specifications.*

LEVELS

Even if two devices share the exact same profile, one or the other might be a more powerful machine or device, or be designed to deal with higher bit rates. Many of the tools for compressing audio or video or reproducing shapes can scale down to cell phone screens and scale up to HDTV. Thus, while profiles specify which subset of tools is being used, *levels* specify how complex the use of those tools is, and what CPU power and data rates are needed to decode them.

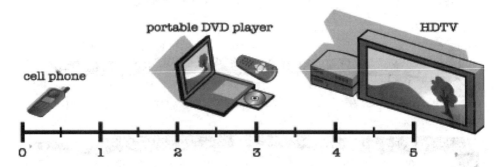

Figure B-2   *Levels specify the appropriate level of technology for the target device.*

CONFORMANCE POINTS

Conformance points are simply a combination of a profile and a level where different products can interoperate (by conforming to that level and profile). If all the cell phones support creation and playback of a simple visual profile at level 0, then any video made by any cell phone can be played back on any other cell phone.

PARTS OF MPEG-4

To understand MPEG-4, it is necessary to understand how extensive and rich in tools it is. The rest of this appendix provides a conceptual overview of each part in the most recent MPEG-4 standard. Some parts (especially the earlier parts) are relevant to our concerns here and are described in detail; other parts require only a light explanation.

> **Note** MPEG (including MPEG 1/2/4/7/21 and future versions) operates within the ISO/IEC Joint Technical Committee. So the intimidating list of acronyms seen in most MPEG-generated standards documents— ISO/IEC/JTC 1/SC 29/WG 11—simply indicates that MPEG is Subcommittee 29, Working Group 11 in the ISO/IEC Joint Technical Committee.

PART 1: SYSTEMS

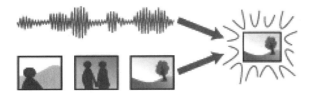

Part 1 of MPEG-4, Systems, mainly describes the tools needed to combine the video and audio into a combined scene. Earlier MPEG only had two kinds of *elementary streams*, roughly defined as the natural audio and video that was compressed with MPEG-2 codecs. Thus, its system layer mostly involved tools for synchronizing the audio and video, and perhaps mixing them together for transport. MPEG-4, however, has many different elementary streams, such as:

- Natural audio, as would be recorded with a microphone
- Synthetic audio, instruments, or voices created electronically
- Natural video, recorded with a camera
- Synthetic video and video elements, such as 2D or 3D renderings, animations, and more
- Backdrops (called *background sprites*)
- 2D still pictures and textures
- 3D shapes and models

- Text
- Triggers for synthetic audio instruments
- Descriptions of how to compose all these elements
- Interactive (user-triggerable) actions
- Metadata about audiovisual elements
- Intellectual property rights information for media elements

MPEG-4 uses the term *stream* to mean that items come in over time according to a timeline. Where a DVD player (MPEG-2) only has to decode a few different video and audio codecs, an MPEG-4 player might have to put together an entire 3D scene and then show it to the user from different camera angles, allow user input, and more. To allow user input requires programmability. And the existence of all these new media elements requires a more complex file format than for MPEG-2 or MPEG-1. Thus, the Systems part defines how the entire system fits together, and defines all the system pieces.

The 3D aspects of MPEG-4, and the capability to describe a complete scene in 3D, are based on a system called *VRML '97* (Virtual Reality Markup Language), a text-based, HTML-like language for describing 3D scenes. MPEG-4 extended the standard to deal with all the MPEG-4 media elements, called *audiovisual objects,* both natural and synthetic. Also, instead of downloading the entire scene at once (as in VRML), the scene description is now required to stream. Finally, the scene description had to be made much smaller than text-based VRML. These features are achieved in BIFS (Binary Format for Scenes), depicted in Figure B-3.

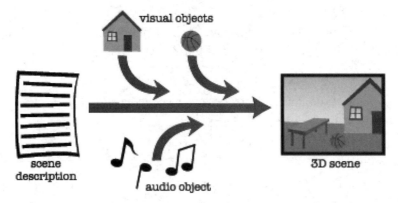

Figure B-3   *BIFS, the binary format for scenes.*

After the playback device receives all these disparate elements, they have to be synchronized in time so that lip motions match audio, for example. Thus, MPEG-4 standardizes a more complex synchronization layer than earlier MPEG, also, more elementary streams than before. If all the data is being sent over a single data connection, these elements need to be *multiplexed* (shuffled together into a single stream, as depicted in Figure B-4). The tools that provide this feature are called *FlexMux*, for flexible multiplexer.

Figure B-4 *With multiplexing, elements are shuffled together into a single stream, then re-synched to a timeline.*

MPEG-2 was always intended to be delivered either from DVD or from satellite, thus the speed of delivery and packet formats were known ahead of time. MPEG-4 decided to support every possible transport mechanism (such as files, network, and wireless connection), so it needed a design that worked independently of any specific mechanism. This was achieved with *DMIF* (Delivery Multimedia Integration Framework), which allows the playback system to simply say, "Get me the video." DMIF then tells the actual transport layer what objects it needs and when and how much delay it can endure, as depicted in Figure B-5. (Technically, the playback system talks to *DAI*, the DMIF Application Interface, but did you need another acronym?) The full DMIF system is defined in Part 6.

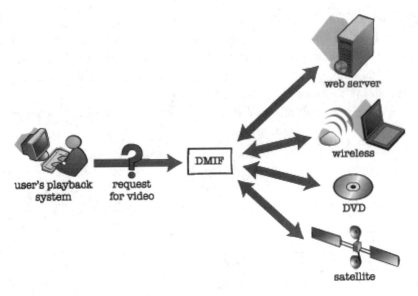

Figure B-5 *DMIF supports multiple transport mechanisms, such as HTTP, 802.11 (wireless), DVD, and more.*

PART 2: VISUAL

As a backwards-compatible standard, MPEG-4 supports many earlier compression codecs including H.263, MPEG-1, and MPEG-2. The first commercially available versions of MPEG-4 simply implemented its enhancements to this earlier line of codecs. These included additional support for lower bit rates, and improvements to algorithm efficiency (by identifying portions of a natural scene as objects instead of simple square blocks and by intelligently compressing them).

MPEG 4 VISUAL PROFILES:

This section discusses the MPEG-4 visual profiles.

Simple is a natural (non-synthetic) video with up to four video rectangles as is sometimes seen on security camera monitors (level 0 can only handle one video rectangle). It can play back earlier H.263 video streams. It uses low bit rates from 9.6Kbps up to 64Kbps (L0 and L1), 128Kbps (L2), and 384Kbps (L3), as shown in Figure B-6. It also has network error-resilience features to deal better with data loss in transit.

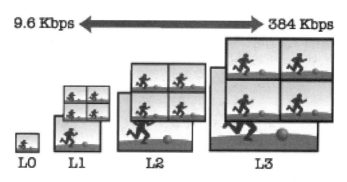

Figure B-6 *The Simple visual profile includes natural video with bitrates of L0-L3.*

Simple Scalable extends the Simple video with *temporal* (frame rate) or *spatial* (resolution) *scalability,* as shown in Figure B-7. In temporal scalability, frames are dropped to match available bandwidth. In spatial scalability, details in the image—not actual frame size—are dropped. *Scalability* is achieved by sending multiple layers, a *base layer* (lower resolution and frame rate) and an *enhancement layer* (adding higher resolution and frame rate). The player can decode only the base layer to reduce complexity or bandwidth. Bit rates range up to 128Kbps (L1) and 256Kbps (L2). This scalability feature can be compared to the stream thinning and distress stream features of codecs discussed in Chapter 2.

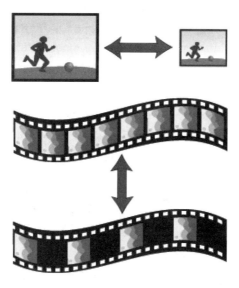

Figure B-7 *The Simple Scalable visual profile allows for variable resolution and variable frame rate.*

Core extends Simple video by adding shapes instead of just rectangular video. Parts of the image can be segmented into shapes and compressed more efficiently as distinct objects, as shown in Figure B-8. Bit rates range up to 384Kbps (L1) and 2Mbps (L2).

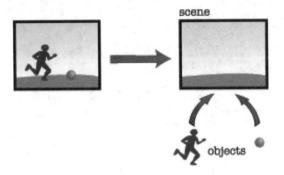

Figure B-8   *The core visual profile defines shape objects that can be separately compressed.*

Main enhances Core video with several television broadcast features: background sprites (used for a relatively unchanging background behind the moving foreground objects), interlacing (for television), and visual object shapes with transparency, which are easier to superimpose and blend with other scenes. Bit rates range from less than 2Mbps (L2) up to 38Mbps (L4). These high bit rates would be appropriate for HDTV, and the backdrop and transparency features can help where additional graphic elements are overlaid on a naturally filmed scene, as is often the case with broadcast television. The Main profile is depicted in Figure B-9.

Figure B-9   *The Main profile incorporates background sprites, interlacing, and object shapes with transparency.*

N-bit extends Core video by allowing a variable *n* different bit depths for color and brightness, ranging down to 4 bits per pixel per color channel (for example, 16 bits total of only 4,096 possible colors) and up to 12 bits per pixel (36 bits total, for a total of 68.7 billion possible colors). Bit rates range up to 2Mbps. This profile is useful where more color depth is needed in video, which is normally 8 bits for each of the three color channels, called *24-bit color*—16.7 million possible colors.

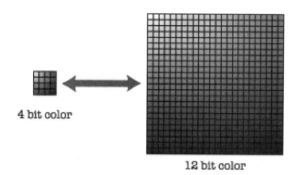

4 bit color

12 bit color

Figure B-10 *The N-bit profile can convey rough or extremely high-resolution color.*

Scalable Texture contains only the Scalable Texture visual object, which compresses still images (called *textures* in MPEG) using *wavelets*, the same compression technique used by JPEG 2000 (see Chapter 2). The simplest description of wavelet compression is that it doesn't break the image into blocky squares like earlier JPEG and MPEG, so images look smoother. In digital camera terms, image sizes are up to 0.4 megapixels (L1), 4 megapixels (L2), and 16 megapixels (L3). This profile can be use by any application that wants to compress still textures in a non-blocky and bandwidth-scalable way. Scalable Texture is depicted in Figure B-11.

Simple Face Animation is the first of the synthetic profiles that includes only simple face visual objects, and is often used for virtual videoconferencing. These 3D facial models can have face textures superimposed on them; the data stream animates the face. Maximum bit rates are 16Kbps for one face at 15fps (L1), and 32Kbps for up to four faces and 30fps (L2). Clearly, conferencing and interactive applications can use this tool. Simple Face Animation is depicted in Figure B-12.

Figure B-11 *Earlier JPEG and MPEG compression created blocky squares (left); the Scalable Texture visual profile uses the smoother "wavelet" compression technique (right).*

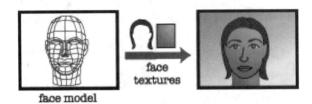

Figure B-12 *The Simple Face Animation profile combines face textures with an animate face model.*

Basic Animated Texture uses the same shapes from the Scalable Texture profile, but maps them to a 2D shape that can be skewed, distorted and moved along with facial animation. It allows up to four textures and 64Kbps (L1), and up to eight textures and 128Kbps (L2). It is depicted in Figure B-13.

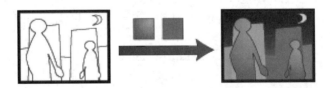

Figure B-13 *The Basica Animated Texture profile maps wavelet-compressed shapes onto a 2D shape.*

The Hybrid combines the Core profile (for natural video) and Basic Animated Texture profile (for synthetic video). This profile allows the full combination of animated synthetic objects on a natural scene, or natural video in a virtual scene.

This can provide, for instance, changing ad banners within a natural video scene. Bit rates are approximately those of Core plus Basic Animated Texture, so 384Kbps for video and 64Kbps for animated textures in L1, and slightly more than 2Mbps for L2. Hybrid is depicted in Figure B-14.

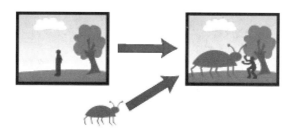

Figure B-14 *The Hybrid visual profile allows a combination of natural video and synthetic (computer-generated) objects.*

Core Scalable, shown in Figure B-15, extends Core video to allow temporal scalability (drop frames) or spatial scalability (lower resolution) of any individual visual object in the scene. Bit rates range up to 768Kbps (L1), 1500Kbps (L2), and 4Mbps (L3).

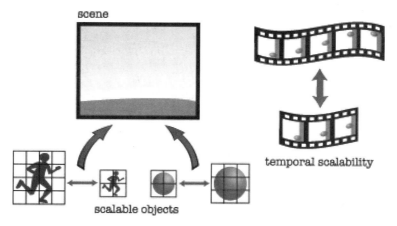

Figure B-15 *The Core Scalable visual profile provides both temporal and resolution scalability for individual objects.*

Advanced Core, shown in Figure B-16, a hybrid profile that extends Core and Advanced Scalable Texture profiles to provide full scalability with both natural video and still textures. Bit rates range up to 384Kbps (L1) and 2Mbps (L2), plus bit rates for delivering the still textures at up to 4 megapixels (L2) and 16 megapixels (L3).

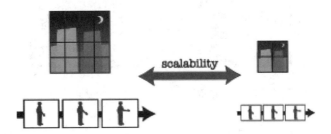

Figure B-16 *The Advanced Core visual profile provides scalability for still textures and natural video.*

Advanced Coding Efficiency extends the Core profile to add optimizations such as *global motion compensation*, which efficiently compresses common global camera motions such as pan, zoom, and rotation. These result in greater compression at the cost of greater playback complexity. Bit rates range all the way from 384Kbps (L1) to 2Mbps (L2), 15Mbps (L3), and 38Mbps (L4). This profile is depicted in Figure B-17.

Figure B-17 *The Advanced Coding Efficiency profile includes better compression for camera motions.*

Advanced Real Time Simple, shown in Figure B-18, is a natural video compression profile designed for real-time applications. It maintains a good frame rate even when encountering packet loss. It also requires a small buffer and thus can start up quickly, allowing fast channel changing. It is an obvious choice for teleconference applications. Bit rates range up to 64Kbps (L1), 128Kbps (L2), 384Kbps (L3), and 2Mbps (L4).

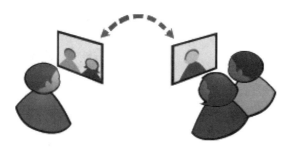

Figure B-18 *The Advanced Real Time Simple profile works well for video conferencing and other real-time applications.*

Advanced Scalable Texture, depicted in Figure B-19, improves the Scalable Texture profile to provide scalability not only for the textures, but the shapes to which they are to be mapped. This profile also provides *error resilience*, which refers to arranging the bits so that even data loss or corruption in transit does not destroy the whole picture. Its tiling feature allows a portion of a picture to be quickly viewed/zoomed in on without having to decode the entire picture, and is useful for slide shows, digital cameras, and more. As with the Scalable Texture profile, the image sizes are up to 0.4 megapixels (L1), 4 megapixels (L2), and 16 megapixels (L3).

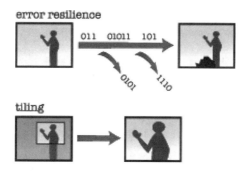

Figure B-19 *The Advanced Scalable Textures profile allows for error resilience and tiling.*

Simple Face and Body Animation, depicted in Figure B-20, extends the Facial Animation profile with a 3D body model, which can be animated at low bit rates. It allows one face and body at 15fps and 16Kbps (L1), and up to four faces at 15–30fps and 32Kbps (L2).

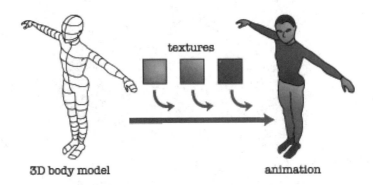

textures

3D body model   animation

Figure B-20 *Simple Face and Body Animation profile provides low-bitrate 3D character animation.*

Simple Studio is designed for use inside movie and TV studios, where MPEG-2 is in broad use. It adds the major MPEG-4 feature of segmenting video into shapes as in the Core profiles. All the frames are stand-alone key frames; thus, data rates are quite high, but working with the video is quicker. Bit depth can be up to 10 (L1 and L2) or 12 (L3 & L4) instead of the normal 8 bits per pixel per color component (YUV—see Chapter 1, "Video Preparation and Capture") for wide-ranging color and brightness. MPEG-2 studio video can be imported directly into MPEG-4 with no loss of quality. Bit rates range up to 180Mbps (L1), 600Mbps (L2), 900Mbps (L3), and 18Gbps (L4). Existing MPEG-2 studio video can be losslessly transcoded to this profile—meaning, it's translated into this format without any degradation.

Whereas MPEG-2 studio was a 4:2:2 format with twice as much luma resolution as chroma channels, MPEG-4 uses a 22:11:11 sampling format (equivalent to a 4:2:2 YUV sampling but for HD resolutions), and can sample 22:22:22 as well (equivalent to 4:4:4 red-green-blue color sampling.) (See Chapter 2 for an explanation of color sampling.) So at the top of the scale, this studio format can do HD quality (1920[ts]1080) or film quality (2048[ts]2048), 22:22:22, full 12-bit color (per RGB color channel for 36 total bits of color depth). Add to this the ability to do 30 frames *progressive* video or 60 interlaced, and even more progressive frames up to the maximum bit rate. The top of MPEG-4 for studios is the top of video quality used today.

Core Studio extends the Simple Studio profile, but supports only 10-bit color depth. It adds in-between frames for increased compression savings (also increasing the computing power needed to use it). It also allows for multiple core studio video streams, up to 4 (L1 and L2) and up to 8 (L3 and L4). The maximum bit rates are 90Mbps (L1), 300Mbps (L2), 450Mbps (L3), and 900Mbps (L4). It's depicted in Figure B-21.

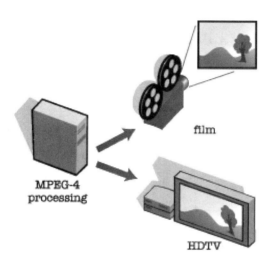

Figure B-21 *The Simple Studio and Core Studio profiles are designed for use in TV and movie studios where the target resolution is either HDTV (1920×1080) or cinematic film resolutions (as high as 4000×2000).*

Advanced Simple, shown in Figure B-22, extends the Simple Visual profile similarly to the Advanced Coding Efficiency profile, with global motion compensation, forward and backwards difference frames (see Chapter 2), and more precise motion detection within the image, for greater compression. Maximum bit rates are 128Kbps (L0 and L1), 384Kbps (L1), 768Kbps (L3), 3Mbps (L4), and 8Mbps (L5).

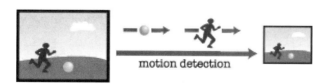

Figure B-22 *The Advanced Simple profile adds better motion compression.*

Fine Granularity Scalability, shown in Figure B-23, extends Simple or Advanced Simple Profiles, adding several additional enhancement layers such that resolution and frame rate can be increased or decreased in fine increments depending on network conditions or player speed. Maximum bit rates are the same as Advanced Simple Profile.

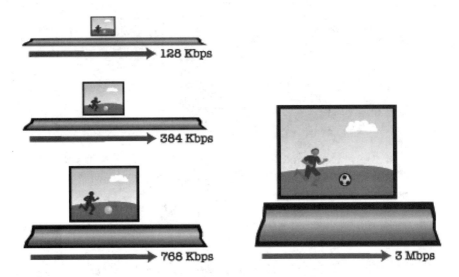

Figure B-23 *The Fine Granularity Scalability profile allows for more variation in resolution/frame rate.*

PART 3: AUDIO

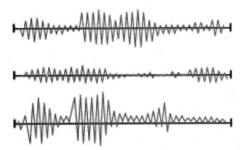

The fundamental change in MPEG-4 audio is that like video, it includes tools for compressing both natural (input from a microphone) and synthesized audio. These include speech synthesis, general MIDI (Musical Instrument Digital Interface), and a highly extensible system for synthetic instruments. In natural content compression, new tools for low-bit-rate applications, such as low bit-rate speech codecs (similar to those used in digital mobile phones) have been added, as well as *parametric* audio codecs, which use parameters (numbers) to deliver recognizable but very low-fidelity sound. It also includes the ability to tightly couple sounds with video by locating the sounds in 3D space (for example, when combined with multiple animated talking heads) and supports far more channels (up to 48) of sound than just stereo.

MPEG-4 AUDIO PROFILES

The Speech profile uses three major tools for reproducing understandable speech at low bit rates, as shown in Figure B-24. *CELP* (Code Excited Linear Prediction) is a scalable speech codec ranging from 3.5Kbps to 24Kbps. *HVXC* (Harmonic Vector eXcitation Coding) is an even lower bit-rate codec, compressing speech between 2Kbps and 4Kbps. *TTSI* (Text To Speech Interface) specifies how to trigger (but does not provide) a speech synthesizer at the audio receiver. TTSI can thus generate speech at a staggeringly low 0.2Kbps–1.2Kbps, as it is mostly sending textual data. TTSI can send phonetic data, so that text in any language can be properly pronounced.

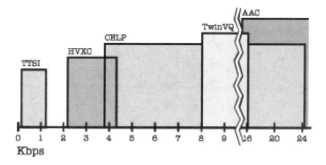

Figure B-24 *Bit rates of various speech codecs.*

The Synthetic profile includes all the synthetic tools for audio. One of these is *General MIDI*, a standard set of digital musical instruments that can be triggered by sending a low bit rate stream of notes and durations. You might have experienced cheesy-sounding web pages due to variations in quality of the built-in MIDI instruments. The solution in MPEG-4 audio is two tools: *SAOL* (Structured Audio Orchestral Language) and *SASBF* (Structured Audio Sample-Bank Format), depicted in Figure B-25.

The Structured Audio profile describes, rather than compresses, audio. SAOL is a complete language for describing the actual algorithm used to produce the sound, so that any kind of computer synthesis can be described (limited only by the complexity of the algorithm and the power of the playback device). SASBF is used to create banks or groups of recordings (samples) of musical instruments.

With these two tools, either sampled or computer-generated instruments can be accurately delivered in such a way that the sound is identical on any device. Then, when a triggering stream such as MIDI or SASL (Structured Audio Score Language) is delivered to the playback device, the sound is reproduced exactly as its author intended, and strange and unacceptable instrument substitutions do not occur. The TTSI speech synthesis tools are also included in the Synthetic profile.

Figure B-25 *The SAOL and SASBF tools can precisely describe a synthetic audio sample so that it plays back exactly as was intended.*

The Scalable profile, as shown in Figure B-26, includes all the tools in Speech as well as *TwinVQ* (Transform domain Weighted INterleave Vector Quantization), which compress natural audio at low bit rates (less than 10Kbps), and scalable *AAC* (Advanced Audio Coding). The scalable AAC, as in scalable video, consists of a basic layer of audio that can be played back. Then, additional enhancement layers (in 8Kbps increments) can be added to the original layer to enhance the sound. If a delivery channel is reduced by bandwidth restrictions, only as many layers as can fit through the delivery channel need to be sent. Using a CELP or HXVC voice stream as the basic layer and then using AAC for enhancement layers can produce a scalable voice stream that sounds good at any bit rate.

The Main profile includes most of the audio tools. The MPEG-4 audio codecs had a tough act to follow with the tremendous success of MP3 (MPEG-1 Layer III audio). MPEG-2 had already standardized the newer AAC codec that supported multi-channel sound, such as the 5.1 surround sound on DVDs. 5.1 sound has six channels of sound. The first five are center, front right, front left, rear right, and rear left. 1 is the subwoofer/bass channel. MPEG-4 has included and enhanced this codec and continues to call it AAC. Main includes many different versions of the AAC codec: low-complexity versions that require less powerful playback processors; error-resilient versions that can endure packet loss; and low-latency versions good for two-way communication. Additional tools are TwinVQ, *HILN* (Harmonic and Individual Lines plus Noise) for low bit rate audio coding in the range of 4Kbps–16Kbps, and *BSAC* (Bit-Sliced Arithmetic Coding), operating in the 48Kbps–64Kbps range. Where each scalable AAC enhancement layer is 8Kbps, BSAC can add many tiny 1Kbps enhancement layers, providing fine grained scalability.

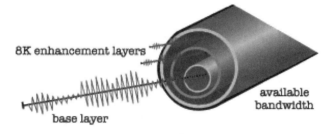

Figure B-26 *The Scalable audio profile allows for more precise quality control; enhancements can be made in 8Kbps increments.*

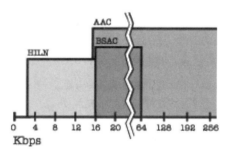

Figure B-27 *Comparison of general audio codecs.*

The High Quality Audio is similar to Scalable, but more complex to process on the playback device. It adds more efficient AAC techniques, as well as network error-resilience features, but does not include the low bit-rate TTSI or TwinVQ, being targeted for higher quality and natural audio compression.

Low Delay Audio, depicted in Figure B-28, contains the low-delay versions of the AAC coder, CELP, and HVXC for speech and network error resilience. It also includes TTSI for text. It is oriented for two-way communication systems where large audio delay is perceivable (and annoying).

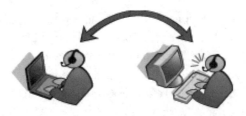

Figure B-28   *The Low Delay Audio profile is well-suited for two-way communication.*

The Natural Audio profile contains only the natural audio codecs: all the AAC variants (low delay, low complexity, scalable, and others), super-low bit-rate TwinVQ, BSAC, HILN, HVXC, and CELP.

The Mobile Audio Internetworking (MAUI) profile contains low-complexity, low-delay, and scalable AAC, as well as TwinVQ and BSAC. It is designed to provide good, but low complexity natural audio compression for mobile communication devices that already have a voice codec (such as cell phones).

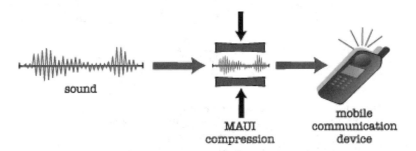

Figure B-29   *Mobile Audio Internetworking is a simple and scalable profile for mobile phones and other communication devices.*

The High-efficiency AAC profile uses a technique called *SBR* (Spectral Band Replication) that is designed to enhance any underlying codec (MP3, AAC, speech codecs) by using a small bitstream to add a quality-enhancing high-frequency signal. A U.S. satellite radio provider has been using high-efficiency AAC at bit rates less than 64Kbps for several years.

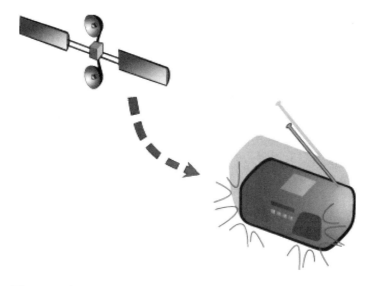

Figure B-30 *The High-efficiency AAC profile is used by commercial satellite radio.*

PART 4: CONFORMANCE

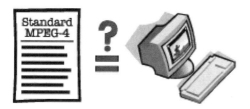

Conformance testing is the process of ensuring that a particular implementation conforms, or properly implements, the standard. Due to the complexity of hardware and software development, it is actually very easy for products to drift away from the standard in the absence of sufficient testing. It is an ongoing process to ensure that all parties supporting a standard actually conform to the standard and interoperability.

For testing playback devices, the obvious solution is to have a set of sample media to test against. For authoring tools that presume to create MPEG-4 content, it is necessary to verify that they always output a conforming bitstream.

As mentioned earlier, the conformance points of the standard are stated as *profile at level*; for instance, a device or software product can claim to support the MPEG-4 Simple Visual profile at level 0. The conformance part of the MPEG-4 specification contains detailed information about the tests to be done to verify that it indeed plays back any valid MPEG-4 stream using Simple Visual at level 0.

Two terms come up constantly when reading through MPEG: *normative* and *informative*. Normative tests, software, descriptions, and other information are required in order to implement the standard. Extra information is informative, such as examples and sample implementations. Conformance does not require adherence to informative portions of the standard.

In addition to sample media and descriptions of tests, the Conformance part includes testing software for encoding, decoding, supporting systems, and more. This software is contained in Part 5.

PART 5: REFERENCE SOFTWARE

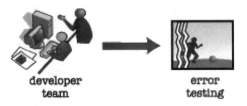

developer
team

error
testing

Many earlier technology standards tended to painstakingly describe in English how a hardware device or software algorithm was to be implemented. Others used *pseudo-code*, a generic expression of software that resembles several programming languages but isn't really written in any of them.

MPEG-4 decided to include simulation software as a key part of the standard. Member companies of the MPEG-4 development effort developed the software in common languages, such as C or C++, and gave it freely to MPEG. Thus, several implementations exist for the various tools in Parts 1 (Systems), 2 (Visual), 3 (Audio), and 6 (Delivery). Luckily, the licensing terms on the software are such that anyone can examine or use it to create their MPEG-4-compliant project.

This code is not optimized, however, and none of it exists as a stand-alone product. For instance, the sample video decoders decode only video, not audio; they do not display it on-screen; and they don't work with standard MP4 files, only the raw video bitstream. To use the reference software commercially, it needs to be optimized to run efficiently on specific operating systems or computer platforms, and it needs to be combined with a lot of other supporting code.

PART 6: DELIVERY MULTIMEDIA INTEGRATION FRAMEWORK

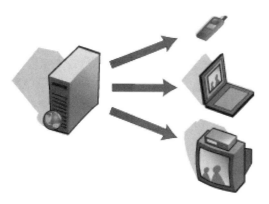

MPEG-2 video was designed for delivery at a relatively high bit rates to a few devices, such as DVD players and digital television receivers. MPEG-4 video is expected to be delivered to everything from cell phones to set top boxes to personal computers to handhelds to studio editing stations—and over far more networks. MPEG-4 can travel over WiFi, cellular wireless (in its many forms), TCP/IP, multicast, and custom protocols, as well as any path that MPEG-2 took.

Different transport systems have different delay, bandwidth, data loss, and feedback characteristics. A DVD player has high bandwidth data loss only due to scratches on the disk and fairly low delay (tenths of a second), but has no feedback mechanism. Cellular networks have fairly low bandwidth, a lot of potential data loss due to signal strength, reasonably low delay, but they have a two-way data channel with a *back channel* for providing real-time feedback to the sender such as, "I'm getting a lot of packet loss; scale down."

Internet networks have more bandwidth than cellular phone networks in general, but have higher or at least more variable delay characteristics, and like cellular, they can have a back-channel where the playback device sends information back to the content source to report on network conditions or even to interact with the content. Multicast delivery on corporate intranets has a certain amount of packet loss, fairly low delay, but no back channel.

MPEG cannot hope to standardize all these. To deal with this variety of transport options, MPEG created a layer between it and the transport layer. So, instead of MPEG having to standardize all the messy details of sending the video over, say, a wireless network, MPEG instead simply standardized the DMIF. The wireless providers seek to deliver MPEG-4 video over their cellular network then design a way to connect DMIF to their wireless protocols.

380 MASTERING INTERNET VIDEO

If you are familiar with programming, you can understand the concept of a layer; the layer provides all the relevant knobs and switches (what the player would like to play, how much bandwidth the player has, how much complexity the player can handle, what kind of packet loss the player is receiving, and so on), and you simply trigger those and don't worry about the details. For DMIF, that layer is called *DAI* (DMIF Application Interface). An MPEG-4 player asks DAI for the various objects and streams that make up the content, and on the other end the DMIF layer pulls the bits off the hard disk or DVD drive, through the air at 1800MHz or 2.4GHz, or off a flash memory stick—all of which transparent to the requesting player.

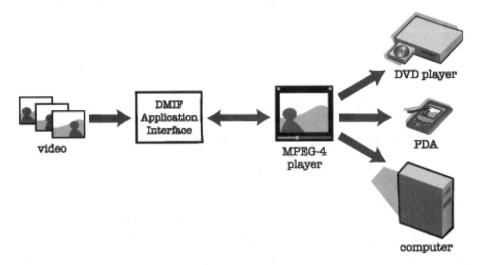

Figure B-31 *DAI is a standardized layer for delivering MPEG-4 video to various devices.*

PART 7: OPTIMIZED SOFTWARE

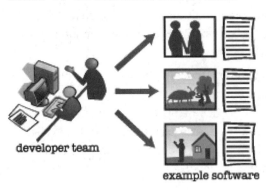

Where Part 5 included unoptimized MPEG-4 software that actually formed the standard, this part includes "informative" example software. This software does not have to be used in order to follow the standard. In other words, Part 7 provides examples of a more "state-of-the-art" implementation of video encoding. To MPEG-4 developers, this example serves as not merely a functional implementation of the standard, but also as a high-performance version.

PART 8: MPEG-4 ON IP FRAMEWORK

Abbreviated *4onIP*, Part 8 specifies how MPEG-4 is to be carried over IP networks—for example, the Internet. Even though Part 6 of the standard does its best to abstract MPEG-4 away from specific transport issues, MPEG wanted to address the strong industry need for standards in this area.

Several things are dealt with in this part of the standard. One is MIME types. MIME (Multipurpose Internet Mail Extensions) categorizes files into standard types, so that programs like a web browser or email client can launch the appropriate application. This part standardizes the MIME types to be used for MPEG content: audio (audio/mp4), video (video/mp4), MPEG-4 streams without audio or video (application/mp4), initial object descriptors, which define the complexity and levels available in a content stream (applications/mpeg4-iod), and finally the XML text version of the initial object description (applications/ mpeg4-iod-xmt).

This part also provides detailed recommendations on how to use the existing IETF standards RTP/RTSP to carry MPEG-4. For more detail, see Chapter 4, "Streaming Media Server Software."

PART 9: REFERENCE HARDWARE DESCRIPTION

Part 9 of the standard provides examples of how to design special computer chips for MPEG-4. Included are blueprints for implementing compressors, decompressors, and other MPEG-4 tools in hardware instead of software.

It is a well-established rule that specialized hardware can perform specific tasks faster than software. State-of-the-art video and audio compression are usually performed for years with expensive hardware before general-purpose computer processors catch up.

As an example, specialized chips could encode and decode MP3 audio for years before PC speeds reached the 100MHz mark, which allowed software to play MP3 files in real time (around 1996). Now, hundreds of MP3 players exist, and none of them use chips as fast as 100MHz. Instead, they use special-purpose chips running at much slower frequencies, using much less power, and doing one thing and doing it really well. Unlike the general-purpose CPUs in a computer, these chips actually have the decompression algorithm for MP3 built in— but they can't do much else. Similarly, dedicated hardware chips allow for the cheap manufacture of cell phones, which are basically audio compressors and decompressors.

It always takes a more powerful general-purpose CPU to do a specialized task. Sure, you can teach an old CPU new tricks through software—but don't expect them to do it fast.

PART 10: ADVANCED VIDEO CODING

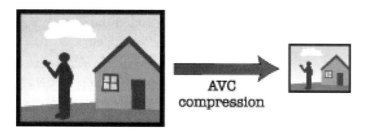

Part 10 of the MPEG-4 standard describes the newest codec addition—*AVC*, or Advanced Video Coding. Also called *H.26L* (during development) and *H.264*, AVC was jointly developed by MPEG and the ITU, and was added to keep MPEG-4 up with the latest in video encoding. ITU calls it H.264, according to its own numbering scheme and as a successor to its H.263 standard.

AVC is essentially twice as good as MPEG-2 at the same bit rate, and thus delivers a similar quality stream at half the bit rate. It is more efficient than the most advanced MPEG-4 Part 2 visual codecs. Because AVC works within the MPEG-4 system and all its existing tools, which in turn work over MPEG-2 transport layers, it is possible that existing MPEG-2 broadcast delivery will be upgraded to AVC by simply plugging in new encoders and upgrading the set top boxes.

AVC is not restricted to broadcast bit rates, however. The codec works at the full range of expected sizes, from small mobile phone video less than 64Kbps to standard HDTV sizes in the 20Mbps–50Mbps range, all the way up to studio bit rates at 240Mbps.

Technical improvements in codecs are hard to describe without delving into mathematics. Visually, AVC improves on all the earlier MPEG codecs by reducing blockiness. Most natural visual codecs in MPEG break the image into 16×16 pixel blocks, analyze how these blocks move from one frame to another, and then send that small bit of motion information instead of the whole block. This is called *motion estimation and compensation* (see Chapter 2). The codec can't really tell that the car is moving; it can only tell that a small patch of color in the tire of the car moved to the right from one frame to the next.

In AVC, the sizes of these blocks can vary tremendously—it can be a 16×16 block, or 16 small 4×4 blocks, or eight 8×4 pixel strips, or something else, as shown in Figure B-32. A separate, more accurate motion description can be sent for each of these subblocks (because motion is tracked based on an object's shape and orientation, and not encumbered by background information). Also, where earlier codecs could make reference to only one other reference frame to use as the basis for moving blocks, AVC can essentially say, "Take this small block from three frames ago and move it here, and this large block from two frames ago and move it here, and this small block from five frames ago and move it here."

Each new frame can be compactly drawn from a large palette of moved, variable-sized blocks from earlier frames. Finally, AVC decoders feature a *deblocking filter* that does just what it sounds like—it goes along the edges between blocks where there are visual artifacts (jaggedness) and smooths them out. All these techniques together greatly reduce the amount of data that AVC needs to send for each frame, and minimize the blocky patterns characteristic of earlier MPEG codecs.

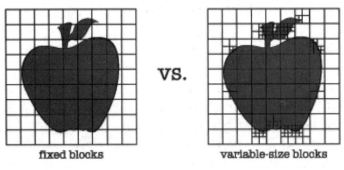

Figure B-32 *A comparison of 16×16 block compression and AVC.*

All these new techniques come at the cost of complexity. The CPU power needed to decode these streams is several times greater than that required for earlier decoders. The encoding is even harder, because there are so many options and there is no right answer—the more time the system has, the more block matching it can do and the smaller the image can potentially become. However, this means that AVC has a lot of room for codec optimization, so that every year the AVC encoders should get more efficient. Like all MPEG standards, only the AVC bitstream for the decoder is specified, so future encoders can keep improving and remain compatible with existing playback systems, due to both increasing computing power and the continuing optimization of the decoding software by competing companies.

PART 11: SCENE DESCRIPTION AND APPLICATION ENGINE

Gradually, pieces of Part 1 (Systems) were breaking off in different revisions of MPEG-4 and getting their own distinct parts in the standard. Part 11 includes the Scene Description tools (BIFS, for composition of 3D scenes) and MPEG-J (Java-based MPEGlets, the application engine), to which were added tools for text/font rendering (using a standard called OpenType) and additional 2D graphics animation tools. This part also includes updates to the system's parts necessary to support multi-user worlds as specified in Part 16.

PART 12: ISO BASE MEDIA FILE FORMAT

Due to a desire to standardize media file formats across different areas, after evaluating competing proposals the QuickTime file format became the basis not only for MP4 (the MPEG-4 file format), but also for any ISO standard media storage. This part of the standard describes how different applications can use the ISO file format in consistent ways so that interoperability is possible, and so that bitstreams that work in different worlds (perhaps a still JPEG 2000 image, or an H.263 video stream) can be displayed no matter what client application happens upon the file.

PART 13: IPMP EXTENSIONS (IPMP-X)

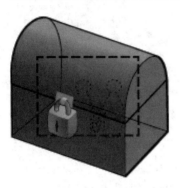

The humorously named *IPMP* standard for *Intellectual Property Management and Protection* was initially standardized in Part 1 (Systems). Its goal was not to standardize DRM for MPEG-4, but rather to standardize the necessary interfaces so that different vendors' DRM tools could coexist cleanly. The initial implementation of IPMP achieved this but did not achieve enough interoperability *between* different DRM solutions. If an MPEG-4-compliant player did not recognize the particular vendor DRM system that the content was encoded in, the player was out of luck and could not decode the stream.

Extensions to the IPMP standard have resulted in an increased degree of interoperability, where the redundancies between different systems have been eliminated (for example, different software using the same encryption techniques can share the same implementation of those techniques). In addition, the interactions between different IPMP tools (DRM systems) have been made smoother, and different IPMP tools can securely communicate and "trust" each other. Figure B-33 depicts the interoperability of IPMP.

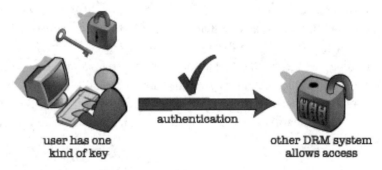

user has one
kind of key

authentication

other DRM system
allows access

Figure B-33 *The IPMP standard has increased the degree of compatibility between various DRM systems.*

The improved component system allows for the replacement of IPMP tools if they become compromised (or hacked). IPMP-X can also work with different rights-description languages, including the upcoming MPEG-21. *Rights description languages* specify for digital media who can play it under what conditions (for example, did they pay?).

PART 14: MP4 FILE FORMAT

Originally described in Part 1 (Systems), this section of the standard updates the description of the standard MP4 file format. ISO created a new a file format, modeled after Apple's QuickTime MOV format (just like MP4), and standardized it as a general-purpose file format. Thus, this part of the standard redefines the MP4 file format and makes reference to the ISO base media format as its underlying framework. This part of the standard is somewhat of a formality, as the file format is essentially unchanged.

PART 15: AVC FILE FORMAT

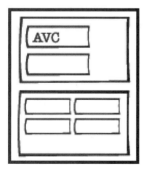

This part of the standard describes how AVC is to be stored in an ISO media format, including how to store multiple AVC streams in the file and how to access AVC scalability features to play the video back at different frame rates and quality levels.

PART 16: ANIMATION FRAMEWORK EXTENSION (AFX) AND MuW (MULTI-USER WORLDS)

The Synthetic-Natural Hybrid Coding (SNHC) group within MPEG-4 started work in the mid 1990s when 3D video cards weren't in broad use. The existing set of MPEG-4 tools for 2D and 3D composition, while extensive, do not provide the visual integration and experiences that is the state of the art in 3D video games today. VRML '97, the basis for BIFS, supports fairly simple shapes and animation techniques compared to the current technology.

Thus, the smooth character animation features in video games are difficult to represent in BIFS, and the common tools used in the industry to create 3D scenes and animations do not export easily to BIFS. In Part 16 of the standard, the SNHC group in MPEG has standardized backwards-compatible extensions to the existing animation frameworks, incorporating modern shape, animation, and rendering features.

In addition to modernizing the 3D toolset, the Multi-User technology specification provides the tools for creating interactive, online 3D worlds where changes made in the world (either by the content author or by actions from the viewers) are propagated to all the viewing terminals.

Because 3D video game technologies are moving in the direction of extremely lifelike, natural-looking video, techniques for delivering these experiences are moving into the video compression domains that are standardized (and patented) in MPEG. As a result, the SNHC group in MPEG is exploring standardization of additional tools for video game development to complete the picture, perhaps opening the door for an industry-standard 3D gaming platform.

PART 17: STREAMING TEXT FORMAT

In coordination with the 3GPP (Third Generation Partnership Project for wireless), the MPEG body has been working to standardize the time-triggered overlay and text rendering with different characteristics and size, and its error-resilient delivery. Still in development, Part 17 primarily standardizes how 3GPP text streams interact with MPEG-4 video and BIFS.

SUMMARY

In this chapter, we presented the MPEG-4 standard as it existed at the time of writing. There will doubtless be new additions to the standard but, as we have seen, by design they will be added in the most backwards-compatible manner, leveraging all earlier MPEG-4 tools and cooperating nicely with relevant external emerging standards.

We have emphasized the natural codecs in our explanations because those who author synthetic video already have a huge compression advantage over natural video, and we assume that most readers are trying to get existing natural video deployed online.

The importance of standardization in the video space cannot possibly be over-emphasized, and the success of earlier MPEG standards makes it very likely that MPEG-4 will achieve this. It has been said that more data currently flows over the MPEG-2 transport layer than flows over TCP/IP.

The major proprietary video codec vendors are likely to converge upon MPEG-4 video standards, which are becoming ubiquitous on the wired Internet and its wireless future.

GLOSSARY

16mm film   Used for student and educational films, and in the past, 35mm films would be converted to 16mm for TV broadcast. A lot of archival material exists on 16mm.

2:2 pulldown   In Europe or other regions that use 50 field per second (fps) interlaced video, the content goes through a process called 2:2 pulldown. In this process, each frame of film (which is 24 fps) is split into two fields, doubling to 48 frames. So what of the other two fields? European systems simply play the films faster. A 50-minute film ends in 48 minutes.

3:2 pulldown   When 24 fps film needs to be converted for broadcast on 60 field per second television, there are not enough frames to fill a second. For every four frames of film, there are 10 fields of video. Thus, a conversion technique was developed to spread 24 frames over 60 fields. It is called 3:2 pulldown because it pulls down film frames into 3 and 2 fields, alternating.

35mm film   The staple film used in cinema today. This is used in a variety of different formats and aspect ratios.

70mm film   Most commercial films are recorded on 70mm film, which offers four times the resolution (double the width and the height) of 35mm film.

8mm film   8mm film and Super 8 were the old home movie formats. A lot of this consumer footage has been converted to video. However, in the video conversion, it was probably copied onto VHS tape, which is interlaced and fairly low quality.

AAC Advanced Audio Codec. The tremendous success of MP3 (MPEG-1 Layer III audio) was a tough act for the MPEG-4 audio codecs to follow. MPEG-2 had already standardized the newer AAC codec that supported multi-channel sound, such as the 5.1 "surround" sound on DVDs (5.1 sound has six channels of sound). The five are center, front right, front left, rear right, rear left. MPEG-4 has included and enhanced this codec and continues to call it AAC. MPEG-4 includes many different versions of the AAC codec—low-complexity versions that require less powerful playback processors; error resilient versions that can endure packet loss; and low-latency versions that are good for two-way communication.

ActiveX Architecture made by Microsoft for making plug-ins for Internet Explorer.

Adobe A software company known for such programs as Photoshop and Acrobat.

Advanced Core The Advanced Core visual profile provides scalability for still textures and natural video.

Advanced Coding Efficiency This profile includes better compression for camera motions.

Advanced Real Time Simple This profile works well for video conferencing and other real-time applications.

Advanced Scalable Texture A profile that allows for error resilience and tiling.

Advanced Simple The Advanced Simple profile adds better motion compression.

AFX Animation Framework eXtension, which is a part of the MPEG-4 standard dealing with multi-user 3D worlds.

algorithm The step-by-step method used by a computer to solve a mathematical problem, such as compression, encryption, and so on.

Amiga A brand of computer that was popular in the late 80's to the early 90's.

Analog When phonographs play back audio, the speakers' vibrations correspond to the indentations on a vinyl record. Essentially, the sound is analogous to the small pits and bumps on the record. When video is stored in an analog form, the frames are stored in an analogous way on a physical medium, such as film or tape.

anamorphic Pertaining to a technique for squeezing widescreen video onto a narrower recording medium such as film or DVD. An anamorphic widescreen movie stored on DVD is stored at 720x480, but the 720 pixels are resampled and stretched (by creating new pixels) to fill 1280 pixels horizontally. Anamorphic cinema squeezes wide (2.35:1) frames onto 35mm film.

ANSI   The American National Standards Institute is an organization that works to form standards in the United States and to ratify international standards for domestic use.

AOL   America Online is one of the largest consumer (ISP) Internet Service Providers in the United States.

API   Application Programming Interface is the array of features available to a computer programmer using a particular software tool, and the methods of communicating with and using these tools.

application layer   This is the top protocol layer. All other Internet protocols used by applications are built upon the transport layer protocols. These protocols make up the application layer. Of course, the most well known of these is HTTP (Hypertext Transfer Protocol). Other familiar protocols include FTP (File Transfer Protocol, ports 21 and 23), SMTP (Simple Mail Transport Protocol), and POP3 (Post Office Protocol, version 3). All of these protocols use TCP as its transport, and each performs the same basic functions: connect, send data, receive data, and disconnect.

artifacting   See mosquito noise.

ASF   Advanced Systems Format is a Microsoft file type for streaming media.

aspect ratio   Aspect ratio is how wide the picture is compared to how tall. Aspect ratios are written in the form horizontal:vertical. A screen with an aspect ratio of 16:9 might be eight inches horizontally by four and a half vertically, or 16 feet wide (horizontal) and 9 feet high (vertical). This ratio can also be boiled down to a denominator of 1. The ratio 1.78:1 has the same value as the ratio 16:9.

ASX   Active Streaming index are those index files compatible with the Windows Media system that refer to ASF files, or other ASX files.

Asymmetric encryption   Asymmetric encryption involves a pair of matched keys: one key to lock the data and another key to unlock it. Usually both keys can lock and unlock; key A can unlock only things locked with key B, and key B can unlock only things locked with key A.

Atari   A company famous for video games also manufactured a Macintosh-like personal computer popular in the late 80's–early 90's.

ATM   Asynchronous Transfer Mode (*not* Automatic Teller Machine) is a low-level protocol used in telecommunications over fiber, copper wire, which has better performance characteristics and bandwidth guarantees than TCP/IP.

atom   Apple's QuickTime movies were designed with a concept of four-character atoms, hierarchical structures containing elements such as index points, durations, and pointers to the media data itself. There is a top-level atom called the movie atom. The MPEG-4 and ISO file formats also use atoms.

audiovisual objects   The 3D aspects of MPEG-4, and the ability to describe a complete scene in 3D are based on a system called VRML (Virtual Reality Markup Language), a text-based, HTML-like language for describing 3D scenes. MPEG-4 extended the standard to deal with all the MPEG-4 media elements, called audiovisual objects, both natural and synthetic.

AVC   Advanced Video Coding is a codec for video and part of the MPEG-4 standard.

AVI   Audio Video Interleaved; a container file format for holding video and audio.

back channel   Any data channel that travels back from the receiver to the sender for providing real time feedback to the sender, such as, "I'm getting a lot of packet loss, scale down."

backbone   The Internet backbone (as much as a large, shapeless, and ever shifting cloud of networks can have a backbone!) consists of long-haul connections that carry large volumes of Internet traffic (packets) across and between continents.

background sprite   A term used for a relatively unchanging background behind the moving foreground objects.

backwards compatible   Sometimes a standard must be added to or improved upon. When these additions are done in such a way that any product built on the improved standard can continue to work with products based on the earlier standard, the standard and new products are said to be backwards compatible. Almost all DVD players (which use MPEG-2 video) also play VCDs (video CDs, which use MPEG-1 video and are popular in Asia) because they were designed to be backwards compatible.

bandwidth   How much traffic a network connection can handle.

base layer   Scalability in bitrate/quality is achieved by sending multiple layers: a base layer (lower resolution and framerate) and an enhancement layer (adding higher resolution and framerate). The player can decode only the base layer to reduce complexity or bandwidth.

Basic Animated Texture   The Basic Animated Texture profile maps wavelet-compressed shapes onto a 2D shape.

best effort delivery   Best effort is the only kind of data transport the public Internet provides. Routers do "the best they can," but if they run out of memory, bandwidth, or have other, more important data to transfer, they can simply discard data packets.

Betacam SP   See BetaSP.

BetaSP   A very high quality professional analog tape.

BGMP   Border Gateway Multicast Protocol is a sparse mode multicast protocol that designates a domain instead of a specific core router as the central coordination point. This allows any router around that domain to serve as the core router, and reduces the dependency on a single router.

bi-directional frame   A frame whose contents are calculated based on both previous and future intraframes or predictive frames. Essentially, this is like a "tween" frame in Flash animation: given a starting frame and an ending frame, the software can calculate the position of the objects in each "in-between" frame.

BIFS   Binary Format for Scenes is part of the MPEG-4 standard that deals with synchronizing video and audio.

bitmap   A kind of image on a computer that consists of simple, uncompressed pixels. It is the "purest" form of an image.

bitrate   We talk about the size of a stream as its bit rate—that is, the number of bits used to represent a second of audio or video. The bitrate is measured in kilobits per second, or Kbps, the same measurement used for Internet connection speeds. This is handy because we can compare a stream's bitrate to the user's bandwidth.

bitrate sensitive delivery   Bitrate sensitive delivery guarantees are essential for applications that operate at a fixed bitrate and are sensitive to packet loss. Certain video conferencing protocols work well with this delivery profile because they were originally designed for fixed-bandwidth, highly reliable data networks (such as leased lines between two locations).

bitstream   In MPEG, the combined statistics for frames per second, bitrate, size, and computational complexity as a standard of quality.

blocking   If you have ever tried using JPEG's low quality setting in a graphic editor, you have probably seen blocking in the image. JPEG takes each channel—Y', Cr , and Cb—splits them into 8x8 blocks, and applies a mathematical process that essentially transforms the individual pixel values in those blocks into a representation of the spatial frequencies of change in the block. The purpose of this transformation is to represent the general pattern or shape of the block without having to transmit the value, luma, and color of every single pixel.

BNC   A type of high quality cable used for high quality analog transmission.

bottleneck   A Three Stooges-type phenomena wherein a large amount of data formerly traveling on a high-bandwidth stream hits a part where the bandwidth lowers. This is analogous to what happens after a "Road Narrows" sign on a busy street; although things were going smoothly before, everyone becomes stuck in this small section of the road.

broadband   The sweeping term for any high-capacity Internet connection, such as DSL or cable, which is "always on."

broadcast   To deliver video publicly and broadly, usually simultaneously to all viewers; or, simply any video that is sent to many people.

brownout   Using the analogy of a public exchange point being a major airport, if it is a "foggy day" at that exchange, the entire Internet that goes through that exchange can be slowed down (brownouts) by the data that cannot take off.

brute force   Computing methods that are redundant and devoid of finesse, such as simply trying every possible combination for a lock rather than picking it or some other alternative.

BSAC   Bit-Sliced Arithmetic Coding is for a codec audio transmission that can decrease or increase in quality by very small increments to adjust to available bandwidth conditions.

BSR   The Board of Standards Review, which is a part of the American National Standards Institute (ANSI).

buffer   The building up of a safety zone for streaming so that the video is not pausing to wait on a slow transmission. Also, the portion of a streaming file that is cached on the playback computer at a given time.

buzzword   An invented term for technology to make it seem more exciting, unique, useful, or proprietary.

caching   Making a local copy of data so it can be accessed more quickly. Caching servers bring content closer to the viewer, either by keeping a copy inside of a company network or keeping a copy near the viewer on their Internet service provider.

Cb   Chrominance-blue. See YCrCb.

CBR   Constant Bit Rate; the video's bit rate stays consistent while its quality varies.

CBT   Core-based Trees; a simple, sparse-mode multicast protocol. New group members send join messages to a designated core router. Any routers that the join message passes along the way also begin to relay the multicast. This builds a tree up as the packets move to the core. The choice of core router location is important because the broadcast tree is rooted at the core.

CCD   Charge-Coupled Device (CCD) is a device in digital cameras that measures brightness and color.

CD   Compact Disc; the standard digital storage format for all manner of data that typically stores approximately 700 megabytes.

CDN   The Content Delivery Network (CDN) is a network of service providers that have rigged up a redundant linking system for streaming or web servers to make file downloads or video delivery more efficient and fail-safe.

CELP   Code Excited Linear Prediction is a scalable speech codec that ranges from 3.5 Kbps to 24 Kbps.

checksum   Checksumming is a technique used to find out whether data has been altered in transit. The receiver can sum (add) up all the data received and check if it adds up to the right number.

chroma keying   The fancy term for the traditional act of using a blue or green screen behind a person and giving them a digital background, such as for weather reports.

chrominance   Essentially, a fancy synonym for color. It is used to describe one of the channels or portions of color sent separately in delivering in a video signal.

CIF   The H.261 video conferencing code works with two video resolutions: common interchange format (CIF) at 352×288 pixel resolution, and quarter common interchange format (QCIF) at 176×144 pixels.

Cinepak   A codec invented in the early 1990's that is still used today. It is possibly the first cross-platform multimedia codec for PCs.

circuit   Telephone calls create a two-way circuit all the way from caller to receiver. The message "all circuits are busy"—usually only heard during disasters or radio call-in concert ticket giveaways—means that the switch does not have any additional slots in which to carry this call.

circuit switching   If there are not enough circuits to place the call, the main barriers to telephone transmission are at the beginning of the call. While a call is in progress, the entire route between the caller and recipient is reserved for their use only—even if there is silence and no one is talking. Telephones use what is called a circuit-switched connection.

CMYK   Cyan Magenta Yellow Black; the four pigments mixed together by most printing presses to create their color range. Compare with RGB.

coaxial   The cable used in "cable" TV and other TV-related services.

codec   Because the compression and decompression steps are closely related, the software that performs these tasks is usually bundled together in a package called codec. The word itself is a combination of compressor and decompressor, and can describe either the technique used to compress the video, or the software on the computer that actually does the compressing and decompressing.

collocation   Having to do with hosting files on multiple servers in different places than one's own business (for instance, at an ISP or telephone company or managed hosting service) for convenience, speed, or reliability.

component   A term for any kind of cable or transmission device wherein the data for brightness and colors are separated onto multiple wires.

composite   A term for any kind of cable or transmission device wherein the data for brightness and colors are compressed onto one wire.

compression   Compression is the process of making a video file smaller.

conformance point   A conformance point is a combination of a profile and a level where different products can interoperate (by conforming to that level and profile). If all the cell phones support creation and playback of a simple visual profile at level 0, any cell phone is able to play back a video made by any other cell phone.

connotations   An idea or meaning implied by or associated with something.

Core   The Core visual profile defines shape objects, which can be compressed separately.

Core Scalable   Core Scalable extends Core video to allow temporal scalability (drop frames) or spatial scalability (lower resolution) of any individual visual object in the scene.

Core Studio   Core Studio extends the Simple Studio profile but only supports 10-bit color depth. It adds in-between frames for increased compression savings (also increasing the computing power needed to use it).

cosine   Cosines are used to measure triangles and to describe waves and frequencies using mathematics.

CPM   Cost per thousand (mil = thousand); the standard measure of how much an advertiser will pay per 1000 viewings of an ad.

CPU   Central Processing Unit, or just processor. This is the main chip in a computer that determines how quickly your computer can run programs, and to some degree, how many programs it can juggle at once.

Cr   Chrominance-red. See YCrCb.

crack   The breaking of an encryption system or other safety measure, or a program that performs the breaking.

cryptography   The art or science of encryption on a computer.

cryptosystem   A system for encryption on a computer.

CSS   Content Scramble System; a method of encryption for DVDs to prevent digital copying.

DAI   Delivery Multimedia Integration Framework (DMIF) Application Interface; an MPEG-4 player asks DAI for the various objects and streams that make up the content. On the other end, the DMIF layer pulls the bits off the hard disk or DVD drive, through the air at 1800Mhz or 2.4Ghz, or off of flash memory, all transparent to the requesting player.

DAT   Digital Audio Tape; in the early days of digital audio recording, CD audio did not yet exist, and digital audio tape was becoming a standard in pro audio. The DAT standard sampled data at a high rate, 48khz, 16-bit sampling, but did not compress it.

datagram   Small bits of data.

data-link layer   The second of the protocol layers is the data-link layer. At this layer, almost every piece of hardware, from wireless to optical, TV cable, telephone, or satellite, all have their own special "language" or protocol with which they intercommunicate.

DCT   Discrete cosine transform is the name of the type of Fourier transform that uses discrete points (as opposed to continuous lines). It uses cosines (sine waves, just shifted to the left half a wave) to do this. DCT is really a lossless part of compressing data; it simply restates the same data in a different way by transforming it.

de facto   Latin for "in fact." A de facto standard is a standard because it beat out the competition, as opposed to being selected by a committee.

decompression   The process of decompressing is essentially the opposite of compressing; whatever steps were done to compress the video are now reversed. Like making juice from concentrate, this is the "just add water" step return to something resembling with the original.

decrypt   To unscramble and retrieve a message that has been encrypted.

DeCSS   A program that was made to remove the CSS protection on DVDs so they could be copied.

delay sensitive delivery   Delay sensitive delivery is appropriate for variable-bitrate video codecs that nonetheless depend on timely delivery of key frames to reproduce an intelligible picture on the network connection's viewing end.

dense mode multicast   A CEO broadcast example is a good example of dense mode multicasting. Just about everyone in the company would want to watch the broadcast, so the system could operate more quickly by simply flooding the video to all the routers and having routers without any viewers specifically ask the parent router to stop sending, or to prune that router. Dense mode protocols make sense only inside a private network, and even then, only when a majority of the computers on the network will receive the multicast.

DES   Data Encryption Standard is an algorithm developed by IBM and evaluated by the National Security Agency.

dialup   The sweeping term for any low-capacity Internet connection wherein you dial through a phone line to your ISPs.

Digest   A digital hash. See hash.

DigiBeta   The dominant standard for filming digital video; a high-quality tape format.

digital   Digital content is represented not by analogous indentations or etchings in some physical media (the vinyl in records or the silver in film), but by a series of numbers, which are then encoded as ones and zeros on physical media.

Digital signature   Digital signatures not only assure the stream's integrity, but also positively verify who sent it. It works as follows: the publisher of the file calculates a checksum, scrambles the checksum, and locks it with a secret key or pass code that only the publisher knows, but that can be unlocked with a publicly available key. The player software uses the public key to unlock the checksum and compares it with the calculated checksum. If they match, the file must not have been altered in transit because only the author who knew the checksum to begin with could have produced it.

distress stream   A low-bitrate stream used to keep streaming media going when low bandwidth or high error conditions prevent the normal stream from functioning.

disparate   Containing or composed of dissimilar or opposing elements.

DivX   Around 1998, movies were converted from DVDs to MPEG-1 files. Just when Microsoft's new MPEG-4 codecs were looking like a more efficient alternative, Microsoft crippled the codec so it would play back only content stored in ASF (Microsoft's Advanced Systems Format) files, which Linux machines could not use. Then a crafty French programmer re-altered the Microsoft MPEG-4 codec so it could once again play content stored in AVI (audio-video interleaved) files. Now, with an even better codec than MPEG-1, a system emerged for ripping movies from DVD. This system consists of Microsoft MPEG-4 v3 for the video, MP3 for the audio, and AVI as the file container. This new rogue "standard" was dubbed DivX.

DMIF   Delivery Multimedia Integration Framework; MPEG-2 was always intended to be delivered either from DVD or from satellite, thus the speed of delivery and packet formats were known ahead of time. MPEG-4 decided to support every possible transport mechanism such as files, network, and wireless connection, so it required a design that worked independent of any specific mechanism. This was achieved with Delivery Multimedia Integration Framework, which allows the playback system to simply say "get me the video;" DMIF then tells the actual transport layer what objects it needs, when, and how much delay it can endure.

DOCSIS   Data Over Cable Service Interface Specification is a protocol used to send data over cable television wiring.

download   In downloading, the entire file is downloaded to the user's machine before he can play a single frame. In the download scenario, a standard web (HTTP) server can be used to serve the media file. The user must have the appropriate player.

down sampling   Reducing the resolution of either an image or a part of the image (such as the detail of color) so as to lower file size.

DPI   Dots per inch. A measure of resolution for printers, scanners, and displays.

digital rights management   Digital Rights Management technological methods of controlling how users consume media they have licensed, downloaded, or purchased.

DSS   Digital Satellite Systems is a specific type of satellite dish broadcasting.

DV   Digital Videotape is a format for digital video recording on magnetic tape.

DVC   Digital Video Cassette; a reminder located on the boxes of certain types of DV tape indicating that this is indeed a cassette for digital video.

DVCam   Two variants of DV tapes are DVCam and DVCPRO. These tape formats store less time on a single tape but are more durable, can survive more playbacks, and degrade less over time. They look the same as DV and miniDV tapes, except that they are labeled DVCam and DVCPRO. These tape formats require special players and do not play back in consumer DV players and cameras.

DVCPRO   See DVCam.

DVD   Digital Video (or Versatile) Disc is an optical data storage disc the same size as a compact disk that can store large amounts of data (feature-length movies and so on). The storage capacity of DVDs can range from 4.7 gigabytes to over 20 gigabytes.

DVI   Digital Visual Interface is a type of interface that provides a completely digital path from computer/DVD player to monitor/TV.

DVMRP   Distance Vector Multicast Routing Protocol is the oldest multicast protocol and is dense mode. Distance vectors are measurements of how many routers lie between the source and the destination. This protocol minimizes the distance vectors (between routers) of the multicast tree.

elementary stream   Earlier versions of MPEG (before MPEG-4) had only two kinds of elementary streams, roughly defined as the natural audio and video that was compressed with MPEG-2 codecs.

encryption   The process of scrambling or concealing data so that it cannot be read without a way to bypass it (either with or without permission).

enhancement layer   In certain audio and video codecs, an enhancement layer provides incremental increases in quality of the signal so it can be adjusted to best use the available bandwidth of the communications channel.

entropy encoding   After other steps have been completed on a JPEG, conventional lossless compression (similar to .ZIP files and so on) is performed on the values. This is called entropy coding, and it shrinks the size of the image without getting rid of any information.

error resilience   A means of arranging the bits of a video stream so that even data loss or corruption in transit does not destroy the whole picture.

Fast Streaming   A group of Microsoft technologies concerned with reducing buffering times when seeking through content. They include the following: Fast Start: Instant-on playback; Fast Cache: Download and cache the streaming content; Fast Reconnect: Automatically reconnect to a stream if interrupted; and Fast Recovery: See forward error correction.

Forward Error Correction (FEC) A system that deals with packet loss from network error without having to resend lost packets.

FGS Fine Granularity Scalability is a profile in the visual part of the MPEG-4 standard that allows for more variation in resolution/frame rate.

field A half-frame is called a field, and it consists of every other line of the video. The odd fields contain lines 1, 3, 5, 7… and so on. The even fields consist of lines 2, 4, 6, 8…and so on.

fingerprint Used figuratively, a "fingerprint" in computers is any set of characteristics used to uniquely identify something, such as a file, an MP3, and so on.

firewall A standard security system blocking access by certain protocols.

FireWire A kind of cable that provides an all digital path from one digital device, such as a camera, to a computer.

FLA A file extension that denotes a video made in Macromedia Flash.

Flash A compression method and player wherein vector graphics are put on screen and animation commands are sent, rather than having the entire picture change each frame.

FlexMux Flexible Multiplexing is a set of tools for multiplexing, or shuffling, a data's video into a stream so it is sent smoothly, and then re-syncing it into the actual video.

flicker The perception that the pictures are flashing on and off like a strobe light.

FLV FLash Video is a file extension that denotes compressed video delivered with Macromedia Flash.

flying spot scanning Currently the highest quality method of film scanning is called flying spot scanning. A bright light (that can be aimed and scanned around) is swept across the picture vertically, and this light is split into red, green, and blue. The intensity of each color for the spot through which the light is shining is measured with a light sensor. The flying spot can be moved finely or coarsely, taking more or fewer samples per inch, as desired.

Fourier transform Named after a French mathematician, Fourier transforms can represent any oddly shaped curve on a graph as the sum of a bunch of sine waves and cosine waves added and subtracted together.

4onIP Part 8 of the standard specifies how MPEG-4 is to be carried over IP networks, that is, the Internet. Although Part 6 of the standard does its best to abstract MPEG-4 away from specific transport issues, MPEG wanted to address the strong industry need for standards in this area.

fps   Frames per second is a way of measuring frame rate.

fractal-based compression   Some of the general techniques in the area of compression were different transforms than MPEG's DCT, such as wavelets and fractal-based compressors, that zoom in on areas of pictures to find repeating data, which is easier to compress.

frame   Video creates the illusion of movement by showing a series of slightly different still images in rapid sequence. These images are called frames.

frame rate   The speed at which the frames are displayed. Frame rates of less than 10 frames per second (fps) basically look like a slide show. At 10 fps, the video conveys motion. Silent movies were filmed at 16 fps. When sound was added to movies, the frame rate was increased to 24 fps to make lips and voice synch up.

FTP   File Transfer Protoco is a protocol that predates HTTP, and is still used for uploading web pages and data files to servers.

future-proofing   Designing something to deal with future problems.

Geocities   A well known "budget" web hosting service.

GIF   A format for images that makes use of a compression scheme that was revolutionary when it was first introduced.

glitch   A sweeping term for any seemingly unexplainable computer phenomena or mistake.

global motion compensation   Advanced Coding Efficiency extends the Core profile to add optimizations such as global motion compensation, which efficiently compresses common global camera motions such as pan, zoom, and rotation. These result in greater compression at the cost of greater playback complexity.

GMP   There have been several versions of protocols for joining the multicast, and there continue to be ongoing developments in this area. The basic protocol for joining multicasts is called the Internet Group Management Protocol, or IGMP. There are three versions of this protocol. Version 1 has only the join message, version 2 adds the leave message, and version 3 adds the ability for clients to "tune in" to a particular data stream when many are being sent to a single group, and filter out all the others (for applications such as Internet TV). Multicast Listener Discovery (MLD) achieves the same goal as IGMP, but it is a part of IPv6, which is the newest version of the Internet protocol (IP). To simplify things, two more acronyms were developed. These and other similar protocols are referred to as Group Membership Protocols (GMP). IGMP version 3 and MLD version 2 are also referred to as Source Filtering Group Membership Protocols, or SFGMPs.

groups of pictures   MPEG streams are composed of interleaved audio and video data that is arranged into sections called groups of pictures. Just like TV, you can "tune in" to the stream at any point; however, unlike hierarchical formats, there is no table of contents, index, copyright information, and so on. In the MPEG-1 and MPEG-2 standards, this data is usually delivered outside of the .mpg file.

GUID   Globally Unique IDs are 128-bit numbers used extensively in Windows operating systems and programs as a handy identifier, sort of like a bar code or a serial number.

hack   1) A unique and insightful way of solving a problem. 2) A method of defeating or getting around some sort of computer limitation. 3) A gag or prank. 4) Illegal or unauthorized trespass into an online computer system.

hash   "Hashes up" a password in a predictable but irreversible way. A new scrambled string comes out of a hash. When someone enters a password to get their e-mail, for example, the password is hashed and turned into a longer string of characters. For instance, one possible hash of the word password is $1$0ZX5WIpr$HbsZvyyyeltL95mVikp831. Hashes are used to avoid storing passwords in plaintext—that is, in clearly readable text. This is why most systems cannot tell you your password if you forget it; instead, you must create a new one. They do not know your password; they only know a hash of your password, from which they cannot retrieve your password.

HD   High Definition. High quality or high resolution.

HDTV   High-Definition Television. A kind of high resolution, extremely detailed television.

headroom   A media file can only be delivered in real-time if the stream's bitrate is somewhat less than the speed of the viewer's Internet connection. For instance, a modem user with a 56K connection cannot watch streams over about 50K. A DSL subscriber with a 384K connection can only watch streams up to about 350K. The difference between the stream bitrate and the user's maximum bandwidth is called headroom. Headroom represents the amount of bandwidth available for other applications while the stream is playing.

HILN   Harmonic and Individual Lines plus Noise is used for low bitrate audio coding in the range of 4Kbps to 16Kbps.

hinting   The process of breaking up the video into chunks is called packetization. To reduce the work of the media servers, the work of organizing the file into these chunks is sometimes done beforehand through a process called hinting. Hinting involves adding additional data to the video file (a hint track) to tell the media server how to packetize it when it is served. Hint tracks contain data concerning not only what chunks of audio and video exist, but also concerning how large a chunk to send over the Internet and at what time intervals. Although similar techniques are used by all media streaming, the term "hinting" is seen primarily in QuickTime streaming.

host   The traditional term for a machine that is connected to the Internet and can both send and receive information.

HTML   HyperText Markup Language is the standard code for creating web pages.

HTTP   Short for HyperText Transfer Protocol, this protocol provides the means of delivering things such as web pages or simple images.

HTTPS   This is short for HyperText Transfer Protocol Secure. It's like HTTP, except it's armed with some sort of security system.

HTTP streaming   Serving media files from a web server in such a way that viewers can view content as it is downloaded.

hub   A hub is a simple device that connects to each computer, router, printer, or other network device, and combines them into one large network. Having been superceded by more efficient switches, hubs are being gradually phased out.

HVXC   Harmonic Vector eXcitation Coding is a very low (between 2 and 4 Kbps!) bitrate audio codec.

Hybrid   The Hybrid visual profile allows a combination of natural video and synthetic (computer-generated) objects.

H.261   A video codec standard that was intended for videoconferencing and video telephone applications.

H.263   Continued to improve upon H.261 with MPEG-like features and higher resolutions.

H.264   Another name for AVC (advanced video codec) in MPEG-4.

H.26L   Another name for AVC (advanced video codec) during its development.

IceCast   A streaming protocol created by Nullsoft for streaming MP3 radio stations.

ICY   There is one other notable streaming protocol. The Shoutcast/Icecast streaming protocols began in 1998 as a simple hack-to-stream MP3 radio station. Using a slightly customized version of the HTTP protocol (called the ICY protocol, with a URL like icy://www…), a company called Nullsoft (now part of AOL) created the Shoutcast server, which can send or receive streamed MP3, or virtually any streamable audio or video codec.

IEC   The International Electrotechnical Commission is another large international standards body that was specifically created for electronics-related standards and overlaps and cooperates with ISO (International Organization for Standardization). ISO and IEC are independent of governments, but governments adopt many of their standards.

IEEE   Institute of Electrical and Electronic Engineers. Creators of the IEEE1394/FireWire/i.Link standard (and many other standards).

IETF   The Internet Engineering Task Force has been formalizing Internet communication protocols since 1986. The IETF documents many of the Internet standards such as TCP, UDP, RTSP, RTP, and so on through the creation of documents called RFCs (Requests for Comments).

IFF   A well-designed, multipurpose file format made by Electronic Arts for audio/video storage on Amiga computers and used extensively for general data storage on computers. Examples of IFF format files are TIFF (graphics) and AIFF (digital audio).

IGMP   Internet Group Management Protocol.

IGMP snooping   While routers must understand multicast for it to work at all, switches must also. IGMP snooping occurs when a switch must look at all the IGMP packets that flow past it to figure out which machines are trying to join a multicast group. Because these messages were designed and directed at a router, the switch must "snoop" and read every single packet as it passes by.

i.Link   Sony's name for their IEEE1394/FireWire connectors.

informative   In MPEG and other standards terminology, informative information does not authoritatively define the standard, but helps illustrate it.

Instant On   Patent-pending QuickTime technology for rapid playback and seeking through files.

Intelligent Streaming   Microsoft's system for scaling down a stream's bitrate, based on real-time network conditions.

interframe   An inter- (between) frame is not a complete frame on its own; it is a smaller partial frame that can be reconstructed into a frame for display by referring to other complete frames at other times.

interlaced   Rather than redrawing the entire image 24 times each second, the inventors of the television chose to redraw half of a frame, 25 to 30 times per second (depending on the country), scanning every other line alternately. You will sometimes see the letter "i" used in conjunction with the number of frames to denote that it is interlaced.

interleaving   The process of weaving together audio and video tracks into a coherent media file.

intermediate frame   Same as interframe.

interoperability   A major standards goal is interoperability, where different companies work together to develop products independently that, when combined, work together smoothly as intended.

interpolate   Lower resolution cameras store 720 pixels, but they interpolate (fill in) the missing pixels by averaging two adjacent pixels and inserting a new pixel between them. This is also called upsampling. As you can imagine, creating new pixels out of thin air does not actually increase the quality; it increases the size and decreases the quality.

interpolated frame   Same as interframe.

interstitial   An ad placed between two bits of video; a regular "commercial."

intraframe   A self-contained (intra = internal), standalone frame; also known as a key frame.

intranet   A local network located in an office or other business.

Inverse Telecine   When 24 fps movies are converted to interlaced television standards, they are *telecine'd*. Inverse telecine reverses this process and restores the original 24 frames, which are more suited to Internet broadcast.

Inverse 3:2 pull-down   A way to reverse 3:2 pull-down. Also called Inverse Telecine.

IP   Shorthand for Internet Protocol, which is the basic networking language for the Internet.

IP v6   Internet Protocol version 6 (IPv6) is often discussed in conjunction with multicast. IPv6 is the newest version of the Internet Protocol, which is the protocol on which the entire Internet runs. Probably the most easily understood aspect of the new protocol is that addresses will go from four sets of numbers (216.250.117.130) to eight sets of letters and numbers: (2023:0000:13AF:0000:0000:09C0:522C:250D).

IPMP   The humorously named IPMP standard for Intellectual Property Management and Protection was initially standardized in part 1 (Systems) of MPEG-4. Its goal was not to standardize digital rights management for MPEG-4, but instead to standardize the necessary interfaces so that different vendors' digital rights management tools can coexist cleanly.

iPod   An extremely popular small portable MP3 player manufactured by Apple Computer.

ISMA   Internet Streaming Media Alliance.

ISO   The International Organization for Standards is the largest international body. They create standards of everything from units of measurement to country codes to freight container dimensions.

ISP   Internet Service Provider. Any company that provides Internet connections to companies or to end consumers.

ITU   The International Telecommunications Union is part of the United Nations and forms worldwide telecommunication (ITU-T) and radio communication (ITU-R) standards. The H.xxx standards, such as the H.263 video codec, are ITU-T standards.

java   A special programming language commonly used in websites.

JavaScript   Netscape's Java language.

join message   A computer joins the group of machines that receive the multicast by sending a join message to the multicast's source. All routers along the way between the intended recipient and the source see this command and know that they should forward this particular multicast to the router from which they received the join message.

JPEG   A file format created by the Joint Photographic Experts Group.

Jscript   Microsoft's Java language for Internet Explorer.

JTC   MPEG (including MPEG 1/2/4/7/21 and future) operates within the ISO/IEC joint technical committee. So the intimidating list of acronyms seen in most MPEG-generated standards document, ISO/IEC/JTC 1/SC 29/WG 11, simply indicates that MPEG is Subcommittee 29, Working Group 11 in the ISO/IEC Joint Technical Committee.

judder   The less-than-smooth motion of objects as they are displayed at slightly changing speeds.

key   A string of text or bytes in security systems that are scrambled with the original message in some way.

key management   Because of all the keys, key management becomes an important part of any digital rights management system. In the case of Internet-based video distribution (our interest here), some of the keys are usually stored securely by the media server or, in the case of some third-party systems, on a separate website with client software to communicate with that website. Sometimes, it is necessary to revoke a key that has been granted—say, to remove Bill's ability to get content when he cancels his subscription, or to prevent him from continuing to view content he has already downloaded. Systems vary in the way they implement this; however, most media digital rights management systems are centralized, so there is not a lot of worry of "checks crossing in the mail."

key frame   A standalone frame that is encoded in its entirety (compressed, of course), and does not depend on information from any other frames. Think of this as a single JPEG image.

last mile   The term last mile was coined to describe the part of the network that connects the end user with the Internet. The last mile comprises the dialup modem, cable modem, DSL, or wireless access between the end user, to the ISP central office, and up to the source of the ISP's Internet connectivity.

latency   Delay on the Internet; lag.

layered protocols   The concept of layered protocols is exciting and important to computer scientists. As an analogy, IP can be likened to letters; TCP and UDP are comprised of many IP packets and can be likened to words; higher-level protocols assemble these words into more complex sentences, paragraphs, pages, and so on.

leave message   When computers want to drop off a multicast, they send a leave message to their local router. When the router sees this message, it knows that it might not need to get the stream anymore.

letterbox   The black boxes below and above a widescreen video when the resolution is changed to fit a screen.

level   Even if two devices shared the exact same profile, one of them might be a more powerful machine or device, or it might be designed to manage higher bitrates. Many of the tools for compressing audio or video or reproducing shapes can scale down to cell phone screens and scale up to HDTV. Thus, while profiles specify which subset of tools is used, levels specify how complex the use of those tools are and what CPU power and data rates are needed to decode them.

license   In a digital rights management system, the decryption key and rules about the content.

live video   1) Video that is viewed while it is happening or seconds afterwards. 2) Video that is viewed simultaneously by all watchers. (For example, Saturday Night Live, which is filmed live and watched simultaneously by everyone except the studio audience.)

load balancing   In web or streaming media servers, having several machines serving the same data and spreading the clients across the different servers.

long-haul   A term for a type of connection that is designed to carry a large amount of data traffic over long distances.

Luma   A fancy word for brightness.

luminance   A fancy word for brightness.

Macromedia   The creators of a variety of interactive multimedia technologies, such as Flash (for web animations), Shockwave (for interactive games and CDs), and servers for video and multimedia delivery.

Macrovision   A type of protection placed on commercially made VHS tapes that distorts the video if someone tries to copy it.

Main   The Main profile incorporates background sprites, interlacing, and object shapes with transparency.

many-to-many   A good example of many-to-many multicast is multi-party video conferencing, which requires everyone to be both a broadcaster and a receiver and contains the same number of receivers as senders.

MAUI   Mobile Audio Internetworking is a simple and scalable profile for cell phones and other mobile communication devices.

Mbone   The Multimedia Backbone is a large group of multicast-enabled networks connected to the public Internet by special software that links these networks through tunnels.

MBR   Multiple Bit-Rate combines all the different bitrate encodings into a single video file.

MD5   Web servers and browsers use MD5 (for "message digest") to hash uniquely identifying content, by creating a digital "fingerprint" that can be quickly checked to see if two files are the same. SHA-1 is more resistant to hacking than MD5 and has replaced MD5 in many applications.

megapixel   A unit of measurement that is equal to one million pixels.

metadata   Data about the content of media files, such as copyright data, authorship, dates of creation, ownership, and so on.

MIDI   Generally known as that cheesy, Casio-sounding prerecorded music you sometimes hear when you visit a Geocities-hosted web page.

MiniDV   MiniDV is pretty much the standard DV tape format. It fits in everything from small handheld video recorders to large digital filmmaker cameras.

MJPEG   Motion JPEG, an animated image format that consists entirely of compressed key frames.

MLD   Multicast Listener Discovery (MLD) achieves the same goal as the multicast Internet Group Management Protocol (IGMP), but is part of IP v6, the newest version of the Internet Protocol (IP).

MMS Microsoft Media Server (protocol). A media transfer protocol created by Microsoft for transporting Windows Media.

MMST Microsoft Media Server protocol for TCP.

MMSU A variant of the MMS protocol, MMSU goes over UDP for the most efficient delivery.

MOD MOD (from *module*) files are a computer multimedia sound format from the late 80's and early 90's, before computers had enough storage or processing power to deal with natural audio codecs, such as MP3. Mod files a combination of sample voices and the capability to embed sound clips.

MOSPF Multicast Extensions to Open Shortest Path First. Another dense mode multicast protocol, MOSPF is based on a routing technique that simply chooses the next shortest unused path (between routers) when building a multicast tree.

mosquito noise An ugly blurring effect that occurs when trying to compress images with high contrast spaces such as text (for example, black on white). Also called artifacting.

motion animation and compensation Most natural visual codecs in MPEG break the image into 16x16 pixel blocks, analyze how these blocks move from one frame to another, and send that small bit of motion information instead of the whole block. This is called motion estimation and compensation. The codec cannot really tell that the car is moving; it can only tell that a small patch of color in the car's tire moved to the right from one frame to the next.

mount point A URL on a media server (Real, QuickTime).

MOV The format of Apple's QuickTime media files (MOVie). MOV files are a flexible multimedia storage format, and have been used as the basis for the MPEG-4 and international standard file formats.

MPEG-1 MPEG-1 is the compression technique used in video CDs, on some game CDs circa the mid-1990's (for example, Playstation), CD-Interactive, and is commonly seen in .mpg files.

MPEG-2 MPEG-2 is probably the most widely deployed digital video standard. It is the standard used by digital satellite systems (DSS), DVD players, and digital cable systems.

MPEG-3 MPEG-3 was originally intended to be the compression system for HDTV, but MPEG-2 out-performed expectations making MPEG-3 unnecessary.

MPEG-4 MPEG-4 (standardized in 1999; the extensions are still being worked on) is a standard encompassing a vast array of tools for coding (digital representation) of audio and video.

MP3 For years MP3, or MPEG-1 Layer III audio, was an obscure audio codec. It was technically part of the MPEG-1 standard, but implementing it required a lot of processor power. MPEG-1 Video and MPEG-1 Layer II audio (MP2!), which did much lighter compression, were used in Video CDs and CD-Interactive; in addition, almost no commercial implementations of MPEG-1, including special chips that implemented it, supported the MP3 part of the standard. MP3 was and still is a good compression format. When people first started using the MP3 codec in the mid 1990's, the Intel 80486 PC computers of the time were not even fast enough to play back MP3s in real-time. MP3 was used as a sort of "zip file" for CDs and imported records; people would take an audio CD and wait many hours for it to compress (like today's video compression).

multicast An important, but limited network technology for efficiently broadcasting live media to large audiences.

multicast group Collections of machines that have indicated their desire to receive a particular broadcast. Today, when multicast is used to broadcast video or audio to an audience, these groups are sometimes called channels.

multiplexing With multiplexing, video elements are shuffled together into a single stream, and then resynched to a timeline.

Narrowcast To deliver video to a niche market on the Internet.

NAT Network Address Translator. A device that allows multiple computers to share one IP address.

natural key frame An obvious place in which a key frame should be placed, such as a clear scene transition.

N-bit The N-bit profile can convey rough or extremely high-resolution color by using a variable N (where N is a number between 4 and 12) bits per color per pixel.

NCSA National Center for Supercomputing Applications.

network infrastructure How a network is set up.

network layer See layered protocols.

Nickelodeon A television channel featuring programming for children and teens and, at night, for nostalgic adults.

normative Two terms constantly come up when reading through MPEG: normative and informative. Normative tests, software, descriptions, and other information are required to implement the standard. "Extra" information, such as examples and sample implementations, is informative. Conformance does not require adherence to informative portions of the standard.

NSV   A recently developed format that is used to contain the video streamed by ShoutCast/IceCast video servers. Like most of the other formats, it can hold audio and video and can be streamed or downloaded.

NTSC   National Television Systems Committee is the TV standard used in the United States, Japan, Canada, parts of South America, and so on. It contains 480 visible horizontal scan lines and 60 interlaced fields per second (60i). It has the highest frame rate of the interlaced formats, and thus the smoothest motion for content recorded on video camera. Note that 60 fields per second is actually usually 59.94 fields per second; therefore, the 30 pairs of fps actually play back 29.97 times per second. NTSC is sometimes incorrectly called 30 interlaced frames per second, but this can be misleading because each field captures a unique moment in time.

NullSoft   A company that developed the highly popular Winamp MP3 player and developed the standard MP3 radio streaming format for the Internet (ShoutCast).

object   All the various file formats are built around a concept of named file segments. AVI calls them segments. QuickTime calls them atoms. ASF calls them objects. Flash calls them tags.

Ogg   A container format developed by ziph.org to house its open-source and patent-free audio and video content.

one-to-many   Broadcasting the same audio or video of a single source to many users. This is in contrast to video conferencing, which can be one-to-one (as in a person-to-person chat) or few-to-few (several people video conferencing).

oscillating frequency   The smooth, repeating wave pattern in the electrical power that flows to homes on a given continent.

outtro   Video shown on the exit of other video; the opposite of intro.

packet   A packet is a chunk of information that flows on a network. Packets generally contain, at a minimum, source and destination addresses, a size, and some data.

packetization   The process of breaking up video into chunks.

packet switching   The path from a website to a web browser is very different than traditional communications such as telephone or television. Conceptually, it is similar to the telephone conversation—it is a two-way conversation in which the browser asks for a document and the server sends it. Unlike the telephone call, however, there is no reserved circuit. Data, in the form of requests and responses, is organized into chunks called packets and sent between the requesting web browser and the web server. In between the requester and the server are a series of routers; these machines route traffic between different, smaller networks. Each time a packet crosses the boundary from one ISP to another, or from one kind of network to another, it goes through a router. The packets "hops" from router to router like a bucket brigade. This type of data transmission is called packet switching (rather than circuit switching). Internet packet switching, as discussed previously, has some attributes that render it both reliable and unreliable.

PAL Phase Alternation by Line is the TV standard used by much of Western Europe, the United Kingdom, and many other parts of the world. Being a newer design, it has better color than NTSC (the North American television standard), and it has 576 visible horizontal scan lines. However, at 50 interlaced fields per second (50i), it is slower. The name comes from the technical description of the way color is transmitted. Brazil uses a slightly different version of PAL that runs at 59.94/60i.

part MPEG standards are divided into parts. These parts are documents, which can include software and even hardware designs. Together, all of these parts define the standard. Each part can be added to over time or have small typos corrected, but it cannot be substantially changed; thus, products that were compliant several years ago are always compliant.

P2P Peer-to-Peer is a networking paradigm that exploits the new reality that users are no longer second-class citizens. The term peer (not to be confused with network peering) describes a machine that is connected to a network and is capable of both serving and consuming content, acting as both a server and a client.

peering The process of connecting a network to the Internet at a public exchange point.

physical layer The first protocol layer consists of the hardware that actually carries the proverbial ones and zeros from one computer to another (such as copper wires, telephone lines, cable, fiber optic, and so on).

PIM-DM Protocol Independent Multicast – Dense Mode is one of the latest dense mode multicast protocols. It is called protocol independent because it does not rely on a particular type of routing protocol, but simply uses the paths determined by the existing routers.

PIM-SM Protocol Independent Multicast – Sparse Mode is the most standard sparse mode multicast protocol.

pixel A tiny sample of light/color stored on a computer as a minute part of an image.

pixel aspect ratio   Film and television do not always use square pixels. As mentioned previously, the horizontal resolution can vary from source to source, and if it is scanned at a different width, the pixels will not have a 1:1 ratio (square). When DVD video was standardized, rather than going with a 4:3 ratio of pixels, a slightly higher 720x480 (U.S., Japan) and 720x576 (Europe) pixel resolution was used. Note that the corresponding aspect ratios for these are 1.5:1 and 1.25:1. Nonetheless, these are displayed at a 4:3 ratio on TV screens, resulting in a pixel aspect ratio of .9:1. These pictures are only 90% as wide as they are tall.

PNA   Progressive Networks Audio. RealNetwork's former transfer protocol, which has now been replaced by the Internet standard Real Time Streaming Protocol (RTSP).

PNM   Progressive Networks Media. RealNetwork's former transfer protocol, now replaced by RTSP.

ppi   Pixels per inch, same as dpi.

predictive frame   A frame whose contents are predicted using information from a previous frame along with new instructions on what to take from that frame. Also called intermediate frame.

preroll   An advertisement or station identification that plays before the media the viewer had requested.

profile   MPEG has a concept of profiles or subsets of tools from the entire set. For instance, you can choose from only natural video encoding tools for video captured with a camera, or only synthetic 3D video tools for creating artificial scenes with 3D models, or a combination of both. Each of these would be described by a different profile, and if many handheld devices used a particular profile, they can share the same MPEG-4 content created for that profile.

progressive   This is the same as non-interlaced. Progressive video, such as that in cinematic film and on computers, is constructed from frames, not interlaced fields like television. It is symbolized by the letter p, such as 30p = 30 progressive frames.

progressive download   QuickTime synonym for HTTP streaming.

protocol encapsulation   In the late 1990s, each major streaming vendor had systems that worked over UDP and could work with impaired performance, over TCP. However, corporations began to restrict their networks so heavily that even general-purpose TCP would not work; now only TCP traffic on port 80 (the normal port for web traffic) works. More restrictive proxy firewalls have made it so that often you cannot even use TCP—only HTTP traffic is allowed. In response to this "only-HTTP" world created by the corporate IT managers, developers had to come up with a way to deliver Internet video into these networks. A technique of tunneling transport protocols within HTTP was developed. With tunneling, all the normal packets that would be sent via UDP are constructed as they normally would be, but are then sent over HTTP connections.

protocol layer   Networking is often described in terms of layers. Software exists for moving information on the Internet at each layer. The Internet has several layers of software that help it operate. Certainly you have at least seen the terms HTTP and TCP/IP; these are protocols (networking languages spoken between computers). See physical layer, data-link layer, network layer, transport layer, and application layer.

proxy   A type of server software that gets network data on behalf of another program. Web browsers and media players use proxies to move data safely and efficiently through firewalls in larger companies.

Public Exchange Points   Existing at various points on continents, these are the major nerve centers where many regional private networks, Internet providers, corporations, schools, and government divisions, both large and small, converge to exchange traffic destined for other points on the Internet.

public key   In certain kinds of encryption, two keys are made: a private and public key. The public key is distributed and used by others to read messages encrypted by the private key, and to encrypt messages so that only the holder of the private key can read them.

publishing point   A URL on a media server (Windows Media 9).

QCIF   A resolution for H.261 videoconferencing, 176×144 pixels.

QOS   Quality of Service describes any technologies that guarantee a certain behavior on the network, such as reserved bandwidth.

Quake   Quake is worth noting as a compression scheme. In Quake, a thin (modem-capable) real-time data stream could not only download textures to the Quake video game, but it could also animate the characters fighting in real time at high enough frame rates for people to compete in vast numbers.

quantization   This is the first lossy step of many video compression algorithms. Quantization is essentially a process of rounding numbers off, to reduce accuracy and save space.

QuickTime   An extensive set of video technologies from Apple computer available on the Macintosh and Windows platforms. QuickTime includes codecs, servers, file formats, and players for a wide variety of audio and video multimedia.

RAM   Real's index file format that simply points to the actual media file's URL.

RealAudio   RealAudio currently describes any media compressed with Real's audio codecs. RealAudio was probably the first audio broadcasting format for the Internet.

RealMedia   The format for Real's streaming media files; it can be extended to hold all types of multimedia. (RM)

RealNetworks   The company that produced RealMedia, RealAudio, and so forth.

RealPlayer   A flexible client-side player program for RealMedia and other codecs. The RealPlayer has been superceded by the RealOne player, which includes subscription models. Most versions of RealPlayers include a heavy advertising component.

RealServer   The type of server made by RealNetworks for running RealMedia.

Real time   "Real time" is an abused term; technical purists would say that it concerns systems that can consistently and without fail respond to requests in tiny fractions of a second. In web marketing speak, it means roughly "really fast," or, "what we'd like to brag as being really fast." It has come to mean that video or audio is playing at normal speed, and that it can play cleanly, without skips or interruptions, because it is downloaded at an acceptably fast rate. In other words, five minutes of video takes approximately five minutes to download and play.

RealVideo   Video that is compressed with RealNetwork's codecs.

redundant   Having more than one (of a given part of a system) to keep a system running in the event of hardware, software, or human failure, or overflow.

reference frame   Same as key frame, as other frames refer to it.

Reference MOV   QuickTime system for linking to multiple bitrate files and having the client decide which one to play based on the viewer-selected bandwidth capabilities.

reflect   The usual arrangement for live streams is that the live stream, from either a play list or a broadcaster, originates from a single machine. This machine is busy with encoding or producing the live stream, so it does not directly take viewer requests, and it is often safely behind a firewall, away from the raw Internet. Instead, it reflects its stream off of another media server or even several media servers—as many as are needed to serve the intended audience. These media servers are situated outside the firewall, or at the collocation facility, and are directly on the Internet.

reflected multicast   Receipt and redelivery of simultaneous video to many viewers via unicast. Not really multicast; simply another term for broadcasting.

relay server   A server designed to retransmit a signal without altering it. Relay servers can be used to serve streaming media through firewalls.

rendezvous point   In PIM-SM, the central router is called a Rendezvous Point (RP).

resample   The process of changing the size or resolution of an image by creating new pixels that are averages of multiple pixels in the original image.

resolution   In the analog world, resolution means how much information a picture contains or how much detail is recorded in the picture. Most commercial films are recorded on 70mm film, which offers four times the resolution (double the width and the height) of 35mm film. In the digital world, resolution is the horizontal and vertical number of pixels that are actually in your video, and the rectangular shape in which the video is shown.

resolve   To measure the horizontal lines of resolution of a particular TV or camera, many parallel black and white lines are put on the screen or camera in increasing density. At a certain number, they blur together and you can no longer see alternating black and white lines. When you can no longer resolve or see these lines distinctly, you have exceeded that TV's horizontal resolution.

revoke   To declare that an encryption key is no longer valid, either because the key or the party is no longer trusted or authorized.

router   Machines operated by ISPs that route packets between machines. Machines on the Internet are sometimes called hosts. When a host needs to send a packet, it sends it to the nearest router. Your ISP provides the router that routes the packets your host (machine) sends to other hosts on the Internet.

RP   See rendezvous point.

RSVP   Resource Reservation Protocol is a network protocol end device (such as the viewing computer) used to request network performance guarantees (such as maximum delay or a minimum bandwidth).

RTCP   Another protocol in the RTP specification, RTCP (Real-time Control Protocol) couples with RTP to provide a control channel that is useful for quality monitoring. Servers send RTCP packets down to all the clients; clients send RTCP packets back periodically (for instance, every five seconds) to let the server know the quality of the stream they receive. The server can then throttle down the quality of the stream, if necessary.

RTP The IETF has produced a collection of protocols for video delivery. The Real-Time Transport Protocol (RTP)—version 1.0 was documented in 1993, RTP 2.0 came in 1996—provides transport and synchronization features for streaming audio and video. RTP is spoken between a media server and a media player application. RTP doesn't actually ensure real-time delivery, but it encodes the different frames of audio and video with enough timing information so they can be synchronized in real-time on the receiving end. RTP is also the standard way to deliver media over UDP on multicast networks.

RTSP Developed in 1996, the Real-Time Streaming Protocol provides the VCR-like controls (play, stop, fast forward, rewind, and so on) for a streaming media server. The protocol is modeled somewhat after HTTP as it was intended to be as good for streaming media as HTTP had been for web pages. RTSP can work in conjunction with RTP; RTSP sets up the connection and then RTP is used to deliver the data. RealNetworks and Netscape both worked on the specification of this protocol. RealNetworks then switched to RTSP for its transport setup, deprecating its earlier PNM (Progressive Networks Media) and PNA (Progressive Networks Audio) transport protocols.

SAOL Structured Audio Orchestral Language is a complete language for describing the actual algorithm used to produce the sound, so that any kind of computer synthesis can be described (limited only by the complexity of the algorithm and the power of the playback device).

SASBF Structured Audio Sample-Bank Format is used to create banks or groups of recordings (samples) of musical instruments.

SASL With SAOL and SASBF, either sampled or computer-generated instruments can be accurately delivered in such a way that the sound is identical on any device. Then, when a triggering stream, such as MIDI or SASL (Structured Audio Score Language), is delivered to the playback device, the sound is reproduced exactly as its author intended and strange and unacceptable instrument substitutions do not occur.

SBR Spectral band replication is a technique designed to enhance any underlying codec (MP3, AAC, speech codecs) by using a very small bitstream to add a quality-enhancing, high-frequency signal.

Scalable Texture Earlier JPEG and MPEG compression created blocky squares; the Scalable Texture visual profile uses the smoother "wavelet" compression technique.

scrubbing The term for any rewind/fast forward functions in video.

SECAM   Systeme Electronique Couleur Avec Memoir is an electronic color system with memory (describing the technical manner in which color is transmitted); it is used in France, Russia, much of Eastern Europe, and everywhere else PAL and NTSC are not used. It has 576 visible horizontal scan lines and 50 interlaced fields per second (50i), like PAL. It differs mainly in the way color is transmitted. Content is usually produced in NTSC or PAL and is only converted to this format at the end.

seek time   The length of time it takes a moving head to swing over the surface of a CD-ROM or hard disk and find a specific piece of data.

segment   All the various file formats are built around a concept of named file segments. AVI calls them segments. QuickTime calls them atoms. ASF calls them objects. Flash calls them tags.

server-based   Streams are server-based content—all the video is kept on the media server, which is only downloaded a few frames of video at a time. The player does not (permanently) save the video to the hard disk; when the stream is over, there is nothing left on the hard disk to watch.

session key   A temporary key used for a secure conversation between client and server, such as an online store.

SFGMPs   There have been several versions of the protocols for joining the multicast, and there are ongoing developments in this area. The basic protocol for joining multicasts is called the Internet Group Management Protocol (IGMP). There are three versions of this protocol. Version 1 has only the join message. Version 2 adds the leave message. Version 3 adds the capability for clients to "tune in" to a particular data stream when many are sent to a single group, and filter out all the others (for applications such as Internet TV). Multicast Listener Discovery (MLD) achieves the same goal as IGMP, but it is part of IPv6, the newest version of the Internet protocol (IP). To simplify things, two more acronyms were developed. These and other similar protocols are referred to as Group Membership Protocols (GMP). IGMP version 3 and MLD version 2 are also referred to as Source Filtering Group Membership Protocols or SFGMPs.

(S,G)   You often see the notation (S,G) in the technical multicast literature. S stands for the IP address of the source of the multicast information, a class A, B, or C address. G stands for the group IP address, a class D address. An (S,G) pair would be stored in a link state table in a router and would indicate that a particular machine wanted to receive data from the source S in the multicast group G. An (S,G) pair would also mean that there was a specific source tree rooted at that source.

(*,G) You might also see (*,G) in the same discussions as (S,G). The asterisk means "anyone" or "all" and is stored in the same link state table, indicating that a machine wants to receive data from any (*) source in the multicast group G. (*,G) also describes a shared tree with a central meeting point.

SHA[en]1 Hashing techniques are used to uniquely identify content, by creating a digital "fingerprint" that can be quickly checked to see if two files are the same. SHA1 (for "secure hashing") is more resistant to hacking than MD5 and has replaced MD5 in many applications.

shared tree A shared tree is a tree where the root router is somewhere in the center of the tree, and multiple senders send their data up to the root, from which data then flows down (through various routers) to all receivers.

ShoutCast A streaming protocol created by Nullsoft for streaming MP3 radio stations.

signature Another common use of hashing is to create what is called a signature (also called a fingerprint or a digest) for a file. This is a small file that can be used to uniquely identify a much larger file. For instance, many file sharing programs use hashes to check whether a file has been successfully downloaded. Thus, hashes are a form of checksum. These hashes are much smaller than the file. Instead of comparing the entire file, they simply compare the two hashes.

Simple The Simple visual profile includes natural video.

Simple Face Animation The Simple Face Animation profile combines face textures with an animated face model.

Simple Scalable The Simple Scalable visual profile allows for variable resolution and variable frame rate.

Simple Face and Body Animation Simple Face and Body Animation extends the Facial Animation profile with a 3D body model, which can be animated at low bit rates.

Simple Studio Simple Studio is designed for use inside movie and TV studios, where MPEG-2 is in broad use. It adds the major MPEG-4 feature of segmenting video into shapes as in the core profiles. All the frames are stand-alone key frames; thus, data rates are quite high, but working with the video is quicker.

Simulated live broadcast Prerecorded video delivered at the same time to all viewers from a video file or playlist of files.

simulcast To deliver video simultaneously to all viewers.

SMIL   Simple Multimedia Integration Language is used by RealPlayer, QuickTime player, and IE to combine different multimedia elements into a time-based presentation.

SNHC   The Synthetic-Natural Hybrid Coding group within MPEG-4 started work in the mid-90s when 3D video cards weren't in broad use. The existing set of MPEG-4 tools for 2D and 3D composition, although extensive, do not provide the visual integration and experiences that is the state of the art in 3D video games today. VRML '97, the basis for BIFS, supports simple shapes and animation techniques compared to the current technology. The SNHC group in MPEG has standardized backwards-compatible extensions to the existing animation frameworks, incorporating modern shape, animation, and rendering features.

Sorenson   A company that develops a variety of state-of-the-art compression technologies. Sorenson creates proprietary codecs (such as QuickTime's Sorenson codecs or Macromedia's Spark video codec) as well as optimized MPEG-4 codecs.

source tree   A source tree or shortest path tree is a tree with the source machine sending the data at its root. The root is the router from which all data flows. This source machine directly sends data to its nearest router, which sends the data through the shortest path (through various routers) to all receivers.

sparse mode multicast   Sparse mode multicasting is required for multicasting on the broad Internet, where most people are not aware of and will not seek the broadcast. It would be foolish to use a dense mode multicast protocol that automatically sent the data to every machine on the Internet, requiring each to then say, "Hey, I didn't want this broadcast."

spatial compression   All video compression boils down to two basic techniques: spatial compression and temporal compression. Spatial compression is about compressing the data within a single frame, much like a JPEG file is a compressed version of a photograph.

SSM   Although multicast originally supported the many-to-many in all cases, this was inherently insecure as designed. Because any machine on the Internet can potentially send to a specified group address (just as anyone can send to any single address), a malicious or mistaken user can send to a group address. If, however, this group address was already received by millions of machines (perhaps a large football game was being video broadcast), every single machine would also start receiving this broadcast as well. Attempts to solve this have resulted in a Single-Source Multicast (SSM) model that eliminates unintended senders. Instead of receiving from a group address G, receivers subscribe to a combination source-group (S,G). They receive only what is sent by the designated source. In SSM, they have also changed the terminology to fit with video broadcasting. Receivers are now subscribers; join and leave messages are now subscribe and unsubscribe; and groups are replaced with a combination of source and group called a channel.

standard   Standards are agreements between large numbers of people or companies about how specific technology should be implemented.

station   A URL on a media server (Windows Media prior to version 9).

Stream Thinning   General description of a technique for lowering the frame rate of a stream to deal with impaired network conditions that relies on both the codec and the streaming server.

SureStream   Real technology for automatic adjustment of stream quality based on real-time network conditions.

SWF   A file format for Flash movies, typically contains vector-drawn animations with scripting controls.

SWV   A file format for Flash movies, typically contains vector-drawn animations with scripting controls.

symmetric encryption   In computer encryption, we take a key of a certain number of bits, say 64 bits, and scramble those bits with the same number of bits from the original content. We then repeat the process on each 64-bit chunk of plaintext. This is called symmetric encryption because the same key is used to lock and to unlock the message. Figure out the key and you have the message, and you have all other messages encoded with the key.

Tag   All the various file formats are built around a concept of named file segments. AVI calls them segments. QuickTime calls them atoms. ASF calls them objects. Flash calls them tags.

TCP   Transmission Control Protocol is the dominant transmission protocol. It's considered a self-healing protocol in that it detects errors and resends packets that were damaged or dropped because of network transmission.

temporal compression   All video compression boils down to two basic techniques: spatial compression and temporal compression. Temporal compression essentially applies compression over time. Rather than send each compressed frame, temporal compression predicts where the people and the moon will be in each incremental frame.

tier   The process of connecting a network to the Internet at a public exchange point is called peering, and connecting to the backbone this way makes one a Tier-1 Internet provider. ISPs that rent their connection from a Tier-1 provider are called Tier-2 providers, and so on.

tiling   Tiling allows a portion of a picture to be quickly viewed/zoomed in on without having to decode the entire picture, and is useful for slide shows, digital cameras, and so on.

transcoder   A coder that translates between two different codecs in the same "family" (MPEG-2 to MPEG-4).

Transform   Shifting between different ways of representing the same information is called a transform.

Transport Layer   The fourth protocol layer. At the network layer, IP controls the movement of packets around the network, and an IP address identifies a particular machine on the Internet. Here at the transport layer, TCP and UDP provide different kinds of information delivery.

Tree   A tree is simply a hierarchical system of routers and computers that has no loops (the data doesn't loop back to the source) and allows efficient multicasting of a data to all interested receivers.

TTSI   Text To Speech Interface is a speech codec that specifies how to trigger (but does not provide) a speech synthesizer at the audio receiver. TTSI can thus generate speech at a staggeringly low 0.2Kbps to 1.2Kbps, as it mostly sends textual data. TTSI can send phonetic data, so that text in any language can be properly pronounced.

tunnel   A data link between network islands for multicasting.

tunneling   Tunneling is the transport of a protocol within another protocol to get it through barriers (such as firewalls or private networks).

TurboPlay   Real's rapid playback and seeking technology for broadband connections.

TwinVQ   Transform domain Weighted Interleave Vector Quantization is a tool that compresses natural audio at low bitrates (<10Kbps).

UDP   The User Datagram Protocol is considered an unreliable protocol. It is a lean protocol that doesn't add a lot of complexity on top of IP.

unicast   To deliver video to a single viewer via a server-to-client network connection.

upsampling   The process of increasing the size or resolution of multimedia by interpolation.

URL   Universal Resource Locater is a web address, such as http://www.masteringinternetvideo.com.

USB   Universal Serial Bus is a kind of connector cable for everything from keyboards and mice to game joysticks and external hard drives.

VBR   Variable Bit Rate is the video's quality, which stays consistent, whereas bit rate varies.

VCD   Video CD is a predecessor to DVD that was very popular in Asia.

VCR   You probably have this sitting on top or near your TV; it's the thing that lets you record TV shows on VHS tapes, and plug video game consoles into the TV.

VGA   Video Graphics Adapter is the name of both the 15-pin connector and the basic video standard for PCs. Additional letters before the VGA (such as SVGA and XVGA) describe successively higher resolutions within this standard.

VHS   Video Home System is the dominant consumer standard and is the tape you put into your VCR.

video   In the early days of film, they called movies "moving pictures;" in fact, the word "movie" is an abbreviation of "moving picture." Video, like film, creates the illusion of movement by showing a series of slightly different still images in rapid sequence.

Video clip   This term usually means a short piece of video, but in this case it means any piece of video. (A two-hour movie served on-demand is still a clip in Real-speak, for instance.)

VOB   A file format for MPEG-1 and MPEG-2 video.

VoD   Video On Demand is one of the most common uses of streaming servers on the Internet to provide video when the user asks for it, as opposed to broadcast television, where content is shown to everyone at the same time. Streaming servers usually designate a folder or directory on their hard disk as the source directory. Without additional configuration, any media that is in this directory can be played back.

VPN   Virtual Private Networks run over normal Internet connections (such as home DSL or cable modem) but keep the data private through encryption, and are "virtual" because they are part of the Internet; they aren't a leased line directly between the office and that household, for instance.

VRML   Virtual Reality Markup Language is a text-based, HTML-like language for describing 3D scenes.

wavelet   The simplest description of wavelet compression is that it is a different approach to compression and doesn't break the image into blocky squares like earlier JPEG and MPEG, so images look smoother.

webcam   Any small and typically low-quality camera for personal use in video chatting, and so on.

webcast   Any "webcast" is simply many unicasts, one to each individual viewer. Each of these unicasts uses up more bandwidth at the source of the broadcast, goes through all the bottlenecks present on the path to the source of the broadcast, and uses additional processor power on the media server for that broadcast.

WiFi   Short for Wireless Fidelity, simply put, it's this specific kind of wireless Internet connection.

Windows Media   Microsoft's brand of media player, codec, and audio/video streaming system.

WM   Windows Media.

WMA   Windows Media Audio (file).

WMF   Windows Media File containing audio or video.

WMV   Windows Media Video (file).

WMX   Windows Media index file used containing a list of URLs of Windows Media files.

wrapper   In computer technology, a wrapper describes any file or protocol or interface that "wraps" and possibly presents a pretty face or adds additional information or functionality to the thing it contains.

In digital rights management, file wrappers offer content providers a measure of control over when and how their content is consumed. This includes password-protected media files, required payment systems, files that expire after a certain time, copy protection, and so on. Digital rights management tends to be implemented by storing all the audio and video data in some sort of digital rights management wrapper, which surrounds and protects the video and audio from unauthorized access.

XML   The eXtensible Markup Language is a human-readable text format and markup language that is used extensively in computers to store settings, preferences, database information, and to facilitate communication between automated systems. It is similar to HTML, but it can be used to mark up (describe or annotate) anything, not just text formatting.

Y'CrCb   Digital compression systems use a color space called Y'CrCb. In this color space, the Y' channel contains a combination of red, green, and blue brightness, or luminance (called luma), and the other two channels carry color information about red (Cr = chrominance-red) and blue (Cb = chrominance-blue) color, without luminance.

VGA   Video Graphics Array is 640 by 480 pixels (1.33:1 aspect ratio) with 4-bit color (16 colors).

YIQ   See YUV.

YUV   YUV is used in European television broadcasting; YIQ is the North American broadcast equivalent. Both of these are similar to Y'CrCb. Often YUV is used interchangeably with Y'CrCb. The only real difference is that they contain slightly different ratios of red, green, and blue. The important thing to know about these color spaces is that they allow us to separate color from brightness and deal with it separately.

MASTERING INTERNET VIDEO WEB BIBLIOGRAPHY

CHAPTER 1—VIDEO PREPARATION AND CAPTURE

PUBLICATIONS

Jones, Frederic H., *How to Do Everything with Digital Video,* McGraw Hill/Osborne, 2002.

Menin, Eyal, *The Streaming Media Handbook,* Prentice Hall PTR, 2003.

Gloman, Chuck, *No-Budget Digital Filmmaking,* McGraw-Hill, 2003.

WEBSITES

720i
> http://www.afterdawn.com/glossary/terms/720i.cfm

A Sound Person's Guide to Video
> http://www.spgv.com/columns/dlp.html

About Video Editing
> http://www.aboutvideoediting.com/articles/web-streaming-video.shtml

Action-Guide: Choosing Converters
> http://action-guide.com/faq/

AMR Wideband
> http://www.ietf.org/proceedings/01mar/slides/avt-8/sld003.htm

AudioVideo101's Audio/Video Dictionary
> http://www.audiovideo101.com/dictionary/line-quadrupler.asp

CEM's Spring 2000 Issue: This Ain't Your Parents' TV!
http://cem.colorado.edu/archives/sp2000/brian.html

Cine-Byte Imaging Video to Film, Data to Film, Trailers and VFX
(416)504-1010
http://www.cinebyte.com/video.htm

Cinefx's Video Technology Primer
http://www.cinefx.com/vidtech.htm

Close-Up with Joe Fedele: DVCPRO and Digital Video Recording
http://www.fedele.com/website/dtv/dvcpro.htm

Codec Central-DV Cameras
http://www.icanstream.tv/CodecCentral/Codecs/DVCamera.html

Color Television, NTSC Tutorials
http://www.ntsc-tv.com/ntsc-index-04.htm

Conventional Analog Television: An Introduction
http://www.ee.washington.edu/conselec/CE/kuhn/ntsc/95x4.htm

DeepSea Power and Light: Video Resolution
http://www.deepsea.com/faq.html

Digital TV 1/1/04
http://alvyray.com/DigitalTV/default.htm

Digital Video Essentials
http://www.videoessentials.com/DVEQ&A.htm
http://www.videoessentials.com/glossary.htm

DV Versus Betacam SP
http://www.dvcentral.org/DV-Beta.html

DVD Benchmark
http://www.hometheaterhifi.com/volume_7_3/
dvd-benchmark-part-1-video-9-2000.html

DVD Player Benchmark—Par—Progressive Scan DVD
http://www.hometheaterhifi.com/volume_7_4/
dvd-benchmark-part-5-progressive-10-2000.html

Film for Television
http://www.rcc.ryerson.ca/rta/tvtech/the_book/chapter14/main.html

Film Scanning Pointers
http://www.ltlimagery.com/film_scanning_pointers.html

Formats of Video Tapes
http://www.high-techproductions.com/formats.htm

Front Street TV and Video, Big screen TV Repair
  http://www.frontstreettv.com/FAQ.html

Grass Valley Dictionary
  http://www.thomsongrassvalley.com/docs/Miscellaneous/Dictionary/
  DictionaryB2_Y.html

Guide.melchman Terms
  http://melchman.net/guides/HDTV.html

HDTV Lingo
  http://skyvision.com/pages/information_center/hdtv_lingo.html

"How Film Is Transferred to Video"
  http://www.cs.tut.fi/~leopold/Ld/FilmToVideo/

Interlaced Video.
  http://www.labdv.com/leon-lab/video/interlace_en.htm

Interlacing: Luke's Video Guide
  http://www.lukesvideo.com/interlacing.html

JVC SR-VD400US D-VHS Recorder/Player, PRO-HD Player
  http://www.ggvideo.com/jvc_srvd400.htm

LabGuy's World—The History of Video Tape Recorders Before Betamax and VHS
  http://www.labguysworld.com/

LabGuy's World—VideOlson Videotape Formats.
  http://www.labguysworld.com/formats.html

"Making SP Look Like Digibeta"
  http://www.tvcameramen.com/studio/studio08.htm

mir DMG: Aspect Ratios and Frame Sizes
  http://www.mir.com/DMG/aspect.html

Movie Theatre Information
  http://hsvmovies.com/static_subpages/formats/shooting_formats.html

My-Symbian
  http://my-symbian.com/uiq/techdata_p900.php

Nicky Pages' Digital Solutions
  http://nickyguides.digital-digest.com/interlace.htm

NTSC
  http://www.high-techproductions.com/ntsc.htm

Open Source Audio and Video
  http://corecodec.org/

Picture Quality
  http://www.terraguide.com/Quality.html

Pro Digital VTR Comparison
http://kensystem.com/kensys/vtr.htm

Pure Motion
http://www.puremotion.com/cgi-local/ikonboard/
topic.cgi?forum=1&topic=485

"So You'd Like to Learn About Aspect Ratios, Scope Films, and Flat Films?"
http://www.amazon.com/exec/obidos/tg/guides/guide-display/
-/2QCDBL5Y4Q5B1/104-8706709-5539938

Solutioneers Persistance.html
http://www.solutioneers.net/cinema/persistance.html

Square and Non-Square Pixels
http://www.lurkertech.com/lg/pixelaspect.html

Streaming Media World—"Creating Quality Streaming"
http://smw.internet.com/video/tutor/videotips/

Streaming Media World—"Screenblast Tips and Tricks"
http://www.streamingmediaworld.com/video/tutor/screentips/index4.html

Streaming Media World—Streaming Basics and Shooting Video for Streaming
http://www.streamingmediaworld.com/video/tutor/streambasics1/index.html

S-video Limited Resolution
http://episteme.arstechnica.com/6/ubb.x?a=tpc&s=50009562&f=67909965
&m=6190999994

Television and Video Resolution
http://members.aol.com/ajaynejr/vidres.htm

The DV, DVCAM, and DVCPRO Formats: Tech Details, FAQs, and Links
http://www.adamwilt.com/DV-FAQ-etc.html#widescreen

The PC Technology Guide
http://www.pctechguide.com/06crtmon.htm

TV Camera Resolution
http://videoexpert.home.att.net/artic1/201res.htm

TVRESOLUTIONS
http://68.60.94.173/TVRESOLUTIONS.htm

"Understanding the Use of Square Versus Non-Square Pixels in AE"
http://www.creativecow.net/articles/gerard_rick/pixel_madness/

Unexposed Film
http://www.jamesarnett.com/1-1-3.html

Video and Scanner Resolution: The Kell Factor
http://members.aol.com/ajaynejr/kell.htm

Video Resolution Test Patterns
http://www.bealecorner.com/trv900/respat/

Video Resolution
http://www.fortunecity.com/victorian/canterbury/222/resolv.htm

Video Standards
http://www.udayton.edu/~cps/cps460/notes/displays/video_standards.html

Video Tape Format Comparison
http://www.matternvideo.com/formats.htm

Videographica: Video Glossary
http://tangentsoft.net/video/glossary.html

Videomaker
http://www.findarticles.com/cf_dls/m0GCO/2_18/106290332/p1/article.jhtml

Videotape Formats
http://graphics.lcs.mit.edu/~tbuehler/video/formats.html

Videotape Formats
http://www.terraguide.com/Formats.html

View as HTML
http://216.239.53.104/search?q=cache:cxH0FzCwoD0J:www.oznet.ksu.edu/
edtech/How_To/PDFs/VideoStreaming2001.pdf+panning+internet+video&
hl=en&ie=UTF-8

Welcome to CVP, Home of the World's Best Video Systems
http://www.creativevideo.co.uk/reframe.php?url=http://
www.creativevideo.co.uk/pages/cvp_info_25fps.htm

"What Became of TV Channel 1?"
http://members.aol.com/jeff560/tvch1.html

What Video Widescreen Entertainment Online Articles
http://www.whatvideotv.com/articles/frame.html?

"Why Are Films Only 24 FPS?"
http://www.movie-fan-
forum.com/movies/Why_are_films_only_24_fps_583571.html

Widescreen-O-Rama!
http://www.thedigitalbits.com/articles/anamorphic/aspectratios/
widescreenorama.html

WolfVision Homepage
http://www.wolfvision.com/wolf/faq.html#1

CHAPTER 2—VIDEO COMPRESSION

PUBLICATIONS

Waggoner, Ben, *Compression for Great Digital Video,* CMP Media LLC, 2002.

WEBSITES

comp.compression Frequently Asked Questions
   http://www.faqs.org/faqs/compression-faq/part1/preamble.html
The Compression Site
   http://www.davesite.com/computers/compress.shtml
Digital Video: Introduction
   http://www.doc.ic.ac.uk/~nd/surprise_96/journal/vol2/sab/article2.html
IGM: Desktop Video #2 Compression Standards
   http://www.insanely-great.com/features/010626.html
MVQ Video Compression Method
   http://www.vtt.fi/tte/samba/projects/mvq/history.html
Solutions
   http://www.idm.ru/wavelets.htm

CODECS/INDEO

Ligos Corporation: INDEO Video
   http://indeo.ligos.com/pi=185.php?&n1=products&n2=indeo&n3=video

MPEG

BMRC
   http://bmrc.berkeley.edu/frame/research/mpeg/mpegfaq.html
BMRC Berkeley MPEG2 FAQ
   http://bmrc.berkeley.edu/frame/research/mpeg/mpeg2faq.html
Introduction to MPEG
   http://www.idm.ru/support.HTM
MPEG . ORG - MPEG Starting Points and FAQs
   http://www.mpeg.org/MPEG/starting-points.html

MPEG FAQ

> http://www.crs4.it/~luigi/MPEG/mpeggeneral-1.html
> http://www.faqs.org/faqs/mpeg-faq/part7/

MPEG Glossary

> http://www.crs4.it/~luigi/MPEG/mpeggloss-l.html

MPEG Moving Picture Expert Group FAQ

> http://www.crs4.it/~luigi/MPEG/

MPEG-4 Industry Forum

> http://www.m4if.org/

MPEG-4.htm

> http://leonardo.telecomitalialab.com/paper/mpeg-4/index.htm

MPEG-4—Codec Comparison

> http://www.extremetech.com/article/0,3396,s=1021&a=4058,00.asp

MPEG-4—Overview and Analysis

> http://www.extremetech.com/article/0,3396,apn=10&s=1021&a=3780&
> app=8&ap=9,00.asp

JPEG

4.2. Video Compression

> http://www.cs.sfu.ca/undergrad/CourseMaterials/CMPT479/material/notes/
> Chap4/Chap4.2/Chap4.2.html

JPEG Algorithm and Associated Data Structures

> http://www.cs.und.edu/~mschroed/jpeg.html

H.261

4.2.2 H.261

> http://www.cs.sfu.ca/undergrad/CourseMaterials/CMPT479/material/notes/
> Chap4/Chap4.2/Chap4.2.html

H.261 Video Coding

> http://www-mobile.ecs.soton.ac.uk/peter/h261/h261.html

"A History of Video Conferencing"

> http://myhome.hananet.net/~soonjp/vchx.html

H.263

H.263 Video Codec
   http://www.4i2i.com/h263_video_codec.htm

H.263 Video Coding
   http://www-mobile.ecs.soton.ac.uk/peter/h263/h263.html

ITU H.xxx Audiovisual and Multimedia Systems
   http://www.itu.int/rec/recommendation.asp?type=products&parent=T-REC-h

QUICKTIME

History and Peregrinations
   http://developer.apple.com/technotes/tn/tn1031.html

Queen's Film Studies Cinepak Examples
   http://www.film.queensu.ca/310/310Cinepak.html

QuickTime History
   http://www.retiariusenterprises.com/documents/quicktime/history.html

Sorenson Versus Cinepak
   http://hcs.harvard.edu/~tabanger/sorenson/

CINEPAK

http://www.csse.monash.edu.au/...dec/cinepak.txt

http://www.csse.monash.edu.au/~timf/videocodec/cinepak.txt

GIF, AIFF, WAV, AND REAL

"Getting the Best Sound Out of RealAudio"
   http://web.archive.org/web/19961220191350/www.realaudio.com/help/
   content/audiohints.html

Real Audio G2 Online
   http://www.geocities.com/ResearchTriangle/Thinktank/4787/main.html

"Real Video: What Is it and How Did it Evolve?"
   http://www.rcc.ryerson.ca/schools/rta/brd038/papers/1997/realvid.htm

RealNetworks Documentation Library
   http://service.real.com/help/library/dokhma.html

RTMW '96
   http://www.w3.org/AudioVideo/RTMW96
Toon Tracker RealAudio Page
   http://www.toontracker.com/realaudio/ttra.htm

APPLE

Codec Central–QuickTime
   http://www.siggraph.org/education/materials/HyperGraph/video/
   architectures/QuickTime.html
Compressors Supplied by Apple
   http://developer.apple.com/techpubs/quicktime/qtdevdocs/INMAC/QT/
   iqImageCompMgr.7.htm

MICROSOFT

EE Times: Forum to Weigh Microsoft's Corona...
   http://www.eetimes.com/story/OEG20011212S0060

DV

DV.com
   http://www.google.com/search?q=cache:4VPkCFkXqHYC:www.dv.com/
   magazine/1998/0698/johnson0698.html+realvideo+4.0+codec&hl=en&ie=
   ISO-8859-1
EBU's Evaluation of DV Formats
   http://www.adamwilt.com/EBU-DV.html
Film Look Deinterlacing for DV: DVFilm Maker
   http://www.dvfilm.com/maker/helpmac.htm

FLASH AND VRML/3D

Internet Pictures Corporation
   http://www.ipix.com/
Web3D Consortium: Frequently Asked Questions
   http://www.web3d.org/fs_faq.htm

MATH

6:5:5 YUV
http://www.halfbakery.com/idea/6_3a5_3a5_20YUV_20display_20mode

CNN
http://download.cnn.com/vxtreme/

Codec Central: List of Codecs
http://www.siggraph.org/education/materials/HyperGraph/video/codecs/
Default.htm

Codec Shootout
http://radio.irt.de/demo/vida/begin.htm

Codec Zone
http://home.earthlink.net/~codeczone/fixes.htm

Discreet Support and Services
http://www.discreet.com/support/codec/

Fractal Image Encoding
http://inls.ucsd.edu/y/Fractals/

Image Compression
http://www.debugmode.com/imagecmp/

Index to Series of Tutorials to Wavelet
http://engineering.rowan.edu/~polikar/WAVELETS/WTtutorial.html

Separate HTML for Basic Foil 5 Wavelet
http://www.npac.syr.edu/users/gcf/RLCIVQMjune96/wavelet/
foilsephtmldir/005HTML.html

Sorenson Media: Quality Video for the Web
http://www.sorenson.com/content.php?pageID=132

Video Objectification
http://www.techreview.com/articles/innovation60402.asp

Wavelet Resources
http://www.mathsoft.com/wavelets.html

Wavelets
http://www.cosy.sbg.ac.at/~uhl/wav.html

The Wavelet Tutorial
http://engineering.rowan.edu/~polikar/WAVELETS/WTpart4.html

Xilinx FAQs
http://www.xilinx.com/ipcenter/color_space_converter_lounge/faq.htm

CHAPTER 3—VIDEO STORAGE FILE FORMATS

The Almost Definitive FOURCC Definition List
  http://www.webartz.com/fourcc/indexcod.htm

Audio and Video
  http://msdn.microsoft.com/library/default.asp?url=/nhp/default.asp?contentid=28000411

AVI File Format and RIFF
  http://www.daubnet.com/formats/AVI.html

AVI File Structure
  http://www.rasnaimaging.com/people/lapus/avi.html

Byte Magazine on ASF Patent
  http://www.byte.com/documents/s=446/BYT20000905S0004/index2.htm

CoreCodec.org
  http://www.corecodec.org/

File Format
  http://fileformat.virtualave.net/ind_wave.htm

File Formats
  http://msdn.microsoft.com/library/default.asp?url=/library/en-us/wcegmm/htm/dshow_102.asp

The Graphics File Format Page (3D specs + Anim)
  http://www.dcs.ed.ac.uk/home/mxr/gfx/3d-hi.html

graphics/avi-faq
  http://www.faqs.org/faqs/graphics/avi-faq/index.html

John McGowan's AVI Overview
  http://www.jmcgowan.com/avi.html

John McGowan's AVI Overview: Chronology
  http://www.jmcgowan.com/avichrono.html

Live Capture and File Format Reference
  http://www.cisco.com/univercd/cc/td/doc/product/webscale/iptv/iptv30/adminug/appa.htm

Microsoft Patents ASF Media File Format
  http://www.advogato.org/article/101.html

MovieToXML
  http://www.hoddie.net/xmltorefmovie/movietoxml.html

MP3 ID3 Tags
  http://www.searchtools.com/info/mp3-search.html

MPEG File Format
    http://rnvs.informatik.tu-chemnitz.de/~jan/MPEG/HTML/mpeg_file.html

MPEG2 FAQ 58 File Format
    http://bmrc.berkeley.edu/frame/research/mpeg/mpeg2faq.html

Multimedia Formats
    http://home.pcisys.net/~melanson/codecs/formats.html

QuickTime and SMIL
    http://developer.apple.com/techpubs/quicktime/qtdevdocs/
    IQT_INTMOV/9qtandsmil/09_intmov_qtandsmil0.htm

VCD Help page
    http://www.vcdhelp.com/tools.htm

Video File Formats
    http://mmdc.jhu.edu/docs/22/

VirtualDub Home Page
    http://www.virtualdub.org/

VirtualDub News
    http://www.virtualdub.org/virtualdub_news

VirtualDub—Codecs
    http://www.virtualdub.org/docs_codecs

Wav Central: Wav Files and Sound Files Database
    http://www.wavcentral.com/

Webopedia
    http://www.webopedia.com/TERM/A/ASF.html

"What is the SWF File Format?"
    http://www.adobe.com/support/techguides/webpublishing/flash/
    whatisflash.html

XMLtoRefMovie
    http://www.hoddie.net/xmltorefmovie/

CHAPTER 4—STREAMING SERVER SOFTWARE

PUBLICATIONS

Sitaram, Dinkar and Dan Asit, *Multimedia Servers,* Morgan Kaufman
    Publishers, 2000.

Sawyer, Ben and Dave Greely, *Online Broadcassting Power!* Muska & Lipman Publishing, 2000.

WEBSITES

"An Introduction to Streaming Video"
http://www.cultivate-int.org/issue4/video/
Streaming Video: The Technology
http://www.ncsu.edu/ced/mentornet/tutorials/video/technology.html

VIDEO WEB INTEGRATION

"Putting Video on Your Web Site"
http://www.webdeveloper.com/multimedia/
multimedia_putting_video_on_website.html

QuickTime 5.0.2 AppleScript Scripts
http://www.apple.com/applescript/qtas.html
Video on Internet (1996)
http://www.rad.com/networks/1996/video/video.htm

CHAPTERS 5—VIDEO TRANSPORT PROTOCOLS

PUBLICATIONS

Hunt, Craig, *TCP/IP Network Administration, 2nd Edition,* O'Reilly and Associates, 2001.

WEBSITES

Apple QuickTime Streaming Server
http://www.apple.com/quicktime/products/qtss/
DMN.TZI.org
http://www.dmn.tzi.org/...mmusic-confarch-03.txt
http://www.dmn.tzi.org/ietf/mmusic/49/id/draft-ietf-mmusic-confarch-03.txt

IETF.org
>   http://www.ietf.org/...-iesg-gap-analysis-00.txt
>   http://www.ietf.org/internet-drafts/draft-ietf-mboned-iesg-gap-analysis-00.txt

MBONE: Multicasting Tomorrow's Internet
>   http://www.savetz.com/mbone/

Network Layers: TCP/IP (Cisco)
>   http://www.cisco.com/warp/public/535/4.html

Network Protocol Layers
>   http://www.rabbitsemiconductor.com/documentation/docs/manuals/TCPIP/Introduction/4layers.htm

openRTSP
>   http://www.live.com/openRTSP/

RTMW '96
>   http://www.w3.org/AudioVideo/RTMW96

RTP, RTSP, and MBone
>   http://www.cs.columbia.edu/~hgs/teaching/ais/slides/

RTSP 1.0 Adopted by Real
>   http://wp.netscape.com/newsref/pr/newsrelease263.html

RTSP FAQ
>   http://www.cs.columbia.edu/~hgs/rtsp/faq.html

RTSP FAQs
>   http://www.rtsp.org/2001/faq.html

TCP/IP and OSI Network Layers
>   http://www.uwsg.iu.edu/usail/network/nfs/network_layers.html

TCP/IP Layer Diagram
>   http://www.rabbitsemiconductor.com/documentation/docs/manuals/TCPIP/Introduction/5protoco.htm

Visualizations of the MBONE
>   http://www.caida.org/outreach/papers/1999/manta/manta.html

Web Video Transport
>   http://www.byte.com/art/9609/sec10/art5.htm

Video Conferencing

Eyematic
>   http://www.eyematic.com/

First Virtual Communications
   http://www.cuseeme.com/
iVisit
   http://www.ivisit.com/

CHAPTER 6—ENTERPRISE MULTICAST

PUBLICATIONS

Maufer, Thomas A., *Deploying IP Multicast in the Enterprise,* 1998.

WEBSITES

Abilene NOC: Enabling IP Multicast with Abilene
   http://www.abilene.iu.edu/mccook.html
Advances in Multicast
   http://www.nanog.org/mtg-0102/ppt/eubanks/sld001.htm
Border Gateway Multicast Protocol (bgmp) Charter
   http://www.ietf.org/html.charters/bgmp-charter.html
Cisco Internet Protocol (IP) Multicast Technology Overview
   http://www.cisco.com/warp/public/cc/pd/iosw/tech/ipmu_ov.htm
Cisco Multicast Quick-Start Configuration Guide
   http://www.cisco.com/warp/public/105/48.html
Core-Based Trees
   http://www.cs.ucl.ac.uk/staff/jon/mmbook/book/node78.html
IETF.org
   http://www.ietf.org/internet-drafts/draft-holbrook-idmr-igmpv3-ssm-05.txt
Jon Crowcroft's Deprecated Work Page
   http://www.cs.ucl.ac.uk/staff/jon/
JTC 036 RPT-to-SPT Switchover Delay
   http://advanced.comms.agilent.com/routertester/member/journal/JTC_036.html
Multicast Group Membership Protocols
   http://www.juniper.net/techpubs/software/junos/junos60/
   swconfig60-multicast/html/mcast-overview18.html
Network Communication Protocol Dictionary, Directory, Reference, and Guide
   http://www.javvin.com/dictionary.html

Network Computing
http://www.networkcomputing.com/1204/1204f1c2.html

NRL Multicast/Traffic
http://tonnant.itd.nrl.navy.mil/jmcoms/iptraffic/sld006.htm

PIM Sparse Mode
http://bmrc.berkeley.edu/courseware/cs294/fall97/lectures/IPMcastRouting/sld015.htm

PIM-DM: Protocol-Independent Multicast
http://www.javvin.com/protocolPIMDM.html

Planning IP Multicasting
http://www.microsoft.com/technet/treeview/default.asp?url=/technet/prodtechnol/windowsserver2003/proddocs/deployguide/dnsbb_tcp_dtot.asp

Preface
http://www.cs.ucl.ac.uk/staff/jon/mmbook/book/node1.html

Reliable Multicast Transport (rmt) Charter
http://www.ietf.org/html.charters/rmt-charter.html

Resource-Reservation Protocol (RSVP)
http://www.cisco.com/univercd/cc/td/doc/cisintwk/ito_doc/rsvp.htm#xtocid1

Secrets of Home Theater and High Fidelity Volume 1, 1994
http://www.hometheaterhifi.com/volume_1_1/v1n1vcrs.html

Source-Specific Multicast
http://www.openmash.org/resources/workshops/Talks/eckert.pdf

The Trouble with RPs
http://www.nanog.org/mtg-0102/ppt/eubanks/tsld006.htm

CHAPTER 7—VIDEO SECURITY AND DIGITAL RIGHTS MANAGEMENT (DRM)

PUBLICATIONS

Schneier, Bruce, *Applied Cryptography,* 2nd edition, John Wiley & Sons, 1996.

WEBSITES

Cipher Block Vhaining
http://searchsecurity.techtarget.com/sDefinition/0,,sid14_gci344945,00.html

CNET News.com
http://news.search.com/search?version=x&tag=ex.ne.fd.srch.ne&q=digital+ rights+management

Cover Pages: XML and Digital Rights Management (DRM)
http://xml.coverpages.org/drm.html

DeCSS Central
http://www.lemuria.org/DeCSS/

DeCSS Central: HAL2001 Speech
http://www.lemuria.org/decss/hal2001.html

Definition of Asymmetric Encryption
http://m-tech.ab.ca/concepts/asymmetric_encryption.html

Digital Asset Management, XML, Rich Media, DRM, and a Traditional Business Value: Profit
http://www.gca.org/papers/xmleurope2001/papers/html/s25-1.html

DRM Glossary
http://www.giantstepsmts.com/drm_glossary.htm

DRM Watch
http://www.giantstepsmts.com/drmwatch.htm

Encryption and Security Tutorial
http://www.cs.auckland.ac.nz/~pgut001/tutorial/

Encryption Example
http://www.insanemind.co.uk/hispec/encryptexample.htm

Encryption Tutorial
http://hotwired.lycos.com/webmonkey/programming/php/tutorials/ tutorial1.html

"Hacker Cracks Microsoft Anti-Piracy Software"
http://news.com.com/2100-1023-274721.html?tag=rn

Index of /tatschl/bilder/symbole
http://www.vindobona.com/tatschl/bilder/symbole/

International Organization for Standardization
http://mpeg.telecomitalialab.com/standards/mpeg-21/ mpeg-21.htm#_Toc23297969

InterTrust Technologies
http://intertrust.com/

Key Topics Cryptography
http://www.itsc.state.md.us/info/InternetSecurity/Crypto/CryptoOverview.htm

Microsoft in Video-on-Demand
http://news.com.com/2100-1023-274547.html?tag=rn

Microsoft's Digital Rights Management Scheme
http://cryptome.org/ms-drm.htm

O'Reilly Network
http://www.oreillynet.com/pub/wlg/2614

Popular Science: The PC-Based Tivo Emulator
http://www.popsci.com/popsci/computers/article/0,12543,385155,00.html

Public-Key Cryptography
http://216.239.53.100/search?q=cache:sfanXHInCfgJ:engr.smu.edu/~nair/
courses/7349/Public_Key_Cryptography.ppt+asymmetric+encryption+large+
primes&hl=en&ie=UTF-8

RealNetworks
http://news.com.com/2100-1023-979792.html

Report: Future Bright for Online File-Sharing
http://www.newsfactor.com/perl/story/19025.html

RSA Laboratories Cryptography FAQ
http://www.rsasecurity.com/rsalabs/faq/

RSA Laboratories Cryptography FAQ Introduction
http://www.rsasecurity.com/rsalabs/faq/1.html

SONICblue Inc.
http://www.diamondmm.com/company/press.asp?ID=595

SSL and TLS
http://www.rz.informatik.uni-muenchen.de/doku/web/sec/v11/ch07s04.html

The Digital Rights Management Dictionary
http://www.info-mech.com/drm_dictionary.html

The IT Pros
http://www.theitpros.net/images/wireless-network-special.gif

The Register
http://www.theregister.co.uk/content/4/22354.html

Video DRM
http://www.sunwebcasts.com/smw/rights/ashida.html

"What Is Encryption?"
http://www.insanemind.co.uk/hispec/encryption.htm

Wired 9.01
http://www.wired.com/wired/archive/9.01/streetcred.html?pg=4

CHAPTER 8—INTERNET VIDEO STANDARDS

AIT RealNetworks
    http://www.ait.iastate.edu/realserver/

CDI: BYU Forum Example
    http://home.byu.net/%7edle2/past/cdi/examples/quicktime/gandhi.html

Composite Media Group
    http://www.research.ibm.com/mpeg4/Projects/MPEG4.htm

Digital Printing
    http://www.acmebook.com/digital/printing/

General Microsoft Trademark Guidelines
    http://www.microsoft.com/mscorp/legal/trademarks/gnlguide.asp

Helix Universal Server Configuration File Reference
    http://service.real.com/help/library/guides/helixserverconfig/
    config_variables.htm

Index of Movies2
    http://commons.ucalgary.ca/movies2/

Internet Video Magazine Home
    http://www.internetvideomag.com/

ISMA: Home
    http://www.isma.tv/home

ISO/IEC JTC 1/SC 29/WG 11 Press Release
    http://www.jtc1.org/FTP/Public/JTC1/
    DOCREG/SC_29_WG_11_Press_Release.htm

Leonardo Standards
    http://www.chiariglione.org/leonardo/standards/mpeg/standards.htm

MPEG-4 Description
    http://www.chiariglione.org/mpeg/standards/mpeg-4/mpeg-4.htm#3.2

MPEG-4 Industry Forum
    http://www.m4if.org/resources/profiles/

QuickTiming.Org
    http://www.quicktiming.org/

QuVIS Press Archives
    http://www.quvis.com/products/Applications/applications.htm

RealNetworks.com
    http://realforum.real.com/cgi-bin/realforum/wwwthreads.pl

Site Updates
   http://developer.apple.com/techpubs/quicktime/qtdevdocs/whatsnew.htm

Sorenson Media
   http://www.sorenson.com/content.php?pageID=132#s3

VBrick: MPEG Television Over IP
   http://www.vbrick.com/

Video-Demystified.com
   http://www.video-demystified.com/

Vlogging Video Weblogs: WebReference Update - 030306
   http://webreference.com/new/030306.html

WM9 to SMPTE
   http://www.streamingmedia.com/r/printerfriendly.asp?id=8501

Appendix A—A Quick List of Problems and Concise Solutions

Chilton's Online
   http://www.chiltonsonline.com/

Appendix B—The MPEG Standard

Publications

Pereira, Fernando and Touradj Ebrahimi, *The MPEG-4 Book*, Prentice Hall PTR, 2002.

Topic, Michael, *Streaming Media Demystified*, McGraw-Hill, 2002.

Walsh, Aaron E. and Mikaël Bourges-Sévenier, *MPEG-4 Jump Start,* Prentice Hall PTR, 2002.

Watkinson, John, *The MPEG Handbook*, Self-published through Focal Press, 2001.

WEBSITES

Composite Media Group
  http://www.research.ibm.com/mpeg4/Projects/MPEG4.htm
H.264
  http://whatis.techtarget.com/definition/0,,sid9_gci934039,00.html
ISO Technical Programme: JTC 1/SC 29
  http://www.iso.ch/iso/en/stdsdevelopment/techprog/workprog/
  TechnicalProgrammeSCDetailPage.TechnicalProgrammeSCDetail?
  COMMID=148
ISO/IEC JTC 1/SC 29/WG 11 Press Release
  http://www.jtc1.org/FTP/Public/JTC1/DOCREG/
  SC_29_WG_11_Press_Release.htm
Leonardo Standards
  http://www.chiariglione.org/leonardo/standards/mpeg/standards.htm
MPEG-4 FAQ
  http://www.chiariglione.org/mpeg/faq.htm
MPEG-4 Industry Forum
  http://www.m4if.org/m4if/banner_ad.php
  http://www.m4if.org/resources/profiles/
MPEG-4 Seminar
  http://mpeg.telecomitalialab.com/events&tutorials/mtx/
  mpeg-4_seminar.htm
MPEG-4 Systems
  http://mpeg.telecomitalialab.com/events&tutorials/mtx/mtx97_oavaro/
  ppframe.htm
MPEG-4 Systems: Overview
  http://mpeg.telecomitalialab.com/events&tutorials/mpeg-4_si/
  3-systems_overview_paper/3-systems_overview_paper.htm

MPEG-4 PROFILES

Coding Technologies
  http://www.codingtechnologies.com/products/aacPlus.htm
  http://www.codingtechnologies.com/products/sbr.htm
Leonardo Standards
  http://www.chiariglione.org/leonardo/standards/mpeg/standards.htm

MPEG Audio FAQ Version 9
  http://www.chiariglione.org/mpeg/faq/mp4-aud/mp4-aud.htm#43

MPEG Systems FAQ
  http://www.chiariglione.org/mpeg/faq/mp4-sys/sys-faq-ipmp-x.htm

MPEG-4 BSAC Standard
  http://www.vialicensing.com/products/bsac/standard.html

MPEG-4 Industry Forum
  http://www.m4if.org/resources.php

MPEG-4 Industry Forum
  http://www.m4if.org/resources/profiles/#MPEG01A

Overview of the MPEG-4 Standard
  http://library.n0i.net/graphics/mp-eg4_overview/

Philips Digital Networks
  http://www.digitalnetworks.philips.com/InformationCenter/Global/FArticle
  Summary.asp?lNodeId=760&channel=760&channelId=N760A2171

ReallyRareWares TwinVQ Encoder
  http://www.rjamorim.com/rrw/nttvqf.html

"What Is MPEG DMIF?"
  http://mpeg.telecomitalialab.com/events&tutorials/mtx/mtx97_vbalabanian/
  ppframe.htm

INDEX

informIT

www.informit.com

YOUR GUIDE TO IT REFERENCE

Articles

Keep your edge with thousands of free articles, in-depth features, interviews, and IT reference recommen-dations – all written by experts you know and trust.

Online Books

Answers in an instant from **InformIT Online Book's** 600+ fully searchable on line books. For a limited time, you can get your first 14 days **free**.

Catalog

Review online sample chapters, author biographies and customer rankings and choose exactly the right book from a selection of over 5,000 titles.

Wouldn't it be great

if the world's leading technical publishers joined forces to deliver their best tech books in a common digital reference platform?

They have. Introducing
InformIT Online Books
powered by Safari.

POWERED BY
Safari

■ Specific answers to specific questions.

InformIT Online Books' powerful search engine gives you relevance-ranked results in a matter of seconds.

■ Immediate results.

With InformIT Online Books, you can select the book you want and view the chapter or section you need immediately.

■ Cut, paste and annotate.

Paste code to save time and eliminate typographical errors. Make notes on the material you find useful and choose whether or not to share them with your work group.

■ Customized for your enterprise.

Customize a library for you, your department or your entire organization. You only pay for what you need.

Get your first 14 days FREE!

For a limited time, InformIT Online Books is offering its members a 10 book subscription risk-free for 14 days. Visit **http://www.informit.com/online-books** for details.

informIT
Online Books

informit.com/onlinebooks

Register
Your Book

at www.awprofessional.com/register

You may be eligible to receive:

- Advance notice of forthcoming editions of the book
- Related book recommendations
- Chapter excerpts and supplements of forthcoming titles
- Information about special contests and promotions throughout the year
- Notices and reminders about author appearances, tradeshows, and online chats with special guests

Contact us

If you are interested in writing a book or reviewing manuscripts prior to publication, please write to us at:

Editorial Department
Addison-Wesley Professional
75 Arlington Street, Suite 300
Boston, MA 02116 USA
Email: AWPro@aw.com

Addison-Wesley

Visit us on the Web: http://www.awprofessional.com